Unreached Peoples 82

Edward R. Dayton
and
Dr. Samuel Wilson,
editors

David C. Cook Publishing Co.
ELGIN, ILLINOIS—WESTON, ONTARIO

The material contained in the Expanded Descriptions and Unreached Peoples Registry may be reproduced or copied in any form, provided appropriate credit is given. Portions of the rest of this book may only be used with written permission from the David C. Cook Publishing Co., 850 North Grove Avenue, Elgin, IL 60120, U.S.A.

Cover design by Graphic Communications, Inc., St. Louis, Mo.
Printed in U.S.A.

ISBN: 0-89191-838-8
LC: 81-69100

Contents

Introduction

Unreached Peoples '82 is the fourth book in a series jointly inaugurated in 1979 by the Strategy Working Group of the Lausanne Committee for World Evangelization (LCWE) and the Missions Advanced Research and Communication Center (MARC). The primary purpose of these annual directories is to inform and motivate the Church toward greater effectiveness in proclaiming God's message throughout the world.

The concept of "unreached peoples," spelled out in *Unreached Peoples '79,* developed as missions strategists began to recognize the importance of dividing the world's population by people groups, rather than by political boundaries. Briefly, a people group is defined as a "significantly large sociological grouping of individuals who perceive themselves to have a common affinity for one another because of their shared language, religion, ethnicity, residence, occupation, class or caste, situation, etc., or combinations of these." (See *Unreached Peoples '79,* page 23.)

This definition was rather arbitrarily established by the Strategy Working Group of the Lausanne Committee for World Evangelization. And, like every definition, sometimes further explanation by example is needed. Is a tribe a people group? Yes. Is an ethnic group? Yes. Is a group living in a particular area? Perhaps. A people group may be any or all of these things, but it can be much more. A people group can be defined by where it lives, the language it speaks, the special situation in which it finds itself (such as refugees), its occupation, its socioeconomic class, to name only a few considerations. The important idea behind the people group concept is the notion of placing boundaries around a particular group of people so those in ministry can adapt their gospel presentation to the subculture.

One advantage of the people group approach to world evangelization is that it permits us to respond in Christian love to a people's total need. Thus, the dichotomy which sometimes separates those who emphasize "social action," and those who stress "evangelism" should be nonexistent. Of course, there is never a question as to whether or not we should attempt to proclaim Christ as Lord and Savior. It is not a question of whether, but a question of when.

Although the Registry of Unreached Peoples (see page 171) is updated with each volume, the focus of each edition varies. *Unreached Peoples '79,* the first in this series, provided an overview and included people groups from all walks of life all over the world. *Unreached Peoples '80* focused on Muslims. *Unreached Peoples '81* highlighted expanded descriptions of Asian peoples. The present volume takes as its special interest, people groups within urban areas.

The special focus of each *Unreached Peoples* edition is evident in every section. First, the case studies deal with individual people groups within the area of emphasis. So do the expanded descriptions (usually 50-80 in each issue). Finally, each year a special effort is made to add new people groups to the registry section from the highlighted area. For example, this *Unreached Peoples* edition includes many urban-dwelling peoples not previously listed in the first three volumes.

The registry (part 4) is drawn from the computerized data bank on unreached peoples at MARC. To the extent that the details are available, the Unreached Peoples Data Bank in 1981 had information on each of the categories listed in the expanded description, *with the exception* of the narrative text. If the reader wants more information than that given in the descriptions in the registry, he or she may write directly to MARC (MARC International, 919 W. Huntington Drive, Monrovia, CA 91016).

As of this volume, 273 expanded descriptions have been published. The volume in which they appear is listed in the Registry of Unreached Peoples which begins on page 171.

The registry now includes some information about 3265 people groups considered by the researcher or reporter to be unreached. It is unlikely that a complete list of all the unreached people groups of the world will ever be compiled, nor is that the ultimate purpose of this series. There could easily be thousands of "people groups" in each major country of the world. For example, one group that is currently being reached is "bus girls in Seoul, Korea." These are young women who come from the country to the city to act as ticket takers in metropolitan bus companies. They live in dormitories of the bus company and form a particular social, occupational group.

The purpose of the registry is to encourage us to look at the people who live around and among us and to take steps to reach them.

FEATURE ARTICLES

In addition to case studies and expanded descriptions, each volume has attempted to describe some of the strategies available for reaching unreached people. The section titled "The Unreached and How to Reach Them" has covered the basic philosophy of the Strategy Working Group and MARC, as well as articles by other missiologists.

THE PRESENT VOLUME

The world of the 1980s is increasing in complexity. Not only is the population growing, but individuals and groups appear to be in constant movement over the face of the globe. With the exception of the American Northeast, almost every major city in the world has seen astounding population growth during the past several years. Why?

Much of the credit for this phenomenon, commonly called urbanization, can be given to the impact radio, television, films, magazines, and newspapers, have had on the world's rural population. People in distant villages and towns have been experiencing ever-rising expectations about the kind of life they should live. Modern advertising creates a dissatisfaction among rural people who contrast their way of life with the (apparently) glamorous world of the cities, which are attracting more and more people toward them. For example, over 50 percent of Latin America now lives in cities.

The end result of urban migration has been the breakup of formerly stable groups into larger and larger numbers of more complex people groups. The physical and spiritual needs of people in a rural village can usually be identified in a short time. But when thousands upon thousands of people are crowded into high-rise buildings and massed into traffic-choked streets, it is very difficult to understand who they are and what their needs may be. The task of identifying a people group in an urban setting is more difficult than in a rural setting, but is needed just as much.

The current volume, therefore, places a special emphasis on people groups within cities. The expanded descriptions in *Unreached Peoples '82* focus on city peoples, as do the case studies. Two obvious gaps exist in the missiological section, for there are no essays dealing forthrightly with the place of the local church in urban evangelism, nor is there an article exclusively addressing the evangelization of the urban poor. This was not by design. Our assigned articles, though solicited, simply did not arrive in time for inclusion.

We owe a special word of appreciation to Dr. Ray Bakke, special consultant for this volume. His perspective as a teaching scholar, as well as a successful inner-city minister, has been invaluable. After ten years of pastoral ministry in an inner-city church, Dr. Bakke has concluded that the fundamental strategic difference between the local church and the parachurch mission agency is one of *starting point*. According to Dr. Bakke's philosophy of city ministry, the mission agency can and indeed must start with community and population analysis, then work back to ministry design. The local church, however, must begin with an inventory of congregational gifts and resources, set priorities, and then work outward to the groups present in the contiguous, then extended, community. An obvious symbiotic relationship exists between the urban church and the urban parachurch, but, he laments, it is seldom obvious in practice.

UNREACHED PEOPLES '83 AND '84

Unreached Peoples '83 will focus on reaching the 16 million refugees spread out across the face of the earth. These peoples have left their homes for any number of reasons, including war and oppression, disaster, and economic disruption. But they all have the same need—Jesus Christ.

Unreached Peoples '84 will center on various peoples of the vast continent of Africa.

HOW TO USE THIS BOOK

Use it for prayer. Select a few people groups for which you can pray regularly.

Use it to motivate. The sheer magnitude of the "task" to evangelize the world calls us to a deeper dedication.

Use it for field selection. Perhaps God is calling you as an individual or as an agency to attempt to reach one or more of these groups.

Use it for group study. Here is a way to open up a whole new world to those who may be ignorant of the needs around the world.

NEW EDITORIAL TEAM

Unreached Peoples '79, '80, and '81 were edited jointly by C. Peter Wagner and Edward R. Dayton. With this edition, Dr. Samuel Wilson, Director of MARC, has replaced

Dr. Wagner. We are especially grateful to the contribution that Peter Wagner has made to this and other attempts to help carry out the great commission.

As always in this series, the entire MARC staff is due grateful mention. This volume is especially the result of the contributions of R. Boyd Johnson, Paul Hawley, Samuel Chao and Kimberly Finn.

Edward R. Dayton

LAUSANNE COMMITTEE FOR WORLD EVANGELIZATION AS OF 1981

One of the outcomes of the International Congress on World Evangelization held in Lausanne, Switzerland, in the summer of 1974 was a mandate from the 2,400 participants to form an ongoing committee. The "Spirit of Lausanne" was a powerful new thrust for completing the task of world evangelization. It was not to die.

The Lausanne Committee for World Evangelization was born at a meeting in Mexico City, January 20-23, 1975. The committee drew up a constitution, named forty-eight charter members, and elected Leighton Ford president and Gottfried Osei-Mensah executive secretary.

During June 16-26, 1980, the LCWE convened a Consultation on World Evangelization at Pattaya, Thailand, to evaluate the work of the committee and to determine its future. Six hundred participants and 250 consultants, observers, and guests were present. As a result of that consultation, the decision was made to reaffirm the mandate of Lausanne and to continue the work of the movement.

The central offices of the LCWE are located in Nairobi, Kenya (P.O. Box 21225). Four working groups carry out its basic ministries—intercession, theology/education, strategy, and communications. The current listing of committee members follows:

Francisco Anabalon, Chile
Ramez Atallah, Canada
*Saphir Athyal, India, *Deputy Chairman*
Peter Beyerhaus, West Germany
Vonette Bright, U.S.A.
Robert Coleman, U.S.A.
Mariano DiGangi, Canada
Nilson Fanini, Brazil

Ajith Fernando, Sri Lanka
*Leighton Ford, U.S.A., *Chairman*
*Andrew Furuyama, Japan
Emmy Gichinga, Kenya
Geziel Nunes Gomes, Brazil
Billy Graham, U.S.A. *(ex officio)*
Fritz Hoffmann, East Germany
C. B. Hogue, U.S.A.
*Donald Hoke, U.S.A., *Treasurer*
Abdel Masih Istafanous, Egypt
Festo Kivengere, Uganda
Victor Koh, Philippines
Gordon Landreth, England
Samuel Libert, Argentina
Branko Lovrec, Yugoslavia
Billy Melvin, U.S.A.
Stanley Mooneyham, U.S.A.
Agne Nordlander, Sweden
*Samuel Odunaike, Nigeria
*Gottfried Osei-Mensah, Kenya, *Executive Secretary*
Pablo Perez, Mexico
*John Reid, Australia, *Intercession Working Group Chairman*
John Richard, India
*John Stott, England, *Theology and Education Working Group
Chairman*
*C. Peter Wagner, U.S.A., *Strategy Working Group Chairman*
I Ben Wati, India
Warren Webster, U.S.A.
James Wong, Singapore
*Thomas Zimmerman, U.S.A., *Communications Working
Group Chairman*

Strategy Working Group
   The Strategy Working Group of the Lausanne Congress on
   World Evangelism has the task of discovering unreached
   groups of people and helping to design strategies to reach
   them.

C. Peter Wagner, U.S.A., *Chairman*
Fouad Accad, Arabian Gulf
Edward R. Dayton, U.S.A.
David Gitari, Kenya
Tom Houston, England
John Y. Masuda, Japan
George Samuel, India
Douglas Smith, Bolivia
James Wong, Singapore

*Executive Committee member

Part 1
The Unreached and How to Reach Them

The Power and Problems of People Group Thinking in World Evangelization

by Samuel Wilson

The idea of thinking about the world in terms of "people groups" is one which has gained prominence only in recent years. There are, apparently, stages of understanding and awareness in the application of the concepts.

Many people still think about a people group as being a tribe or some ethnic group. It is more difficult to get to the stage where one can identify people groups in the complexity of urbanized or so-called "modern" societies.

In this article, a revision of a paper originally presented to a group of Europeans, Dr. Wilson uses a number of illustrations from Europe which show how to go about identifying people groups within more cosmopolitan arenas.

THE PLACE OF PEOPLE GROUP THINKING

The idea of approaching world evangelization in terms of people groups is gaining more and more acceptance. The initial work done by MARC in the late sixties, the International Congress on World Evangelization at Lausanne in 1974, the subsequent work of the Lausanne Committee on World Evangelization, plus the insight and enthusiasm of Dr. Ralph Winter which led to Edinburgh '80, have all contributed to helping missions strategists recognize the value of segmentation by people groups.

Prior to the people group approach, unreached peoples were categorized primarily in national units—in other words, all the people living within the borders of a particular country, were often lumped together without regard to ethnic and cultural differences. Consequently, evangelistic efforts which met with some success with some peoples, would totally miss the mark with others.

Why should we be interested in people *groups*?

The easy answer is, of course, because all people have a place in God's Kingdom. The Church of Jesus Christ takes on form and gives vital witness to and through her human social circumstances.

Individuals develop cutural patterns in the groups in which they find a sense of community. These patterns include ways of thinking and acting. Groups are significant not only because they can enhance or hinder evangelism, but because they can effectively hide whole segments of human population from the view of potential evangelists.

Advantages of People Group Thinking
1. Thinking in terms of people groups is helpful because it corresponds to the way God has chosen to work in the world. Jesus said he would build his Church; the Church is a new people, the community of faith. It should surprise no one that in practice this new community tends to grow most readily along the lines of human relationships already active in the lives of individuals, even as it breaks down human barriers by transcending them.

2. People group thinking helps do away with the harmful split in emphasis on social versus evangelistic activity. Consider what happens if one starts with a people group, first defining its needs, and then attempting to prayerfully respond to it. The social conscience natural to the true Christian in whom the love of God dwells responds to human need when hunger, thirst, or nakedness exists. Loneliness will be sensed and companionship given in Jesus' name. When a group is sated with material things, love will offer a witness which suggests that life can have meaning only in God's service.

A strategy of the Spirit unique to each people group will evolve from that group's present situation and setting, growing "from inside out." There will be no need to choose between social action and evangelism. A strategy springing from the needs of the group will faithfully incorporate both. So, as Edward Dayton has already pointed out in his introduction, it will not be a question of whether Christ will be proclaimed in all His fullness, but when.

3. *People group thinking can fulfill the standard of scripture to overcome social barriers.* The people group approach to viewing the world has been criticized for potentially leading the Church toward racism. But the fact is, people group thinking is the only hope for bringing individuals out of the social narrowness into which we naturally decline. Every local church has a tendency to develop its own built-in culture, to gradually fall into thinking that its way of believing and doing is the one right way.

The one sure way to avoid chauvinism and racism is to call on the Church to transcend these limits by focusing on the tremendous variety of God's world. A congregation can capture the missionary spirit and enthusiasm by being called to go beyond itself. Missionary vision and the fulfillment of the scriptural ideal to reach every tribe, people, tongue, and nation can only result from learning to see people groups and plant the Church among them.

THE TASK AND PROBLEMS OF IDENTIFYING PEOPLE GROUPS

The "Easy" Part

Some people groups are not difficult to see. Others are obscured among familiar faces, familiar surroundings, and places where it appears Christianity has already taken root. Europe is a good example.

As we undertake the task of identifying the people groups of

Europe within which no church exists, our minds and hearts will automatically turn to those groups that most clearly shout by their presence: "We are different."

For instance, recent estimates place as many as 15 million known migrants in Western Europe alone. Guesses beyond that claim there are at least another half million employed illegals. These figures do not include the thousands of Surinamese and Antillese in Holland on Dutch passports, who remain uncounted by official estimates. Gypsies wander and call attention to themselves by their unique customs. Mosques under construction and unfamiliar sounds on production lines call Germany's attention to almost 600,000 Turks, 470,000 Yugoslavs, and 370,000 Italians.

All these groups lift a clamor of tongues and customs; the Church can either ignore and pass them by (and thus allow them to remain unreached) *or* can make a special effort, a missionary effort, to reach them.

The gospel must take a form adapted to the lifeways of each people group—every conceivable human division—or many thousands in Europe will have no chance of redemption.

For this part of the task, a part I have (maybe mistakenly) chosen to call easy, one can count on considerable help.

Almost every government can provide statistics that at least identify major groupings of ethnic peoples. Migrants are tracked because of their influence on the labor market. Holland can give three different sets of statistics through the Ministry of Social Welfare, the Ministry of Justice and the Central Bureau of Statistics. This will at least name and locate significant migrant groups.

The Minority Rights Group, an international research and information unit registered in Great Britain, has published forty-six reports in brochure form. It makes available helpful films such as "The Turkish Rubbish Collectors of Frankfurt." These are typical of many published and public sources which can serve as a basis for evangelistic effort.

It will also be fairly easy to take into consideration the divisions which left their mark on Europe's history. Someone has said that the national boundaries and nationalism of Europe are the result of a common hatred of enemies and a common error about ancestry. Such political divisions and loyalties may be the basis for identifying real groups. Every traditional political party in Belgium (except the Communist) has divided into Flemish and Walloon wings as a result of the linguistic/regional problems. The lines along which evangelism must proceed in Yugoslavia are readily identifiable. Someone has written, "It is a combination of six republics, two autonomous regions, eight major national groups, three religions and two alphabets." Even in Serbia, strong minorities of Albanians, Hungarians, Croats, Muslims and Montenegrins exist. Serbs comprise only 72 percent of Serbia.

A Harder Challenge: Identifying People Groups Which Are Not Ethnolinguistic

Working data will be most incomplete if it centers only on social groupings related to nation, language, and migration. We are aware of these major ethnolinguistic differences because of the great contribution anthropology continues to make to the Kingdom. But social distance can be as great and more difficult to transcend than ethnolinguistic distance, and can be devastatingly effective in keeping groups hidden and unreached.

Many great minds have wrestled with questions about the characteristics of so-called modern societies. German sociologist Georg Simmel goes to the heart of our problem by making a basic distinction about the character of groups.

In a traditional society, Simmel relates, the individual can be viewed as the smallest of a series of concentric circles. The individual is at the center of a family. The family in turn belongs to a village, which belongs to a clan, which belongs to a tribe, which is itself a people group or may be part of a larger people group. There is no conflict at any level that produces confusion for the individual as to identity (who am I?) or behavior (how should I act?). This kind of understanding, where all the groups to which an individual belongs are in perfect agreement, Simmel calls "inclusive."

But Simmel then goes on to note that modern industrial society has spawned a breed of people who draws their identity in pieces from a plural set of groups—groups that are often in conflict with one another. This he classifies as "intersective."

For example, a typical Western family may have four brothers. Three become professionals. But as a lawyer, a dentist, and a medical doctor, they learn different codes of professional ethics, travel in different company, and share an outlook on life partly with the family, but also strongly with fellow professionals. A fourth brother, perhaps the oldest, who may have had to work to help the others through school, and retains the family religion by tradition, is an embarrassment on grand social occasions and illustrates the nonintersection of life with the brothers' friends and social circles. Any club, business partnership, or political party can increase the divergence of viewpoint.

In our modern world every one of us is an intersection of the many groups to which we belong. Each group is potentially useful in explaining how we think about life and how we might have been won to the Lord and to the Church. Each has its own construction of reality and its own attitude toward religion, Christianity, and the gospel.

Where groups multiply, persons get a stronger sense of individualism, sometimes even oppressive loneliness. Alienation may be most complete where societies are most pluralistic. People become trapped economically, socially, and psychologically. Consequently, people groups in the major cities of Europe are characterized each by their own kind of social pluralism.

This means that no final listing of unreached peoples in Europe is possible because of this proliferation of groups and the problem of overlap. But it also means that when one approach to thinking of reaching individuals fails, an alternative approach based on another group may be significantly successful. An alternative strategy based on *another* group can include the *same* individual! If this assessment appears to be relative, we shall have to live with that. It really offers more hope than coming face-to-face with a politically hostile, closed group where penetration is impossible.

The Church must learn to employ the tools of thinking "peoples." However, most church congregations or sets of congregations have been severely limited, particularly in their outreach, to one or a few people groups similar to themselves. One way out of this situation is to introduce the concepts of people groups in terms of groups that *are* being reached. It is characteristic of human nature that people are better able to draw careful distinctions among those who most nearly share their own lot in life. Conversely, we tend to lump together those who are the most distant socially. Yet it is also true that people in highly pluralistic societies (many "intersective" people groups) can become blind to all distinctions on a conscious level. When the Church is taught to see those it has been reaching, she may be able to overcome its blindness to those not being reached.

When the Church is urged to integrate people-group thinking into its ministry, it tends to view the bulk of society as homogeneous. The undefined majority that is viewed as the object of ministry efforts is seen as an irreducible whole. Koreans, for example, have insisted to us that Korea is homogeneous, that there are no recognizable people groups—they are *all Koreans*.

A further difficulty is that the continent of Europe has worked Christianity into many national identities. The nations of Europe face the particular problem of national identity which is married to a state church. To be a Swede may mean to be a Lutheran. This is understood as being a Christian, whether or not one has an experience of God's grace or lives in fellowship with God's true children, spiritually born from above. Any assessment of the state of evangelism must confront the fact that many people groups hidden to the good news exist among those who are Christians in name only.

Fortunately, the social distance from the Christians in the churches to most of these unconsciously hidden groups is not great. When there are congregations of people like these unreached, normal evangelism can be carried on.

Let me cite some illustrations to help clarify things. The National Initiative in Evangelism in England (NIE) has broken some good ground in this regard. They now have made available a series of discussion papers which are based on several helpful ways of looking at society.

"Discussion paper number one" deals with residents of council housing estates. Here, the group is defined by the intersection of a number of possible ways of looking at the population. Most evident is the spatial neighborhood. These people are defined as groups because of where they live, that is, on the council estates. However, some inhabitants of the not so clearly defined estates were not conscious of being "on the estate," and others, particularly those with their own town center, had a greater sense of community. Therefore, one must not automatically associate community with geographic neighborhood.

Another dimension which molds life is social class. Some of the estates are clearly one-class societies. In some of the lower class, working-class estates, the people may lack any sense of community. Here it would be possible to adopt a ministry and evangelistic strategy which concentrates on building a sense of community through the church fellowship.

Other papers in the NIE series deal with senior citizens, young people at risk, and weekend leisure seekers. The significance of stage in the life cycle, social class, time, and other dimensions are evident immediately in these titles. Being aware of the many ways people are "like" other people may help in showing what needs to be done.

THE FUTURE OF PEOPLE GROUP THINKING

A five-step process helps us see a people group from a viewpoint of evangelistic strategy.

1. *Identification:* Where are they? Who are they? Research work is needed. The anthropologically defined groups will require resources, but the sociological groups present more of a challenge.

2. *Verification:* Is this really a people group? The discussion of intersective groups points to a problem: We can describe categories of people who do not form groups that have meaningful impact on our evangelism. Baldness, left-handedness, color blindness may all have very real effects on the feelings of an individual, but it will be a rare church that finds that baldness as a group membership definition enables it to break new ground

in evangelism. Bald men simply do not feel part of a significant group because of their hairless state. So realize that not all descriptive categories define missiologically meaningful groups.

The urban poor do not necessarily exist as a meaningful group, even in a given locality. Some sense of belonging and community which affects one's sense of identity will be necessary if the category listing is to be verified as a group that needs a strategy for evangelism. Do they meet and change one another? Is there mutual influence on behavior because the individuals sense likeness?

At this stage, one must raise the major question touched on earlier: Is there a viable church ministering within the people group? Can it carry witness forward? If so, the group has been penetrated. If not, the group is hidden or unreached.

3. *Determination of feasibility:* How can this people group be reached? It is not enough to know a group can be named and to know whether a church exists within it. It is necessary to become familiar with a group's needs as a means of defining the appropriate way to approach the group. This is dealt with in rather extensive literature published by MARC and the Strategy Working Group.

Here, questions of receptivity and resistance, government reaction and secular contexts will all need to be considered. It can be readily seen that this step requires information far beyond merely cataloging the name, size, and existence of a group.

4. & 5. The other two steps deal with *Mobilization* and *Penetration*. Since these are action steps, each requires some new level of information, but together they constitute our real goal: to see churches planted among all unreached people groups to the glory of Christ.

Samuel Wilson is director of MARC (Missions Advanced Research and Communication Center), a division of World Vision International. He has served on the mission field in Peru for over a decade, and following his doctoral work in sociology at Cornell University, served for eight years as a professor at Nyack College and the Alliance School of Theology and Missions.

A Contemporary Perspective on the Evangelization of World Class Cities

by Raymond J. Bakke

A major thrust of this essay is to suggest that rationale for an urban mission evangelization priority comes partly from an understanding of the global nature and mission dynamics of world class cities* themselves. By the structures they assume and the roles they play, and primarily by the gigantic increases in their size and international significance, large cities must now become a strategic priority for local churches and mission agencies.

Given the pluralism of cities, the writer suggests a broad range of mission strategies both in and to cities. Lest urban evangelists, pastors, and missionaries be overwhelmed by the complexity and diffuse nature of urban evangelization, a theological meaning system is proposed to enable people to see global significance in the tasks of daily urban mission.

In the process, the church is made to see that not only is fleeing the city an untenable option, but preparing for and ministering in the cities is the only aggressive preparation for future faithfulness.

*Cities of international significance and populations of at least a million.

THE CITY DEFINED

Definitions of cities fall into two broad categories. Some urbanologists, like Louis Wirth, define cities by *forms*—i.e., by structural criteria such as size, density, or heterogeneity.[1] Others, like Lewis Mumford, define cities by *functions,* stating that "the unique office of the city is to increase the variety, velocity, extent, and continuity of human intercourse."[2] Both of these categories contribute significantly to our understanding of contemporary cities.

The term *urban* in itself connotes both places and processes. Los Angeles, for example, certainly qualifies as an urban place, but that does not exhaust its roles or functions. Every time entertainers use Los Angeles as a stage setting for television or movies which go into the homes of rural America, they in some measure urbanize rural areas. Via the media they export urban experiences and values, create new language, and change expectations. One might call this "the Los Angelization of America." In other words, urbanization goes beyond places with boundaries to processes that affect us all.

Extended Urban Influence

To suppose, then, that a numerical decline in the population of major cities means that the world is becoming less urban is misleading—at least in the developed world of technologically significant nations. With notable sun belt exceptions, most large cities in postindustrial societies are indeed losing people. But far from witnessing a decline of urbanization, large cities are extending their influence over greater and greater spheres of life. As forms or places, large cities may be regarded as becoming less significant, but as functions or processes major cities represent continued growth and accelerated significance.

ROLES OF THE CITY

Urban anthropologists sometimes classify cities by roles: cultural, economic or administrative. These categories enable us to see obvious differences between most cities. For example, Chicago, São Paulo and Bombay are clearly economic or industrial cities. Boston, Benares and Rio de Janeiro have primarily cultural roles in their respective countries. Washington, D.C., New Delhi, and Brasilia assume roles of governance.

No one can doubt that the structures of community life, histories, ethos, population profiles and expectations of these cities are broadly shaped or influenced by the roles they play in the larger society. On a smaller scale, numerous port cities, and market or county-seat towns, maintain similar roles with equal regional significance for those seeking to design ministry strategies within them. At a fundamental level, then, the differences between large cities and small cities or towns are of degree and not kind. By comparison, the large city contains more human variety and functions at such speeds that its social life resembles the work of time-lapse photography.

Extension of Roles

Realistically, then, a culture-wide decentralization of American and other Western world cities represents not a decline in urbanization, as some might hopefully or nostalgically suppose, but rather a new reality. The same forces which brought significance to Chicago, Detroit, and Miami "have come hither also." Suburban sprawl and the growth of formerly rural mountain towns represent an extension of cities and not an escape from them. Because the societal roles which belonged almost exclusively to cities in the past are now being distributed broadly throughout the developed world, the social matrix in which God's church worships and evangelizes therefore seems to be vastly different from most people's perception of it. The import, however, of these perceptions for worldwide urban evangelization can only be summarized here as basic to formulating a threefold rationale for the concerted evangelization of world class cities. These three elements relate to the demographic, prophetic, and strategic perspective of the city.

DEMOGRAPHIC PERSPECTIVE OF THE CITY

Worldwide urban growth has been pegged at 7.2 percent a year. At that rate, city populations will double in a decade. Seen concretely, the birth-over-death rate alone is creating a new Chicago *and* Los Angeles (6 million people) in the world every month. Mexico City has passed Tokyo and Shanghai to become the world's largest city with a current growth rate of about eighty thousand persons a month, the equivalent of a million a year. A little more than half of this growth is by birth, the balance by immigration.

The demographics of African cities are no less startling or consequential. Cairo, the largest African city, went from 4 to 8 million people in the 1970s. Lagos, the capital of Nigeria (the most populous of the continent's forty-nine nations), grew in a little more than a decade from a community smaller than Rockford, Illinois, to become a city larger than Chicago. Other data show that nearly sixty thousand Africans are male, urban, and unemployed. Perhaps even more significant is the great number of Africans who are also male, urban, and *underemployed,* thereby creating an urban condition described by Kenyan President Daniel Arap Moi as "a social time bomb."

Young Population of Old Cities

Numbers alone do not tell the whole story, however, as a closer look at Mexico City and at many other rapidly developing cities in the "Two-Thirds World" reveals. Although in the United States the median age of city residents is nearly thirty and rising, the median age of Mexico City is approximately fourteen and holding. Seen another way, there is a city under fourteen years of age larger than New York that lives within Mexico City.

Economically, this means that Mexico must create more than a million new jobs a year just to keep pace with teens entering the job market. Socially, it reminds us that a very old world class city can be growing younger and older at the same time. In terms of international relations, it puts pressure on the two-thousand mile border between the United States and Mexico, showing that there is "no getting away" from the new urban realities.

Changing Expectations

Revolutions do not occur when things are as bad as they can be, but rather when expectations for improvement outpace reality. In this view, the real inflation impacting world class cities is less monetary than it is the inflation of expectations. Jakarta, now a city the size of New York in the island world of the South Pacific, has a toxic garbage problem. If they bury the garbage, it will poison the water. If they burn it, it will pollute their air. Neither specter is pleasant. The consequences for life, ministry, and evangelization for this urban population are significant.

Growth and the Economy

Contemporary urban growth in the developing world is characterized by three fundamental differences from the growth of large cities like New York or London a generation ago. First, current urban growth in developing nations is built upon a huge and rapidly increasing birthrate. It is not just transfer growth from rural areas. Rural areas are simultaneously exploding in population.

Second, cities everywhere are shifting from labor-intensive to capital-intensive economies. The jobs needed to serve these growing populations just do not exist and will not exist for millions of people who come to the city hoping for a better life than in barrios or tribal lands. But current data shows that massive reindustrialization for the sake of creating urban jobs worldwide is not happening. It is very unlikely that it ever will happen.

Limited Resources

Finally, cities of recent generations have assumed there were neither limits to energy, nor constraints on their environments. Now cities know better, and the prospects of many for dealing with these realities are not hopeful.

Seen globally, then, in terms of numbers or demographics, our world of 4.3 billion people is nearly 50 percent urban. The more developed world has been urban, while the rest of the world is in the process of urbanization.

A PROPHETIC PERSPECTIVE OF THE CITY

The City as Microcosm

A second aspect of a rationale for the study and evangelization of cities is based on the role of cities as the research and development component of society as a whole. What shows up in cities today, whether new kinds of crime or new discoveries for medical care, will arrive in noncity areas tomorrow. Therefore, the future for rural and small-city dwellers is visible in large cities today. Mission strategists have not been quick to recognize this. Neither have they taken innovative and aggressive action in the face of these urban realities.

Seminaries now use psychiatric wards and hospital settings to train students for effective counseling ministries. The assumption is not that the patients in these psychiatric settings are so different than the rest of us, but rather that routine behavior is exaggerated there. Given this assumption, a hospital setting makes more visible the normal human behaviors we all experience. It makes them easier to identify for teaching purposes.

By analogy then, students of evangelization should be taught how to exegete the city. This is not because the city is so different from rural or small-town places, but because the routine roles of space and time are accelerated in the city. Thus it is easier to diagnose actual contextual realities and to design increasingly effective evangelization strategies.

The organization of ministry strategies borrows heavily from management perspectives for programming in an institutional urban matrix. Sociological, historical, and anthropological disciplines assist in locating and understanding people in need. Political and psychological awareness enables wise and sensitive implementation of our strategies in diverse urban contexts. Urban work leans heavily on all God's gifts to his church.

The City as a Testing Ground

For practical reasons, any constructive scenario for evangelism training then might test ministry design and skills in the urban context before projecting it upon the culture at large.

In rural areas, nearly every relationship is a primary or emotionally significant one. Neighbors in a rural setting generally have socially, geographically, vocationally, and often biologically significant relationships. Class and other boundaries exist (often tyrannically so), but almost everyone has a general relationship to everyone and everything in a routinized fashion.

Not so in the city. There we choose relationships, and life is much more specialized. Urban experience quickly teaches formerly rural people how to put boundaries around their lives to cope with the daily demands of the metroplex. Thus, people for whom life was formerly a series of primary relationships must adapt to a life of mostly secondary relationships. This produces all sorts of specialized, pluralistic behavior and belief systems. In this setting, training can generate and test a variety of new stratgies for evangelism.

The Ghetto, Symptom of Urbanization

Ghettos (and there are many kinds) show up first in cities usually as responses to some of the dynamics just described. But ghettos *per se* (even the most pathological ones) are not the real problems of our times but are visible symptoms of fundamental, systematic processes. To treat ghettos as the basic urban disease, or even to make them special targets of evangelization strategies as the *sine qua non* of urban ministry, is like treating a sick person's temperature, rather than the disease.

Christians need strategies to cope with broad urban realities, a plethora of tactics, models, and styles. Obviously, no one form of ministry constitutes adequate response to urban pluralism.

Strategies for Evangelism

Lamentably, we observe many single-strategy evangelization options for large cities. In these cases the evangelists, representing a host of churches and agencies, do not recognize the need for multiple responses to the urbanization of the world. Moreover, while Christian ministry strategies and responsibilities obviously begin with evangelism, they certainly do not stop there. God's people should seek to minister not only *in* the city, but *to* it as well.

Cities have inherited an unusual share of all our problems and problem peoples who have dropped out of other places. As the old saying states, "All roads lead to Rome . . . and all sewers also." Large numbers of urban individuals and institutions lie in ruin. Evangelism is most effective when the passion for evangelistic effectiveness is adorned with broad-ranging concerns and goals for the renewal of the whole of city life.

As in the days of old, urban evangelization is most effectively accomplished by those within the city itself. Jeremiah told the Babylonian exiles to ". . . build houses and settle down . . . and . . . seek the . . . prosperity of the city to which I have carried you into exile. Pray to the Lord for it, because if it prospers, you too will prosper" (Jer. 29:5f). After the exile, Isaiah told the rebuilders of Jerusalem, "Your people will rebuild the ancient ruins and will raise up the age-old foundations; you will be called repairer of broken walls, restorer of streets with dwellings" (Isa. 58:12).

Is it not ironic that many contemporary Christians who claim a high view of scripture continue to ignore the biblical truth stated plainly in hundreds of Old and New Testament texts dealing with urban mission? Surely "the blessed hope" is the Lord's intervention, not the church's continued flight from the presence and task of urban evangelization.

If our analysis is correct, evangelization of the cities today will impact the countryside tomorrow. Surely the cost accountants of mission budgets cannot fail to see the significance of urban mission as a high-growth investment, even though in the short run it often costs more than ministry in rural areas.

A STRATEGIC PERSPECTIVE OF THE CITY

For nearly two thousand years the church has possessed the mandate to disciple all the peoples or nations of the world. Now, in this very generation, we are discovering where these peoples and nations are located: in the large cities of the world. Urban pastors and missionaries need a global perspective to interpret the modern city. They need international skills to live and serve there. This I believe and base my belief on personal experience. Among the nearly 60,000 residents (1980 census) in my own inner-city Chicago neighborhood and nearby public high school, about fifty nations of the world are now represented within an area little more than one square mile. Theologically, one might ask, "What is God trying to accomplish by the urbanization of his world and the internationalization of our cities?" The fact that he's doing it is undeniable. Could it be his way of showing us the priority now for urban evangelization?

"The Empire Strikes Back" is more than the title of a recent movie. It is European urban reality. Without exception, capital cities of Europe which served as administrative centers for empires in the colonial world abroad now are experiencing the usually painful custodial roles for formerly colonialized peoples who have come from the colonies to the new cheap labor markets. Although the dynamics involved create enormous problems for old urban establishments in London, Paris, Amsterdam, Berlin, and other cities, they also create exciting new potential for urban ministry and international evangelization. Every city now has links with populations "back home." To reach out to a person in the name of Jesus Christ in East London is to simultaneously reach out to the Punjab. In Paris it is to impact Algeria. Reaching out in Amsterdam affects Surinam, Goa, or Indonesia. In Berlin, it affects Turkey and other places.

A BIBLICAL AND HISTORICAL PRECEDENT FOR URBAN EVANGELIZATION

The drama behind Paul's epistle to Philemon, the apostle's only personal letter in the New Testament, effectively illustrates this principle of urban ministry for international evangelism:

The Repatriation of an Urban Refugee in Five Acts.

Act I. **Paul in Ephesus**—Acts 19—Two evangelization strategies and over two years' ministry are mentioned. "All Asia" is impacted (v. 10). People, like Philemon, who live one hundred miles upriver in Laodicea or Colossae are converted too. **Time:** Early 50s

Act II. **House Church** in Laodicea (or Colossae, the Lycus valley). Church planting in a small market or regional

city, probably as a result of the Ephesus evangelization ministry. **Time:** Still early 50s

Act III. **Paul in Rome**—Stealing money from his house
church host and master, Onesimus (like the urban
prodigal) goes "where all roads lead"—to Rome.
There he contacts Christ through another, and yet
different urban strategy of Paul, who disciples him
with his urban ministry team. **Time:** Early 60s

Act IV. **Back in Laodicea**—Paul has written a three-
hundred-and-thirty-word (Greek text) cover letter,
hand-carried by Onesimus and Tychicus, explaining
that Onesimus should be welcomed back and recon-
ciled into the family as a brother and not as a slave.
Paul gives a theological perspective to account for
this urban migration. **Time:** Still early 60s, just before
Paul is executed.

Act V. **Back in Ephesus**—A New Testament Postscript:
Ignatius of Antioch, en route to Rome and martyr-
dom, stops at Smyrna and pens a pastoral letter to
Onesimus, now the leading pastor of Ephesus and
successor to the apostle John (banished in 96),
where our drama began some sixty years before in
Acts 19. **Time:** 110 A.D.

Many Bible scholars have concluded that the Onesimus of the
Ignatian letter is the same slave of the Philemon letter. This
sequence presents a marvelous example of the social significance of New Testament evangelism. More than being instru-
mental in the simple repatriation of another urban refugee,
Paul's letter to Philemon provides a lens through which we today
may view the dynamics of contemporary urban reality.

Needed: A Hermeneutic to Interpret and Give Significance
Urban evangelists and pastors, like church leaders everywhere,

need a hermeneutic to interpret and give significance to their ministries in cities. To understand the global context and international significance of urban neighborhoods provides a significant meaning system for those engaged in evangelization of world-class cities. The changing roles of contemporary cities tend to overwhelm pastors by the pluralistic and conflicting demands amid turbulent immigrant and migrant streams. A new understanding of these same macrodynamics could give pastors a new vision of what could or should happen in urban evangelization and provide the theological motivation and psychological energy to get on with the task.

HISTORICAL PRECEDENT FOR URBAN EVANGELISM

In scripture there are hundreds of references to cities and ministries within them. Moreover, the church was born in the city and followed the contours of the urbanized Roman Empire. Examples of the early church, of the thousand-year exchange of African urban churches for European rural ones (500 to 1500 A.D.), of the Reformation in cities, and the resurgence of uniquely urban forms of ministry in the nineteenth and twentieth centuries, are all included in the written record of the church, indicating that God's Spirit has given unique gifts to his urban churches. These examples are worthy of our thoughtful examination, along with other examples of cross-cultural mission.

SUMMARY

Though a declining population is characteristic of some world class cities, others are experiencing rapid growth. Meanwhile, the rest of the world is in the process of urbanizing. With their large and international populations, major cities have become a microcosm of the world and thereby provide a place to develop and test strategies of world evangelism.

Cities continue to challenge churches and mission agencies to develop specialized structures and functions. That a plethora of mission structures, church models, and personal styles exist in most world-class cities is well known. But by no means can most cities be classified as evangelized. Even if they were "reached" today, at the rate cities recycle peoples and cultures, they may be "unreached" by tomorrow.

Every city has a unique ethos. So also does every neighborhood, group, or person within it. Therefore, the ongoing task of urban evangelization requires that we seek to exegete our cities as faithfully and fully as we do the scriptures. Then the whole gospel can engage the whole city to the glory of God and the building up of his urban Kingdom.

NOTES

1. Louis Wirth, *Ghetto* (Chicago: University of Chicago Press, 1956).
2. Lewis Mumford, *Culture of Cities* (New York: Harcourt, Brace, Jovanovich, Inc., 1970).

Dr. Raymond J. Bakke is a professor of ministry at Northern Baptist Theological Seminary in Lombard, Illinois, and is co-founder of the Seminary Consortium for Urban Pastoral Education (SCUPE). He is a graduate of Moody Bible Institute, Seattle Pacific College, Trinity Evangelical Divinity School, and has two degrees from McCormick Theological Seminary. He has taught Bible at Trinity College, Church History and Urban Ministry at McCormick and has over twenty years of urban ministry experience, including a ten-year inner city pastorate. In 1980, he served as the international coordinator for the large city mini-consultation at COWE in Pattaya, Thailand.

The Scope of Mass Evangelism

by H. Norman Pell

Following an introduction to the broad function of mass evangelism–to break down "the wall which separates the church from the masses"–the author summarizes what he considers to be the essential philosophy and theological rationale for mobilizing the whole church in large urban centers. Pell's definition of mass evangelism centers on the efforts of the whole people of God to penetrate every sphere of life in the social structure. He rightly sees in his succinct definitional statement the need for God's people to be active in opening these spheres to strategic witness.

Unique to this essay is the outlined presentation of five contemporary models of mass evangelism with some assessment and criteria for their use.

While the editors applaud his recognition of the crusade mode as an opportunity for penetrating these distinct spheres, at this point the use of people group concepts to enhance "normal" (E-1) evangelism, and the identification and development of strategies for unreached people groups, could make tremendously valuable contributions.

The acute reader will notice how, without articulation, each of these modes of crusade has adapted in some way to the constraints of group thinking. For example, "Evangelism as Celebration" builds separate group needs into the progression and culminates in total celebration.

FUNCTION OF MASS EVANGELISM

These words are written on the refectory wall in a theological seminary for home mission priests at Lisieux, France: "I have not to search for the subject of my meditation. It is always the same. There is a wall which separates the church from the masses; the wall must be broken down at whatever cost to give back to Christ the crowds who are lost to him."

Mass evangelism aims to do just that—break down the wall which separates the church from the masses. It seeks to give back to Christ the crowds who are lost to him. In this sense, the term "mass evangelism"—the gathering together of people for the purpose of proclaiming the gospel—is not a misnomer. The term may be misunderstood, however, unless we point out that we engage in mass evangelism so that people may come into the Kingdom of God.

PHILOSOPHICAL BASIS FOR MASS EVANGELISM

The objection is sometimes raised that a large percentage of those who attend evangelistic meetings are already church-going people. How does this relate to the goal of reaching those who are separated from the church? Several aspects of the question need to be examined.

1) Far more people come to a commitment to Christ from outside the church, even when the audience for the most part comprises church-attending people, than is generally appreciated. Dr. Robert Ferm found in his study of 14,000 Graham Crusade converts living on four continents, that 46 percent were unchurched prior to their decisions.

2) Some time ago Archbishop William Temple stated, "We cannot separate the evangelization of those without, from the rekindling of devotion of those within." It is obvious to the objective mind that evangelism must begin among those within the framework of the church before it can have a significant impact on those outside. In a mass evangelistic meeting, there is unparalleled potential for communication to both groups.

3) The number of people separated from the church who are present at a mass evangelistic meeting is ultimately the responsibility of the local congregation. If the participating churches

have motivated and mobilized their congregations effectively, large numbers of unchurched people will be present.

4) The impact of a series of mass evangelistic meetings is not confined to the meeting time. Such meetings open the way for the gospel to be communicated by radio, television, and newspaper to every possible area of the city and surrounding communities. The evangelistic team and other Christian workers take the message to schools, service clubs, offices, factories, and other strategic social structures not normally open to such a witness. In other words, the venture should be seen not as people attending a series of meetings for a set time, but as the whole people of God penetrating every possible sphere of life that may be opened to receive the witness of the gospel during the designated period.

THEOLOGICAL BASIS FOR MASS EVANGELISM

Mass evangelism finds its source in the great commission of Matthew 28: 19-20: "Go preach . . . make disciples of all people." The population explosion means that in the world today, there are more people than ever before who know nothing of Jesus Christ.

Yet the Lord Jesus never gave a command that could not be fulfilled. His great commission can be achieved, but only if the Body of Christ functions as its Lord intended (cf. Ephesians 4: 1; 1 Corinthians 12—14; Colossians 1: 24—2: 7).

Ken Strachan of the Latin America Mission made a study of the fastest-growing movements in their field: the Communists, the Jehovah's Witnesses and the Pentecostal churches. Their common denominator was obviously not their message. The three groups are respectively an anti-Christian ideology, a heretical cult and a Christian fellowship. Strachan concluded that the growth of any movement is in direct proportion to its ability to mobilize its entire membership for continuous evangelistic action.

Mass evangelism provides a basis for the mobilization of the whole church. It calls all believers to rediscover the power of personal and group prayer. Prayer cells are multiplied in churches and homes across the area while Christians are equipped to share their faith. Contacts with non-Christians are encouraged as believers try to build bridges of friendship to those who are separated from the church. People are enlisted to sing in the choir, usher, or serve in a variety of ways that relate to their particular gifts.

For the first time in many congregations, Christian leaders learn that the church is a body of related believers called to achieve God's purpose through discipleship and witnessing. The church is summoned to action—to advance against the enemy, tear down Satan's strongholds, and establish the Kingdom of God.

When the Body of Christ rises to its true calling, the oneness of the church is demonstrated by the believers' love for each other (cf. John 13:34, 35). In other words, Christians best express the nature of the church when they work together in evangelism. Mass evangelism provides an excellent basis for a demonstration of Christian love and unity.

FIVE MODELS OF MASS EVANGELISM

Model A—Mass Evangelistic Effort as Climax of Preparation

One approach to mass evangelism views the evangelistic effort at the climax of a defined period of preparation. This approach is expressed in the crusades conducted by Billy Graham and his associates around the world.

When the Billy Graham Evangelistic Association works with local churches in a given city or area, the two basic objectives of a crusade are to evangelize the community, and to strengthen the local churches. The four phases in this method of mass evangelism are labeled preliminary, preparation, penetration and preservation.

In the *preliminary* stage, churches which desire to cooperate in a given city or area are drawn together to communicate the good news of Jesus Christ to as many people as possible through a corporate witness. At this point, a crusade committee may be formed, agreement reached concerning the evangelist to be invited, the location and dates for the crusade decided, and responsible working committees established (prayer, finance, counseling and follow-up, visitation, Operation Andrew, youth, publicity, ushers, choir, etc.).

Next follows the *preparation* period designed to lay a foundation for the whole crusade effort. A network of prayer cells is established. Plans are implemented to raise the budget. People are trained in special classes to share their faith and counsel inquirers who will respond in the crusade meetings. Visitation of the total area is organized to invite people to attend the crusade. Believers are encouraged to follow the example of Andrew, who brought Simon Peter to Jesus, and invite their friends to attend. Young people are urged to bring their peers. Ushers are recruited for the meetings. Practical details of the auditorium setting are given proper attention. Publicity and advertising to promote interest in the witness is planned and developed, with special attention given to mass media communication.

When the crusade starts, the *penetration* phase begins. The focus centers on the evangelist's message. It also opens other areas of opportunity for the gospel to penetrate the life of a city. Doors are opened to the evangelist and his team which are not normally open to local believers. High schools, college campuses, service clubs, factories, office canteens, and homes provide a basis for community penetration because interest has been aroused by the crusade event.

As Christian people work together, the media take notice. Access to radio, television, and newspapers normally generated by a crusade provides an excellent forum for bringing the gospel to people who have not planned to attend the crusade.

The *preservation* phase begins when the first inquirer indicates an interest in making a commitment to Christ. This person is counseled personally so the way of salvation is clear. The counselor also takes the person's name, address, and other pertinent information to aid a local congregation in their follow-up. The new Christian, then, is usually guided into a neighborhood Bible study or local church. Because the goal of evangelism is the formation of mature Christians (cf. Colossians

1:28), the work of the crusade only begins with a person's commitment to Christ.

Model B—Evangelism as an Ingredient of Comprehensive Witness

A second approach sees mass evangelism as one ingredient in the mobilization of the church with all its resources for a comprehensive witness in the world. The movement responsible for laying the foundation of this concept is known as Evangelism in Depth (EID). It had its formal inception in an experiment in the Republic of Nicaragua in 1960.

The Latin America Mission has prepared the following outline stating the basic presuppositions, principles, and program of Evangelism in Depth:

1) Presuppositions or Convictions. a) Abundant reaping requires saturation sowing. b) Christians can and must work together in evangelism. c) When Christians pool resources for evangelism, God multiplies those resources. d) A dedicated minority can make an impact on an entire nation.

2) Principles. a) Mobilization of every Christian in witness. b) Mobilization within the framework of the church. c) Mobilization by local leadership. d) Mobilization with global objectives.

3) Program. a) Principles of determining methods—match resources with needs. b) Basic program elements are prayer, training, visitation, special projects (including social action projects), evangelistic meetings, and continuation.

Mass evangelistic meetings form an important part of the EID program. These meetings include local campaigns in each church, a united campaign in each city, and regional campaigns in which churches of surrounding cities cooperate. The climax of the year is a national campaign when Christians converge on the capital city for a great parade and final meeting.

However, the flip chart of the EID movement comments:

It is often surprising to the person first hearing about

Evangelism in Depth to learn that before the evangelistic meetings even began more than half the total of new converts of the year have already made their decision for Christ. It is well to keep in mind that all the phases of the program which precede the evangelistic meetings are in themselves evangelistic efforts and are not to be construed simply as preparation for the evangelistic meetings.

The theological foundation of Evangelism in Depth could be described as an ellipse whose two foci are the great commission of the church and the unity of the Body of Christ.

The basic philosophy of the Evangelism in Depth movement has been crystallized in the following statement:

In-depth evangelism is two things: a set of biblical goals rooted in the fundamental purpose or mission of the church; and a plan for moving a church toward these goals. The first goal is total evangelism, which has to do with mission. The second goal is total mobilization, which describes the church functioning as the Body of Christ. The third goal is visible unity, emphasizing the need for making visible the oneness of the Body of Christ.

In the years that followed the 1960 Nicaraguan experiment, the strategy was developed in Costa Rica, Guatemala, Honduras, Venezuela, Bolivia, Peru, Colombia, and Ecuador. What happened in Latin America subsequently inspired similar efforts by Christians in other parts of the world.

Almost simultaneously with the Evangelism in Depth developments in Latin America came the New Life For All movement in Nigeria. This indigenous evangelistic effort aimed to bring the gospel to every person, first in Nigeria and then in all of Africa. It was born in the heart of the Reverend Gerald O. Swank, a missionary of the Sudan Interior Mission, who worked at that time in the Bible Institute at Kagoro, Nigeria. The burden for total evangelization of Nigeria arose out of Jesus' words: "My meat is to do the will of him who sent me and to finish his work." Also, "I have finished the work which Thou gavest me to do" (John 4:34 and 17:4).

Dr. George Peters points out that the secret behind the

47

movement, besides the gracious and sovereign ministry of the Holy Spirit, was the rediscovery of some simple and basic scriptural evangelistic principles. These, in turn, demanded a drastic rethinking of the method, gradually leading to a new pattern of evangelism.

Those principles may be stated in two basic formulas: 1) The total church worshiping must become the total church militant in Christian witness and evangelism. Total evangelization of the lost requires the total mobilization of all believers. 2) The practice of centripetalism must be changed into the practice of centrifugalism if the task is to be accomplished. The church must become a "going" and "sending" church. It must cease living to itself.

The method by which this idea could be realized gradually developed in the mind of Mr. Swank. In 1962 he met with Dayton Roberts of the Latin America Mission. He was encouraged by the similarities between the Evangelism in Depth movement and New Life For All, as it was unfolding. Later, as New Life For All progressed and matured, the formula for evangelization was stated as "mobilization X witness."

The plan followed in implementing this understanding was based on these premises: 1) Every Christian, without exception, according to talents and circumstances, is called upon to be a witness for Christ. The first goal, then, even though the final result may fall short, is the mobilization of the total membership. 2) Every Christian's fellowship must center in the fellowship of the local church. The church then begins to function as it should. 3) This personal and church witness must relate to the total witness of the entire Body of Christ in the area or city. Therefore, in some practical way, a living witness must be given to the unity of the Body of Christ. There is only one gospel, so it is imperative that those who believe in Christ should unite in their testimony to him. 4) The aim must be nothing less than total and complete outreach. Therefore, we should think in terms of natural geographic or language areas. In this way, we can face the problem of fulfilling our responsibility.

A city-wide evangelistic campaign is recommended in the manual for the New Life For All movement toward the end of the year's efforts. But again the manual sounds a warning:

> It has happened that the churches in a city have thought of the City Campaign as being the entire program of New Life For All. In these cases, they did not reap the benefits they would have if they had established the work on a proper basis and carried through all the steps as outlined. The City Campaign must be considered as the climax only of a long, persistent and determined effort to reach everyone in it.

Model C—Evangelism as an Extension of Celebration

A third approach to mass evangelism enables evangelism to become an extension of celebration. This is a current model of mission being developed by African Enterprise around the concept, "Festivals of Faith."

Michael Cassidy is founder and South African Team Leader of African Enterprise, an interracial organization dedicated to evangelization. In the 1970s he was joined in this task by Bishop Festo Kivengere of Uganda, who became the leader of a team of nine evangelists in East Africa.

The idea of a Festival of Faith developed from a discussion that Michael Cassidy had with Dr. Ralph Winter, Director of the United States Center for World Mission. Winter expressed the view that the church ought to have moments when it could really perceive, feel, and experience its togetherness. "Why," asked Dr. Winter, "don't you try to mount a sort of combination of a country fair and an evangelistic campaign?"

The idea appealed to Cassidy. He observed that in a number of parts of the world the term "festival" has greater appeal than that of "mission" or "crusade." This title for mass evangelism has been used by other evangelists, such as Leighton Ford, who found it more acceptable in the affluent North Shore area of Chicago than the term "crusade." To many people, it is a less threatening title and depicts more succinctly the concept of Christian togetherness as the context for evangelism and mission. In this way, evangelism becomes an extension of celebration.

Kimberley, South Africa, was the location of Cassidy's first "festival" experiment. The organizations involved were pleased with the result. Here was instituted the plan for having a meeting each night of the week in a different community, followed by one meeting when all gathered at a central stadium on the weekend for an experience of Christian celebration.

This model of mass evangelism may be especially appropriate to South Africa. It helps to overcome the problem of how to have a major campaign in an area where the residential restrictions make it difficult for blacks to get to a central meeting area in the middle of a town. At the same time, it provides the opportunity for Christians of all races to experience togetherness.

In Kimberley, for example, four thousand people were present for the closing Communion service and some two thousand stayed the whole afternoon for the music festival. Michael Cassidy comments, "South Africans in many ways seem starved for this kind of experience and they basically need and long for opportunities to relate. Perhaps our Festivals of Faith can constitute at least one type of opportunity."

Model D—Evangelism for Church Growth and Church Planting

Still another approach may aim to use mass evangelism in the context of church growth plans for existing churches, as well as for actually starting new churches. One exciting experiment along these lines has been undertaken in Argentina, Uruguay, and Bolivia in crusades conducted by Luis Palau.

Objectives for these city-wide evangelistic crusades were the growth of participating churches and strategic planting of new churches in Rosario, Argentina.

Specific goals were delineated in a workshop held fourteen months prior to the crusade. The combined membership of the twenty participating churches was 1769. Six months after the November 1976 crusade, these twenty churches had grown to 2566—a 42.5 percent increase in seventeen months, the equivalent of a 25.3 percent annual growth rate; in contrast, during the previous ten-year period, the annual growth rate was 1.4 percent. But more significantly, the participating churches planned for external as well as internal growth. They started 42 new congregations now thriving in strategic sections of the city.

Similar efforts to achieve church growth were made in Uruguay and Bolivia and succeeded in combining church growth approaches with mass evangelism. Luis Palau comments:

> I consider this a real breakthrough in mass evangelism. We've concerned ourselves primarily with moving vast acres of grain, i.e., securing public decisions. Far too often these have resulted in gleaning only a few sheaves of responsible members. We've considered follow-up as something that takes place after the evangelistic harvest is over. What we really need is to build into every phase of our evangelistic planning a goal-oriented concept of follow-through. And the difference is more than semantics. It's the basic difference between gathering grain into barns or leaving it in the fields to rot.

Model E—Evangelism as a Catalyst of Continuing Outreach

A recent variant on all these approaches has utilized mass evangelism as a catalyst to develop evangelistic outreach to the community on a continuing basis.

In addition to continuing with Model A, Leighton Ford and his team have recently developed another model which seeks to enable the local congregation to develop a life-style of reaching out. In this concept, the crusade phase becomes a catalyst to inspire continuing evangelism, rather than the climax of efforts.

The theme of this reach-out process is "Reach Out Now" (cf. John 4:35), and all activity points to that end. It is hoped that this life-style may be achieved by a local congregation prior to the celebration or crusade phase. The crusade then becomes one more way for the local church to reach out to others, rather than the expression of the sum total of the church's evangelistic endeavor over a period of time.

Principles of the reach-out process are based on the understanding that the church is the extension of the Incarnation. It must therefore embody in its life and ministry the principles of the ministry of Jesus (cf. Matthew 9:35-10:7; Luke 10:17-22).

These principles have been defined as:

1) *Establishing Specific Objectives.* Helping the local congregation (not just the leadership) to discover together what specific goals the Lord is calling them to achieve in the Kingdom of God.

2) *Identifying People's Needs.* Assisting the local congregation to break through the barriers which isolate the church from people in the community and enable Christians to "build bridges of friendship" to people.

3) *Equipping the People of God.* Motivating the entire congregation to be the people of God and enabling them with confidence to share their faith.

4) *Reaching Out and Discipling.* Encouraging Christians to relate to people in their life situation, with special emphasis on the use of the Christian home in this connection, sharing their friendship and faith in a way that will stimulate spiritual growth.

5) *Celebrating and Evaluating.* Joining together in worship and thanksgiving to celebrate God's working in his world and to reach out to others in the context of praise and fellowship.

Reach-out resources have been developed which are offered to enable churches to implement the principles outlined.

The effect of these concepts upon the crusade is to provide Christians with a keen sense of participation arising from their prior involvement at the congregational level. They are less inclined to come to the crusade as "spectators" of what others are doing, having already experienced the joy of reaching out to others.

Another important aspect of the reach-out process is that after the crusade, in the context of the celebration phase, less of a letdown is experienced by the participants than in Model A. Christians return to their churches and continue to implement the principles to which their congregation is committed, having regarded the crusade as another enabling resource.

CRITICISMS OF MASS EVANGELISM

1) *Concerning the method.* Despite its use by our Lord and by great evangelists of the past, there are some critics of mass evangelism who would describe it as a social anachronism with

limited appeal in the contemporary world.

While mass evangelism will not appeal to every person, it does provide an opportunity for non-Christians to hear an explanation of the gospel within the context of a crowd and without becoming self-conscious. Rarely does another opportunity exist to do this in today's society.

The appeal of mass evangelism to a wide cross section of the community, including young people, depends largely upon those planning each program. It must relate to each subculture it seeks to reach.

2) *Concerning the messenger.* There are those who claim that mass evangelism fosters a personality cult which many people find distasteful. Let us agree that mass evangelism at this point is open to the obnoxious self-promotion of the charlatan. But if an evangelist is carefully chosen whose authenticity and integrity are above question, there is no reason why the New Testament formula cannot be repeated. "They heard John speak and followed Jesus" (John 1:37).

Some claim that apart from Billy Graham very few evangelists have sufficient charisma and drawing power to attract whole communities to mass meetings. But is personal charisma an essential qualification of an evangelist? Surely the response in attendance should arise basically from the action taken by the Christians in the churches sponsoring the evangelistic witness. Any added contribution made by the personality of the evangelist is a plus factor.

3) *Concerning the message.* Critics of mass evangelism often state that the evangelist's message is too simplistic and void of social relevance. The question is, "What is the gospel?" The Lausanne Covenant described this "objective thrust of the Gospel," this "good news," this way: "that Jesus Christ died for our sins and was raised from the dead according to the Scriptures, and that as the reigning Lord he now offers the forgiveness of sins and the liberating gift of the Spirit to all who repent and believe."

The Lausanne Covenant goes on to state: ". . . We affirm that evangelism and sociopolitical involvement are both part of our

Christian duty. . . . The salvation we claim should be transforming us in the totality of our personal and social responsibilities. Faith without works is dead."

A basic premise is, then, that the central message of evangelism is personal as it relates to the individual. The outworking of the response to this message must be seen in society as obedience to Christ, incorporation into the church and responsible service in the world. These three emphases should find expression in evangelistic preaching as they highlight the nature of Christian discipleship; otherwise, the evangelist's preaching may produce decisions but not disciples.

SUMMARY

The foregoing outline of various mass evangelism models being implemented around the world today highlights the importance of urging churches to carefully seek the guidance of the Holy Spirit in discerning the following: 1) What are the objectives desired? 2) Which model of mass evangelism embodies the approach most appropriate for the participating churches at this time? 3) Which evangelist will present the gospel in a way that is relevant to the receiving community, and make the demands of Christian discipleship an integral part of the message communicated? 4) How can the most help be given local churches to mobilize their congregations for the ventures contemplated?

This brief survey of the various models of mass evangelism has highlighted one factor above others: that the effectiveness of any mass evangelism model is ultimately measured, under the blessing of the Holy Spirit, by the extent to which Christians in local congregations can be motivated and mobilized to be the people of God and achieve established objectives.

Normal Pell is currently the international coordinating director of in-depth evangelism programs for the Leighton Ford evangelistic team—a position he has held for the last seven years. An ordained Baptist minister, he is also general superintendent of the Baptist Union of Victoria in his native Australia.

He, his wife Dorothy, and son Allan, live in Melbourne.

Urban Missions: Reaching the City of Amsterdam

by Floyd McClung

While most mission organizations are overwhelmingly rural or small town in their orientation, Youth with a Mission (YWAM) is almost exclusively urban in its history and loci of activity. Begun nearly two decades ago primarily as an outreach ministry to alienated youth, drug-culture "dropouts," and those who attend urban events such as the Olympic Games and world fairs, YWAM illustrates an evolving mission strategy seeking now to embrace both urban persons and places.

Youth with a Mission's uniqueness is due partly to its charismatic and flexible style and partly to its compassionate, creative, young urban staff leadership who seem to adapt as well to city life as pioneer missionaries did to jungles a generation ago. Youth with a Mission's intentional modeling projects function as a research and development component for other mission organizations planning ministry in large cities.

Within the last thirty years the greatest mass migration in human history has taken place—a migration to the city. The populations of Third World cities alone have increased by 400 million people to 26 with over 1 million. Current figures also indicate that there are 178 cities worldwide with more than 1 million people.

At the present rate of migration, in twenty years, there will be

650 million people living within 60 of the world's cities. The human race is fast becoming an urban species.

This burgeoning urban population represents intense human need and reflects increasingly complex problems of poverty, crime, oppression, hunger, unemployment, and inadequate housing. It is estimated that a fifth to a half of all urban people in the Third World live in slums or shantytowns. Basic services— such as sanitation, water, and electricity—may be grossly inadequate or even completely lacking. Loneliness, fear, violence, instability, and alienation are a part of the city dweller's life day after day.

BIBLICAL PERSPECTIVES ON THE CITY

In light of the biblical perspectives and the reality of human need in the densely populated urban areas, a response is required from the Church of Jesus Christ.

Luke's description of Jesus' ride into Jerusalem (Luke 19:41) includes the strong feelings of compassion which the Lord expressed as he wept over the city that killed prophets and stoned those sent by God. Jesus cared deeply for this city which had broken its covenant with God and resisted his desire to gather its people. He cried openly for this city that would crucify him. He loved the people of this city who knew no peace, were oppressed by the Romans, and unmindful of the long-awaited Messiah in their midst.

In the Old Testament, the gentile city of Nineveh had no covenant with God to compel him to care, as did Jerusalem. Yet God saw 120,000 people who were confused and lost. Jonah's confession reveals God's characteristic grace and extension of mercy toward the repentant city: ". . . I knew that Thou are a gracious God and merciful, slow to anger, and abounding in steadfast love, and repentant of evil" (Jonah 4:2).

Cities of the world today need to experience these attributes of God's character. The people of the cities need to be reached with the gospel of God's saving grace.

BIBLICAL MODELS FOR EVANGELIZING THE CITY

One method in God's strategy for reaching the city becomes

clear from our reading the Book of Jonah. The Lord uses prophetic proclamation to call people to himself. Nineveh faced certain judgment by God for its sinfulness. But the people heard God's message through Jonah, and the city repented.

There is something here of a biblical antidote for the overwhelming pessimism toward efforts to reach cities for Christ. There is hope for the cities, in spite of all their problems; for even Nineveh repented and turned to the Lord. He saw the influence of this Assyrian capital. He focused his love and grace on it to cause a change.

Today there are similar cities with influence far beyond their geographic boundaries. They are headquarters for principalities and powers, places of evil and strife, initiators of trends, fashions, and ideas that captivate wide interest. Like Nineveh, many of the world's cities take on a strategic import because of their great influence. Just as God spotlighted Nineveh for Jonah's special attention, God calls his people today to focus special care and effort on reaching the Ninevehs of our world with the message of his love and grace.

The strategies God uses to reach the cities may change from one city to another. For Nineveh, God used a proud prophet to preach. In Babylon, God directed his people to "build houses . . . plant gardens . . . seek the welfare of the city where I have sent you . . . and pray to the Lord on its behalf, for in its welfare you will find your welfare" (Jeremiah 29:5-7). Infiltrating and inhabiting the Babylons of our world is another strategy God uses for reaching the cities through his people who live there as salt and light.

In Antioch, God directed the early church to use still another strategy. An apostolic center of body life and missionary activity was established. Its purpose was twofold: to penetrate one of the most influential commercial centers of that day with the gospel of Jesus Christ; also, to serve as a base for sending out the good news with mission teams—such as those who went out with Paul and Barnabas. According to Acts (chapters 11, 13-16), the church at Antioch was marked by these characteristics:

(1) It was an integrated church, made up of blacks, whites,

    Jews, Greeks, rich, and poor.

(2) It was a growing church, with "great numbers" of people involved.

(3) It had a solid base of teaching, including an outreach ministry to keep it from being ingrown.

(4) It was charismatic, in the best sense of that word, open to the prophetic gifts (as distinguished from the teaching gifts).

(5) It cared for the poor, responding to the exhortations of the Holy Spirit by providing practical help to them.

(6) It had a plural leadership, allowing a diversity of ministries to function.

(7) It had a strong devotional life, spending time in fasting and worship.

(8) It was an apostolic center, training, sending, and supporting its best members in missionary activity without trying to control them.

(9) It had a rich life of fellowship and provided strong pastoral care for its members.

These biblical models from Nineveh, Babylon, and Antioch identify some of God's strategies for us today and provide a theological basis for continuing work among urban populations. Sensitivity to God's great heart of love toward the cities of people without Christ provides immense motivation to care and be involved in urban ministries.

MARKS OF THE URBAN MISSIONARY

Because scripture clearly presents God's deep concern for people in urban areas, we have an imperative to care and respond with action. Reaching the cities for Christ will require the efforts of thousands who are committed to minister the love of Christ—with all that may mean to the city dwellers of the world.

An urban ministry sometimes calls for personal sacrifice and perhaps suffering on the part of those who minister. Much of what is considered to be the normal requirements and rights of life must sometimes be laid aside in order to care for and witness to needy city people. Doing without what some consider to be necessities (washing machine and dryer, refrigerator, owning a home or a car, having meat in the diet, having hot water and even heated living facilities) must be done voluntarily and without resentment. Willingly giving up the right, and even any expectation, of having these things is essential, or it will cause bitterness toward God and those with whom and to whom we minister.

The new wave of urban missionaries must see no dichotomy between evangelism and practical love. They must be secure and dedicated enough to flesh out the gospel through daily life-style, bold and zealous enough to preach the gospel through creative proclamation. They must see the roles of the doctor, the evangelist, the teacher, the carpenter or any other—each as an equally legitimate expression of God's love; for there are different ministries in the body of Christ, but each one to be done in humility as a part of the team or the community. The lone missionary cannot provide an alternative to the impersonal loneliness of the city. Christian service in the urban setting has its greatest effect when done as the expression of a loving body of believers.

"URBAN MISSIONS" LAUNCHED BY YOUTH WITH A MISSION

Youth with a Mission's Urban Missions has its roots in a ministry we began in 1971 in Kabul, Afghanistan, to help American and European "hippies" traveling through the city. Although at first we saw ourselves as an evangelistic team, we soon discovered that approach was ineffective in reaching people. What was needed was a loving Christian community which offered love and acceptance to alienated, wounded young people whom we sought to reach. This approach did work, and the result was the conversion of several hundred young people.

In 1973, we moved to Amsterdam and became concerned with reaching a broader spectrum of humanity than the young people we had grown accustomed to helping. We saw that the whole city was alienated from God and from one another. Only 3 percent of its population were churchgoers. The "impersonal-ness" of big-city living overwhelmed us. We saw that our evangelism had to be rooted in a caring community of believers, devoted to becoming involved in the lives of others.

Against the background of this experience, which had alerted us to the great and varied needs in the city, leaders of Youth with a Mission prayerfully decided to launch a new program to reach great cities. In 1978, I was asked to initiate a new ministry focusing on urban evangelism. After two years of prayer and planning, "Urban Missions" was launched.

Immediate Goals and Long-Range Objectives

The goal of Urban Missions is to reach urban people with the gospel and establish them in reproducing fellowships of believers. A priority is to train local converts to lead the churches that are planted and instill in them a vision to reach another city, neighborhood, or people group with the gospel.

The long-range objective is to send pioneering teams to the world's 300 great cities. It is projected that a minimum of 5000 workers are needed to accomplish this objective. With God's help and blessing, this can be done through a spontaneous multiplication of churches that are planted, and through recruiting, training, and sending urban missionary teams.

Focus on Amsterdam

At present Urban Mission's project is focused on the city of Amsterdam. Eighty staff workers are involved in a variety of evangelistic outreaches and church planting programs. These include coffee bars, street preaching, social work with prostitutes, drop-in centers, drama teams, an elementary school, literature distribution, home Bible studies, concerts, and a live-in community. The goal is to plant churches in the unreached neighborhoods and among the unreached people groups of Amsterdam, and, at the same time, to provide programs that give practical care for needy people such as alcoholics, runaways, and prostitutes.

Amsterdam provides an ideal training ground for preparing teams for cross-cultural missionary work. There are 115 nationalities in the city and over 40 ethnic neighborhoods, ranging from Chinese to Egyptian, Surinamese to Indonesian. Not only does Amsterdam lend itself as an ideal international training site because it is the world in microcosm, but, unlike American cities, its ghettos are in the suburbs rather than the inner city. This helps prepare workers who will be trained and placed in teams for ministry in the great Third World cities with their sprawling suburban slums in the next two to five years.

Structure of the Ministry

Urban Missions has four live-in communities in Amsterdam. Each community has its own group of leaders responsible for the various projects. Because our ministry is still evolving, with definite goals not yet fully worked out, we find it important to meet regularly as community leaders.

The leadership couples from each of the four communities meet weekly for fellowship over a meal, to share needs, to pray, and to coordinate our ministries. These times together facilitate our function as an eldership and provide the quality time needed to build the relationships essential to unity and mutual upbuilding.

All our workers in Amsterdam meet regularly as a body for worship, recreation, outreach ministry, and teaching.

Leaders in each community are responsible for the pastoral care of our body. When the communities number from twenty to thirty people, small groups are formed. People are trained in special seminars to counsel and lead Bible studies for these groups. These training seminars also help group leaders stimulate their gifts and grow in various areas of responsibility.

We look upon ourselves more as a body than as an organization, though aspects of both are present. Youth with a Mission functions more as a community missionary movement than as an administrative organization. Leaders of the various teams, communities, and fellowships are selected from those called to full-time involvement in YWAM ministries. These leaders work closely and in counsel with godly businessmen and other mature Christians in the Body of Christ.

Recruitment and Training for Ministry

Most of those involved with us as workers in urban ministries have heard about the ministry from a friend, or they have heard one of our leaders speak. We believe God can use young people in mission work, so we challenge them to give a summer, or one or two years to the Lord's work. Most of our full-time workers are people who stayed on after a short-term experience.

In Amsterdam we hold an outreach each summer, as well as a summer School of Missions. Through these short-term programs, people get firsthand experience in overseas work. They often get a world vision and are spoiled for the ordinary! Our recruiting endeavors are augmented by regular newsletters and other printed information.

A six-month period at our Discipleship Training School provides a screening and training process for applicants. This program stresses formation of Christian character and focuses upon seven basic areas foundational to the Christian life: Bible study and prayer, knowing God, relationships, spiritual warfare, servanthood, gifts and ministries, evangelism, and missions. Prayer groups meet daily to pray for the nations of the world. Students participate in practical work programs or local outreach ministries each afternoon and also in a month of outreach experiences usually held somewhere outside Holland.

Training for work with Urban Missions is based on a philosophy of practical discipleship. We try to implement the method Jesus used in discipling the twelve:

(1) He did it and they watched.
(2) He did it and they helped.
(3) They did it and he helped.
(4) They did it and he left!

This requires time-consuming and demanding personal involvement of leaders in the lives of the recruits.

How Ministry in Community Works

The Ark was the first ministry we established in Amsterdam, and it has proven the fruitfulness of our live-in community approach.

The Ark is a healing community of about fifty people who minister through a Sunday evening service, friendship evangelism, Bible studies, and a consistent emphasis on relationships. Through the Ark's ministry, one hundred to two hundred people have come to the Lord each year.

More recently, we have emphasized creativity in evangelism. For example, a drama team presents the gospel in discos, nightclubs, student centers, and on the street. Colorful proclamation of the gospel may be accompanied by Jewish folk dancing and mime, attracting large crowds of people on the main squares of the city. Sometimes a coffin is carried through the red-light district to prophetically protest death in the city.

On Friday and Saturday nights a small group goes out to witness to the prostitutes, who number as many as fifteen thousand in Amsterdam's inner city. This activity has led to many dramatic conversions. It also reminds us of people's resistance to the gospel. Further, these experiences strengthen our conviction that the city is best penetrated by a praising, loving community that raises questions in people's minds by the love, creative evangelism, and practical care within the community. The questions raised can be answered through the community's proclaiming and teaching.

THE CHALLENGE

In Urban Missions, all our workers have been inspired by the two young men, ages nineteen and twenty-one, sent by General Booth to open the work of the Salvation Army in New Zealand. Both had been Christians less than three years when Booth commissioned them to "take New Zealand for Christ!"

Upon arrival in Wellington, one young man suggested that the other "take the North Island, and I'll take the South Island." When the two met again nine months later, they had 5,000 converts between them, 500 newly converted workers in Salvation Army uniforms, and barracks established in every major city in New Zealand. They had taken New Zealand for Christ!

We believe God can use Urban Missions to do similar mighty exploits for him as we are willing to give ourselves to reach the

Ninevehs, Babylons, and Antiochs of our day. It won't be easy. It may cost us our lives. But it is worth it all to see the light of the gospel shine into the darkness that hangs like a cloud over our cities. After all, we know that he is ". . . a gracious God and merciful, slow to anger, and abounding in steadfast love" (Jonah 4:2, RSV).

For more information about YWAM's urban ministries, write:

> URBAN MISSIONS
> Youth with a Mission
> Prins Hendrikkade 50
> 1012 AC Amsterdam

Floyd McClung is director of Urban Missions, a division of Youth with a Mission. Urban Missions is a program of urban evangelism and church planting in several world-class cities. He presently lives in Amsterdam, Holland.

Part 2
Case
Studies

National Evangelism Support Team (NEST) in the South Bronx

by Dale W. Cross

The "Bold Mission Thrust" emphasis of the Southern Baptist Convention contains a "Key 22 Cities" denominational plan, part of which is described in this report on the National Evangelism Support Team (NEST).

Perhaps the most noteworthy and commendable feature of the article is the intentional reduction by a successful, powerful, and visible mission organization, to a lowered profile. The resultant cooperative arrangement, along with its sensitivity to local dynamics and indigeneous persons, is characterized, in addition, by a willingness to accept risk, and by a nontriumphal spirit. This is a comprehensive joint-action project in the South Bronx, New York, to test the rationale, philosophy, and strategy design.

A number of key elements are suggested here. They include a powerful challenge to laity for involvement at practical levels in urban mission and evangelism, dramatic integration of evangelism with the broader agenda of rebuilding an entire urban community, and a candid assessment of events to date.

The planners built from a realistic data base, program cost, and problem analysis.

THE BIRTH OF NEST

National Evangelism Support Team (NEST) was born as the

result of lay revolution among Southern Baptists. It is the channel by which creative, turned-on Christian lay people link up with one another to give purposeful expression to their strong call to mission.

In recent years, many Southern Baptist lay people have experienced new spiritual life through renewal weekends, lay witness missions, evangelism schools, and special mission action projects sponsored by Brotherhood and Women's Missionary Union, the denomination's men's and women's mission societies. After these action projects or training periods have concluded, people have expressed a keen interest in accelerating their mission participation. But as they sought to give expression to their dreams, ideas, and projects, frequently the established systems of the church and denomination have been unable to provide the counsel, support, and affirmation they needed.

Meanwhile, a denominational emphasis called Bold Mission Thrust (BMT) was organized to evangelize and congregationalize America. Bold Mission Thrust's goals are to present the gospel to every person in America and to establish new churches in communities which have no evangelistic witness. Twenty-two cities have been targeted as key points of major emphasis. Other emphases focus on communities in transition, ministry projects with ethnic groups and blacks, and cooperative ministries with other Christian groups.

A massive denomination-wide promotion was launched, emphasizing the need for bold, creative planning for the future. This promotion was internalized by the bold new laity becoming evident in the Southern Baptist denomination. They began calling for Convention leadership to match their rhetoric with real boldness in planning and action.

Parachurch evangelism and mission groups sometimes come into being as a direct result of the local church or denomination's failure to provide ways for the laity to actualize their dreams and goals and participate directly in mission. In order to avoid this eventuality, the Southern Baptist Convention formed NEST to capture and channel the great surge of lay energy.

NEST IN THE STRATEGY OF BMT

In the national strategy for implementing the Bold Mission Thrust, the NEST concept is applied to key cities where the needs demand new energy, creativity, and resources. On file at the Convention's National Evangelism Office are the names of those who have participated in their Lay Renewal or witness training programs. Some participants have previously registered concern for particular cities. From across the nation these persons are called together.

Some of these lay people have skills which make them valued consultants in designing strategy. All bring a new sense of excitement and hope concerning the Bold Mission Thrust in the cities. On weekend tours into the cities they see the needs and learn about the projects to which they might relate. They meet with local Southern Baptist leaders to be briefed on the BMT strategies for the specific city.

On one of these weekend tours in New York City, a NEST tour group was introduced to a project in the South Bronx called the Bronx Shepherds Restoration Project. The Shepherds project has since become a primary model for NEST and is providing valuable lessons in how to open new avenues for meaningful lay participation in urban mission.

THE BRONX SHEPHERDS RESTORATION CORPORATION

The Bronx Shepherds Restoration Corporation (BSRC) is the culmination of efforts by a group of ministers and lay people who remained in the South Bronx after other major institutions abandoned the area. This group felt the ultimate rebuilding of the South Bronx as their task. Together they discussed approaches, goals, and objectives. They agreed that the organization's objective should be the physical, spiritual, social, and economic rehabilitation and revitalization of the Bronx.

The Shepherds serve as a change agent to develop and stabilize the target community. The major goal is to improve the quality of life by creating a stronger housing stock, rehabilitating and reinforcing community infrastructure, upgrading commercial centers, and developing jobs and economic activity.

Representatives from eighty-seven churches in the South Bronx comprise the membership of the Bronx Shepherds. The group is interdenominational, including representatives of National Baptist, Methodist, Church of Christ, African Methodist Episcopal, Lutheran, and Southern Baptist churches. There are no restrictions on membership, and any church in the area may belong. The churches provide the seed money to operate this organization.

On the second Saturday of each month, the Shepherds meet to discuss business. All members are urged to attend, to express their comments, and to voice their concerns and those of their constituents. A representative member may bring two members of his/her congregation to emphasize the congregation's concerns and complaints.

Another vehicle for accountability in the Shepherd projects is the board of directors who meet monthly to address concerns brought to their attention. If any issue is not resolved, it is brought before the general body for resolution.

Devastation in the South Bronx

The South Bronx, according to many witnesses, is probably the most devastated area in any of the nation's cities. Some consider it to be in worse condition than Berlin and other major German cities at the end of World War II. Some term it a wasteland, for one block after another is littered with strewn rubble and abandoned buildings.

During the last ten years the area has experienced marked deterioration. Within this time, the South Bronx has seen: 1) the loss of 200,000 jobs, 2) the loss of every major form of employment other than manufacturing, 3) an unemployment rate of 18 percent, 4) abandonment of 40 percent of its housing, 5) an increased illiteracy rate (35 percent of the population has less than eight years of school), 6) a substantial increase of aged persons (10 percent of the family heads are sixty-five years or older), 7) 35 percent of families are headed by a female, 8) 28 percent of the population is below the poverty level, and 9) a marked reduction in income to a median level of $4000 per family.

Nevertheless, the South Bronx has not been totally abandoned as some had predicted. But through the aid of groups like the Bronx Shepherds Restoration Corporation, the community has seen some lessening of the devastation.

Strategy of Revitalization

The Shepherds' revitalization strategy has been to create islands of strength within the South Bronx. This has involved identifying institutions that represent strength—like churches, schools, hospitals—and making them the locus of a development effort. The rationale is that revitalization and rehabilitation may be achieved by anchoring a development with a proven source of strength.

The Shepherds' strategy assumes that as each island of strength is developed, the concentric circles for expansion of such areas would meet, eventually rehabilitating the whole area. The Shepherds also believe that when the process begins around the islands of strength, others will see the trend and move also to rehabilitate and revitalize.

One reason McKinley Square is such an important piece in the Shepherds' strategy is its central and highly visible location. A move to rehabilitate it would be seen by the other inhabitants as a signal that the area is coming back. As a result, they would begin to revitalize their own homes and buildings.

Each Shepherds' target area focuses on a site in proximity to churches, schools, etc. In the case of churches, the congregations are made aware of the Shepherds' efforts and their support is enlisted. Their actions are expected to have a domino effect.

The South Bronx Shepherds have focused on improved housing as a strategy for the spiritual and physical resurrection of the South Bronx. But the level of devastation requires creative solutions that juxtapose the resources of government, civic and social groups, corporations, and the church. Unfortunately, solutions to the problems have to date been too little, too late, and too lethargic.

Problems and Procedures of Rehabilitation

Restoration costs are nearing $50,000 per housing unit, while new construction is fast approaching $65,000. Costs like these have frightened away most concerned groups, individuals, and organizations. Yet, if spiritual and physical resurrection is to occur, the problem of substandard and devastated housing must be addressed. This is one reason the Bronx Shepherds Restoration Corporation is proposing a model for housing development that will make rehabilitation less costly and provide a blueprint for churches all over the nation to replicate.

The local church housing redevelopment effort is designed to take advantage of one of the most plentiful resources the church has—workers. Each church requests its membership to tithe five days of their time each year. The skills of representatives from participating churches are assessed, and they are assigned to various tasks (i.e., furring, taping, painting, flooring, etc.).

When buildings in need of renovation are identified, cost estimates and work plans are developed. The labor force of 100 church volunteers working under the guidance of skilled artisans provides the unskilled and semiskilled labor required to moderately rehabilitate each building. The major tasks of plumbing, electrical wiring, and heating are left to the experts.

Labor costs comprise anywhere from 70 to 80 percent of total construction costs. By using tithed labor, the Shepherds should be able to substantially rehabilitate a housing unit for $10,000 to $12,000, compared to the current market rate of $50,000.

Benefits of the Shepherds' Plan

Significant benefits come to the South Bronx as a result of the proposed program. First, by being able to substantially rehabilitate a unit for as little as $10,000-$12,000, the Shepherds make the possibility of renewing a deteriorated neighborhood attractive to prospective and current residents.

Second, churches and other groups can afford to rehabilitate several housing units, since a twenty-unit building would cost $200,000 to rehabilitate rather than $1,000,000. Moreover, the Shepherds would have a substantial "sweat equity" investment of $800,000 that could be utilized at a later date.

Third, the rents charged by the Shepherds could be less than market price since debt service and interest costs would be substantially less than that required by traditional means.

Fourth, people would once again be attracted to the area because of the positive steps being taken to rebuild it.

Example of Project Cost

The projected costs for a project are outlined below using a fifty-unit building as an example. Suitable ratios are expected to occur with smaller buildings ranging from ten to forty-nine units.

PROJECTED COSTS

	INSTALLED COST	CPU
EXPERT SERVICES		
New Power Plants	$ 90,000.00	$ 1,800.00
Plumbing	25,000.00	500.00
Electrical	20,000.00	400.00
Roof	25,000.00	500.00
TOTAL EXPERT SERVICES	$160,000.00	$ 3,200.00
OTHER MATERIALS		
Sink/Medicine Cabinet	3,750.00	75.00
Toilet Bowl	3,125.00	62.50
Kitchen Sink/Cabinet	10,000.00	200.00
Faucet	1,875.00	37.50
Cabinets/Top	10,000.00	200.00
Tub	10,000.00	200.00
Tile	1,250.00	25.00
Flooring/Sheetrock/Lumber	150,000.00	3,000.00
Stove/Refrigerator	30,000.00	600.00
Miscellaneous	20,000.00	400.00
TOTAL OTHER COSTS	$240,000.00	$ 4,600.00
TOTAL COST MATERIALS AND EXPERT SERVICES	$400,000.00	$ 7,800.00

TOTAL ESTIMATED COST: *1.25 x TOTAL MATERIALS & EXPERT
SERVICES =
1.25 x $400,000 = $500,000

*Factor for inefficiency, escalation in prices, etc.

NEST'S INVOLVEMENT IN THE BRONX

The National Evangelism Support Team in the South Bronx is now composed of fifty to seventy-five persons from outside New York City. They are supporting the project in numerous ways:

1. They support it through financial investment. A commitment of $20,000 was made by the NEST group to assist in the opening of the Shepherds' administration office. This was the first financial commitment made to the newborn organization and in some measure helped to bring two other grants of $50,000 and $40,000 to the Shepherds.

2. The Shepherds' office building was opened in June 1980 through the services of a layman from South Florida who moved with his wife to the Bronx. While living in the community, he personally did much of the refurbishing of the office center. In addition, laymen from three of the Shepherds' member congregations gave many hours of work to upgrade their own church buildings.

In March 1981 the first work crew began work on apartment units in one of the eight buildings which the Shepherds have on rehabilitation contract. This work crew included a pastor and nine laymen from Charlottesville, Virginia, and two other laymen: one from Cleveland, Ohio, and the other from Butte, Montana.

Other work groups are being enlisted through NEST and through the state convention director of Brotherhood, the Southern Baptist mission organization for men. The major focus for 1981 is to enlist 220 lay people who have skills in rehabilitating housing to volunteer at least one week of work with the Shepherds.

3. A multimedia presentation on the Shepherds' project has been produced through the NEST coordinator's office of the Southern Baptist Home Mission Board. This show is available to local church gatherings and regional meetings of laity, and to business and service groups which may be interested in the Shepherds' project.

A new group is emerging from NEST that will deal essentially with resource development. "Friends of Evangelism" is comprised of business people concerned about the cities.

4. One of the primary needs acknowledged by the Shepherds' leaders is for a concerted prayer support effort. The first thing each NEST participant must do is build a base of prayer for divine wisdom, courage, and patience essential for the Shepherds to achieve their goals.

5. NEST gives its support through direct involvement in evangelism training, evangelistic witness and encouragement in the Bronx. The Shepherds' organization has an evangelism committee led by a layman from one of the area's churches.

In September 1979, a conference on evangelism in the South Bronx was jointly sponsored by NEST and the Shepherds. There were sixteen participants from outside New York and several hundred lay persons and pastors from the Bronx in the weekend conference.

The program was designed to provide a theological framework for the development of strategies. Dr. George W. Webber of New York Theological Seminary was the resource person for theological input. Resource persons from the New York Baptist Convention and the Southern Baptist Home Mission Board assisted in evangelism training. Small groups dialogued about the nature of the churches and communities in the Bronx and the appropriate design for effective evangelism in that setting.

Sunday morning, persons representing NEST worshiped and shared testimonies in the Shepherds' churches. On Sunday afternoon, a rally celebrated the commitment of NEST and the Shepherds to move together, to risk, and to learn.

Evangelism Through Relationships

The lay persons who come to the Bronx as volunteers in the housing rehabilitation project are encouraged to maximize the spiritual impact of their ministry. On arrival they are given orientation to the Bronx by community residents. They also receive some basic training in sharing their faith through personal testimony. They are provided marked New Testaments to assist them in witnessing opportunities. They are encouraged to build relationships with community people through involvement in the worship and ministry activities of one of the Shepherds' churches.

Project volunteers are also alerted to the possibilities of meaningful interaction with residents in or near the buildings where they are working and in restaurants, stores, etc. There is great sensitivity to the need for low-profile evangelism, which acknowledges the necessity of building credibility in the community. The level of involvement of the NEST volunteers with local community people is expected to increase with each new work crew. By the last quarter of 1981, we hope to see a significant evangelistic impact on the community.

Assessment of NEST Involvement
The NEST involvement in the Shepherds' project was initiated without any specific expectations for success. It has been an open-ended developmental relationship since the first encounter in May, 1978. If the Shepherds' project is to be judged on the growth and maturing of the Shepherds, the expanding participation by NEST volunteers, and the development of a significant trust level between the Shepherds and the NEST, there is strong basis for affirming the experiment.

CHALLENGES AND PROBLEMS
The primary challenge is learning how to be involved in this project without replicating the paternalistic, dehumanizing patterns of the past. Persons from a white middle-class orientation inevitably come to the Bronx with a mind-set reflecting racism and paternalism. While a few unfortunate encounters have caused us to lose some credibility, we have been spared the kind of destructive failures which fracture relationships.

Another ongoing problem has been communication. The NEST is not intended to be an organized structure, but rather a facilitative fellowship. Communicating this concept within the highly organized denominational structure continually prompts questions about accountability, continuity, and legitimacy. There is a tendency for denominational clergy workers to depreciate anything that is beyond their control and comprehension. There is also an inherent fear of the laity's participation outside "normal" lines of mission participation. Consequently, to communicate the concept of NEST to the denominational constituency, as well as to Shepherds' leaders, is a continuing challenge.

Coordination of travel schedules, housing arrangements, materials on job site, and numerous other support details has been difficult. The frustration generated by the mix-ups, both for the NEST people and the Shepherds, could have aborted the experiment if not for the conviction that this is the right kind of thing for us to do. We also realize that some difficulties in communication are inevitable.

Perhaps the most challenging dimension of this project has been the difficulty of gaining a sense of focus for our efforts together. Every person who comes to the Bronx comes with a different set of expectations for involvement. Because participation of Southern Baptists with the Shepherds was initiated from the office of Metropolitan Evangelism, there have been expectations of great numbers of conversions as a result of the project. Though there have been conversions and renewed commitments directly attributable to the NEST participation, they have been few. The expectation of the primary leaders of both the Shepherds and NEST has never been to blitz the Bronx with a direct evangelistic thrust. Rather, it has been to move cautiously to find practical ways of assisting in the project which the Christians in the Bronx have competently planned.

The Needs of Those Who Minister

From the beginning we have acknowledged that Southern Baptists bring to their ministry in the Bronx some real needs of their own. In many ways they are needier than those to whom they minister. Like other white middle-class Christians in America, Southern Baptists need to be freed from their racism, exclusivity, pride, and pat answers for questions they do not really understand. The Shepherds project in the South Bronx is a learning lab which may equip lay people, pastors, and denominational leaders to be genuine, effective representatives of Christ in this urban world.

SUMMARY

Concerned Southern Baptist lay people band together in NEST to work with the Bronx Shepherds Restoration Corporation to rehabilitate a devastated key city area. They give practical testimony through their work, leaving most of the job of direct evangelism to South Bronx Christians.

The complexity, confusion, and chaos which seem to be inherent in projects such as this one are a problem. But this is the stuff of which the urban world is made. Unless we learn to incarnate the good news of Jesus Christ in places like the South Bronx, our brand of gospel will be suspect among the masses of the earth's unreached peoples.

Dale W. Cross is director of metropolitan evangelism strategy for the Southern Baptist Home Mission Board, a position he has held since 1977. Prior to that, he served as director of associational services for the Greater Detroit area, and the Chicago Metro Baptist Association.

An ordained minister, he has pastoral experience in both Texas and Michigan. He also has worked with young people as a public school teacher.

Reaching Adelaide's Nominally Protestant or Anglican City Dwellers

by Dean Drayton

As part of the preparation for the Consultation on World Evangelization (COWE) in Pattaya, Thailand, in June 1980, many grass-roots groups were organized to study and strategize in major cities around the world. This report from an Adelaide Churches Crusade Subcommittee was one of dozens of reports sent to the International Coordinator for the large city mini-consultation at COWE.

While the special focus of this study was "reaching nominal Christians" in their city (a large number in many cities), the unique contribution of this Adelaide report is that it shows the value of comprehensive historical analysis as a basis for developing a renewal strategy for the whole church in a given context. The generational analysis provides an excellent base for the next necessary step, moving to the specifics of responding to group needs with a tailored evangelistic plan. The article makes an excellent beginning in this regard. Coincidentally, it demonstrates the value of the people group approach, whether or not the people are unreached.

Moreover, the summary conclusion of this report ("We have the necessary organizations for evangelism, but we lack clarity of aim") reminds us all that new, expensive, or avant-garde strategies or programs may not be needed for the evangelization of large cities. Rather, refocusing the resources and gifts of grace we already possess will accomplish the task of reaching our cities with the gospel of Jesus Christ.

THE CITY OF ADELAIDE

Adelaide, capital of South Australia, stands on a fertile plain which slopes gently from the Mount Lofty Ranges to the shores of the Gulf of St. Vincent.

Adelaide is the fourth largest city in Australia with a population in 1976 of 900,433. Located south of the River Torrens, the city proper is surrounded by a belt of parkland separating it from the suburbs. Within easy access from Adelaide by train, tram, bus, or auto, are recreational facilities of the Mount Lofty Ranges behind the city; and on the coast in front of the city are the seaside resorts.

RELIGIOUS AFFILIATION IN SOUTH AUSTRALIA

In the province of South Australia, from the formation of the province in 1836 until after World War II, the religious composition of the population was remarkably stable. Since that time the percentage of people indicating a church preference has declined, and the number of those listed in census records as having no religious preference has greatly increased. Of those who listed a church preference, few actually attended church.

	1866	1901	1921	1947	1976
Anglican	30.2%	29.4%	33.6%	29.2%	22.0%
Uniting (Churches)	34.0%	33.6%	32.8%	32.0%	19.5%
Independent, Baptist, Church of Christ, Lutheran	11.8%	14.7%	13.4%	10.0%	8.2%
Other Protestant	4.5%	2.7%	4.0%	2.3%	6.3%
Not stated, Object, No religion	5.9%	5.2%	3.6%	13.8%	21.0%
Other religions	1.0%	1.0%	1.0%	1.0%	1.0%

RELIGIOUS AFFILIATION IN ADELAIDE

In the city of Adelaide, the figures are comparable to those for the province as a whole: (figure 2)

Religious Preference	Percentage of Population	Actual Numbers
1. Protestant Denominations	28.5%	257,498
2. Church of England	23.5%	212,199
3. No religion stated	22.0%	196,418
4. Roman Catholic	22.0%	194,600
5. Other groups:		
Greek Orthodox	3.0%	30,307
Sects	0.5%	5,338
Non-Christians	0.5%	4,073

For the purposes of this study, the first three groups may be considered as nominally Protestant city dwellers. Since Gallup polls confirm that 80 percent of the world's population believes in God, the 22 percent who did not answer the census question on religion, or answered "none," are included among those considered in our study as nominal.

The total of those in these first three categories indicates that 666,115 is the number of nominal Christians in Adelaide's population of 900,500. With 24 percent of the nominal Christians under age fifteen, we have a total of 501,911 adults, in a total adult population of 671,939, as the target population for evangelism.

Three out of every four of these adults can be reached without crossing major cultural or denominational barriers. They are people who consider themselves Christians, or who are agnostic about the Christian faith. From their perspective, they have heard the gospel and have either affirmed it or called it in question.

Affiliation Patterns by Age Groups

Among these nominal Christian adults, the religious census indicates the existence of two distinct groups. Those over age fifty have maintained nominal church ties without involvement in a church community. Denominational affiliation was included in the census as a part of their identity whether they attended church or not.

Among those aged twenty-five to forty, increasing numbers are writing "none" in the religious census information. In this group, 36.5 percent of those aged twenty-five to thirty-four and 29.8 percent of those aged thirty-five to forty-five no longer consider themselves as identified with a denomination.

Answers to the census question on religion are open to many possible interpretations because people interpret religion in many ways. For some it means a specific denomination; for others it is a larger category, such as Christian. For some it is a private matter, and they list nothing at all. Whatever the individual understanding of the question, writing "none" indicates rejection of the institutional church.

It seems that the local congregation is the problem. The majority of adults "belong" to a church they stay away from. This points to the quality of congregational life as being critical in an age which is becoming more and more skeptical. The congregation's perception of its role and life-style is the first help or hindrance to those who would be open to hear, see, and share in the reality of the gospel. The congregation—individually and corporately—is responsible, therefore, for opening the way into the faith and fellowship of God's people.

Nominal Christians—An Unreached People Group

Among these who categorize themselves as Christian, how many are actually practicing Christians? (For our definition, a practicing Christian is one who belongs to a church community.) As a matter of record, actual attendance in Adelaide churches is comparable to the real membership or number of communicants. The following chart derived from census data indicates the difference in numbers between those who see themselves in a denominational context and those who are by our definition, practicing Christians.

Of the approximately 500,000 adults, almost 100,000 are members or communicants of a church or religious group. That means one in five is involved in a church community. Based on the definition of an unreached people as a population that is less than 20 percent practicing Christian, even the nominal Protestant (including Anglican) adults might be classified as an unreached people group.

	Anglican	Uniting	Lutheran	Baptist	Church of Christ	Totals
Census Adults	275,337	242,171	62,344	22,004	20,260	622,116
(76%)	209,256	184,050	47,381	16,723	15,398	472,808
Members	16,252	34,000	31,983	5,700	5,800	93,735
Involvement	7.77%	18.4%	67.50%	34.08%	37.66%	

GENERATIONAL PERSPECTIVE

A Five-Generation View

The most helpful insight into reaching nominal Christians in Adelaide came from the discovery that there have been five distinct generations of people in South Australia. This insight provides a specific and helpful way to tackle the question of nominal belief.

A combination of at least three factors has led to a series of five distinctive generations. These factors may be identified as: 1) the surges of migration; 2) the policy of encouraging young families to migrate; and 3) the occurrence of World Wars I and II at the peak times of birthing new generations. In South Australia each of these factors reinforced the others, resulting in the following sequence of five distinctive generations, each with its own unique experiences, particularly in times of change.

1. 1850-1860. First immigrants settle in South Australia.
2. 1858. First generation born in the province.
3. 1885. Second generation born in the province during the second wave of immigration.
4. 1914. Third generation born in the province during the third wave of immigration.
5. 1945. Fourth generation born in the province at the beginning of the fourth wave of immigration.

Since its inception, the province of South Australia has been growing rapidly and developing from within. From without it has been impacted by the technological revolution in the Western world.

Each generation, then, has specific characteristics. For our purposes, it is apparent that they have each had a definite attitude to the church and the gospel and have left their impact on the composition and size of the churches. An evidence of this is the congregational growth of established and dissenting churches with the first two indigenous generations until 1914.

World War I had a dramatic effect on the second indigenous generation born in 1885. Circumstantial evidence suggests that after World War I, the church ceased to expect the conversion of adults or the winning of them to the church. As a result, the rate of growth in all congregations slowed remarkably until the mid-1920s. According to Anglican and Methodist figures, there followed a decade of increased growth until the mid-1930s.

During the next twenty years, after the third indigenous generation (beginning in 1914) had surged through the Sunday school, church membership in all major denominations plateaued or declined. Apparently the Sunday school became the chief evangelistic arm of the church. Since the mid-1950s, growth in most denominations seems directly attributable to migration and the confirmation of fourth-generation adolescents passing through the Sunday school and into the church in the sixties. Since that time the Anglican and the uniting churches have experienced a marked decrease in fourth-generation adolescents of the fifties as they passed through denominational Sunday schools into the church in the sixties. By the end of the 1960s the drop in communicants or membership within the larger denominations was marked. It seems that those confirmed from the fourth generation had second thoughts in their twenties and opted out of congregational life.

The Challenge of Two Key Generations
Reaching the two distinctive World War I and World War II generations is the challenge continuing to face the church. Born

during World War I, the first of these generations lived through the Great Depression during their adolescence, and through World War II in their twenties. During this same period, the radio, automobile, telephone, and airplane (as well as compulsory primary school education) compressed a mobility of mind and thought into a generation that also suffered the consequences of international war and inflation.

At one time regarded as one of the most significant institutions in any community, the church was bypassed by the WW I generation and was labeled as irrelevant by popular alternative views. The church initially reached this 1914 generation primarily through the Sunday school, but when their adolescent years were passed, few of them joined the church as adults. Those who joined as teenagers, however, usually stayed.

The growth of secondary industries and the resulting rise of cities, along with the newly developed international perspective which the wars brought to many of this generation's parents, were factors providing a new context for the church. In most cases, local congregations were left at one side, edged out of most people's day-by-day lives and society's concerns. The adults who had grown up in the church did not know how to reach out into a community. The church tried, however, by speaking louder, or inviting people to come and hear the gospel. In these times of radical change, the institutional church was called into question by society. By its very tradition, the church was slow to respond and to adapt. A tradition-conscious generation within the church was left with the Sunday school as its primary method of outreach to its own and its next generations.

This is the first generation to have had a complete, compulsory, and free primary and secondary education; the first generation to own their own cars during adolescence; the first to grow up on the wider world of television and the pill; a generation with the highest expectations of what is needed in a home; a generation waiting longer to have fewer children; a "silver spoon" generation which has received from its security-conscious parents the surest environment to grow up in of any previous generation.

The World War II generation also enrolled in Sunday schools, but most dropped out of the Sunday school in their early teens. Some were confirmed in the church, but few became involved with worshiping congregations.

CURRENT RELIGIOUS INTEREST

It is the fourth generation of indigenous Australians which is actively and enthusiastically involved in religious groups today in a way rarely seen since the founding of the province. A new impetus for evangelism is coming from fourth-generation couples in their mid-thirties.

This group gives two reasons for their search for God. One is the emptiness and meaninglessness of life in an age of affluence. A second reason stems from the difficulties and problems of marriage in an era that rates self-expression more important than relationships.

The two most common means this generation of thirty-year-olds has used to find the reality of God are the sharing process in small groups, and an emphasis on receiving and knowing the Holy Spirit. These fourth-generation couples are now giving birth to the next generation, who will likely contribute to an explosion of the Sunday school, similar to the one in the late 1950s.

It is interesting to note that this "silver spoon" generation has not yet faced personal, national, or international calamity. Indications are that the very privilege of their generation is cause for concern as they prepare a world for their children. As the world's major problems of resources, development, and power threaten international conflict, the question of meaning may be raised in a new, fundamental way. Meanwhile, the increasing problems with individual and family relationships, plus the need to be responsible parents, all provide new opportunities for evangelizing this and the next generation.

Census figures showing the rapid increase in those who list no religious association indicate that religion has become a question rather than a formality. This new generation of articulate Christian parents will undoubtedly have a powerful ministry to their own children and to those of their own generation.

REACHING THE UNREACHED OF ADELAIDE

A Statement of the Problems

Two basic problems exist: First, the traditional, institutional church has yet to face the imperative of evangelism in the twentieth century. Although organizations and methods for evangelistic use are available, the church has not used them. Indeed, the church is marked by a lack of aim and direction in their outreach, and a general withdrawal and separation from society.

A second problem is related to the two distinct generations living in Adelaide. The older generation, those fifty years and older, has expressed the need (in the last census) to identify themselves with a denomination whether they attend regularly or not. The young to middle-aged generation, those twenty to forty years, has generally chosen to look elsewhere for self-definition. Both generations have tended to drift away from the traditional, institutional church.

These two factors have apparently combined to discourage the church in concerted outreach and aggressive evangelism. On the one hand, people with a general feeling of emptiness are searching for definition. On the other hand, the church, which could provide definition and offer fulfillment through the gospel, stands at one side as though unable to reach out.

Toward Some Solutions

The church itself, with God's empowering, is central to the solutions. The nature and purpose of the local church's fellowship must face honest self-evaluation and its implications for change. Individual congregations need to see themselves as a family of families, thus improving the quality of life within the congregation.

The church must also reach out and go to the people, inviting them to become parts of its local church family, instead of waiting for the people to come to it. A corporate evangelism strategy is needed to reach whole families at a time. Central to the success of future outreach is intergenerational and intra-family evangelism. For this task resources need to be prepared to aid the family in discovering the gospel, to nurture them in faith and equip them for witness within and beyond their families.

In a world of constant change, the local congregation needs to be creative and flexible in its outreach. Learning to adapt is essential for the survival of the church and for the health of its evangelistic arm. To ready itself and maintain a strong evangelistic outreach, the church must disciple its own; the faithful must continue to grow. This requires the church's willingness to educate all its members in the basics of the faith, in the context of faith. Further, the church needs an openness to face social issues realistically at the congregational level and devise means for its people to be involved in appropriate group action. Undergirding the education for Christian faith and social concern, the church must provide an accepting climate for small groups to share and develop the individual in his/her need for the reality of God in the relationships of life.

The youngest generation has not yet been scarred by the tragic world events which have affected older generations. There is much hope that this present generation will find ways to bridge the generation gap to reach and pastor these generations. The church must help this youngest generation to reach its parents, a task the church has not been able to do.

What Is Working

Churches in South Australia have the necessary organizations and methods for evangelism, but the aim has been unclear. There yet remains the need for continuing, active consultation to help church groups forge an effective ministry through which generations may be won to the Lord and his church.

In spite of the inertia in most churches, many young families are being reached. Sunday schools are again becoming evangelistic in their outreach. Small groups have formed in some churches to enable members to be part of a supportive group—sharing their concerns, caring for and encouraging one another in their Christian walk and witness. This process holds promise. Also, the charismatic emphasis on knowing and receiving the Holy Spirit has strong evangelistic appeal.

SUMMARY

Within Adelaide's nominally Christian community, two major factors exist. First, the majority of adults have drifted away from the institutional church. Second, these adults comprise two groups. The older group defines itself as having a specific denominational preference whether it attends church or not. The younger group has chosen to look outside the church for self-definition and spiritual identification.

Methods and organizations for evangelism do currently exist in the institutional church, but the church lacks aim and direction in its outreach. It has been unable to demonstrate to a growing percentage of South Australians the necessity of belonging to a worshiping community.

While Gallup polls indicate that 80 percent of the population believes in God, South Australia's fifth and present generation searches for definition in a world otherwise empty of meaning. Through supportive sharing in small groups and the ministries of the charismatic movement, young adults are being reached with the gospel. These young couples are becoming articulate Christian parents of the next generation and may well become the backbone of a new evangelistic thrust whereby the church will innovatively reach out to reach the city of Adelaide with the gospel.

Reaching the Toronto Italian Community for Christ

by Victor Adrian and Mariano OiGangi

Because ethnic pluralism is the essence of world-class cities, "Reaching (any ethnic group) for Christ" became a universal urban evangelization strategy. Fortunately, many inspiring examples of evangelism and ethnic church growth do exist in many large cities on every continent.

"Reaching the Toronto Italian Community for Christ" represents a positive model ministry. It represents the ongoing study and strategy of a competent and compassionate group from several church organizations concerned for the whole metropolitan region.

This report shows appreciation for, and sensitivity to, the Italian people and their history, unique culture, and contribution to the city.

This report gathers and interprets data, and begins to show its significance for evangelization. To do this, it combines theory and practice and provides a helpful bibliography.

This report affirms those diverse groups who are doing the ministry, rather than competing with others.

Finally, this report illustrates how evangelists might think theologically and design an evangelistic message tailored to the unique values and world view of the group to which that message is directed. It leads us to the point of building actual strategies, and sets the stage for future evaluation and mid-course correction. When these occur, it will be a valuable basis for a case history.

EFFORTS FEW AND FEEBLE

The large Italian population of metropolitan Toronto can be considered a people group built by immigration to the North American continent largely during the past fifty years. Since World War II, Toronto's Italian population has multiplied by a factor of ten. In 1971 this group made up at least 12 percent of the city's total population of more than 2.5 million, and continues to grow significantly. It is not only Toronto's largest ethnic group, but the current estimate of nearly half a million Italians is the largest first generation, non-British ethnic population in the city. An Italian businessman writes:

I am convinced that the Italian community of Toronto is possibly the largest mission field open to the church of Christ in Canada. Efforts to evangelize them have, so far, been few and feeble. There are great possibilities if Canadian churches were to catch the vision and dedicate as much effort to winning the Italians of Toronto as they put into doing missionary work in some of the smallest nations of the world.

IMMIGRATION AND DENSITY FACTORS

At the turn of the century, barely one thousand Italians lived in Toronto. Over the next three decades this number slowly grew to about thirteen thousand (a number one-third that of the Jewish community at the time). And like their Jewish counterparts, they have settled in ethnically concentrated areas, primarily in the northwest quadrant of metropolitan Toronto where they make up approximately 39 percent of that area's population. In some areas of this section, density of the Italian population reaches as high as 76 percent.

World War II ushered in a period of stress for Italian immigrants. As Canada's general population began to see them as representatives of the enemy abroad; immigration dropped by a third. But the end of the war brought a complete reversal of this trend, and for more than twenty years an average of some twenty thousand Italians entered Canada annually.

In 1967, Canada introduced the point system, assessing potential immigrants on the basis of their education and occupational skills. New Italian arrivals gradually declined in number through the late sixties to the present level of three to four thousand each year.

By the census year 1971, Canada had an Italian population of 730,520, nearly two-thirds of whom chose Ontario as their province of residence. Twenty-three percent settled in the province of Quebec, and 13.7 percent scattered throughout Canada.

Most immigrants chose to settle in the cities. Toronto, the center of Ontario's industrial heartland, became a major place of settlement. In 1971, of the 469,570 Italians in Ontario, 275,637 (58.7 percent) were living in Toronto. This number represents 37 percent of the entire Italian population of Canada.

SOCIOECONOMIC FACTORS

Most Italian immigrants prior to inauguration of the point system came from the rural villages of southern Italy, which includes the islands of Sicily and Sardinia. Historically, this area has been the country's most economically deprived region. Clearly, the dominant motive for leaving the homeland and immigrating to Canada has been the search for economic stability.

Kinship Networks

Typically, Italian immigrants who came to Toronto before establishment of the point system came with others of the same rural community, where closely knit kinship circles prevailed. These culturally male-dominated kinship networks led to the immigration of virtually entire villages and continue to be the major orientation of the immigrant social structure.

A crucial factor in understanding the nature of the Italian social system in Toronto is what has been designated as "chain migration." Under the early sponsorship system, newcomers settled near their sponsors. Then they in turn became sponsors, and those they sponsored settled near them. This led to ethnic segregation and limited contact with the general population except for formal, impersonal relationships.

Intra-community Divisions

Italian immigrants seldom participate in non-Italian organizations, and only a few belong even to Italian organizations. There are, nevertheless, many Italian clubs and societies, but they usually involve regional or village loyalties (even kinship networks) as a requirement for membership. Few embrace the wider Italian community. In spite of an apparently uniform cultural environment at home and at work, traditions inherited from the homeland tend to divide the Italian immigrant population quite consistently along kinship and regional lines.

The lack of cohesive central loyalty is confirmed by Italian attitudes toward leadership. Research in Canada and the United States has confirmed what interviews with Italians in Toronto have revealed. They are basically skeptical of those who profess to be their leaders, considering such claimants as self-appointed and self-seeking.

Lack of any group consensus and expression of confidence in leadership arises not only from regional differences, but also from attitudes which traditionally distrust and downgrade anyone from outside the kinship circle who attempts to take a leadership role. Some individuals perform leadership roles which benefit the Italian community, but most of them are not in the public eye.

This tendency toward traditional attitudes can be traced primarily to the poverty-stricken peasants of rural villages in southern Italy, where outside influences are considered to be self-seeking and exploitive. Dependence is focused on recognized kinship networks.

In an adopted country, this distrust of non-family members extends to all non-Italians and non-Catholics. It has reinforced the self-segregation of Italians in their neighborhoods. Italian suppliers of distinctively ethnic goods and services have exploited this exclusivism by establishing "little Italys"—self-sufficient Italian business and residential areas, like those also evident in major cities of the United States.

Religious Factors

Some believe that the claim by most (96 percent) Toronto Italians to be Catholic should strengthen their sense of unity. But unlike the Jewish community, which is ethnically exclusive, the Roman Catholic Church is not. Several ethnic groups claim allegiance to Catholicism.

Further, there is not a sufficient number of Catholic parishes to serve the large Italian community, and most first-generation immigrants with their familial orientation are reluctant to participate in non-Italian parishes. Consequently, adherence to the Roman Catholic Church does not seem to be a significant integrating force.

Being a Christian, as one Italian businessman expressed it, is equivalent to being a human being. Catholicism is part of the religious heritage passed down through the centuries and is generally taken for granted by most Italians. Meanwhile, the family-oriented kinship circle plays the determining role in influencing attitudes and behavior.

Educational Factors

Because their rural society has not placed a high value on formal education, most Italian newcomers were lacking in education in comparison to Canadian standards. Forty percent of the adults had not reached grade five, 70 percent had not reached grade nine, and 90 percent had not reached grade ten, the educational level for two-thirds of the total metropolitan labor force.

Part of this deficiency was the result of age differentials. One-quarter of the Italian immigrant population was under 10 years of age, and over half were under 25, making the median age 26. By comparison, the median age of the total Canadian population was 31.7, almost 6 years above the Italian median.

Aside from the age differential, the low level of education among the Italians has proven a severe handicap for adults seeking employment. Four-fifths of the Italian labor force is concentrated in unskilled or low-skilled employment and in a limited number of occupations. These generally include the construction trades, machining, product fabrication, and some of the service industries.

In the factories and service industries of Canada, the men are joined by women, a practice almost unheard of in their southern Italian villages. For both men and women, unskilled or low-skilled employment means a low level of income. Sixty percent of the men earn less than their counterparts in the total Canadian labor force. Italian women earn even less.

Lower incomes, however, have not hindered home ownership. Eighty-four percent of Italians own their homes, as compared with only 54 percent of Canada's total population. Credit for this accomplishment goes to the extended family or kinship networks which have led to extensive mutual assistance.

The majority of Italian parents believe that the educational system in Toronto emphasizes the roles of the British and the French, to the almost total neglect of other ethnic groups who have contributed much to Western civilization. One impact of this belief is the development among second and third generation Italians of a disrespect for the Italian culture and language, creating further division within the Italian population. Some school boards have tried to soften the cultural conflict by subsidizing Italian classes and giving more attention to European history.

Language Factors

Limited fluency in English has not only been a handicap for Italians seeking employment, it has also limited relationships with the broader society. Minimum education has affected the acquisition of skills needed in acquiring a second language. In addition, patterns of residence and employment limit the exposure of Italians to the English-speaking environment and allow them little time to attend English classes. The tradition which keeps many Italian women in the home also keeps them from acquiring a proficiency in English.

Motivation to learn English is weakened not only by these factors but also by the availability of Italian daily and weekly newspapers and Italian radio and television stations. The 1971 census indicates that a fourth of the Italian population spoke neither English nor French, the two official languages of Canada. Italian is unquestionably the second most widely used language in Toronto and is spoken almost exclusively in 70 percent of the Italian homes.

GENERAL CANADIAN ATTITUDES TOWARD ITALIANS

Growth of the Italian population was so gradual during the early years of the century that other Canadians were not threatened. Prejudice was minimal and discrimination rare until animosity erupted during World War II. Although this has cooled, a stereotyped image of the Italian as a poorly educated, unskilled laborer persists.

News media coverage of criminal activities involving the Sicilian mafia in the United States also tends to label Italians in ways they deeply resent. In spite of continuing efforts to change its image for the better, the Italian community in its exclusivism finds it difficult to eradicate the negative attitudes developed toward them over the years.

THE ITALIAN COMMUNITY AT THE CROSSROADS

The major characteristic of the Italian population in Toronto is its comparative isolation from the mainstream of urban life. But there are signs of change. First, Italian immigration has fallen to a new low, so fewer first generation Italians are being added to the population. This factor will gradually lessen the cohesion that now characterizes the kinship-based social structure.

A second sign of change is becoming evident as the result of second and third-generation Italians receiving their education in Canadian schools. These Italian-Canadians make up a large proportion of the 30 percent who live scattered through the city since they prefer ethnically heterogeneous neighborhoods to the solidly Italian ones in which most of them were raised.

A third sign that change is in the wind is increasing intermarriages with non-Italians. A rare exception among first-generation Italian families, this is not uncommon among the Canadianized second and third generations.

The fact that English is already the primary language of the children indicates that it will soon become the primary language of the Italian community as a whole.

Although these changes bring new stresses, the pressures for change are not new to the Italian community in Canada. As immigrants, they have been struggling with the transition from a rural European background to the social and economic structures of urban living in North America. They have had to face the demands of a highly industrialized, urban society, with its requirements of working hours and disciplined toil. Since they come as immigrant groups, with primary ties limited to their own distinctive kinship networks, the Italians who have settled in Toronto lack the historical, ethnic, or religious tradition of collective responsibility which would embrace the entire group. Divisions between kinship circles, and the rift between northern and southern Italy's peoples, still persist as a continuation of a long, historical tradition.

The Italian community is at a crossroads, but few outside the community are concerned with what direction the future will take. The Protestant church is not yet awake to its responsibility for those who do not find Catholicism a viable spiritual orientation. A comprehensive strategy for evangelizing this people group has yet to be articulated.

OBSTACLES TO ITALIAN EVANGELIZATION

Virtually all Italians at home and abroad are related to the Roman Catholic Church, but more than two-thirds do not practice their faith with any consistency. The growth of the Communist Party, tolerance of divorce, and permission for abortion in Italy during the past decade prevails despite the articulate, strong opposition of the Catholic Church.

This does not necessarily mean the field is white for harvest.

Many obstacles, some of them formidable, still hinder the conversion of Italians to Christ:

1. *Sacramental Soteriology:* The idea that once you have been baptized you are automatically regenerated and become a Christian militates against a positive response to the gospel.

2. *Formal Adherence:* Although many Italians do not participate regularly in confession and the mass, most of them say, "I was born Catholic, and I'll die Catholic." They retain formal adherence for baptisms, first communions, weddings, and funerals. They have a ritual observance, rather than a moral commitment which affects life-style.

3. *Theological Ambiguity:* Catholicism and orthodox Protestantism have common elements. Among these are belief in the Trinity and in Christ's deity, virgin birth, atoning death, bodily resurrection, ascension, and return in judgment. Catholicism also acknowledges the Bible as inspired and authoritative. But customs and doctrines drawn from ecclesiastical tradition obscure the uniqueness of Christ as mediator and the sufficiency of faith in him alone for salvation.

4. *Charismatic Renewal:* Like the encouragement to read scripture in the vernacular, charismatic renewal among Catholics holds great potential for good if it leads to a closer walk with God and personal trust in the Savior. However, it may result in deeper devotion to Mariolatry and the mass. Furthermore, on the basis of shared charismatic experience, Protestant evangelicals may feel it is no longer urgent to evangelize Catholics. We must remember that basic questions of vital differences still remain: a) Is tradition of equal value with scripture as the rule of faith and practice, or should we look to the Bible alone as our authoritative guide? (b) Is salvation by grace alone received through faith, or must we rely on ritual observances and draw on human merit as well to

be saved? (c) Is a priestly class still valid, or do we now have a priesthood of all believers edified by a pastoral ministry?

5. *Anticlerical Approach:* If theological ambiguity and charismatic renewal are counterproductive to effective evangelization, so is the anticlerical approach on the part of Protestants. The fact that Italians are dissatisfied with "The Church" and spend much of their time criticizing the priesthood does not make them evangelicals. It only indicates their anticlerical inclination. To encourage such an attitude is to follow a questionable approach. A considerable amount of so-called evangelization among Italians in previous generations (both in Canada and the U.S.) was distorted because ex-priests without adequate evangelical retraining were turned loose on immigrant populations with a polemic attitude that did not give due preeminence to the crucified and risen Redeemer.

The foregoing observations arise not merely from the study of Reformation history, but particularly from one who has a Roman Catholic background, pastoral experience in an Italian congregation in Montreal, and annual involvement in Bible ministry on the Mediterranean island of Sicily.

STEPS TOWARD EVANGELIZATION OF ITALIAN IMMIGRANTS AND IMPLICATIONS FOR MISSION TO ITALIANS ABROAD

Italian Christians living in Toronto burdened for reaching fellow Italians for Christ believe Christian workers must learn to speak the Italian language. The Italian community in Toronto will not be evangelized merely with radio evangelism, although that work is necessary. It will not be won with television programs, though these can be helpful. The Italian community will not be won by trying to attract them to the Italian-speaking churches in the cities, although a few might be won in that manner.

What is needed is a number of full-time Italian-speaking workers dedicated to winning others on a one-to-one basis. These should seek to infiltrate the Italian organizations in the community and learn to win the respect of the Italian community.

Eventually the Canadian-born Italians in the next generation or their children may be reached through normal channels of the evangelical churches in the city. But if the present first generation immigrant is to be reached, Italian-speaking workers must be found, perhaps among evangelical Christians in Italy.

Reaching Toronto Italians for Christ could also assist in evangelizing Italy abroad. There are daily flights leaving Toronto with full passenger loads for Italy. As Italians are increasingly evangelized, they could take the message to their families at home.

Most of the present evangelical churches in Italy have been started as a result of a small number of Italian immigrants accepting Christ in Chicago. These went back and gave their witness to those at home. A concern for reaching the Italian community in Toronto needs to incorporate in that vision the prospects for reaching Italians in their homeland.

SUMMARY

Factors of population density, common problems in adjusting to an urban society, plus a less than vital commitment to a Catholic religious orientation, all offer opportunities for speeding the evangelization of Italian immigrants in metropolitan Toronto.

A missing ingredient for accomplishing this goal is a viable evangelization strategy which has yet to be articulated by either the Protestant church or parachurch groups. At this writing, there appears to be little sense of urgency for this work by either.

The foregoing case study by a committee of concerned Christians offers an analysis of the harvest field and indicates a sparse crop has resulted from the evangelization process used thus far. The fact that a significant part of the field is literally being eroded as the first generation Italians become elderly and are dying without Christ is only implied. The imperative of limited time for this group and for the ever-increasing Italian population of second and third generation Italians colors the picture "urgent."

A secondary yet major benefit from the evangelization of Toronto's Italian community is the mission-level evangelization of Italy-based families and friends by the frequent travels of Toronto's Italians to the homeland. Italian Christians evangelizing Italians in Canada, the United States, Italy, and wherever immigrant concentrations remain suggest an obvious but untapped source for seed planting and harvesting.

Victor Adrian is president of Toronto Bible College and Ontario Theological Seminary.

Mariano DiGangi is a professor at Ontario Theological Seminary.

Reaching Ethnic Cambodians in Bangkok

by Ronald Hill

The "Cambodian Holocaust" is a contemporary fact. No more anti-urban regime can be documented than the one which systematically sought to kill or relocate millions of urban persons, including a few hundred known Christians, from Phnom Penh since 1970.

A massive turning to Christ about 1975, simultaneous with the persecution and relocation of many of these people in Thai refugee camps, succeeded in spreading church growth all over Southeast Asia and on to other nations. Strong growth has been seen in these overseas locations.

*Since the days when Jeremiah instructed the Jerusalem exiles to live and serve Babylon because God had **sent them there** (Jer. 29), urban refugees have represented a remarkably strategic group for evangelization and church renewal. This case study reminds us that large cities do not exist as ends in and of themselves, and that effective evangelization of urban refugees requires sensitivity both to a cluster of "pull" factors that drew them to that place, and to the "push" factors that expelled them from their sending environments.*

In the fall of 1979, television screens around the world were filled with haunting images of tens of thousands of sick and mal-nourished Khmer refugees staggering into Thailand. This tragic exodus, combined with reports of massive food shortages and continuing internecine fighting inside Cambodia, raised serious questions about the very survival of the Khmer race. A year later, when a semblance of order had come about within the country and reports indicated the food situation was much improved, the question still remained as to how the bulk of the Khmer race could be evangelized and discipled for Christ.

Although reports from Phnom Penh said a few Khmer Christians were meeting together, and some were even making first timid contacts with Christians from outside Cambodia, the fact remained that only in the Thailand refugee camps were serious efforts under way to bring Cambodians to Christ. This study deals with efforts to reach another part of the Khmer race—ethnic Cambodians in Thailand.

MASSIVE RESPONSE OF CAMBODIANS TO THE GOSPEL

Out of the holocaust in Cambodia has come an encouraging story of a massive response by the Cambodians to the gospel for the first time in history. When Christian and Missionary Alliance missionaries went back into Phnom Penh in 1970 after General Lon Nol had taken over from Prince Norodom Sihanouk, they found only 300 to 500 Christians. This was the visible, measurable result of some forty years of C.M.A. work in the country. The Cambodian race up to that time had proven to be one of the most resistant in missions history.

As the Communist noose tightened around Phnom Penh between 1970 and 1975, a miracle took place in the besieged city. Estimates by Christian and Missionary Alliance and Overseas Missionary Fellowship missionaries in early 1975 placed the number of Christians in the city, which by then had a population of 2 million, at more than 10,000. A taxi driver in Phnom Penh, who was not a Christian, once told me in February 1975 that he was seriously considering becoming a Christian, and that "soon at least half the people in Phnom Penh will be Christians." Missionary Andrew Way of O.M.F. said at that time, "I have never seen people so open to the gospel. Everybody is ready to talk about Jesus!"

Response in Refugee Camps

Then came the takeover by the Khmer Rouge in April, 1975, and so began the flight of thousands into Thailand. News from the church in Cambodia was almost completely cut off, but the Khmer in Thai refugee camps proved to be remarkably responsive. In the three camps where Southern Baptists ministered in the Chanthaburi area, over 2500 were baptized between 1975 and 1979. Hundreds, perhaps thousands of others came to know Christ in other border camps.

Most of these new Christians have since moved on to countries such as Australia, France, Canada, and the United States. A congregation of over one hundred Cambodians with strong lay leadership is a part of the South Main Baptist Church in Houston, Texas. Reports from many other Cambodian believers indicate that they are active in evangelical churches within the countries to which they have gone.

Response in Holding Centers

The massive response to the gospel has continued since the mass flight of Cambodians into Thailand at the end of 1979, when Vietnamese troops invaded Cambodia, installed a new government in Phnom Penh, and drove the Khmer Rouge troops to the western mountains. Vigorous Christian groups are actively witnessing in each of the holding centers, where a total of almost two hundred thousand await repatriation to Cambodia when conditions permit. A few with direct family connections in third countries are being allowed to migrate and be reunited with their families.

Most remarkable is the movement towards Christ at Khao I Dang, largest of the holding centers. Beginning with the witness of two pastors and a few other Christians who were a part of the refugee flood, the number of believers had grown to between ten thousand and twenty thousand by the end of 1980. Forty house churches, in addition to one large central church, were reported to be meeting regularly.

Primarily an indigenous movement, the Cambodian response to Christ since 1970 has been aided with literature and teaching by missionaries from Overseas Missionary Fellowship and the Christian and Missionary Alliance.

A PERSPECTIVE ON THE RESPONSIVENESS OF ETHNIC CAMBODIAN RESIDENTS IN BANGKOK

Does this same response extend to the estimated 1 million ethnic Cambodians who are permanent residents in Thailand? A work begun between 1978 and 1980 among these people in Bangkok gives preliminary evidence that it does.

The Khmer—Cambodian Residents of Bangkok

In 1980, Bangkok was a city of more than 5 million, the only world class city in Thailand. Because it is not only the capital but also the business and manufacturing center of the country, it is a mecca for Thai villagers seeking economic salvation. It has become a patchwork of disparate ethnic, economic, and class groups stitched onto the basic fabric made of the Thai governing group and the Chinese business community. Not insignificant among these groups in Thailand is the Khmer minority.

Most of the Khmer live in the provinces of Buriram, Surin, and Srisaket in northeast Thailand, bordering northern Cambodia. Although they speak Khmer in their home villages, most can also speak Thai. All are considered Thai citizens, and the young people attend Thai schools. In recent years, many Khmer have migrated to Bangkok to look for jobs, along with tens of thousands of other northeastern Thailanders.

A Christian Witness to the Khmer

Through the witness of John Ellison and other C.M.A. missionaries, two sisters and a first cousin came to study at the Thailand Baptist Theological Seminary in Bangkok in 1975. They became members of Immanuel Baptist Church during their seminary days, and on graduation, the two sisters became teachers in Immanuel's kindergarten. The cousin began working at the Community Center of Prachakom Church, a Baptist church in the Din Daeng area. The up-country Khmer living in Bangkok were seen by them as a people group.

Through the witness of the two Cambodian sisters, an older Cambodian woman in the community was won to Christ. As a key person in obtaining jobs for up-country Khmers when they first arrived in Bangkok, she soon had placed several new-comers as domestics in the homes of Immanuel Church members. This was doubly beneficial, for church members were happy with dependable workers; the employees were in homes where they heard the gospel and were encouraged to attend church. Through this woman's continuing witness, others in the community also became Christians and were brought into the group.

With the encouragement of the pastor, Boonkrong Pitakanon, and the leadership of the seminary graduates, weekly meetings in the Khmer language were begun. These featured Bible study, singing, fellowship, and the latest news from the home villages in the provinces of Surin and Buriram. As an outgrowth of these Thursday night meetings, more than twenty were soon attending a Khmer Sunday school Bible class and the Thai worship services of Immanuel Church.

A STRATEGY FOR EVANGELIZING
THE KHMER IN THAILAND

Although the Thai and Cambodian cultures have borrowed extensively from each other, Pastor Boonkrong nevertheless encouraged the group to maintain its Khmer identity. He understood that peoples come to Christ most readily in their own cultural surroundings. Boonkrong also gained the aid of missionary Bill Smith (a member of Immanuel and later elected to be its outreach chairman), who was experienced in using the Southern Baptist Bangkok Urban Strategy to evangelize two neighborhoods there.

Laying the Foundation

Initially, Boonkrong and Smith took two key steps in laying a foundation for the Khmer work: First, they surveyed the Khmer community in Bangkok and discovered a population of several thousand (no exact figures available). They found that Khmer most often worked at the least desirable jobs—on construction gangs, road repairs, and waterworks projects—which paid poor wages and offered little security. It was difficult to maintain a consistent follow-up effort with the Khmer people because their living quarters were but temporary shacks and they moved frequently.

In their second step to build a workable strategy, Boonkrong and Smith visited Surin Province where the home villages of most of the Khmer people attending Immanuel Church were located. There the people received them warmly. The two men decided at this point that in light of the high mobility of the Khmer population, it would be strategic to work both in Bangkok and in Surin Province. Since that initial survey visit by Pastor Boonkrong and Bill Smith, the two seminary-trained girls (who are also teaching in the church kindergarten) regularly make trips to minister in the home villages.

Thus, a beginning has been made in reaching the ethnic Khmers in Bangkok. The work is related to a strong local church, with a pastor who understands and supports the people-group concept of evangelization. It has had the benefit of trained leadership, although Pastor Boonkrong has sensed that in the Khmer culture, strong male leadership will be necessary to build a growing, stable group. His hopes for this have risen with the coming of a younger brother of the two seminary-trained girls to study in the seminary. Immanuel Church is supporting him, and Pastor Boonkrong is spending time teaching and working with him.

Building for Growth
Before the work grows beyond this original small Khmer congregation within Immanuel Church, other steps are necessary. First, a comprehensive and statistically specific survey must be made to *determine the felt needs* of the Khmers in Bangkok, the kinds of approaches and ministries they will respond to, and

whether they are as ready as are the Khmers in refugee camps or in Cambodia to respond to the gospel.

Further, a plan to *intensively disciple each Khmer convert* must be developed, preferably in the Khmer language, unless research shows that these people are more literate in Thai and that materials should therefore be prepared in that language. Some Khmer materials developed for the extensive evangelistic work in the refugee camps are already available. For follow-up with those who have completed these evangelistic Bible study lessons, discipleship materials developed by the Bangkok Urban Strategy for use with new Thai Christians now need to be reworked in the Khmer language.

A third step in the strategy is to *develop lay leadership,* not only for this first Khmer group at Immanuel, but also for the anticipated rapid multiplication of other groups of Khmer Christians.

Another step in building for growth is to *strengthen the connections with evangelizing the home villages.* A Southern Baptist missionary couple now studying Khmer are training to help in this follow-up work in the villages and thereby move toward accomplishing this goal.

SUMMARY

The burgeoning Khmer population in the Bangkok area is a people group, uprooted from the security of home villages and seeking a new life in a strange urban milieu. They are part of a larger people that at long last is proving responsive to the gospel after centuries of resistance. Not yet established in a living pattern for their Bangkok situation, they are still open to new ideas. They need help in coming to grips with their new life in the city.

The Bangkok branch of the ethnic Khmer are still intimately related to the 1 million "cousins" in the home villages, and when evangelized, may well prove to be a bridge for taking the gospel to their own village people.

Reverend Ronald Hill is a missionary of the Southern Baptist Convention working in Bangkok, Thailand.

Part 3
Unreached Peoples — Expanded Descriptions

The following section contains descriptions of forty-nine urban people groups in alphabetical order. Each group has a data table printed above the written description, containing information based on questionnaires completed by persons in the same country or otherwise knowledgeable about the people group. (Please see Appendix A for a sample of this questionnaire.)

In the data table, the most common name of the people group is given first, followed by the name of the country in which the group is located. Stars in front of the name indicate receptivity to the gospel: ★★★ = very receptive, ★★ = receptive and ★ = indifferent.

The following is a summary of the remaining data categories:

Alternate names: Any alternate names or spellings for the people group.

Size of group: Latest population estimate of the group.

MARC ID: An identification number by which information on that particular group is filed. Any correspondence sent to MARC dealing with a group, sending corrections, updates, additions, or requests for further information should refer to that number.

Distinctives: Distinctive features that unify this group. Many different things may make a group distinct or cause them to consider themselves a people. Often several factors give them some kind of affinity toward one another, or make them different from other groups. Respondents to the Unreached Peoples questionnaire were asked to indicate the relative importance of various factors in making the group distinctive. Those factors were: speaking the same language, common political loyalty, similar occupation, racial or ethnic similarity, shared religious customs, common kinship ties, strong sense of unity, similar education level, common residential area, similar social class or caste, similar economic status, shared hobby or special interest, discrimination from other groups, unique health situation, distinctive legal status, similar age, common significant problems, and "other(s)."

Social change: This represents an estimate of the overall rate at which culture and social change is taking place in the group—very rapid, rapid, moderate, slow, and very slow.

Languages: Primary languages. Multilingual communities often use different languages in different situations. They may learn one language in school, another in the market, and yet another in religious ceremonies. Respondents were asked to indicate the major languages used by the group as well as the place or function of each language. These functions are indicated by the following codes:
V—vernacular or common language
T—trade language or lingua franca

S—language used for instruction in schools

W—the language used for any current or past Christian witness

G—the language most suitable for presentation of the gospel

P—the language used in any non-Christian ceremonies

The percentages listed next to the headings *speak* and *read* indicate the percentage of the total group that speak and read the language listed.

Scripture: Indicates the availability of various forms of biblical literature in the main language of the group.

Recordings: Indicates the availability of recordings, records, or cassettes in the main language of the group. Recordings can include Bible readings, Bible stories with gospel applications, culturally adapted gospel messages, or basic Christian teaching, as well as music. (Detailed information on recordings in specific languages can be obtained from Gospel Recordings U.S.A., 122 Glendale Blvd., Los Angeles, CA 90026, U.S.A.)

Christian literacy: This indicates the percentage of Christians among the people (if any) over 15 years of age who can and do read in any language.

Religion: This indicates the primary religion(s) found among members of the group. The percentage shown next to "adherents" estimates the percentage of the group who would say that they follow the religion(s) listed. The percentage next to "practicing" indicates the number who actively practice the religion(s) listed (in the opinion of the researcher or reporter). The determination of the percentage of those adhering to a certain religion versus the percentage of those practicing their faith is admittedly a subjective judgment. This figure is important, however, when considering Christian populations, because the definition of "unreached" used here is a group that is less than 20 percent *practicing* Christian."—1 percent" means less than one percent practicing, and is used when the Christian population is extremely small and difficult to estimate.

Churches and missions: This indicates the primary Christian churches or missions, national or foreign, that are active in the area where the people group is concentrated. The figure under "membership" is the approximate number of full members of this church or mission denomination from the people group. The figure under "community" is the approximate number of adherents (including children) to the denomination or mission from the people group. These are not *all* the churches and missions among this group—only the ones that have been reported.

Openness to religious change: This is an estimate of how open the group is to religious change of any kind. Categories are: very open, somewhat open, indifferent, somewhat closed and very closed.

Receptivity to Christianity: This is an estimate of the openness of the group to Christianity in particular. Categories are: very receptive, receptive, indifferent, reluctant and very reluctant.

Evangelism profile: People tend to come to Christ in more or less well-defined steps. This scale (based on a scale developed by Dr. James Engel of the Wheaton Graduate School) indicates the approximate percentage of the group at various levels of awareness of the gospel. The scale ranges from people with no awareness of Christianity to those who are active propagators of the gospel. A further explanation of this useful tool may be found in Edward Dayton's article "To Reach the Unreached" in *Unreached Peoples '79.*

Not Reported (nr): Whenever this appears in any category, it indicates that the information has not yet been received by the MARC computers. In future volumes of this series, information will be added as it becomes available.

Validity Code: An estimate of the accuracy and completeness of the data on a scale from one to nine. The code is:

1. The only information available at this point is the group name, country, language, population and primary religion. The percentage listed under practicing Christians is at best a rough estimate.

2. There has been more data collected than the "baseline" information in 1, but it is scanty or of poor quality.

3. About half of the information on the Unreached Peoples questionnaire (Appendix A) has been collected, and information on the Christian community, if any, is missing or probably inaccurate.

117

4. Almost all the data on the Unreached Peoples questionnaire has been collected *or* the source document has supplied most of the necessary information.

5. Information has been supplied by a completed Unreached Peoples questionnaire and at least one other document.

6. In addition to 5, there is enough detailed information about the people group to write an accurate, up-to-date description.

7. There exists an extensive description of the people group in secular or Christian literature.

8. There has been a major research study (thesis or dissertation quality) done on the group which includes detailed information on the Christian community.

9. In addition to 8, the study includes a thorough exploration of evangelism strategy for the particular group, based on firsthand experience.

Following the data table with the basic information about the people group are several paragraphs further detailing the characteristics of the group.

A complete listing of all unreached people groups currently identified in the MARC files can be found in Part 4. For many of these groups there is more information available. To obtain the data on a particular group, just send in the reply page located in the back of this book.

INDEX OF PEOPLE GROUPS WITH DESCRIPTIONS IN *Unreached Peoples '82*

Page Number

EXPANDED DESCRIPTIONS

Aborigines in Brisbane (Australia)

ALTERNATE NAMES: not reported

SIZE OF GROUP: 8,000   MARC ID: 5000

DISTINCTIVES: ethnicity; sense of unity; social class; discrimination

SOCIAL CHANGE: rapid

LANGUAGES: English (95% speak; V)

SCRIPTURE: Bible; RECORDINGS : yes

CHRISTIAN LITERACY: 90%

RELIGION: Secularism (80% adherents/80% practicing); Protestant (10% adherents/3% practicing); Roman Catholic (10% adherents/3% practicing)

CHURCHES AND MISSIONS	BEGAN	MEMBERSHIP	COMMUNITY
Uniting Church	1950	175	nr
Aborigine Evang. Fellowship	1960	150	nr
Aborigine Inland Mission	1970	35	nr

OPENNESS TO RELIGIOUS CHANGE: indifferent

RECEPTIVITY TO CHRISTIANITY: reluctant

GROWTH RATE OF CHRISTIAN COMMUNITY: slow growth

EVANGELISM PROFILE:
- 3% No awareness of Christianity
- 70% Aware that Christianity exists
- 10% Some knowledge of the gospel
- 9% Understand the message of the gospel
- 2% Personally challenged to receive Christ
- 2% Decision to accept Christ
- 3% Incorporated into a fellowship of Christians
- 1% Active propagators of the gospel

VALIDITY: 6

Australia's consciousness of the Aboriginal people results from both their distinctive ethnic grouping and their social class. They are entitled to government social welfare aid for the disadvantaged. Race is a more significant factor of their group unity than is religion. Most of the Aborigines have left their tribal "dreamtime" customs as they have become absorbed into the Western urban culture. About 3% of the Aboriginal community consider themselves to be practicing Christians; regular church attendance is at about 1%. There is only one Aboriginal congregation in Brisbane at the present time, with 150 members. Fellowship in the areas of high-density Aboriginal housing should be encouraged.

Urban Australian Aborigines have proved to be resistant to the gospel. By using existing "bridges" and not overwhelming them with massive outreach programs, evangelism should be successful. Cooperation with the Brisbane church and its existing ministries--and increasing awareness of missionary opportunity and responsibility--should result in more Aborigines being won for Christ.

EXPANDED DESCRIPTIONS

Ahmadis in Lahore (Pakistan)

ALTERNATE NAMES: not reported

SIZE OF GROUP: 60,000   MARC ID: 5016

DISTINCTIVES: religion; discrimination; sense of unity

SOCIAL CHANGE: not reported

LANGUAGES: Urdu (V); Panjabi (V)

SCRIPTURE: Bible; RECORDINGS : yes

CHRISTIAN LITERACY: not reported

RELIGION: Islam (100% adherents)

CHURCHES AND MISSIONS: not reported

OPENNESS TO RELIGIOUS CHANGE: somewhat closed

RECEPTIVITY TO CHRISTIANITY: reluctant

GROWTH RATE OF CHRISTIAN COMMUNITY: not reported

EVANGELISM PROFILE: not reported

VALIDITY: 6

The Ahmadia Muslim sect was founded by Mirza Ghulan Ahmad. In 1890 he claimed to be the Messiah and Mahdi (the "Expected One" of the Muslims), and that he had been born of Mary, the mother of Christ. After his death in 1908 there were two claimants to his position as self-proclaimed caliph, both of whom migrated to Pakistan in 1947 when India was partitioned: Ghulan Ahmad's son settled in the town of Qadian, while the other came to Lahore. This sect may be called a people group because of their religious beliefs and solidarity as a persecuted sect of Islam.

In 1974 the National Assembly passed a constitutional amendment declaring the Ahmadis to be a non-Muslim minority in Pakistan. While this action placed the movement and its members in a position of some embarrassment, it also stimulated interest in the movement, which has been growing faster since the persecution began.

Ahmadis will usually have well-informed arguments against Christian interpretations of biblical events and teachings. However, at times some have been open to the gospel, and some converts have become mature, loyal Christians. Such receptivity was evident in 1974 during a period of open agitation and violence against them. While some mission and church groups within Pakistan have worked with individual Ahmadis, the most effective approach would probably be through a national missionary movement to support converted Ahmadis in efforts to win their peers to Christ.

This sect can be called a "counterfeit Christianity" because it gives a distorted picture of the gospel and because its founder called himself Jesus Christ, the Messiah. This is the sect that has proclaimed that Jesus was revived after crucifixion, lived to the age of 120, and then died and was buried in Srinagar, Kashmir. If Ahmadis can be convinced of the historical death and resurrection of Christ, there is every likelihood that they could become Christians.

Anatolian Turks in Istanbul (Turkey)

ALTERNATE NAMES: not reported

SIZE OF GROUP: 2,000,000   MARC ID: 5041

DISTINCTIVES: social class; education; religion

SOCIAL CHANGE: moderate

LANGUAGES: Turkish (V, G)

SCRIPTURE: Bible; RECORDINGS : yes

CHRISTIAN LITERACY: not reported

RELIGION: Islam; Islam-Animist

CHURCHES AND MISSIONS: not reported

OPENNESS TO RELIGIOUS CHANGE: indifferent

RECEPTIVITY TO CHRISTIANITY: indifferent

GROWTH RATE OF CHRISTIAN COMMUNITY: not reported

EVANGELISM PROFILE: not reported

VALIDITY: 5

Turkish society is divided principally between rural and urban sectors. Rural Turks live the life of peasant cultures worldwide and adhere strongly to tradition in the villages. By contrast, urban Turks desire a modern life-style, live in high-rise apartments and travel on broad city avenues.

Officially, Turkey is a secular republic and has no caliphate or religious courts or schools, but Islam is still a strong influence in individuals' lives. Rural and urban Turks maintain the formal practice of Islam. They feel the need to show religious observance, chiefly the fast of Ramadan. Modern Turkish city dwellers, however, practice many customs unacceptable to Islamic purists. City officials may include a blood sacrifice in the ceremony of laying a cornerstone, and mothers may hang bits of cloth in sacred trees near the mosque to help their married daughters become pregnant. University students offer chickens in sacrifice to ensure better marks on an examination.

While there is some friction between different sectors, Turkish society is basically egalitarian. However, there is a clear distinction, even antipathy, between urbanite and villager, rich and poor. Certain powerful Turkish families control the government bureaucracy, and those in high military ranks are a privileged class. Still, class distinctions do not split the community: all Anatolian Turks share a feeling of brotherhood as Turks and Muslims.

Turkey is one of the least Christianized and most resistant countries in the world: it is estimated there are less than 200 Christians in this country of nearly 40 million. A first strategic step in evangelization of the Anatolian Turks must be prayer, so that this hard and rough ground will be watered and softened to receive a witness offered in friendship and love.

Arab Immigrants in Bangui (Central African Republic)

ALTERNATE NAMES: not reported

SIZE OF GROUP: 5,000   MARC ID: 5045

DISTINCTIVES: ethnicity; religion; kinship; sense of unity; social class; occupation

SOCIAL CHANGE: not reported

LANGUAGES: Arabic (V, G); Ngambaye (T); French (T)

SCRIPTURE: Bible; RECORDINGS : yes

CHRISTIAN LITERACY: not reported

RELIGION: Islam (100% adherents)

CHURCHES AND MISSIONS: not reported

OPENNESS TO RELIGIOUS CHANGE: very closed

RECEPTIVITY TO CHRISTIANITY: very reluctant

GROWTH RATE OF CHRISTIAN COMMUNITY: not reported

EVANGELISM PROFILE: not reported

VALIDITY: 5

Bangui as a whole is 35% Christian. Like many other growing cities around the world, it has a predominantly young population, part of which consists of migrant Arabs from North Africa. These Arabs are merchants and are relatively homogeneous as a group. Their social structure in Bangui has been complicated by their leaving the economic institutions of rural and town life. Their goal in the city is to join the growing middle class of professional people, bureaucrats, clerical technicians and industrialists, goals that may be realized only by their children. They have experienced a radical shift as their cultural patterns undergo the changes imposed by urban life.

Considerable political turmoil has occurred in the Central African Republic over the last several years, although there is more stability since the "Empire" has reverted to a republic. There have not been any comprehensive evangelistic efforts made in this city, and the Christian population is divided along missionary lines. The churches apparently need to move evangelistic efforts outside the church buildings and to concentrate more on training lay people to work in personal evangelism.

Good cross-cultural roles to reach the Arabs in Bangui would be as educators and literacy teachers, medical teams, and disciplers for leaders and evangelistic workers. There is also a small force for evangelism in this city at Bangui Evangelical School of Theology. These North African Arabs represent only one aspect of the growing influence of Islam in the Central African Republic; another challenge to comprehensive evangelism is growing African intellectualism, which often views Christianity as a force opposing true African growth and self-expression.

Arabs in New Orleans (United States of America)

ALTERNATE NAMES: not reported

SIZE OF GROUP: 1,000   MARC ID: 5008

DISTINCTIVES: language; ethnicity; religion; kinship; sense of unity

SOCIAL CHANGE: not reported

LANGUAGES: Arabic (100% speak; V); English (T)

SCRIPTURE: Bible; RECORDINGS : yes

CHRISTIAN LITERACY: not reported

RELIGION: Islam; Orthodox

CHURCHES AND MISSIONS	BEGAN	MEMBERSHIP	COMMUNITY
Greek Orthodox Church	nr	nr	nr

OPENNESS TO RELIGIOUS CHANGE: somewhat open

RECEPTIVITY TO CHRISTIANITY: receptive

GROWTH RATE OF CHRISTIAN COMMUNITY: not reported

EVANGELISM PROFILE: not reported

VALIDITY: 5

In 1981 there were approximately 1000 Arab people living in metropolitan New Orleans. This number has doubled in the past decade as relatives have come to join those who were already here. They have come from Egypt, Jordan, Saudi Arabia, Kuwait and other Middle Eastern countries.

They speak Arabic and are a mixture of Muslims and a small number of Christians who belong mainly to the Greek Orthodox church. A small Egyptian congregation uses the facilities of an Episcopal church for a monthly meeting. A priest flies in from Boston or Chicago for the service on the first Saturday of each month. This group enjoys fellowship, but there is not much evidence of evangelism among them. They do not have contact with each other in the intervening weeks.

Several members of this group have expressed interest in regular weekly Bible study meetings. This is a great challenge for someone who will take advantage of this evangelistic opportunity.

There is also a large group of Arab people in the Baton Rouge area. It might be possible to combine these two groups to encourage each other. The Baptist Association in New Orleans has expressed some interest in evangelizing Arabs, but nothing has been done in an organized effort.

Auberge Crowd in Geneva (Switzerland)

ALTERNATE NAMES: International Students

SIZE OF GROUP: 150   MARC ID: 5002

DISTINCTIVES: education; age; hobby or interest

SOCIAL CHANGE: rapid

LANGUAGES: English (V, S, G); German (V); French (V); Arabic
      (V)

SCRIPTURE: Bible; RECORDINGS : yes

CHRISTIAN LITERACY: not reported

RELIGION: Secularism (100% adherents/100% practicing)

CHURCHES AND MISSIONS	BEGAN	MEMBERSHIP	COMMUNITY
Youth For Christ	1980	nr	nr

OPENNESS TO RELIGIOUS CHANGE: somewhat open

RECEPTIVITY TO CHRISTIANITY: receptive

GROWTH RATE OF CHRISTIAN COMMUNITY: not reported

EVANGELISM PROFILE: not reported

VALIDITY: 5

In Geneva, Switzerland, there is an international community
of approximately 35,000 foreigners in a city of 300,000. Most of
these people speak English either as a mother tongue or as their
working second language. The so-called Auberge crowd comes out
of the large number of English-speaking children and teenagers
who attend the International School of Geneva. The approximately
150 students in this group hang out at the English-speaking pubs
and cafes in Geneva.

These young people are called the Auberge crowd because they
spend much of their time at the Auberge de la Poste, across from
the International School. These intelligent and well-educated
students come from upper middle-class families, and most will
attend the best American and European universities. Their
activities center around liquor, electronic games and drugs.
They are united by these activities as well as by friendships,
language, their international experience and their desire for
excitement on weekends.

Most come from secular homes, while some come from nominal
Christian homes. A few come from Muslim backgrounds, though
these are mostly nominal also. Few have anyone to speak with
concerning spiritual and practical life issues.

Westerners and people with an international background are
easily accepted by this group. Prior to 1980 no strategy of
evangelism had been directed toward them. One Campus Life worker
regularly contacts the students at the Auberge de la Poste. A
coffeehouse ministry or a ministry to the whole person would work
well when combined with cultural sensitivity.

Bachelors in Lagos (Nigeria)

ALTERNATE NAMES: not reported

SIZE OF GROUP: 26,000   MARC ID: 5013

DISTINCTIVES: significant problems; economic status; age

SOCIAL CHANGE: moderate

LANGUAGES: English (T); Tribal Languages (V)

SCRIPTURE: Bible; RECORDINGS : yes

CHRISTIAN LITERACY: not reported

RELIGION: Secularism; Folk Religion; Islam; Christianity

CHURCHES AND MISSIONS: not reported

OPENNESS TO RELIGIOUS CHANGE: somewhat open

RECEPTIVITY TO CHRISTIANITY: receptive

GROWTH RATE OF CHRISTIAN COMMUNITY: not reported

EVANGELISM PROFILE: not reported

VALIDITY: 6

A recent survey found that of 26,000 bachelors in Lagos, 18,000 were under 25 years of age. These young men are in a difficult situation because of the "lag" between traditional African customs and the forces creating change in contemporary Africa. There is great cultural pressure to take a bride, but the traditional "bride price" has risen greatly in recent years to reflect supply and demand. Since there is high value placed on a bride who is a virgin, even less costly brides (widows, divorced, separated or unwed mothers), are ruled out by young men trying to make their way in the urban world.

Most young bachelors live with married relatives who provide shelter and meals. The greatest struggle for them has proved to be loneliness, especially for the few Christian bachelors. They are vulnerable emotionally, physically and spiritually and feel helpless in the midst of a culture that honors polygamy, virginity and fertility.

As urbanites, those bachelors in search of a religion are seeking one that reflects the blend of African and Western cultures. Africans have a tremendous respect for power, both political and spiritual. In the city one is tempted to strive for power by political and economical manipulation. Christians need to present the power available in Christ to conquer loneliness and rejection by others and give them the assurance that God will meet their needs.

Bahais in Teheran (Iran)

ALTERNATE NAMES: not reported

SIZE OF GROUP: 45,000   MARC ID: 5037

DISTINCTIVES: religion; sense of unity; discrimination;
    social class; significant problems

SOCIAL CHANGE: rapid

LANGUAGES: Farsi (100% speak; V, G, S)

SCRIPTURE: Bible; RECORDINGS : yes

CHRISTIAN LITERACY: not reported

RELIGION: Bahaism (100% adherents)

CHURCHES AND MISSIONS: not reported

OPENNESS TO RELIGIOUS CHANGE: not reported

RECEPTIVITY TO CHRISTIANITY: not reported

GROWTH RATE OF CHRISTIAN COMMUNITY: not reported

EVANGELISM PROFILE: not reported

VALIDITY: 6

Bahaism is a messianic faith that recognizes prophets of all established religions as true messengers of God. It was founded just over 100 years ago in Iran by Mirza Husayn Ali, known as Bahaullah, who proclaimed himself prophet in 1863. However, orthodox Muslims believe Muhammad was the final prophet and consider Bahaullah's teachings a gross heresy.

The Bahai religion has been persecuted in Iran from its birth. It has its headquarters and main temple in Haifa, Israel, which has made it easy for Iran's Islamic militants to condemn Bahai pilgrims to the shrine as Zionist spies. Many Bahai leaders in Iran have disappeared since the 1979 revolution. They are usually charged with treason, drug smuggling or sexual malpractice, though their faith rigorously forbids all three. Bahais do not drink, take drugs or marry without their parents' consent: in fact, they are strongly exhorted to "strict obedience to one's government."

Under the secular-minded Shah, Iranian Bahais were able to land well-paying jobs and were left relatively alone since they, too, had no great love for the Muslim clergy. Since the Iranian revolution, however, the mullahs have risen to power and seen their chance to equalize the situation. The Bahais must often face the choice of exile, prison or remaining in Iran but converting to Islam and sometimes refunding their salary, even from several years past.

Although Bahais are the largest religious minority in Iran, they seem to have suffered most. Strategies to reach them must emphasize the unique and unrepeatable position of Jesus Christ as God's final Word to humanity. This, unfortunately, is the greatest stumbling block to their acceptance of the Christian faith and must be addressed in a clear manner.

Barbers in Tokyo (Japan)

ALTERNATE NAMES: not reported

SIZE OF GROUP: 220,000   MARC ID: 5009

DISTINCTIVES: language; occupation; ethnicity; sense of
     unity; education; social class; economic status

SOCIAL CHANGE: not reported

LANGUAGES: Japanese (100% speak/100% read; V, S, G, W)

SCRIPTURE: Bible; RECORDINGS : yes

CHRISTIAN LITERACY: 100%

RELIGION: Buddhism (40% adherents/30% practicing); Secularism
     (5% adherents/5% practicing); Other (52% adherents);
     Protestant (3% adherents/1% practicing)

CHURCHES AND MISSIONS: not reported

OPENNESS TO RELIGIOUS CHANGE: indifferent

RECEPTIVITY TO CHRISTIANITY: indifferent

GROWTH RATE OF CHRISTIAN COMMUNITY: slow growth

EVANGELISM PROFILE: not reported

VALIDITY: 6

The barbers in Tokyo provide a welcome refuge and social
gathering place both winter and summer. They are organized as a
tight group and work 12 to 14 hours per day with their own
society of contacts. Since Sunday is the free day for most of
their clientele, the barbers take Monday off.

There are many possible strategies for reaching this people
group. Different areas of Tokyo could be assigned to interested
churches, with specifics regarding the barber community there.
Personal relationships are extremely important in Japanese
culture; therefore, the first contact might best be made late
Tuesday morning, when barbers are most available and proper
introductions would be feasible. Sample literature might be left
with the master of the shop, and a follow-up visit could include
an offer of the monthly magazine Gospel for the Millions to be
left on the reading table. This attractive magazine directed to
non-Christians is inexpensive enough for the average Japanese
church to include in their budget. This would provide a monthly
contact with the staff and the many guests waiting for service.
With proper contacts, most owners would probably give permission
for Christian tapes to be played in their shops. The Akira
Hattori tapes are produced for this kind of pioneer evangelism.
Rotating these tapes each month would give still another point of
contact for the local church.

Since Monday is a free day for the barbers, special meetings
could be prepared to present the claims of Christ and establish
friendships. Social activities, golfing, etc., might take place
during these times. The barbers of Tokyo as a people group need
creative approaches to discipling and promise good results if
such strategies are undertaken.

EXPANDED DESCRIPTIONS

Bengalis in London (United Kingdom)

ALTERNATE NAMES: not reported

SIZE OF GROUP: 15,000   MARC ID: 5038

DISTINCTIVES: language; ethnicity; religion; kinship;
    discrimination; significant problems

SOCIAL CHANGE: rapid

LANGUAGES: Bengali (V, G); English (T, S)

SCRIPTURE: Bible; RECORDINGS : yes

CHRISTIAN LITERACY: not reported

RELIGION: Islam; Islam-Animist

CHURCHES AND MISSIONS: not reported

OPENNESS TO RELIGIOUS CHANGE: somewhat closed

RECEPTIVITY TO CHRISTIANITY: reluctant

GROWTH RATE OF CHRISTIAN COMMUNITY: not reported

EVANGELISM PROFILE: not reported

VALIDITY: 5

   London's East End community of Spitalfields is an area where
immigrant populations have historically settled down with their
families to work. Spitalfields' Bengalis number about 15,000 (up
from 3500 in 1971), and are crammed in council housing around
Brick Lane, the scene of racist rioting in 1978. Unlike the
transitory, single exiles who congregate in Soho, London's
Bengalis need more policing for their own protection. The
Bengalis of Spitalfields suffer miserably from the racism of
their neighbors; the East End gives the neo-Nazi National Front
many of its votes and recruits.
   The majority of Bengali men are engaged in the rag trade,
long an East End staple. This livelihood allows many to get by
without learning English, which is the first step toward
assimilation and leaving the ghetto. Many of the young leave
school without qualifications or even competence in English.
   The extent of unemployment is difficult to determine in this
neighborhood because the Asian community makes few calls on
official agencies for social benefits. The Inner London
Education Authority already provides English language tuition
outside work hours, but the Bengali community is too fearful of
attacks from white neighbors to make good use of it. Some
Bengali clothing workers even insist that their bosses lock their
factory doors from the inside before the start of the night
shift.
   This Muslim community, uprooted from its own cultural
surroundings in south Asia and discriminated against and even
hated by many of its neighbors, is a desperately needy field for
the gospel. Christian workers must be aware that Christianity
will probably be associated by these Bengalis with English
society. Their receptivity depends on a Christ-centered message
which can call their attention from the behavior of those around
them to the Person and mission of Christ for their lives.

Bus Girls in Seoul (Korea, Republic of)

ALTERNATE NAMES: not reported

SIZE OF GROUP: 15,000   MARC ID: 5023

DISTINCTIVES: occupation; language; education; residence;
     age; economic status; hobby or interest

SOCIAL CHANGE: moderate

LANGUAGES: Korean (100% speak/100% read; V, S, G, W)

SCRIPTURE: Bible; RECORDINGS : yes

CHRISTIAN LITERACY: 100%

RELIGION: Secularism (76% adherents); Protestant (11%
     adherents/6% practicing); Roman Catholic (4% adherents/1%
     practicing); Orthodox (9% adherents/1% practicing)

CHURCHES AND MISSIONS   BEGAN MEMBERSHIP   COMMUNITY
     Circle of Evangelism   1974   nr   nr

OPENNESS TO RELIGIOUS CHANGE: somewhat open

RECEPTIVITY TO CHRISTIANITY: receptive

GROWTH RATE OF CHRISTIAN COMMUNITY: not reported

EVANGELISM PROFILE: not reported

VALIDITY: 6

There are some 15,000 girls working for the bus companies in
Souel, Korea, usually from 18 to 25 years old. They are in a low
economic bracket, to say the least. Few Christians take an
active concern for them, although they are a pitiful group. They
are despised and abused to the point where a manager will order a
body search on suspicion of one of them stealing. At times one
will commit suicide to show her honesty. Even Christians, after
they take this job, have difficulty attending church because of
Sunday working hours; currently about 5% of this group attend
church regularly. They suffer misfortune and deprivation, there
is prejudice against them in the city, and many have suffered
mental and emotional stress because of their depressing
environment. They yearn for a life of stability in the midst of
adversity and uneasiness. In short, they are not treated with
dignity as human beings created in God's image.
     An important aspect of reaching bus girls is to focus on the
key individuals in their lives. If her superiors are opposed to
Christianity, it is difficult for a bus girl to keep Christian
faith. On the other hand, a Christian superior not only would
allow discipleship to take place among the workers but might even
take part.
     Since 1974, two groups have attempted to reach them. One is
the Korean Urban Industrial Mission Band; the other is the
Circle of Evangelism, a group of students in Hankook Theological
Seminary. The first group has met difficulty since 1979. They
attempted to mobilize the bus girls to stand up for their rights.
This resulted in a strike by the bus girls, encouraged by the
Mission, which created a social sensation but did not secure any
benefits. Dispite this problem, the prospects are good for a
future increase in the number of Christians in this people group.

EXPANDED DESCRIPTIONS

Cape Malays in Cape Town (South Africa)

ALTERNATE NAMES: not reported

SIZE OF GROUP: 150,000   MARC ID: 5006

DISTINCTIVES: language; ethnicity; religion; sense of unity;
    residence; discrimination

SOCIAL CHANGE: slow

LANGUAGES: Afrikaans (90% speak/85% read; V, G, S, W); English
    (G, W)

SCRIPTURE: Bible; RECORDINGS : yes

CHRISTIAN LITERACY: 85%

RELIGION: Islam (87% adherents/87% practicing); Protestant (3%
    adherents/1% practicing); Other Christian (10% adherents/6%
    practicing)

CHURCHES AND MISSIONS	BEGAN	MEMBERSHIP	COMMUNITY
Apostolic Faith Mission	1910	1,000	1,200
Reformed Church	nr	nr	nr

OPENNESS TO RELIGIOUS CHANGE: very closed

RECEPTIVITY TO CHRISTIANITY: reluctant

GROWTH RATE OF CHRISTIAN COMMUNITY: not reported

EVANGELISM PROFILE: not reported

VALIDITY: 6

The Cape Malays are part of the Coloured people in South
Africa. The vast majority live in the Cape Peninsula,
particularly in Cape Town's well-known Malay Quarter. They are
descended from Muslim people introduced by the Dutch East India
Company from their eastern possessions. The Cape Malays as a
group have remained faithful to Islam. Originally independent
artisans known for their skill and reliability, they have been
forced out of their traditional trades and into factory work by
recent industrial development. About 90% speak Afrikaans.
    The Cape Malays are moderately resistant to the gospel,
though few have had any real contact with it. One reason appears
to be that no mission activity has been directed specifically to
reaching Afrikaans-speaking Cape Malay Muslims, but only to the
Coloured people in general. There are positive indications that
Cape Malay Muslims are reachable: communities of Christian
people will help to solve the problem of ostracism for new
converts. Religious freedom means that Muslim converts need not
fear political retribution or persecution. There is no language
barrier for the general population, and plenty of literature in
Afrikaans is available.
    Workers must be trained to see how the distinct culture of
Malay Muslims affects the way they understand and respond to
Jesus. Converts from among them must be enlisted, if possible,
as the best potential evangelists to their own people. Possibly
the most successful tactic would be to establish a Christian
Muslim mosque. This will be a contextualized Bible-believing
fellowship drawing liturgical elements from local Malay culture,
particularly music. This fellowship should be established with
an openness to manifestations of God's Spirit in action, as well
as a sensitivity not to alienate these people by repeating past
mistakes in evangelizing Muslims.

132

Casual Laborers in Atlanta (United States of America)

ALTERNATE NAMES: not reported

SIZE OF GROUP: 3,000   MARC ID: 5048

DISTINCTIVES: occupation; significant problems; economic
    status; social class; education

SOCIAL CHANGE: rapid

LANGUAGES: English (100% speak; V, G, S)

SCRIPTURE: Bible; RECORDINGS : yes

CHRISTIAN LITERACY: not reported

RELIGION: Secularism; Christianity

CHURCHES AND MISSIONS: not reported

OPENNESS TO RELIGIOUS CHANGE: indifferent

RECEPTIVITY TO CHRISTIANITY: indifferent

GROWTH RATE OF CHRISTIAN COMMUNITY: not reported

EVANGELISM PROFILE: not reported

VALIDITY: 5

A ritual occurs daily in many cities across the USA as unemployed men go to the same unkempt corners and wait for anyone seeking workers for a day or an hour. It is called "catching-out." The jobs they land or "catch" range from dishwashing to construction, from unloading produce to sweeping chimneys. They are picked up, delivered and paid in cash by the day.

In Atlanta, catching-out is a "skid row" phenomenon. While there is an element of choice as these men avoid traditional job hunts, this choice is often based on problems such as alcoholism. Some of these men are known as quality workers, but one view is that because they tend to be older, they can work hard for a day or two but cannot maintain that pace. Others like avoiding payroll deductions for income taxes and social security; some receive welfare and unemployment checks as well.

Trucks that appear to hold the promise of a job always cause the men to perk up. At times three or four attempt to board a truck where only one worker is wanted. Many give up after a few hours and return to the solace of the bottle. Many simply need to catch one good job to buy a car and qualify for a "real job."

These social and labor-market outcasts (and their families, if any) are a growing harvest field for the gospel. They need witnesses willing to share their life-style and hardships, who are sensitive to their impressions of the gospel gained from inner-city "rescue missions." There is also an opportunity for churches to participate with them in their struggle with physical and economic needs and to make them welcome in the broader society.

EXPANDED DESCRIPTIONS

Chicanos in Denver (United States of America)

ALTERNATE NAMES: not reported

SIZE OF GROUP: 121,000   MARC ID: 5029

DISTINCTIVES: ethnicity; language; kinship; sense of unity;
     social class; discrimination

SOCIAL CHANGE: rapid

LANGUAGES: Spanish (V, G, W); English (T, S)

SCRIPTURE: Bible; RECORDINGS : yes

CHRISTIAN LITERACY: not reported

RELIGION: Roman Catholic; Secularism

CHURCHES AND MISSIONS: not reported

OPENNESS TO RELIGIOUS CHANGE: somewhat open

RECEPTIVITY TO CHRISTIANITY: receptive

GROWTH RATE OF CHRISTIAN COMMUNITY: not reported

EVANGELISM PROFILE: not reported

VALIDITY: 5

Nearly one-fourth of Denver's population are
Chicanos--Hispanic Americans. The average household income in
the city in 1977 was $12,200; despite their numbers, in the same
year the Chicano median household income was $8,000, and 32% were
listed as poverty-level in income.

Housing is overcrowded, and rising housing costs lead to
Chicano relocation and displacement. The Chicanos often feel
victimized by the system, and their social difficulties are
compounded by a high percentage of school dropouts.

They are described as "openly receptive to the Word of God."
Denver's Chicanos are familiar with the concepts of sin,
repentance, faith, the Trinity, the authority of Scripture and
life after death. They show a strong interest in a God who
cares, helps and sides with the oppressed. On the other hand,
major decisions are usually made jointly, so individual
commitments to changed life-styles are weak. Catholic tradition
discourages religious activity outside the Roman Catholic Church,
where nominalism is much in evidence.

Chicanos are attracted to churches whose membership is
mostly minority and/or low-income, that teach clearly drawn
concepts of right and wrong regarding life-style and morality and
where worship is emotional, exciting and expectant. It has been
found helpful to press for a decision and not to be distant from
the people one is trying to reach, although the evangelist should
remain an authoritative figure.

Discipling ministries require particular sensitivity.
Chicanos must be encouraged to become involved in some ministry.
A nucleus of stable, supportive Anglos and minority persons may
help to provide encouragement and close fellowship, but there
should be Chicano leadership at all levels. Chicanos should
decide on topic selection, music and style of worship. Bible
teaching must be concretely applied to home and job situations.
The issues of people's physical well-being and social justice
must be consciously addressed to retain disciples and help them
grow; this may even extend to fostering and supporting
enterprises owned and managed by Chicanos.

Chinese in Boston (United States of America)

ALTERNATE NAMES: not reported

SIZE OF GROUP: 20,000   MARC ID: 5019

DISTINCTIVES: language; occupation; ethnicity; kinship;
     residence

SOCIAL CHANGE: moderate

LANGUAGES: Cantonese (V); Mandarin (V); English (T)

SCRIPTURE: Bible; RECORDINGS : yes

CHRISTIAN LITERACY: 75%

RELIGION: Secularism (90% adherents); Buddhism (5% adherents);
     Protestant (4% adherents/3% practicing); Roman Catholic (1%
     adherents/1% practicing)

CHURCHES AND MISSIONS	BEGAN	MEMBERSHIP	COMMUNITY
Boston Chinese Evang. Church	1961	275	nr
Chinese Bible Church	nr	250	nr
Chinese Christian Church	nr	100	nr
Holy Trinity Catholic Church	nr	200	300

OPENNESS TO RELIGIOUS CHANGE: somewhat open

RECEPTIVITY TO CHRISTIANITY: receptive

GROWTH RATE OF CHRISTIAN COMMUNITY: rapid growth

EVANGELISM PROFILE: not reported

VALIDITY: 6

The so-called "Chinatown" in Boston is the fourth largest in
the USA. Not only do many Chinese people live there, it is the
focal point for the entire New England Chinese Community. As
such, the Chinese in Boston are a significant people group bonded
together by a common language, ethnic background and culture.

The first Chinese settled in the Boston area in the late
1880s. They planned on earning money and then returning home.
Because they saw themselves as temporary residents, they didn't
attempt to learn English or become acculturated to American life.
This produced a barrier which was compounded by cultural and
racial discrimination by others around them. Gradually, the
Chinese who stayed adapted and have done better than their
ancestors, though the community as a whole keeps to itself.

The majority of Boston's Chinese residents are secularists
or humanists; few retain traditional Buddhist beliefs and
practices. All of the 20,000 in Chinatown are known to speak
English. There are four active Chinese churches in the area,
totaling approximately 600 full-time members. The younger
Chinese generation is much more receptive to Christianity than
are the older people. Almost all of them have an awareness of
the existence of Christianity, though unfortunately few have an
adequate understanding of the gospel.

Circassians in Amman (Jordan)

ALTERNATE NAMES: Adyge

SIZE OF GROUP: 17,000   MARC ID: 5018

DISTINCTIVES: religion; kinship; education; economic status

SOCIAL CHANGE: moderate

LANGUAGES: Circassian (100% speak; V); Arabic (V)

SCRIPTURE: Bible; RECORDINGS : yes

CHRISTIAN LITERACY: not reported

RELIGION: Islam

CHURCHES AND MISSIONS: not reported

OPENNESS TO RELIGIOUS CHANGE: somewhat closed

RECEPTIVITY TO CHRISTIANITY: reluctant

GROWTH RATE OF CHRISTIAN COMMUNITY: not reported

EVANGELISM PROFILE: not reported

VALIDITY: 5

Amman, Jordan, the youngest metropolis in this part of the Middle East, has grown to a population of some 800,000. It has a mixed population rather than the "quarters" found in most Middle Eastern cities. The larger established urban population has no unified cultural outlook and little relation to the indigenous society of the area.

In the late 1800s Ottoman rulers established several small colonies of Circassians--Sunni Muslims who had fled from the Russian Caucasus in the 1860s and '70s. This provided an element loyal to the Ottoman sultan, who was despised locally as a foreign oppressor.

Circassians and Christians (rather than Muslim Transjordanians) dominated Amman before the incursion of the Palestinians, who since the late 1970s amount to between 60% and 80% of Amman's population. Also, increasing numbers of rural villagers are slowly changing the city's atmosphere. Growing urban population, partly due to drought, has prompted new urban development in Amman and planning studies for other Jordanian cities.

There are 15,000 to 20,000 people in the Circassian community now. Despite their small numbers they have long been prominent in government, landowning, commerce and industry. While there are still many in the senior military ranks, they have probably declined in other areas with the influx of Palestinians and improved Jordanian education. Intermarriage has furthered some Circassian assimilation into the general population, along with their sharing the religion of the majority, Sunni Islam.

The Circassians, like other Muslim peoples in this area, have traditionally opposed Christianity. Strategies for evangelism should include a high regard for the culture of this proud people. Workers should test the idea of a Circassian mosque of "Muslims for Jesus."

Coloureds in Eersterust (South Africa)

ALTERNATE NAMES: not reported

SIZE OF GROUP: 20,000   MARC ID: 5040

DISTINCTIVES: ethnicity; residence; social class; economic
     status; discrimination; significant problems

SOCIAL CHANGE: moderate

LANGUAGES: Afrikaans (V, G, W); English (T)

SCRIPTURE: Bible; RECORDINGS : yes

CHRISTIAN LITERACY: 70%

RELIGION: Secularism; Folk Religion; Islam; Christianity (20%
     adherents/15% practicing)

CHURCHES AND MISSIONS	BEGAN	MEMBERSHIP	COMMUNITY
Evangelical Bible Church	nr	nr	nr
Lyynwood Baptist Church	nr	nr	nr
Eersterust Mission	nr	nr	nr

OPENNESS TO RELIGIOUS CHANGE: somewhat closed

RECEPTIVITY TO CHRISTIANITY: indifferent

GROWTH RATE OF CHRISTIAN COMMUNITY: not reported

EVANGELISM PROFILE:
     0% No awareness of Christianity
     0% Aware that Christianity exists
     20% Some knowledge of the gospel
     30% Understand the message of the gospel
     35% Personally challenged to receive Christ
     0% Decision to accept Christ
     10% Incorporated into a fellowship of Christians
     5% Active propagators of the gospel

VALIDITY: 6

     Planned Coloured and Black townships in and around large
cities of South Africa provide labor for industry. The
government has fostered education and vocational opportunities in
these townships. Eersterust has an unemployment rate of between
25% and 60%. A housing shortage in the community leads to
overcrowding and tensions. Crime is a major problem, and street
gangs are motivated by revenge. Popular gathering places are the
shebeens, which are taverns and often houses of prostitution.
     Unfortunately, the gospel is associated with Afrikaaner
political domination, which hinders receptivity. Despite
familiarity with Christianity, the sociopolitical context results
in skepticism. Coloureds view the gospel as a "call to become
religious," although some are eager to study Scripture and become
active in church.
     Successful church planting must start by identifying with
them as an oppressed and alienated people. Those leading the
work should live within the community. Heads of families can
keep those within their family from receiving the gospel; and
the general violence, drunkenness and gambling within the
environment creates strong opposition to spiritual growth.
Successful church planting and church growth should be initiated
by mature local leadership.

EXPANDED DESCRIPTIONS

Danchi Dwellers in Tokyo (Japan)

ALTERNATE NAMES: not reported

SIZE OF GROUP: 2,500,000   MARC ID: 5005

DISTINCTIVES: residence; language; economic status

SOCIAL CHANGE: rapid

LANGUAGES: Japanese (100% speak; V, S, G)

SCRIPTURE: Bible; RECORDINGS : yes

CHRISTIAN LITERACY: 100%

RELIGION: Secularism (40% adherents); Buddhism (40% adherents);
   Roman Catholic (1% adherents/1% practicing); Protestant (2%
   adherents/1% practicing); Other (17% adherents)

CHURCHES AND MISSIONS	BEGAN	MEMBERSHIP	COMMUNITY
Evangelical Alliance Mission	1965	nr	nr
FEGC	1968	nr	nr
Tokyo Evangelistic Church	1968	nr	nr
Southern Baptist	nr	nr	nr

OPENNESS TO RELIGIOUS CHANGE: somewhat open

RECEPTIVITY TO CHRISTIANITY: indifferent

GROWTH RATE OF CHRISTIAN COMMUNITY: stable

EVANGELISM PROFILE: not reported

VALIDITY: 5

"Danchi" refers to Japanese multiple apartment and
condominium housing started about 1960 by the county government
in Japan. "Tama-newtown," a danchi constructed about 1965 near
Tokyo, is a typical example, with 250,000 residents. It is made
up of buildings from 5 to 11 stories high and will accommodate
400,000 when completed. Residents are chosen by lottery and
enjoy modern facilities throughout the structure.
    The typical danchi family is a young couple about 30 years
old with one child. The husband is a businessman or executive,
taking a train to and from work, since the danchi is usually
located in a rural suburb of newly developed land. He works six
days a week, returning home by 8 p.m. His wife will be caring
for the small child, watching TV and shopping by day.
    The new social and family situation permits the wife to
accept religious changes more readily than the rest of the
family. Seldom do families participate in the traditional
Japanese religious activities. Religion and philosophy are
interesting subjects for them. They are among the ripest harvest
fields in Japan, thanks to strong social and economic pressures.
Nevertheless, some major difficulties remain: (1) foreigners may
not live in danchis; (2) no religious meetings are normally
allowed in the recreation areas (meeting halls are scarce, and
other spaces are impossible to rent); and (3) danchis offer a
sense of community--dwellers are unwilling to travel far for
church services.
    Some missionaries have been successful in handing out
Christian tracts and in the process have found a few Japanese
Christians living in the danchis. Other cross-cultural events
such as teaching English, cooking, sports and handicrafts to
housewives could be a basis for evangelism among the many
thousands of non-working mothers there.

Dead-End Kids in Amsterdam (Netherlands)

ALTERNATE NAMES: not reported

SIZE OF GROUP: 30,000   MARC ID: 5034

DISTINCTIVES: significant problems; age; discrimination;
    economic status

SOCIAL CHANGE: rapid

LANGUAGES: Dutch (100% speak; V, S, G, W)

SCRIPTURE: Bible; RECORDINGS : yes

CHRISTIAN LITERACY: not reported

RELIGION: Secularism

CHURCHES AND MISSIONS	BEGAN	MEMBERSHIP	COMMUNITY
Youth With A Mission	nr	nr	nr

OPENNESS TO RELIGIOUS CHANGE: somewhat closed

RECEPTIVITY TO CHRISTIANITY: reluctant

GROWTH RATE OF CHRISTIAN COMMUNITY: not reported

EVANGELISM PROFILE: not reported

VALIDITY: 6

In cities all over Western Europe, aimless young people are
creating a separate culture--or perhaps anticulture--that
perplexes and frustrates the older generation. This rebellion
began in Amsterdam, where homeless young dropouts entered
abandoned apartment buildings to camp on bits of crumbling floor
space. Riots, rock-throwing crowds and demonstrations have
expressed this destructive violence in many cities (Zurich, West
Berlin, Vienna, London and Paris). This youthful anger appears
to be directed at the welfare state and its concern for
cleanliness, order and prosperity.

Events such as a coronation in Amsterdam have led to marches
and riots; at other times, these appear to have been
spontaneous. The movement is strongly antipolitical, but
elements of the radical left and right have been in evidence.
Another side of this movement is expressed not in rioting but in
resignation. The "anti-everything" message often leads to
alcoholism, drug abuse and suicide, which have increased sharply
among those under 30 in Western Europe. The disorder is
spreading.

These young people suffer what has been called "anomie," a
feeling of lostness and hopelessness, separated from roots and
from relationships and values which give meaning and significance
to life. These young people in rebellion against society's norms
have experienced deprivation at home and can look forward to a
shortage of housing and work opportunities. Their failure and
boredom is reinforced by underachievement in school and
unemployment.

The dead-end kids have rarely heard the gospel, and they
resist considering it seriously because of their ideas of
Christianity and Christians. Only if they have contemporaries
who are Christians do they begin to take notice; some are
attracted by the image of Jesus. There are many ways Christians
can become involved with these people and present the gospel to
them, but they must become vulnerable, willing to share failures,
lives, homes and families with them.

EXPANDED DESCRIPTIONS

Deccani Muslims in Hyderabad (India)

ALTERNATE NAMES: not reported

SIZE OF GROUP: 500,000   MARC ID: 5027

DISTINCTIVES: language; ethnicity; religion; kinship

SOCIAL CHANGE: not reported

LANGUAGES: Dakhni (V, G); Telegu (T)

SCRIPTURE: not reported

CHRISTIAN LITERACY: not reported

RELIGION: Islam (100% adherents); Islam-Animist; Secularism

CHURCHES AND MISSIONS: not reported

OPENNESS TO RELIGIOUS CHANGE: somewhat closed

RECEPTIVITY TO CHRISTIANITY: reluctant

GROWTH RATE OF CHRISTIAN COMMUNITY: not reported

EVANGELISM PROFILE: not reported

VALIDITY: 6

Before 1948, urban Muslims in India's Deccan Plateau dominated government and military services and worked in trade and commerce. The 1948 partition of India immediately reversed this situation. Many emigrated to Pakistan, and those who remained became a new minority under Hindu rule. The old Muslim palaces and compounds either are crumbling or have been leveled to make room for public buildings and roads. The former servants of the established Muslim government and nobility are living on small pensions or meager incomes of family members. The mass of Muslims in the Deccan are now engaged in small trade as laborers in industry and as carpenters, blacksmiths, tanners, shopkeepers and rickshaw drivers. Muslim professionals have adjusted more easily to the new situation, entering banking, business, central government service and employment as scientists and teachers.

Most of the approximately half million Deccani Muslims speak Dakhni, a variant of Urdu. However, the official language of Andhra Pradesh is now Telegu, which has left the Muslims with a strong feeling of cultural loss, since Urdu does not retain even the status of a secondary language. The language and literature are preserved in a few newspapers and in cultural centers.

Middle-class, educated Muslims have a more secularized outlook and modern attitude toward personal law, Muslim education and minority status, and often must bridge social and educational gaps to communicate with the more conservative Muslim community and religious leaders. Deccani Muslim culture differs from north Indian Muslim culture because it embraces Hindu and Muslim elements to a large degree (although this is less true in the cities). Worship of saints is common among this people group.

In missionary outreach to the Deccani Muslims it is important to recognize that the breakdown of Muslim culture under the legal and governmental system presents a unique opportunity to reaffirm their identity as a people. The possibility of reviving mosques around Muslims who have decided to follow Jesus should be carefully considered.

Deviant Youth in Taipei (Taiwan)

ALTERNATE NAMES: Young Drifters; Prostitutes

SIZE OF GROUP: 80,000   MARC ID: 5044

DISTINCTIVES: age; significant problems; social class; discrimination; sense of unity; occupation

SOCIAL CHANGE: rapid

LANGUAGES: Mandarin (100% speak; V, G); Taiwanese (80% speak; V)

SCRIPTURE: Bible; RECORDINGS : yes

CHRISTIAN LITERACY: not reported

RELIGION: Folk Religion (49% adherents); Secularism (49% adherents); Roman Catholic (1% adherents); Protestant (1% adherents)

CHURCHES AND MISSIONS: not reported

OPENNESS TO RELIGIOUS CHANGE: somewhat open

RECEPTIVITY TO CHRISTIANITY: indifferent

GROWTH RATE OF CHRISTIAN COMMUNITY: not reported

EVANGELISM PROFILE: not reported

VALIDITY: 5

It is estimated that approximately 4% of Taiwan's youth between the ages of 15 and 24 are either juvenile delinquents or young prostitutes--a total of around 80,000 in Taipei alone. Although these two groups are somewhat different, there are common bonds: both are social deviants and are outside the scope of present Christian outreach. New government regulations may have reduced the estimated 40,000 prostitutes in Taipei. A Catholic nun has attempted some personal work among these girls, and one Protestant coffeehouse was open for a time to minister to the young drifters.

Taipei churches, with their desire to attract "good" people, seem unable or unwilling to reach out to either group. One engineer burdened for reaching these youth feels they are more receptive than college students because of their low self-esteem and broken family backgrounds. However, Taipei now lacks any structure like the Teen Challenge program in the United States that could build churches adapted to youth from this background. Dr. Harvie Conn's success with wayward girls in Korea suggests that a similar approach would work here if people were found committed to such a ministry. Two seminary women were recently assigned to work with girls sent to detention centers, but this "captive audience" approach has had minimal results.

The deviant youth of Taipei are sorely in need of people who accept and believe in them, and can offer them meaningful work opportunities in a highly competitive society. Apart from individuals, the Friendship Center is the only ministry in Northern Taiwan currently reaching out to them. This Center handles some youth on parole as a church-related institution. Any ministry among these young people, along with presenting the gospel and nurturing disciples, must also help to reunite them with the surrounding society.

Drug Addicts in Sao Paulo (Brazil)

ALTERNATE NAMES: not reported

SIZE OF GROUP: 200,000   MARC ID: 5022

DISTINCTIVES: significant problems; health situation; legal
     status; discrimination; economic status

SOCIAL CHANGE: rapid

LANGUAGES: Portuguese (100% speak; V, G, W)

SCRIPTURE: Bible; RECORDINGS : yes

CHRISTIAN LITERACY: not reported

RELIGION: Roman Catholic; Secularism; Folk Religion

CHURCHES AND MISSIONS	BEGAN	MEMBERSHIP	COMMUNITY
Presbyterian Church	nr	nr	nr
Pentecostal Church	nr	nr	nr
Movement to Recuperate Lives	nr	nr	nr
Salvation Army	nr	nr	nr

OPENNESS TO RELIGIOUS CHANGE: indifferent

RECEPTIVITY TO CHRISTIANITY: indifferent

GROWTH RATE OF CHRISTIAN COMMUNITY: not reported

EVANGELISM PROFILE: not reported

VALIDITY: 5

Drug addiction is an increasing problem around the world.
In Sao Paulo, a city of seven and a half million people, over
200,000 addicts consume an estimated 80 kilos of cocaine and
about a ton of marijuana per month! As in other cities, this has
contributed to a rising crime rate and presents a significant
challenge to the church.

Sao Paulo is known to be receptive to religious change, and
most religions find the city to be "fertile soil." Brazilians are
by tradition Roman Catholic, although the major religious force
is known as "Umbanda." This is a form of spiritism (reflecting a
Brazilian heritage) combined with African and Amerindian concepts
under the Catholic umbrella.

Several Protestant churches have developed and worked
independently of each other in Sao Paulo, beginning with the
Presbyterians. The largest and fastest growing are the
Pentecostals. At present, they represent 69% of the members of
Protestant churches. The most effective evangelistic efforts are
being initiated by parachurches, several of whose ministries
include neighborhood Bible studies, personal witnessing,
counseling, etc. The Movement to Recuperate Lives and the
Salvation Army are working among drug addicts, unwed mothers,
prostitutes and people with drinking problems.

Drug addicts in Sao Paulo must deal with basically the same
financial problems, emotional hurts and social stress met by
addicts in any urban setting. Those who help to meet their needs
are those who can introduce them to the love of Jesus Christ by
means of personal contact and genuine friendship. Addicts do not
go to religious gatherings or church; thus, the church must
reach out to them.

Ex-Mental Patients in New York City (United States of America)

ALTERNATE NAMES: not reported

SIZE OF GROUP: 20,000   MARC ID: 5007

DISTINCTIVES: discrimination; health situation; significant
    problems

SOCIAL CHANGE: rapid

LANGUAGES: English (V); Spanish (V)

SCRIPTURE: Bible; RECORDINGS : yes

CHRISTIAN LITERACY: not reported

RELIGION: Secularism; Roman Catholic; Protestant; Judaism

CHURCHES AND MISSIONS: not reported

OPENNESS TO RELIGIOUS CHANGE: somewhat open

RECEPTIVITY TO CHRISTIANITY: receptive

GROWTH RATE OF CHRISTIAN COMMUNITY: not reported

EVANGELISM PROFILE: not reported

VALIDITY: 5

Every city in America now contains a subculture composed of
persons who have spent time in a mental institution. Because of
the change in government policies and because of the extreme lack
of facilities, many people who were once institutionalized and
otherwise still would be are now out on the streets. A
generation ago the chronically mentally ill were kept in state
hospitals. Now a large percentage have been de-institutionalized
in the hope that they will be integrated into society. This has
yet to happen. The chronically mentally ill are usually not
capable of holding steady jobs and leading normal social lives.
Nor is society (including their families) ready to receive them.

The situation is getting worse. Urban centers attract the
majority of these people. The traditional "rescue missions" are
not equipped to handle them. They live in third-rate hotels and
apartment houses. They eat poorly, are fearful and vulnerable to
attack and exploitation, and sometimes get into trouble.

Very little evangelism is taking place among these people.
When the majority of the mentally ill were institutionalized,
some work was done by hospital chaplains, etc. Now that they are
out on the streets, few Christians seem to know how to go about
reaching them.

According to Sojourners magazine there are more than 20,000
de-institutionalized mentally ill people in New York City, and
the number there, as in all American cities, is increasing.
State mental hospitals are being closed and used for other
purposes. Out-patient services do not nearly make up for the
loss in care for the mentally ill¼ Lcap enr Ymga ne raYKdoa deh
azbaomaeua wca YneaYmeaQQ nK QnumdY oaXauwmne¼

Expatriates in Riyadh (Saudi Arabia)

ALTERNATE NAMES: not reported

SIZE OF GROUP: not reported   MARC ID: 5024

DISTINCTIVES: social class;   residence;   economic status;
    significant problems

SOCIAL CHANGE: rapid

LANGUAGES: English (V)

SCRIPTURE: Bible; RECORDINGS : yes

CHRISTIAN LITERACY: not reported

RELIGION: Secularism

CHURCHES AND MISSIONS: not reported

OPENNESS TO RELIGIOUS CHANGE: indifferent

RECEPTIVITY TO CHRISTIANITY: indifferent

GROWTH RATE OF CHRISTIAN COMMUNITY: not reported

EVANGELISM PROFILE: not reported

VALIDITY: 5

The government of Saudi Arabia is committed to maintaining a strong Islamic presence in this Middle East kingdom. Riyadh, the capital city, is undergoing rapid change as the country spends massive earnings from its oil fields, but even with technological advances, conservative social and religious practices remain.

Expatriates (foreigners) are kept under close scrutiny because of their potential "immoral influence." Visas are granted for one year only in most cases, and those who enter for professional reasons find their activities tightly controlled. Any discovery or suspicion that one is behaving contrary to Islamic beliefs is cause for quick expulsion. It is interesting to note that Mormons are readily granted entry because of their reputation for "clean living." Proselytizing on their part, however, or by followers of any religion except Islam, is strictly forbidden.

Christians have managed to enter Riyadh in small numbers because of their professional skills. Saudi Arabia is making tremendous efforts at this time to catch up with the fast-developing Western world. The most successful attempts by Christians to reach the expatriate population have been by those who have arrived independently and for professional reasons. Effectiveness greatly depends on language skills, cultural familiarity and sensitivity. Because of the church's low profile in Riyadh, knowledge about the size of the expatriate and national Christian communities and the extent of their evangelistic outreach is extremely difficult to acquire.

Favelados in Rio de Janeiro (Brazil)

ALTERNATE NAMES: not reported

SIZE OF GROUP: 600,000   MARC ID: 5043

DISTINCTIVES: residence; education; social class; economic
    status; health situation; significant problems

SOCIAL CHANGE: not reported

LANGUAGES: Portuguese (100% speak; V, G, W)

SCRIPTURE: Bible; RECORDINGS : yes

CHRISTIAN LITERACY: not reported

RELIGION: Christo-Paganism; Folk Religion; Roman Catholic;
    Secularism; Christianity (-1% practicing)

CHURCHES AND MISSIONS: not reported

OPENNESS TO RELIGIOUS CHANGE: indifferent

RECEPTIVITY TO CHRISTIANITY: indifferent

GROWTH RATE OF CHRISTIAN COMMUNITY: not reported

EVANGELISM PROFILE: not reported

VALIDITY: 5

Over 14% of the metropolitan population of Rio de Janeiro
live in 300 "favelas," the generic Brazilian term for squatter
settlements. These areas have been growing at 7.5% per year.
The number of jobs in Rio has not been expanding at nearly the
same rate, meaning that "hyperurbanization" is in effect.

Many favelados are not listed as unemployed since they have
never worked in industrially oriented activities. Therefore,
they are officially listed as "inactive" rather than as an
unemployed part of the economically active population.
Occasionally one family member holds more than one job at a time,
and favelados usually are more than willing to work in any
capacity to earn some money. Any individual in a family who can
find work takes a job, so it is not uncommon to have several
members working at different times and places with little contact
among family members. Often entire families become enslaved in
the task of finding and keeping jobs, with children scavenging in
heaps of garbage for salable items and even food.

Between 4% and 8% of all favelados are of Indian ancestry
and preserve animistic beliefs of spiritism. Receptivity to
Christianity varies because traditions are highly valued in light
of the many changes in environment, social interaction and work
activities. Christo-paganism has increased significantly as
Christian doctrines are combined with animism.

The opportunity for Christian witness among favelados begins
with ministering to their many felt needs, incarnating the gospel
as good news in every aspect of their lives. These hillside
communities are subject to natural disasters like flooding and
fire, as well as the deprivations resulting from the city's
inability to provide basic amenities such as water, electricity
and sewers. The decentralized house church model seems the only
practical approach in this environment. Living with this people
group and sharing their life-style and burdens should make a big
difference in their receptivity to the gospel.

Gays in San Francisco (United States of America)

ALTERNATE NAMES: not reported

SIZE OF GROUP: 150,000   MARC ID: 5010

DISTINCTIVES: sense of unity; residence; discrimination;
significant problems

SOCIAL CHANGE: rapid

LANGUAGES: English (100% speak/100% read; V, S, G, W)

SCRIPTURE: Bible; RECORDINGS : yes

CHRISTIAN LITERACY: not reported

RELIGION: Secularism

CHURCHES AND MISSIONS	BEGAN	MEMBERSHIP	COMMUNITY
Love In Action	nr	nr	nr
First Covenant Church	nr	nr	nr
Agape Ministries	nr	nr	nr

OPENNESS TO RELIGIOUS CHANGE: very closed

RECEPTIVITY TO CHRISTIANITY: very reluctant

GROWTH RATE OF CHRISTIAN COMMUNITY: not reported

EVANGELISM PROFILE: not reported

VALIDITY: 6

Estimates of the gay (homosexual) population range from
150,000 in the city of San Francisco to 800,000 in the whole San
Francisco Bay Area. Those openly identified with the community
are mostly male; the organization and participation of the
female gay (lesbian) population has lagged behind.

Current outreach efforts take several forms. Street
evangelism and literature distribution occur weekly in gay
neighborhoods, and up to 200 Christians take part in a large
periodic outreach, with one-to-one witnessing, street worship and
preaching. Love in Action, Gospel Outreach and Church of the
Open Door have Christian houses where ex-gays can live while
moving to full church involvement. Several full-time workers
counsel gays and ex-gays in person and by mail.

Many homosexuals admit to deep feelings of spiritual need.
Many also know the Bible teaches that homosexuality is sinful;
however, being unwilling to give up homosexuality, or feeling
that they cannot, they refuse the gospel. Members and pastors of
"gay churches" are often former members of evangelical and
Pentecostal churches where they did not find an understanding
attitude toward homosexuality. Resentment and feelings of
rejection stay with homosexuals and increase their resistance to
the gospel.

Loneliness and rejection typify the gay life-style.
Frequently, this is the cause of deep depression and even
suicide. Certain aspects of Western society are more tolerant of
the gay culture, among them the arts. Christians involved in
theater, music, and other forms of human expression would
probably be better bearers of the gospel to this particular
people group. It is crucial to respect confidences, refrain from
expressing judgment, and avoid preconceived ideas. There are
challenges and rewards for those who will persist and see gay
people brought to salvation and incorporated into the community
of believers.

Geishas in Osaka (Japan)

ALTERNATE NAMES: not reported

SIZE OF GROUP: not reported   MARC ID: 5025

DISTINCTIVES: occupation; language; ethnicity; education;
     social class; economic status

SOCIAL CHANGE: slow

LANGUAGES: Japanese (100% speak/100% read; V, G, S)

SCRIPTURE: Bible; RECORDINGS : yes

CHRISTIAN LITERACY: not reported

RELIGION: Secularism; Buddhism; Folk Religion

CHURCHES AND MISSIONS: not reported

OPENNESS TO RELIGIOUS CHANGE: not reported

RECEPTIVITY TO CHRISTIANITY: not reported

GROWTH RATE OF CHRISTIAN COMMUNITY: not reported

EVANGELISM PROFILE: not reported

VALIDITY: 5

Osaka is a city that has been called "intrinsically
Japanese." Though Western kinds of entertainment are increasingly
popular, the most characteristically Japanese form of
entertainment--the geisha--remains. In the West pictures of
geishas are as much a symbol of Japan as Mount Fuji, though the
Japanese are not proud of this. Despite this familiarity, most
Westerners when invited to a geisha party (whatever they expect)
are disappointed.

A visit to one of these famous houses does not include the
pleasures commonly associated with the word geisha. One does not
just visit a geisha house when the mood strikes. An introduction
is necessary, and a visit to a leading establishment is a social
occasion--more important to Japanese than to foreigners. The
geisha house itself is not much more than a beautiful building.
No geishas regularly live there, food is not prepared, and
customers do not spend the night.

Geisha literally means "artist," and aspiring geishas
undergo long training in singing, dancing and samisen playing.
They are expected also to entertain guests with their wit and by
tricks with fans or sake cups. Geishas, especially in the
cities, are usually the daughters of geishas and grow up in a
quarter where many geishas live. Formerly a girl would become a
maiko (trainee) at the age of eleven or twelve, but the school
laws now mean she must wait to take up the profession until she
is about fifteen. Today the women at the recognized geisha
establishments in the cities are definitely artists; the geisha,
however, usually has a patron to whom she is expected to be
"faithful." Geishas sometimes marry their patrons and lead quiet,
domestic lives.

EXPANDED DESCRIPTIONS

Gypsies in Jerusalem (Israel)

ALTERNATE NAMES: not reported

SIZE OF GROUP: 300   MARC ID: 5042

DISTINCTIVES: social class; ethnicity; occupation; religion; kinship; sense of unity; discrimination

SOCIAL CHANGE: not reported

LANGUAGES: Arabic (V, T, G); Romany Dialect (V)

SCRIPTURE: Bible; RECORDINGS : yes

CHRISTIAN LITERACY: not reported

RELIGION: Islam (100% adherents)

CHURCHES AND MISSIONS: not reported

OPENNESS TO RELIGIOUS CHANGE: somewhat closed

RECEPTIVITY TO CHRISTIANITY: reluctant

GROWTH RATE OF CHRISTIAN COMMUNITY: not reported

EVANGELISM PROFILE: not reported

VALIDITY: 5

    Gypsies have spread throughout the Middle East, adopting the language and religion of many Arab communities where they have settled. Jerusalem's Gypsies arrived in the last century as tent-dwelling nomads, then moved into huts, then were relocated by the British into the Baab al Nuta section of the Old City in 1939. During Jordanian rule, they gave up metal working for street sweeping; most now work for the Israeli muncipality of Jerusalem. The Gypsies who migrated to Gaza became entertainers, and their women are often paid by the Arabs to dance at weddings and feasts. Since Gypsy entertainers at times include prostitutes, even the metal workers suffer from the reputation earned by the dancers. Arabs very seldom marry Gypsy women.

    A casual visitor might mistake the Gypsy neighborhood in Jerusalem for another Arab corner of the teeming Old City. The Gypsy families speak Arabic, although the older ones still speak a Gypsy tongue among themselves. The older people dress in traditional Arab styles, while the young (like Arab youth) dress in jeans and T-shirts. Few young Gypsies get beyond grade school in the local Arab language school system. An exception is Abu Selim, the scribe and muktar (headman) of Jerusalem's 300 Gypsies. He is the historian of his tribe and has set down the tales of his people's wanderings. He was selected as muktar in part because he can read and write, rare among Gypsies of his generation. He also works for the city as a scribe, writing down documents for people with city business and interceding with the city authorities on behalf of his fellow Gypsies.

    While Jerusalem Gypsies no longer wander and "keep company with the dog and the wolf," they are outcasts among the Arabs who surround them. Church planting among this group should follow the model of the Gypsy Evangelical Church in Western Europe, a thoroughly indigenous movement among Gypsies which is growing rapidly. Its key appears to be a reproducing leadership and the affirmation of Gypsy life-styles wherever they are found.

Hazaras in Kabul (Afghanistan)

ALTERNATE NAMES: not reported

SIZE OF GROUP: 300,000   MARC ID: 5021

DISTINCTIVES: ethnicity; religion; sense of unity; language; discrimination

SOCIAL CHANGE: not reported

LANGUAGES: Hazaragi (V); Dari (T); Farsi (T)

SCRIPTURE: none; RECORDINGS : yes

CHRISTIAN LITERACY: not reported

RELIGION: Islam (100% adherents)

CHURCHES AND MISSIONS	BEGAN	MEMBERSHIP	COMMUNITY
Int'l Afghan Mission	nr	nr	nr

OPENNESS TO RELIGIOUS CHANGE: somewhat open

RECEPTIVITY TO CHRISTIANITY: receptive

GROWTH RATE OF CHRISTIAN COMMUNITY: not reported

EVANGELISM PROFILE: not reported

VALIDITY: 6

The Hazara are a Mongolian people who apparently are descendents of the troops of Genghis Khan, who overran this part of the world in the 12th century. At present they are mainly found in the central highlands known as the Hazarajat, though many are living in Kabul, the capital of Afghanistan.

The language and history of the Hazara give them a sense of pride and unity. They have a general reputation for being faithful servants, honest in dealings and hard-working. As of 1981 the Russian occupation of the cities of Afghanistan had suppressed Muslim social control, giving local Christian believers more freedom to evangelize and inquirers more opportunity to learn about Christianity. Persons with knowledge of Farsi/Dari have the chance to contact Hazara people in Pakistan or India and prepare for the day when they can return to Afghanistan.

Through education many Hazara have risen to the status of merchants or government employees and officers. The traditional means of living and working in Afghanistan has been as professionals under contract with the Afghan Government, since they are needed to conduct development projects. It is hoped that the future will bring more opportunity for church planting. Persons of some Mongolian background would probably be more effective than Westerners to do this work. Overseas Chinese or individuals of the Northeast India hill tribes would be ideal.

Indian Tamils in Colombo (Sri Lanka)

ALTERNATE NAMES: not reported

SIZE OF GROUP: not reported   MARC ID: 5004

DISTINCTIVES: language; ethnicity; religion; kinship; social
    class; economic status; significant problems

SOCIAL CHANGE: slow

LANGUAGES: Tamil (100% speak; V, G)

SCRIPTURE: Bible; RECORDINGS : yes

CHRISTIAN LITERACY: not reported

RELIGION: Hindu-Animist

CHURCHES AND MISSIONS: not reported

OPENNESS TO RELIGIOUS CHANGE: somewhat open

RECEPTIVITY TO CHRISTIANITY: receptive

GROWTH RATE OF CHRISTIAN COMMUNITY: not reported

EVANGELISM PROFILE: not reported

VALIDITY: 5

    Housing and employment have lagged far behind recent
population growth in Colombo, Sri Lanka. Slum housing usually
consists of two-room tenements, old houses sublet to lower-income
workers, or shanties of cast-off material built in squatter
settlements on unauthorized land. Nearly 351,000 people (62% of
the city's population) live in Colombo's slums; 79% of them are
under 35 years of age.

    Brought to Sri Lanka by the British, the Indian Tamils
originally worked on the tea, coffee and rubber plantations.
When the plantations were nationalized in 1948, their descendants
became a surplus labor force. They continued to follow Hindu
doctrines and maintain their Tamil language and cultural
patterns. Their political, economic, social and religious
background have set them apart and made them a unique people
group in Sri Lanka. At present, the number of Indian Tamil slum
dwellers in Colombo is unknown.

    This people group is reported to be open to new friends and
associations. A door-to-door survey of the people in a proposed
target area can lead to home meetings based on family groupings.
Neighborhood house churches can bring a sense of belonging and
offer healing for lonely, insecure and frustrated slum dwellers.
Youth must be reached and challenged for the ministry before they
graduate from high school. One suggestion is a drop-in center
with Bible studies, media presentations, counseling, clinic
facilities and evangelistic outreach. This center would attract
and nurture youth and channel them into house churches or more
established churches. There is also the opportunity for these to
plant new churches among the rural families of slum Indian Tamil
workers.

Indians in Dubai (United Arab Emirates)

ALTERNATE NAMES: not reported

SIZE OF GROUP: 24,000   MARC ID: 5047

DISTINCTIVES: occupation; religion; kinship; sense of unity;
     social class; legal status

SOCIAL CHANGE: rapid

LANGUAGES: Hindi (V, G); English (V, G); Urdu (V, G);
     Malayalam (V, G)

SCRIPTURE: Bible; RECORDINGS : yes

CHRISTIAN LITERACY: not reported

RELIGION: Hinduism (90% adherents); Christianity (10%
     adherents/6% practicing)

CHURCHES AND MISSIONS	BEGAN	MEMBERSHIP	COMMUNITY
Indian Brethren	nr	60	140
Indian Pentecostal	nr	60	140
Mar Thomite	nr	200	300
Roman Catholic Church	nr	nr	nr

OPENNESS TO RELIGIOUS CHANGE: not reported

RECEPTIVITY TO CHRISTIANITY: not reported

GROWTH RATE OF CHRISTIAN COMMUNITY: not reported

EVANGELISM PROFILE: not reported

VALIDITY: 5

The oil-rich sheikdoms and small states of the Persian Gulf
area have the world's highest proportion of migrant workers to
total population. Three-quarters of the United Arab Emirates'
population is made up of foreign workers, the vast majority of
whom dwell in the cities of Dubai and Abu Dhabi. These thousands
of immigrants have imported a mosaic of values and cultures which
is eroding the desert traditions which have sustained the locals
for centuries. There are signs that recent clampdowns on illegal
aliens (especially in Kuwait) may mean the oil boom is cooling
down in some of these small states, with the era of huge
construction projects just about over.

The Indians of Dubai, though a small percentage of the
foreign population, are a prominent group. Most of them are
merchants, professionals, artisans and skilled workers;
English-speaking Indian clerks and accountants are particularly
numerous. They view employment in the UAE as a means of
providing support for their families in India, although this is a
mixed benefit. Often their families lose contact with these
breadwinners, and the mother must work, borrow and beg to supply
the family's needs. This economic benefit to families in India
has also resulted in a rise in prices for consumer goods.

It is hard to say how stable this population of migrant
Indians is in Dubai. Rather than planting settled churches here,
a more productive strategy may be to concentrate on small group
and individual discipleship, preparing for the day when these
migrant workers will move on or return home. This time of
displacement is a prime opportunity to present the gospel and
transform the values and outlooks of these workers. Those who
face deportation are a particularly needy and ripe harvest field.

Jews in Venice (Italy)

ALTERNATE NAMES: not reported

SIZE OF GROUP: 650   MARC ID: 5046

DISTINCTIVES: religion; ethnicity; kinship; sense of unity

SOCIAL CHANGE: slow

LANGUAGES: Italian (100% speak; V, G)

SCRIPTURE: Bible; RECORDINGS : yes

CHRISTIAN LITERACY: not reported

RELIGION: Judaism (100% adherents)

CHURCHES AND MISSIONS: not reported

OPENNESS TO RELIGIOUS CHANGE: not reported

RECEPTIVITY TO CHRISTIANITY: not reported

GROWTH RATE OF CHRISTIAN COMMUNITY: not reported

EVANGELISM PROFILE: not reported

VALIDITY: 5

Venice's ghetto dates back more than four centuries and is the source of the word "ghetto." About 700 Jews were first forced into Venice's ghetto in 1516, and their number increased to more than 4000 by the 17th century.

The narrow entrances to the ghetto are no longer closed off by gates, but it is still the center of Jewish life in Venice. There are five synagogues, all dating to the 16th century, along with a Jewish community center, museum and home for the aged. The synagogues mark the waves of immigration and were built by immigrants from Germany and later by Sephardic Jews. Each is located on the second floor of a building intentionally designed to conceal the presence of a place of worship. Often they contain treasures of gold carvings and gilt decoration. Only two are used for regular services, and only on Yom Kippur are two of them open for services at the same time. During these holidays, hundreds of Jews return to the ghetto. While temporary rabbis have been in charge for years, a new permanent rabbi was installed in 1981.

The 60 or 70 Jews who still live in the ghetto do so by choice. They have relatively modest incomes, while the lawyers and professionals are dispersed through the city. Many have chosen to live on the Lido, a rich historic area of the city and a center of the Jewish contribution to its history. Others prefer the ghetto as a quiet and convenient area and a good place to bring up children.

Under Mussolini's rule, racist legislation in 1948 forced Jews out of many jobs. With the German invasion the Holocaust itself swept into Italy. However, Jews today note that in Venice there is little discrimination. The evangelistic approach to these Jews should be governed by the principles employed in planting "messianic synagogues" in other parts of the world. In this close-knit community, evangelism among friends and relatives would likely be the most effective method.

Kae Sung Natives in Seoul (Korea, Republic of)

ALTERNATE NAMES: not reported

SIZE OF GROUP: 20,000   MARC ID: 5015

DISTINCTIVES: kinship; discrimination; sense of unity

SOCIAL CHANGE: slow

LANGUAGES: Korean (100% speak/100% read; V, S, G, W)

SCRIPTURE: Bible; RECORDINGS : yes

CHRISTIAN LITERACY: 100%

RELIGION: Buddhism (70% adherents/50% practicing); Secularism
    (27% adherents/27% practicing); Christianity (3%
    adherents/1% practicing)

CHURCHES AND MISSIONS   BEGAN MEMBERSHIP   COMMUNITY
    Young Nak Presbyterian   50   200   nr

OPENNESS TO RELIGIOUS CHANGE: indifferent

RECEPTIVITY TO CHRISTIANITY: very reluctant

GROWTH RATE OF CHRISTIAN COMMUNITY: slow growth

EVANGELISM PROFILE: not reported

VALIDITY: 5

Although Korea is thought of as a monocultural nation, many small pockets of people maintain their unique identity and unity, particularly in resistance of the gospel. The Korean War brought many refugees from North Korea, among them those who came from Kae Sung, a city less than 200 miles from Seoul. These have kept their ways of life, food, customs and trade strongly intact. Mostly Buddhists, they intermarry with few exceptions. "Kae Sung people" in Korean means "smart ones"--diligent, good at making money and careful in spending it--and they are tightly bound to one another. Some feel that their concern with money (earning it, lending it for interest, inheriting and bequeathing it) keeps them "too busy" for religion.

One young woman from this Kae Sung community welcomed a witness for Christ and became a zealous Christian. Without another Christian in her entire family or circle of friends, she encountered persecution when sharing her faith. However, she has led several individuals to Christ in spite of the fact that her mother is the present head of the Buddhist Women's Association.

The highly insular character of this group makes it difficult to reach out to them by any other means than friendship. A cross-cultural missionary, even a Korean from the same city, would need to identify closely with the Kae Sung people in a way that would bring a credible witness, and then to disciple the few Christians in the group, enabling them to share the gospel with their relatives and friends.

EXPANDED DESCRIPTIONS

Mestizos in La Paz (Bolivia)

ALTERNATE NAMES: Middle-Class Mestizos; Cholos

SIZE OF GROUP: 400,000   MARC ID: 5001

DISTINCTIVES: education; residence; social class; economic status

SOCIAL CHANGE: not reported

LANGUAGES: Spanish (100% speak; V)

SCRIPTURE: Bible; RECORDINGS : yes

CHRISTIAN LITERACY: 100%

RELIGION: Christo-Paganism (40% adherents/40% practicing); Roman Catholic (56% adherents/2% practicing); Christianity (4% adherents/2% practicing)

CHURCHES AND MISSIONS	BEGAN	MEMBERSHIP	COMMUNITY
Assemblies of God	nr	nr	nr
Roman Catholic Church	nr	nr	nr

OPENNESS TO RELIGIOUS CHANGE: somewhat open

RECEPTIVITY TO CHRISTIANITY: very receptive

GROWTH RATE OF CHRISTIAN COMMUNITY: rapid growth

EVANGELISM PROFILE: not reported

VALIDITY: 5

The Spanish-speaking Mestizos (people of mixed Indian and Spanish descent) represent 25% of Bolivia's population. Many are located in the country's cities, 400,000 in La Paz alone, where they rank second on the socioeconomic scale to the 10% white Europeans of Spanish descent. Together these two groups have run the nation in a series of civilian and military governments, averaging one revolution per year since independence. Because the other major ethnic groups lack incentive to migrate to urban surroundings, La Paz does not have the constant influx of rural people found in other South American cities.

The lower-middle-class Cholo-Mestizo population of the city has shown the best church growth among the urban people groups. Over 13,760 believers gather in 155 churches among their neighbors. They are 3.5% reached, a little more than the national level. This level could be increased to 4% by adding the 2240 Catholic charismatics meeting in two groups. Within the next five years, by continuing present growth, these figures should grow to 22,200 Mestizo believers in 250 churches.

The centrally located Assemblies of God Church took part in a continuous evangelism and discipleship program to the Mestizos from 1968 to 1977. Twenty-five new churches resulted among both the Mestizos and the Aymara Indians. However, the relocation of several leaders has left this program inoperative. Hopefully, reapproaching these people in each neighborhood zone and denomination will lead to revival so that people group churches will grow and discover how to better meet felt needs of their changing environment. This will help them focus and balance the three basic Christian priorities important in any culture: the encounter and commitment to God in worship, the equipment of the saints toward commitment to Christ's Body and the extension of Christ's Kingdom in the world through His Body in mission.

Middle Class in Mexico City (Mexico)

ALTERNATE NAMES: not reported

SIZE OF GROUP: not reported   MARC ID: 5014

DISTINCTIVES: social class; education; language; significant
    problems

SOCIAL CHANGE: moderate

LANGUAGES: Spanish (100% speak/100% read; V, S, G, W)

SCRIPTURE: Bible; RECORDINGS : yes

CHRISTIAN LITERACY: not reported

RELIGION: Roman Catholic; Secularism

CHURCHES AND MISSIONS	BEGAN	MEMBERSHIP	COMMUNITY
Roman Catholic Church	nr	nr	nr

OPENNESS TO RELIGIOUS CHANGE: indifferent

RECEPTIVITY TO CHRISTIANITY: receptive

GROWTH RATE OF CHRISTIAN COMMUNITY: not reported

EVANGELISM PROFILE: not reported

VALIDITY: 5

    Mexico City has a strong, growing middle class, reflecting
Mexico's increasing role in the world economy. Around industrial
centers in Mexico City, new housing projects are springing up
each year in the suburbs, expecially in the north and northwest.
These have no established witness--no street-corner church--but
receptivity is evident among the residents in these projects.
    This second-generation middle class is not struggling to
maintain a newly found social status, nor are they suspicious of
evangelistic efforts--they are not threatened by the new. In
fact, they are often quite curious about the Bible, even willing
to open their homes for Bible study. Although skeptical of
organized religion, they have no other foundation for personal
security amid the uprootedness and impersonality of life in
Mexico City. They are open to Christ to meet their needs for
purpose, dignity and a sense of belonging in a caring body.
    A decentralized church should be planted among these people.
Several small groups can form a larger congregation that meets
weekly but is not the central focus. These churches should
foster lay leadership, developing their spiritual gifts to
benefit the whole body. The church planting force must stress
discipling new believers, using materials tailored to the needs
of the people and the new Christian community.
    There are obstacles to this kind of church planting.
Inertia is caused by the time needed to travel to new areas. It
is hard to settle in one housing project for two years and then
start over again elsewhere. Acquiring a church building often
leads the community to forget its responsibility to the world--to
spend time and energy constructing and maintaining a building and
then developing programs for the building. The traditional
demand for a pastor as a paid professional expert brings the
danger of slipping into the comfortable pattern of a central
church with a central leader. If lay people take active
responsibility in the church, they are less likely to lose their
vision for planting new churches and reaching out into the
community.

EXPANDED DESCRIPTIONS

Muslim Gypsies in Skoplje (Yugoslavia)

ALTERNATE NAMES: not reported

SIZE OF GROUP: 23,000   MARC ID: 5026

DISTINCTIVES: religion; ethnicity; kinship; sense of unity;
    economic status; significant problems; language

SOCIAL CHANGE: not reported

LANGUAGES: Romany Dialects (V, G)

SCRIPTURE: RECORDINGS : yes

CHRISTIAN LITERACY: not reported

RELIGION: Islam (100% adherents)

CHURCHES AND MISSIONS: not reported

OPENNESS TO RELIGIOUS CHANGE: somewhat closed

RECEPTIVITY TO CHRISTIANITY: reluctant

GROWTH RATE OF CHRISTIAN COMMUNITY: not reported

EVANGELISM PROFILE: not reported

VALIDITY: 5

Gypsies are found in many areas of the world, and there are
Muslim Gypsies in every nation of the Middle East, Central Asia
and North Africa, as well as the southern Balkans and
northwestern India. Over the years differentiation has occurred
between these various groups, and Gypsy customs are mixed with
those of the people among whom they travel or have settled. In
some ways Gypsy society resembles a caste or a group of closely
related castes.
    The Gypsy mother tongue is Romany, a relative of Sanskrit.
Muslim Gypsies speak dialects of Romany or composite languages
partially derived from Romany. Some others no longer speak
Romany, especially sedentarized Gypsies, except in recent or
quite large settlements.
    Suto Orizare, a suburb of Skoplje, is perhaps the largest
Gypsy settlement in the world. Urban Gypsies often leave their
previous occupations, such as smithery and metal working,
entertainment, livestock trading, fortune-telling, petty trade,
and producing cottage craft products like bricks, tambourines,
baskets, etc. They are frequently employed in occupations of low
esteem: they work as garbage collectors, porters, shoeblacks,
street sweepers, carriers, cleaning women and (formerly)
executioners. Some are now employed in factories, and a few have
overcome discrimination to become doctors, teachers, engineers
and other professionals. In the socialist nations of the
Balkans, special opportunities are available to Gypsies, but only
in Yugoslavia have they been allowed to choose a traditional
Gypsy lifestyle.
    The highly insular character of Gypsy society presents
problems for cross-cultural workers, unless they are willing to
whole-heartedly share Gypsy life-styles and outlook on people in
general. However, for successful witness to Gypsies workers must
recognize their feeling of ill treatment by other sectors of
society and be willing to treat them with acceptance and respect.
A great need is for adequate vernacular translations of
Scripture.

Newar in Kathmandu (Nepal)

ALTERNATE NAMES: not reported

SIZE OF GROUP: 100,000   MARC ID: 5030

DISTINCTIVES: language; ethnicity; religion; kinship

SOCIAL CHANGE: slow

LANGUAGES: Newari (100% speak; V, G, W)

SCRIPTURE: portions; RECORDINGS : yes

CHRISTIAN LITERACY: not reported

RELIGION: Buddhism; Buddhist-Animist; Hindu-Animist;
    Christianity (-1% practicing)

CHURCHES AND MISSIONS	BEGAN	MEMBERSHIP	COMMUNITY
United Mission to Nepal	nr	nr	nr

OPENNESS TO RELIGIOUS CHANGE: not reported

RECEPTIVITY TO CHRISTIANITY: not reported

GROWTH RATE OF CHRISTIAN COMMUNITY: not reported

EVANGELISM PROFILE: not reported

VALIDITY: 5

The Newar are believed to be the original inhabitants of the
Kathmandu Valley, where Kathmandu, Nepal's capital city, is
located. They make up half of Kathmandu's population of 200,000
and are Nepal's leading traders and contributors to commerce.
They are respected for their craftsmanship and art.

The Newar are distinguished as a people group due to their
shared culture, ethnic background and Buddhist-animist faith.
The women are "married for life" symbolically to the Hindu god
Vishnu as little girls; thus, they never have to suffer the
stigma of divorce or widowhood. Christian proselytizing is
forbidden by law, though a few small churches exist and are
growing slowly through person-to-person contact.

Modern mission in Nepal started with the rebuilding of the
country after the political revolution of 1950-1951. There are
now nearly 600 known Newar Christians in Kathmandu. Various
organizations are active in evangelism and discipling, village
evangelism and church planting, student evangelism and training,
literature distribution, social work and anthropological
research. The local churches in Nepal are proving to be the most
effective evangelistic force. Artists, farmers, artisans,
traders and humanitarians all have credible face-to-face
witnessing potential.

There are difficulties still to be overcome in reaching the
Newar of Kathmandu. The deep-seated religious traditions and
conditioning of the Newar make it difficult for non-Newar
witnesses, and political opposition to evangelism remains a
barrier and even a threat. It seems that the church among these
people must grow quietly for the present through one-to-one
witnessing and a "web" growth pattern, where individuals win and
disciple those in their immediate context.

Nurses in St. Louis (United States of America)

ALTERNATE NAMES: not reported

SIZE OF GROUP: 3,200   MARC ID: 5031

DISTINCTIVES: occupation; education; economic status; significant problems

SOCIAL CHANGE: moderate

LANGUAGES: English (100% speak/100% read; V, G, W, S)

SCRIPTURE: Bible; RECORDINGS : yes

CHRISTIAN LITERACY: 100%

RELIGION: Secularism; Christianity (-1% practicing)

CHURCHES AND MISSIONS	BEGAN	MEMBERSHIP	COMMUNITY
Nurses Christian Fellowship	nr	nr	nr

OPENNESS TO RELIGIOUS CHANGE: somewhat closed

RECEPTIVITY TO CHRISTIANITY: reluctant

GROWTH RATE OF CHRISTIAN COMMUNITY: slow growth

EVANGELISM PROFILE: not reported

VALIDITY: 5

There are almost one million registered nurses in the United States. They make up the largest health profession in the country, a people group that shares a common occupation, unique problems, and a particular world view.

St. Louis, a city of one and a half million people, has a generally good healthcare system due to the presence of two university teaching hospitals for nurses. The approximately 3200 nurses work in hospitals, nursing homes, clinics, schools, home healthcare and businesses. They are mainly women because of tradition, but the number of men in the profession (now approximately 3%) is growing.

Nurses have a somewhat unique lifestyle due to their working hours. The three shifts are 7 a.m. to 3 p.m., 3 p.m. to 11 p.m., and 11 p.m. to 7 a.m., the first being the most desirable. Those who work the later shifts often have difficulty in adjusting their schedules to their friends and families. This has led to a heavy "burn-out" factor, where nurses eventually quit their jobs. This is made worse by the pain and death that nurses see every day. Many find it difficult to cope and are given little help or counseling to deal with the feelings that this daily contact arouses.

Nurses Christian Fellowship has attempted work in St. Louis, but so far there has been little response. One way to reach nurses would be to provide counseling services for their coping needs, combined with Christian activities at non-traditional hours. Jesus Christ should be presented as a role model of the compassionate servant who dealt best with human suffering.

Parsis in Bombay (India)

ALTERNATE NAMES: not reported

SIZE OF GROUP: 80,000   MARC ID: 5039

DISTINCTIVES: religion; language; ethnicity; kinship; sense
    of unity; economic status

SOCIAL CHANGE: not reported

LANGUAGES: Parsi (V, G, S); Marathi (T)

SCRIPTURE: Bible; RECORDINGS : yes

CHRISTIAN LITERACY: not reported

RELIGION: Zoroastrianism (100% adherents)

CHURCHES AND MISSIONS: not reported

OPENNESS TO RELIGIOUS CHANGE: indifferent

RECEPTIVITY TO CHRISTIANITY: indifferent

GROWTH RATE OF CHRISTIAN COMMUNITY: not reported

EVANGELISM PROFILE: not reported

VALIDITY: 6

The settlement of 80,000 Parsis in Bombay is the largest
community both of Parsis and of Zoroastrians in the world. Their
ancestors migrated from Persia, beginning in the eighth century.
They now have a near monopoly on wealth in large Indian cities
and dominate electrical appliances, textiles, steel mills,
trucking, chemicals and hotels.

One Parsi manufacturing magnate in Bombay has a township of
housing blocks and schools where two-thirds of his 12,000 workers
live. His goal is to "transform the so-called working classes
into middle classes." Parsis in Bombay believe in philanthropy
and civic responsibility and have funded hospitals, schools and
scientific research institutions.

These Parsis retain the religion of Zoroaster. Among their
other religious practices, they leave their dead exposed for
carrion birds in one of the seven Towers of Silence on Malabar
Hill. According to orthodox beliefs, they must be taken there by
a hereditary caste of non-Parsis. However, high-rises have now
penetrated the invisibility that these towers were meant to
maintain. Some Parsis now cremate their dead to circumvent this
problem and to prevent accidental spreading of remains by birds.

The municipal education officer of Bombay speaks of the
obligation to teach children in the language they speak at home.
The public school system teaches in ten langauges; Parsi
children are taught in their own language in schools supported by
wealthy Parsis. Meaningful evangelism among these people must
take adequate account of their unique religion and culture and
the redemptive keys they contain.

Pension Students in Madrid (Spain)

ALTERNATE NAMES: not reported

SIZE OF GROUP: 1,500   MARC ID: 5032

DISTINCTIVES: education; residence; sense of unity; hobby or
    interest; age

SOCIAL CHANGE: not reported

LANGUAGES: English (V, G); French (V, G); Italian (V, G);
    Spanish (T, S)

SCRIPTURE: Bible; RECORDINGS : yes

CHRISTIAN LITERACY: 100%

RELIGION: Secularism; Christianity

CHURCHES AND MISSIONS: not reported

OPENNESS TO RELIGIOUS CHANGE: somewhat open

RECEPTIVITY TO CHRISTIANITY: reluctant

GROWTH RATE OF CHRISTIAN COMMUNITY: slow growth

EVANGELISM PROFILE: not reported

VALIDITY: 5

Foreign students arrive from all over the world to attend
the University of Madrid's "Program for Foreigners." Most seek
housing in a residencia or pension (boarding place) located in
Madrid near the University. In spite of their various language
and ethnic backgrounds these students have several things in
common: they participate in the same study program at the
University (many in the same proficiency level), most are very
near in age, they are all foreign to the Spanish culture and
language (and thus are dealing with the same emotional and
cultural adjustments), and most of them live and socialize in the
same parts of the city with each other.
    For approximately 10,000 pesetas (US$200) a month, each
student receives a bed, a wardrobe-type closet and three prepared
meals. A room and bath are shared with two or three others of
the same sex. All meals are prepared at certain hours each day,
and everyone eats together in a common dining area. Also, they
can expect their clothes to be laundered once a week.
    Once settled into a routine, they form new friendships, and
much time out of class is spent sightseeing and socializing
together. For Christians to reach these students, they must go
where their friendships are formed and nurtured. They live in a
world of intellectual stimulation, high ideals and worthy causes
to defend; sensitivity to this is essential for evangelism. As
for religion, they don't readily accept traditional ritual and
doctrine without question; it must make sense logically and
scientifically. Students are typically transient, so it is best
not to structure outreach programs that require long-term
commitments to any one location (e.g., church planting).
Successful activities in the past have included campouts,
retreats, musical events, home gatherings and tutoring in
Spanish. The best strategies all require being accessible to
lonely, displaced young people.

Prisoners in Antananarivo (Madagascar)

ALTERNATE NAMES: not reported

SIZE OF GROUP: 10,000   MARC ID: 5012

DISTINCTIVES: legal status; significant problems; residence;
    discrimination

SOCIAL CHANGE: very slow

LANGUAGES: Malagasy (100% speak; V, G, W)

SCRIPTURE: Bible; RECORDINGS : yes

CHRISTIAN LITERACY: not reported

RELIGION: Folk Religion (80% adherents/80% practicing);
    Secularism (10% adherents/10% practicing); Roman Catholic
    (5% adherents/1% practicing); Protestant (5% adherents/1%
    practicing)

CHURCHES AND MISSIONS: not reported

OPENNESS TO RELIGIOUS CHANGE: not reported

RECEPTIVITY TO CHRISTIANITY: indifferent

GROWTH RATE OF CHRISTIAN COMMUNITY: not reported

EVANGELISM PROFILE: not reported

VALIDITY: 5

    People are in prison in Madagascar both for criminal and
political offenses. In the city of Antananarivo there are
approximately 10,000 such prisoners. Some know they have brought
shame to their families and home areas. Often when they enter
prison, their lives are in total chaos and they have no idea of
what will happen to them. Almost all still practice the
traditional animism and spiritism widespread on the island.
    Malagasy traditional religions revolve around fear and
worship of deceased ancestors rather than any organized teaching
or priesthood. Nature spirits and spirits of unknown dead people
are feared for their ability to cast a spell or even possess
people in ecstatic experiences. Many traditional beliefs are
traceable to Islam, and some are strong enough that even
professed Christians continue to practice witchcraft and
participate in the ancestor cult.
    Since traditional religions often take on a nation's
individual characteristics, Christianity is often considered a
foreign religion. This viewpoint is somewhat weakened in prison,
however, as is the cohesion of traditional worshipers through
family and national loyalty. This lessened resistance, plus fear
and bewilderment about the future, give Christian workers some
promising openings for witness.
    A two-pronged approach might bear good fruit. Personal
problems and fears could be confronted directly through power
encounter, leading to open consideration of the claims of Christ.
At this point simple, clear, direct gospel messages would give a
basis for reconciliation spiritually as well as with families and
neighbors. Christians should also investigate the possibility of
literacy programs, job training and other forms of social aid.
These might offer additional opportunities to bring a witness of
Christian love to these prisoners.

Pro Hockey Players (United States of America)

ALTERNATE NAMES: not reported

SIZE OF GROUP: 560   MARC ID: 5020

DISTINCTIVES: occupation; sense of unity; hobby or interest; age

SOCIAL CHANGE: not reported

LANGUAGES: English (100% speak/100% read; V, S, G, W)

SCRIPTURE: Bible; RECORDINGS : yes

CHRISTIAN LITERACY: 100%

RELIGION: Secularism (90% adherents); Christianity (10% adherents/5% practicing)

CHURCHES AND MISSIONS	BEGAN	MEMBERSHIP	COMMUNITY
Hockey Ministries Int'l	nr	nr	nr

OPENNESS TO RELIGIOUS CHANGE: somewhat open

RECEPTIVITY TO CHRISTIANITY: receptive

GROWTH RATE OF CHRISTIAN COMMUNITY: not reported

EVANGELISM PROFILE: not reported

VALIDITY: 6

There are approximately 560 professional hockey players belonging to the National Hockey League, forming 21 teams that travel all over the USA and Canada. Because of the prestige of being a professional athlete, hockey players constantly face a barrage of fans, glamor, demanding travel schedules and grueling games. In society's eyes they seem to have everything going for them. Unfortunately, these culturally desirable assets are the very things that prevent hockey players from regular or meaningful contact wth the church.

At present, one known ministry is directed specifically to Canadian and USA hockey players. Hockey Ministries International was founded by a former professional hockey player. Chapel programs consist of periods of worship, reflection, inspiration and often brief talks that relate the Christian message to the life of professional athletes. About 25 Christian professional players are involved in maintaining the chapel program. The second phase of the ministry is a number of Christian Athlete Hockey Camps. These summer gatherings, held in 1980 in five Canadian and one American center, brought several young boys together for six days of instruction and inspiration. Most of the instructors are Christian hockey players whose names are familiar to the young campers.

Athletes so far are the most effective missionaries to athletes (as is the pattern in almost all people groups). Professional teams, especially those originating in the West, accept new concepts not as a group but, if at all, as individuals. The best way to approach them with the good news is to earn first their respect as a participant in the sport, then their trust as a friend and finally their interest as a Christian.

Rajasthani Muslims in Jaipur (India)

ALTERNATE NAMES: not reported

SIZE OF GROUP: 3,500   MARC ID: 5033

DISTINCTIVES: religion; language; kinship; social class

SOCIAL CHANGE: slow

LANGUAGES: Jaipuri (V, G); Hindi (T)

SCRIPTURE: not reported

CHRISTIAN LITERACY: not reported

RELIGION: Islam (100% adherents)

CHURCHES AND MISSIONS: not reported

OPENNESS TO RELIGIOUS CHANGE: somewhat closed

RECEPTIVITY TO CHRISTIANITY: reluctant

GROWTH RATE OF CHRISTIAN COMMUNITY: not reported

EVANGELISM PROFILE: not reported

VALIDITY: 6

Except for the Meo subcommunity, the Muslims of Rajasthan in north India are a people group concentrated in urban centers. United by a common heritage, culture and world view, they fall into three subcategories: Rajput converts, service castes and Muslim traders.

The Rajput elite historically established friendly contacts with Muslims, and some were converted to Islam. However, such conversions were not welcomed locally, and most Muslim Rajputs left Rajasthan. They are distinguishable because of their pride in Rajput ancestry, retention of many Hindu customs and strict endogamy. They are tolerated in predominantly Muslim environments because of their high economic status.

The second subgroup is the service castes, including bangle sellers, dyers, butchers, water carriers and musicians. These were emigrants from the Ganges River valley who came during Muslim rule preceding the British colonial period. Under Rajput patronage they preserved and enhanced the ancient raja traditions of India. These Muslims accommodated their Hindu patrons in a variety of ways: they spoke local dialects, adopted many Hindu customs, remained loyal against Muslim invaders and maintained the Hindu temple for generations as a hereditary right.

The most influential Rajasthani Muslims are the traders, most of whom have migrated from Gujarat during the past 200 years. The Muslim traders, some 15% of Rajasthani Muslims, are believed to be mostly converts from the Hindu trading castes. They have remained isolated from the main stream of Muslim culture in northern India because of their association with Shiism. They have maintained separate identities by forming distinct communities. This trading community may offer the most promise for church planting and Christian growth. They are self-identified as Muslims, but not so much as part of the broader Muslim community. A messianic mosque approach might be effective in simultaneously affirming this community's separate identity and bringing a messianic fulfillment of their religious hope.

Sindhi Muslims in Karachi (Pakistan)

ALTERNATE NAMES: not reported

SIZE OF GROUP: 350,000   MARC ID: 5036

DISTINCTIVES: sense of unity; language; social class; hobby
   or interest

SOCIAL CHANGE: slow

LANGUAGES: Sindhi (100% speak; V, G)

SCRIPTURE: Bible; RECORDINGS : yes

CHRISTIAN LITERACY: not reported

RELIGION: Islam-Animist; Islam

CHURCHES AND MISSIONS: not reported

OPENNESS TO RELIGIOUS CHANGE: somewhat closed

RECEPTIVITY TO CHRISTIANITY: reluctant

GROWTH RATE OF CHRISTIAN COMMUNITY: not reported

EVANGELISM PROFILE: not reported

VALIDITY: 6

   The people who call themselves Sindhi number nearly 10.5
million, most living in Pakistan, with some 1.5 million living in
Gujarat, India. Nearly all Pakistani Sindhis are Muslim, while
nearly all Indian Sindhis are Hindu.
   In the cities a sizable literate portion of the Sindhi
population are merchants, physicians, apothecaries, lawyers,
teachers in local schools and Sindh University, and workers in
other white-collar occupations. Islam also gives employment to
divines, and Sindh contains a large number of miracle-working
hereditary saints who sell advice and magical talismans to their
followers. To be a landlord is a position of pride, and further
prestige comes from having family members (even daughters)
formally educated and working in a profession. Possessing
political power also gives prestige.
   Hindu influence is apparent in Pakistan, for example, in the
songs of the popular Sindhi poet Shah Abdul Latif (born 1690),
and in the social structure, which contains caste-like hereditary
occupational groups. These groups form endogamous lineages
called "zats." At times these zats are found living together in
wards where adjoining compounds occupied by closely related
families may be entered without using the street.
   Sindhi men center their social life in an otak (special
building) which is not enclosed in compound walls as the homes
are. Here the miracle workers and landlords aspiring to local
power meet their followers. Friends join together here to drink
refreshments including batel nut mixtures, alcoholic beverages
and bhang, a drink prepared from marijuana and other substances
infused in milk or water. Men with leisure play cards, watch
cockfights and in the evening enjoy professional musicians or
female dancers hired for the occasion. Though their Muslim faith
is thus clearly a nominal one, their cultural ties keep them from
viewing Christianity as a viable option.

Street Vendors in Saigon (Viet Nam)

ALTERNATE NAMES: not reported

SIZE OF GROUP: not reported   MARC ID: 5035

DISTINCTIVES: occupation; language; education; economic
    status; social class

SOCIAL CHANGE: slow

LANGUAGES: Vietnamese (100% speak; V, G, S)

SCRIPTURE: Bible; RECORDINGS : yes

CHRISTIAN LITERACY: not reported

RELIGION: Buddhist-Animist; Roman Catholic

CHURCHES AND MISSIONS: not reported

OPENNESS TO RELIGIOUS CHANGE: somewhat closed

RECEPTIVITY TO CHRISTIANITY: reluctant

GROWTH RATE OF CHRISTIAN COMMUNITY: stable

EVANGELISM PROFILE: not reported

VALIDITY: 5

The poor families of Saigon (now known as Ho Chi Minh City)
nearly all subsist on one form or another of street vending.
Many are women whose husbands have either deserted them or spend
most of their time away from the home and family. The vendors'
daily responsibilities include at least a half day of working at
their trade and then taking care of the family (cooking meals,
sewing, cleaning and mending clothes, doing housework and staying
in touch with others in the neighborhood). The women street
vendors who sell edible wares usually do not bake their own but
rather buy them from other vendors, who can afford to make them
more appealing visually and therefore more marketable. This
makes them similar to manual laborers who purchase or rent their
own materials and make a marginal profit after selling their
completed goods.

The housing for these poor families is usually quite small;
a 9 by 25 foot room will serve for a family, with cloth drapes as
partitions to form more "rooms." In the slum areas there is a
continuous threat of flooding, particularly in the rainy season.
The slum residents are basically friendly and tolerant of the
mixture of southern, northern and central Vietnamese in the
neighborhood.

Many families will "adopt" children from other families for
one of two reasons: to confuse evil spirits by changing parents
and homes (which is thought to lessen the risk of illness and
poor health), or to obtain financial assistance from the foster
children's organization.

Buddhism dominates the religious life of the street vendors,
but it is a type of Buddhism unique to Vietnam: a combination of
folk religion, animism, Confucianism, Taoism and Buddhism. Some
are Catholic, but in most cases their religion is identical to
that of their Buddhist neighbors except for somewhat different
relics used in their home worship. Evangelism should address the
physical needs of these people and stress Christ's ability to
bring about a life of wholeness without fear.

Tamil Laborers in Bombay (India)

ALTERNATE NAMES: not reported

SIZE OF GROUP: 3,000   MARC ID: 5017

DISTINCTIVES: language; occupation; ethnicity; religion;
     kinship; sense of unity; social class; economic status

SOCIAL CHANGE: moderate

LANGUAGES: Tamil (100% speak; V, S, G, W)

SCRIPTURE: Bible; RECORDINGS : yes

CHRISTIAN LITERACY: not reported

RELIGION: Hinduism; Secularism; Christianity (-1% practicing)

CHURCHES AND MISSIONS   BEGAN   MEMBERSHIP   COMMUNITY
     Tamil Methodist Church   nr   nr   nr

OPENNESS TO RELIGIOUS CHANGE: indifferent

RECEPTIVITY TO CHRISTIANITY: receptive

GROWTH RATE OF CHRISTIAN COMMUNITY: not reported

EVANGELISM PROFILE: not reported

VALIDITY: 5

Bombay is the fifth largest city in the world. Most residents are either migrants or descendants from other Indian states. Fifteen major languages are each spoken by more than 10,000 people. A 1979 survey estimated that 100,000 people in Bombay are homeless and sleep in the streets.

Tamil laborers work at the National Rayon Corporation and earn the equivilence of 50 cents per day. Totaling 3000, they live on Ambivli Hill just outside of Kalyan. About 400 children in this group have no schooling and instead are taught to beg in nearby colonies; all are illiterate.

Many Tamil laborers began to attend church services in Kalyan but were discriminated against because their clothing and habits were disagreeable to those around them. Subsequently, Ambivlians requested a separate church in their own area; money was collected, a crude chapel was constructed, and a Rev. Harris led the first service. There are now 43 baptized converts who are active Christians. In addition, there has been personal contact by representatives of the Tamil Methodist Church, and open-air gospel meetings have been held.

Many evident needs among these people stem from urbanization: loneliness, severance of family ties, altered religious traditions, a new life-style subject to rapid change, and language barriers which influence the formation of ethnic residential groupings. Christian outreach concentrated in South Bombay (the old city) needs to be spread to these and other northern suburbs. A decentralized church based on home meetings could successfully avoid the discomfort which many newcomers experience in church buildings. Missionary help is needed for training Christian leaders and discipling new believers. In all this, it must be noted that a Western-style "casual" life-style is a poor witness to strict Hindus; cross-cultural workers must be prepared to share many of the cultural scruples of the Hindus they are ministering to.

Tamil Muslims in Madras (India)

ALTERNATE NAMES: not reported

SIZE OF GROUP: 50,000   MARC ID: 5028

DISTINCTIVES: religion; ethnicity; language

SOCIAL CHANGE: not reported

LANGUAGES: Tamil (V, G, S)

SCRIPTURE: Bible; RECORDINGS : none

CHRISTIAN LITERACY: not reported

RELIGION: Islam (100% adherents)

CHURCHES AND MISSIONS: not reported

OPENNESS TO RELIGIOUS CHANGE: not reported

RECEPTIVITY TO CHRISTIANITY: not reported

GROWTH RATE OF CHRISTIAN COMMUNITY: not reported

EVANGELISM PROFILE: not reported

VALIDITY: 6

The Tamil-speaking Muslims of Tamil Nadu, India, are the descendants of Arab traders and local converts. They are known throughout the state as shopkeepers and traders, and their prominence in these pursuits goes along with their high degree of urbanization--more than twice that of the state as a whole.

This community exhibits a harmony with Hindu neighbors that is unique among the Muslim peoples of India. In general they identify themselves culturally with their Tamil neighbors. In Madras, however, the Muslim community is more insular and is defined specifically in terms of Muslim behavior rather than following a status code based on wealth, occupation and personal character as in the broader Tamil Muslim community.

The Tamil Muslims' view of society in the urban environment differs sharply from that of their Hindu neighbors. Rather than being hierarchical, interdependent and leisure-oriented, the Muslim community stresses egalitarianism, economic independence and the kind of success that flows from hard work and frugality. In recent years they have undergone a pronounced shift away from their Hindu neighbors in religious practices. Islamic ritual in the countryside has a strong admixture of Sufi saint worship and other nonorthodox features which are viewed with skepticism in the city, where Muslim orthodoxy is the measure of personal prestige and status. These same urban people, however, return to the rural area and take part in the same saint festivals as their former neighbors.

The Tamil Muslims of Madras have harmonious relationships with their Hindu surroundings, unlike Muslims in the north who often view themselves as a threatened population. The caste system does not dictate the organization of the urban Tamil Muslims but is overshadowed by the influence of mercantilism, urbanism and Islamic values. The gospel could profitably be presented to these Tamil Muslims as a means of further reaffirming their "peoplehood" and as a true fulfillment of their Islamic value system and religion.

EXPANDED DESCRIPTIONS

Turks in Basel (Switzerland)

ALTERNATE NAMES: not reported

SIZE OF GROUP: 3,000   MARC ID: 5011

DISTINCTIVES: language; ethnicity; religion; sense of unity; significant problems; discrimination

SOCIAL CHANGE: very slow

LANGUAGES: Turkish (100% speak; V, S, G, W); Kurdish (15% speak; V); German (W)

SCRIPTURE: Bible; RECORDINGS : yes

CHRISTIAN LITERACY: not reported

RELIGION: Islam (95% adherents); Orthodox (5% adherents)

CHURCHES AND MISSIONS: not reported

OPENNESS TO RELIGIOUS CHANGE: very closed

RECEPTIVITY TO CHRISTIANITY: very reluctant

GROWTH RATE OF CHRISTIAN COMMUNITY: not reported

EVANGELISM PROFILE: not reported

VALIDITY: 6

In Basel there are approximately 3000 Turks. Only 5% are Greek Orthodox; the remainder are Muslim. Most speak only their mother tongue, Turkish. Because they are undocumented workers and in a few years will return to Turkey, they usually don't make the effort to learn German. This tends to set them apart from others in Basel. Many would like to integrate themselves into Swiss society but do not succeed. This results in a certain resignation and isolation into their own group. Sometimes this is also a defense against what they consider to be the shameless life-style of the European society around them.

Turks are almost by definition Muslim, and this influences most parts of their lives. Because they know that the Swiss often eat pork, Turks find it difficult to accept an invitation to a meal, even though they would probably appreciate the opportunity to socialize. Often Turks, offended by the unfamiliar demands of a new employer in this new country, give up and return to their homeland.

Because Turks tend to have tight family units, individual responses to Christ are rare even though an individual may respect the validity of Christianity. Also, when reaching out to Turkish immigrants, one must remember to be sensitive to their distinction between men's and women's roles. In their eyes a woman could be deemed "immoral" if she were led to Christ by a man--especially a man from another culture.

Hospitality is highly valued by Turkish people. Turks love to gather together for tea and snacks during the day. Small home Bible studies would be a good way of incorporating this much-loved socializing with some essential sharing of the Word.

Universitarios in Rosario (Argentina)

ALTERNATE NAMES: University students

SIZE OF GROUP: 10,000   MARC ID: 5003

DISTINCTIVES: education; social class; hobby or interest;
     age; significant problems; sense of unity

SOCIAL CHANGE: moderate

LANGUAGES: Spanish (100% speak; V, S, G)

SCRIPTURE: Bible; RECORDINGS : yes

CHRISTIAN LITERACY: 100%

RELIGION: Roman Catholic (80% adherents/1% practicing);
     Secularism (18% adherents); Protestant (2% adherents/1%
     practicing)

CHURCHES AND MISSIONS	BEGAN	MEMBERSHIP	COMMUNITY
Methodist Church	1870	30	nr
Baptist Church	1900	100	nr
Plymouth Brethren	1875	50	nr
Pentecostal Church	1930	10	nr
Roman Catholic Church	nr	nr	nr

OPENNESS TO RELIGIOUS CHANGE: indifferent

RECEPTIVITY TO CHRISTIANITY: indifferent

GROWTH RATE OF CHRISTIAN COMMUNITY: slow decline

EVANGELISM PROFILE: not reported

VALIDITY: 6

     Rosario is a Spanish-speaking European-type metropolis in
Argentina. The entire population (except for a recent small Arab
minority) are European descendants. They are immigrant whites
who began arriving early in the 19th century. Because Rosario's
inhabitants are reserved, conservative and somewhat
materialistic, religious or spiritual interest is not strong
     This lack of interest is particularly true among the 10,000
or so university students enrolled at the two universities
located in the city, the Pontifical Catholic University of St.
Mary and the State University of Rosario. They are
conscientious, well-educated young people from a similar economic
background (most of them from upper and middle-class families).
However, they are proving to be indifferent to the gospel.
     Inter-Varsity, Campus Crusade and other parachurch
organizations have begun work in the community surrounding the
universities. Due to political problems and other intervening
circumstances, they have been unable to operate on the campuses,
so they have had to redirect their main evangelistic efforts to
other people in the city. Rosario now urgently needs trained
young men and women of similar educational level and background
to begin reaching students on their own turf, within the campus
boundaries. Successful evangelistic strategies include small
concerts, to present Christ through music, encounters with
students in coffeehouse settings, small group Bible studies, and
short evangelistic films with time for discussion. All of these
could eventually guide converts into local active Christian
fellowships.

Part 4
Registry
of
the
Unreached

The information on the 3265 unreached peoples in the registry is presented in five different lists. Each list organizes the information differently. Only the first list, which indexes the peoples alphabetically by group name, includes the estimated percentage of those that practice Christianity and a code that indicates the overall accuracy of the data.

Groups are also listed by receptivity to the gospel, principal professed religion, language, and country. All five lists indicate those groups reported to be very receptive (***), receptive (**), or indifferent (*). There is also another code (79, 80, 81, or 82) attached to the group name to indicate that a description has been written about this people group in *Unreached Peoples '79* (79), *Unreached Peoples '80* (80), *Unreached Peoples '81* (81), or *Unreached Peoples '82* (82).

A comparison with the indices in previous volumes in this series will show that some early data has been changed. In a few cases the group has been removed because of more accurate information. This reflects the ongoing nature of this data collection and research.

A more detailed explanation of the information contained in each of the following lists may be found at the beginning of the appropriate sections.

Index by
Group
Name

INDEX BY GROUP NAME

This is the basic listing of people groups in this registry. Peoples are listed by their primary *name,* and effort has been made to standardize names and use the most commonly accepted English spelling. This listing includes the *country* for which the information was provided, principal vernacular *language* used by the group, population estimate of the *group size* in the country listed and principal professed religion (*primary religion*), which in some cases is less than 50 percent of the total group membership.

In addition, this index includes the estimated percentage of the group that practices Christianity in any recognized tradition *(% Chr).* Included in this percentage are Protestant, Roman Catholic, Orthodox, African Independent, and other Christian groups. Excluded in this percentage were Christo-pagans and Christian cultic groups. It is important to note that this figure is the estimated percentage of *practicing* Christians within the group. If the group was listed in *Unreached Peoples '80* or earlier, the figure recorded here will most likely be different, because those volumes recorded the percentage of professing Christians (or adherents), which most often will be a higher number. Thus, these figures should not be compared or used as a time series, since the changes indicate a different kind of data. Differences might also be due to a new and better data source or revised data, since we are continually updating our files.

The index also lists a validity code *(V)* which estimates the accuracy and completeness of the data on a scale from 1 to 9. The code is:

1 — The only information available at this point is the group name, country, language, population, and primary religion. The percentage listed under practicing Christians is, at best, a rough estimate.

2 — There has been more data collected than the "baseline" information in 1, but it is scanty or of poor quality.

3 — About half of the information on the Unreached Peoples questionnaire (Appendix B) has been collected, and information on the Christian community, if any, is missing or probably inaccurate.

4 — Almost all the data on the Unreached Peoples questionnaire has been collected *or* the source document has supplied most of the necessary information.

5 — Information has been supplied by a completed Unreached Peoples questionnaire and at least one other document.

6 — In addition to 5, there is enough detailed information about the people group to write an accurate, up-to-date description.

7 — There exists an extensive description of the people group in secular or Christian literature.

8 — There has been a major research study (thesis or dissertation quality) done on the group which includes detailed information on the Christian community.

9 — In addition to 8, the study includes a thorough exploration of evangelism strategy for the particular group, based on firsthand experience.

The final column in this section indicates the year of the volume of *Unreached Peoples (Vol U.P.)* in which a description of the group appears.

NAME	COUNTRY	LANGUAGE	GROUP SIZE	PRIMARY RELIGION	% CHR	V	U.P.
"Au"ei	Botswana	"Au"ei	5,000	Animism	0%	1	
Abaknon	Philippines	Abaknon	10,000	Christo-Paganism	-1%	1	
Abanyom	Nigeria	Abanyom	3,850	Animism	-1%	1	
Abau	Indonesia	Abau	3,390	Animism	-1%	1	
Abau	Papua New Guinea	Abau	3,400	Animism	-1%	1	
Abazin	Soviet Russia	Abazin	25,000	Islam	0%	1	
Abe	Ivory Coast	Abe	28,500	Islam-Animist	-1%	1	
Abialang	Sudan	Abialang	7,200	Islam	0%	1	
Abidji	Ivory Coast	Adidji	23,000	Islam-Animist	-1%	1	
Abie	Papua New Guinea	Abie	580	Animism	-1%	1	
Abkhaz	Soviet Russia	Abkhaz	83,000	Unknown	0%	1	
Abkhaz	Turkey	Abkhaz	1,000	Islam	-1%	1	
Abong	Nigeria	Abong	1,400	Islam	-1%	1	
Aborigines in Brisbane	Australia	English	8,000	Secularism	6%	6	82
Abou Charib	Chad	Abou Charib	25,000	Islam-Animist	-1%	1	
Abu Leila	Sudan	Abu Leila	4,100	Islam	0%	1	
Abua	Nigeria	Abua	24,000	Animism	-1%	1	
Abujmaria in M.P.	India	Abujmaria	11,000	Hindu-Animism	-1%	1	
Abulas	Papua New Guinea	Abulas	33,000	Animism	-1%	1	
Abure	Ivory Coast	Abure	25,000	Islam-Animist	-1%	1	
Ach'ang	China	Ach'ang	10,000	Traditional Chinese	-1%	1	
Achagua	Colombia	Achagua	100	Animism	-1%	1	
Achehnese	Indonesia	Achehnese	2,200,000	Islam	1%	6	80
Acheron	Sudan	Acheron	1,300	Islam	0%	1	
Achi, Cubulco	Guatemala	Achi, Cubulco	15,000	Animism	-1%	1	
Achi, Rabinal	Guatemala	Achi, Rabinal	21,000	Animism	-1%	1	
Achipa	Nigeria	Achipa	3,600	Islam	-1%	1	
Achode	Ghana	Achode	4,890	Islam-Animist	-1%	1	
Acholi	Uganda	Acholi	nr	Animism	-1%	1	
Achual	Peru	Achual	5,000	Animism	-1%	1	
Adamawa	Cameroon	Fulani	380,000	Animism	-1%	5	
Adele	Togo	Adele	200,000	Animism	0%	1	
Adhola	Uganda	Adhola	80,300	Islam-Animist	2%	4	
***Adi	India	Adi	3,000	Animism	-1%	1	
Adiyan in Kerala	India	Adiyan	2,500	Hinduism	5%	4	
**Adja	Benin	Ge	250,000	Animism	0%	1	
Adjora	Papua New Guinea	Adjora	2,100	Animism	-1%	1	
Adygei	Soviet Russia	Adygei	100,000	Islam	0%	1	
Adyukru	Ivory Coast	Adyukru	50,450	Islam-Animist	-1%	1	
Aeka	Papua New Guinea	Aeka	3,000	Animism	-1%	1	
Aeta	Philippines	Aeta	3,000	Christo-Paganism	-1%	1	
*Afar	Ethiopia	Afar	300,500	Islam-Animist	1%	6	79
*Afawa	Nigeria	Afanci	10,000	Animism	1%	6	80

Afitti	Afitti	Sudan	3,000	Islam	0%	1
**AfO	Eloyi	Nigeria	25,000	Animism	1% 6	80
**African Students in Cairo	Various dialects	Egypt	700	Islam	9%	4
Afshars	Afshari	Iran	290,000	Islam	0%	3
Agajanis	Agajanis	Iran	1,000	Islam	0%	1
Agarabi	Agarabi	Papua New Guinea	12,000	Animism	-1%	1
Agariya in Bihar	Agariya	India	11,790	Hinduism	0%	1
Age	Age	Cameroon	5,000	Animism	0%	1
Aghem	Aghem	Cameroon	7,000	Animism	-1%	1
Aghu	Aghu	Indonesia	3,000	Animism	-1%	1
Agob	Agob	Papua New Guinea	1,100	Animism	-1%	1
Agoi	Agoi	Nigeria	3,650	Animism	-1%	1
Aguacateco	Aguacateco	Guatemala	8,000	Animism	-1%	1
Aguaruna	Aguaruna	Peru	22,000	Animism	0%	1
Agul	Agul	Soviet Russia	8,800	Islam	-1%	1
Agutaynon	Agutaynon	Philippines	7,000	Animism	-1%	1
Agwagwune	Agwagwune	Nigeria	20,000	Animism	-1%	1
Ahir in Maharashtra	Ahir	India	132,520	Islam	0% 6	79
**Ahl-i-Haqq in Iran	Kurdish dialects	Iran	500,000	Islam-Animist	0% 6	82
Ahlo	Ahlo	Togo	2,900	Islam-Animist	-1%	1
Ahmadis in Lahore	Panjabi	Pakistan	60,000	Islam	0%	1
Aibondeni	Aibondeni	Indonesia	150	Animism	-1%	1
Aiku	5907	Papua New Guinea	800	Animism	-1%	1
Aikwakai	Aikwakai	Indonesia	400	Animism	-1%	1
Aimol in Assam	Aimol	India	110	Hindu-Animist	-1%	1
Aiome	Aiome	Papua New Guinea	850	Animism	-1%	1
Aion	Aion	Papua New Guinea	800	Animism	-1%	1
Airo-Sumaghaghe	Airo-Sumaghaghe	Indonesia	2,000	Animism	-1%	1
Airoran	Airoran	Indonesia	350	Animism	-1%	1
Aja	Aja	Sudan	1,000	Islam	-1%	1
Ajmeri in Rajasthan	Ajmeri	India	580	Hindu-Animist	-1%	1
Aka	Aka	India	2,257	Animism	0%	3
Akan, Brong	Akan, Brong	Ivory Coast	50,000	Islam-Animist	-1%	1
Akawa-o	Akawaio	Guyana	3,000	Christo-Paganism	-1%	1
Ake	Ake	Nigeria	300	Animism	-1%	1
**Akha	Akha	Thailand	9,916	Ancestor Worship	1% 6	79
Akhavakh	Akhavakh	Soviet Russia	5,000	Unknown	0%	4
***Akhdam	Arabic	Yemen, Arab Republic	nr	Islam-Animist	0%	1
Akpa-Yache	Akpa-Yache	Nigeria	15,000	Animism	-1%	1
Akpafu	Akpafu	Ghana	8,300	Islam-Animist	-0%	1
Akrukay	Akrukay	Papua New Guinea	150	Animism	-1%	1
Alaba	Alaban	Ethiopia	50,000	Islam	3%	4
Aladian	Aladian	Ivory Coast	14,770	Islam-Animist	-1%	1

179

NAME	COUNTRY	LANGUAGE	GROUP SIZE	PRIMARY RELIGION	% CHR	V	VOL U.P.
Alago	Nigeria	Alago	35,000	Animism	2%	5	
Alak	Laos	Alak	8,000	Animism	1%	5	
Alamblak	Papua New Guinea	Alamblak	1,500	Animism	1%	5	
Alangan	Philippines	Alangan	6,000	Christo-Paganism	0%	4	
*Alars	India	Allar	400	Folk Religion	0%	5	
Alas	Indonesia	Gayo	30,000	Islam-Animist	0%	1	
Alatil	Papua New Guinea	Alatil	400	Animism	0%	1	
Alauagat	Papua New Guinea	Alauagat	300	Animism	0%	1	
*Alawites	Syria	Arabic	600,000	Islam	0%	6	79
*Albanian Muslims	Albania	Albanian Tosk	1,700,000	Islam	0%	6	80
*Albanians in Yugoslavia	Yugoslavia	Albanian (Gheg)	1,500,000	Islam	1%	5	
Alege	Nigeria	Alege	1,200	Animism	1%	1	
Algerian (Arabs)	Algeria	Arabic	8,000,000	Islam	1%	6	80
Algerian Arabs in France	France	Arabic	804,000	Islam	0%	3	
Alôr, Kolana	Indonesia	Alur, Kolana	90,000	Animism	1%	5	81
Alur	Zaire	Alur	19,000	Animism	0%	1	
Alutor	Soviet Russia	Alutor	2,000	Unknown	1%	1	
Ama	Papua New Guinea	Ama	380	Animism	1%	1	
Amahuaca	Peru	Amahuaca	1,500	Animism	1%	1	
Amaimon	Papua New Guinea	Amaimon	370	Animism	1%	1	
Amanab	Indonesia	Amanab	2,800	Animism	1%	1	
Amanab	Papua New Guinea	Amanab	2,800	Animism	1%	1	
Amar	Ethiopia	Amar	22,500	Animism	1%	1	
Amarakaeri	Peru	Amarakaeri	500	Animism	1%	1	
Amasi	Cameroon	Amasi	10,000	Animism	1%	1	
Ambai	Indonesia	Ambai	6,000	Animism	1%	1	
Ambasi	Papua New Guinea	Ambasi	500	Animism	1%	1	
Amber	Indonesia	Amber	300	Animism	1%	1	
Amberbaken	Indonesia	Amberbaken	5,000	Animism	1%	1	
Ambo	Zambia	Ambo	1,000	Animism	0%	4	
Ambonese	Indonesia	Ambonese	80,000	Animism	1%	1	
Ambonese	Netherlands	Ambonese	30,000	Animism	2%	4	
*Americans in Geneva	Switzerland	English	45,000	Secularism	1%	4	
*Ami	Taiwan	Ami	99,000	Buddhist-Animist	2%	5	81
Amo	Nigeria	Amo	3,550	Animism	1%	1	
**Ampeeli	Papua New Guinea	Ampale	1,000	Christo-Paganism	1%	4	
Amsterdam Boat Dwellers	Netherlands	Dutch	7,500	Secularism	0%	3	
Amto	Papua New Guinea	Amto	200	Animism	1%	1	
Amuesha	Peru	Amuesha	5,000	Animism	1%	1	
Amuzgo, Guerrero	Mexico	Amuzgo, Guerrero	20,000	Christo-Paganism	1%	1	
Amuzgo, Oaxaca	Mexico	Amuzgo, Oaxaca	5,000	Christo-Paganism	1%	1	
Ana	Togo	Ana	36,000	Islam-Animist	0%	3	
Anaang	Nigeria	Anaang	246,000	Animism	1%	1	

Group	Country	Name	Population	Religion	%
Anal in Manipur	India	Anal	6,590	Animism	-1% 1
*Anatolian Turks-Istanbul	Turkey	Turkish	2,000,000	Islam	0% 5 82
Andarum	Papua New Guinea	Andarum	64,650	Animism	-1% 1
Andha in Andhra Pradesh	India	Andha	9,000	Animism	0% 1
Andi	Soviet Russia	Andi		Unknown	-1% 1
Andoque	Colombia	Andoque	100	Animism	-1% 1
Anem	Papua New Guinea	Anem	1,000	Animism	-1% 1
Anga in Bihar	India	Anga	423,500	Hinduism	-1% 1
Angaataha	Papua New Guinea	Angaataha	750	Animism	-1% 1
Angal Heneng, South	Papua New Guinea	Angal Heneng, South	15,000	Animism	-1% 1
Angal Heneng, West	Papua New Guinea	Angal Heneng, West	25,000	Animism	-1% 1
Angal, East	Papua New Guinea	Angal, East	100,000	Animism	-1% 1
Angas	Nigeria	Angas	1,800	Animism	-1% 1
Angaua	Papua New Guinea	Angaua	1,250	Animism	-1% 1
Angor	Papua New Guinea	Angor	4,250	Animism	-1% 1
Angoram	Papua New Guinea	Angoram		Animism	0% 1
Animere	Togo	Animere	1,500	Islam-Animist	0% 1
Ankave	Papua New Guinea	Ankave	10,000	Animism	0% 1
Ankwe	Nigeria	Ankwai	580	Animism	1% 4
Anor	Papua New Guinea	Anor	3,000	Animism	-1% 1
Ansus	Indonesia	Ansus	52,000	Animism	-1% 5
Anuak	Ethiopia	Anuak	30,000	Animism	4% 5
Anuak	Sudan	Anuak	3,000	Animism	-1% 1
Anuki	Papua New Guinea	Anuki	100	Islam-Animist	0% 1
Anyanga	Togo	Anyanga	87,100	Animism	-1% 1
Apalai	Brazil	Apalai	11,000	Folk Religion	11% 4
**Apartment Residents-Seoul	Korea, Republic of	Korean	12,000	Animism	1% 8
**Apatani in Assam	India	Apartani	210	Christo-Paganism	9% 6
Apayao	Philippines	Isneg	1,000	Animism	-1% 1
Apinaye	Brazil	Apinaye	75,000	Animism	-1% 1
Apurina	Brazil	Apurina	5,000	Islam	-1% 1
Ara	Indonesia	Ara	13,000	Islam	0% 5
Arab Immigrants in Bangui	Central African Republic	Arabic	16,000	Islam	0% 3
Arab-Jabbari (Kamesh)	Iran	Arabic	200	Islam	0% 3
Arab-Shaibani (Kamesh)	Iran	Arabic	5,250,000	Islam	-1% 1
Arabela	Peru	Arabela	1,000	Islam	1% 5
Arabs in Morocco	Morocco	Arabic dialect	520,000	Islam	1% 4 82
**Arabs in New Orleans	United States of America	Arabic	1,080	Islam	0% 1
Arabs of Khuzestan	Iran	Arabic	600	Animism	nr 4
Arafundi	Papua New Guinea	Arafundi	2,000	Hindu-Animist	1% 5 82
Arandan in Tamil Nadu	India	Arandan	310	Animism	-1% 1
Arandai	Indonesia	Arandai		Animism	-1% 1
Arapaco	Brazil	Tucanoan		Animism	-1% 1

NAME	COUNTRY	LANGUAGE	GROUP SIZE	PRIMARY RELIGION	% CHR	V	VOL U.P.
Arapesh, Bumbita	Papua New Guinea	Arapesh, Bumbita	2,000	Animism	-1%		1
Arapesh, Mountain	Papua New Guinea	Arapesh, Mountain	5,000	Animism	-1%		1
Arapesh, Muhiang	Papua New Guinea	Arapesh, Muhiang	8,070	Animism	-1%		1
Arawa	Nigeria	Hausa	200,000	Islam	-1%		4
Arawak	Guyana	Arawak	5,000	Christo-Paganism	-1%		1
Arawe	Papua New Guinea	Arawe	2,200	Animism	-1%		1
Arbore	Ethiopia	Arbore	2,000	Animism	-1%		1
Archin	Soviet Russia	Archin	900	Unknown	0%		1
Arecuna	Venezuela	Arecuna	14,000	Animism	-1%		1
Argobba	Ethiopia	Argobba	3,000	Animism	-1%		1
Arguni	Indonesia	Arguni	200	Animism	-1%		1
Arifama-Miniafia	Papua New Guinea	Arifama-Miniafia	2,150	Animism	-1%		1
Arigibi	Papua New Guinea	Arigibi	300	Animism	0%		1
Arinua	Papua New Guinea	Arinua	1,700	Animism	0%		1
*Arnatas	India	Aranatan	1,700	Animism	-1%		4
Arop	Papua New Guinea	Arop	1,500	Animism	-1%		1
Aruop	Papua New Guinea	Aruop	470	Animism	0%		1
Arusha	Tanzania	Arusha	110,000	Animism	8%		5
Arutani	Venezuela	Spanish	100	Animism	0%		1
Arya in Andhra Pradesh	India	Arya	2,590	Hinduism	-1%		1
Asaro	Papua New Guinea	Asaro	12,000	Animism	-1%		1
Asat	Papua New Guinea	Asat	660	Animism	-1%		1
Asienara	Indonesia	Asienara	700	Animism	-1%		1
*Asmat	Indonesia	Asmat	30,000	Animism	7%	6	79
Assamese	Bangladesh	Assamese	10,000,000	Islam	-1%		1
Assumbo	Cameroon	Assumbo	10,000	Animism	-1%		1
Asu	Tanzania	Asu	110,000	Animism	0%		1
Asuri in Bihar	India	Asuri	4,540	Animism	-1%		1
Ata	Papua New Guinea	Ata	1,000	Animism	-1%		1
*Ata of Davao	Philippines	Manobo	10,000	Animism	4%	4	4
Aten	Nigeria	Aten	4,000	Animism	-1%		1
Ati	Philippines	Ati	1,500	Christo-Paganism	-1%		1
Atoc	Sudan	Islam	5,200	Islam	0%		1
Atruahi	Brazil	Atruahi	500	Animism	-1%		1
*Atta	Philippines	Atta	1,000	Animism	-1%		5
Attie	Ivory Coast	Attie	160,000	Islam-Animist	-1%		1
Atuot	Sudan	Atuot	8,000	Islam	0%		1
*Atye	Ivory Coast	Atye	210,000	Animism	9%	4	4
Au	Papua New Guinea	Au	3,900	Animism	-1%		1
**Auberge Crowd in Geneva	Switzerland	Arabic	150	Secularism	0%	5	82
Aunalei	Papua New Guinea	Aunalei	1,800	Animism	0%		1
Auyana	Papua New Guinea	Auyana	6,500	Animism	-1%		1
Avatime	Ghana	Avatime	10,400	Islam-Animist	0%		1

Name	Language	Country	Population	Religion	%		
Avikam	Avikam	Ivory Coast	7,940	Islam-Animist	-1%	1	
Avukaya	Avukaya	Sudan	5,200	Islam	-0%	1	
Awa	Awa	Papua New Guinea	1,500	Animism	-1%	1	
Awar	Awar	Papua New Guinea	570	Animism	-1%	1	
Awara	Awara	Papua New Guinea	900	Animism	-1%	1	
Awin	Awin	Papua New Guinea	6,500	Islam	-1%	1	
Awngi	Awngi	Ethiopia	50,000	Islam	-1%	1	
Awutu	Awutu	Ghana	85,000	Islam-Animist	-0%	1	
Awyi	Awyi	Indonesia	400	Animism	-1%	1	
Awyu	Awyu	Indonesia	18,000	Animism	-1%	3	
Ayana	Ayana	Kenya	5,000	Islam-Animist	0%	5	
*Aymara	Aymara	Bolivia	850,000	Animism	7%	5	
Aymara, Carangas	Aymara, Carangas	Chile	20,000	Christo-Paganism	0%	1	
Ayoreo	Ayoreo	Paraguay	700	Animism	-1%	1	
Ayu	Ayu	Nigeria	4,000	Islam	-1%	1	
Azera	Azera	Papua New Guinea	360	Animism	-1%	1	
**Azerbaijani	Azerbaijani	Afghanistan	5,000	Islam	0%	5	80
Azerbaijani Turks	Azerbaijani Turkish	Iran	6,000,000	Islam	2%	6	79
***Azteca	Nahuatl, Hidalgo	Mexico	250,000	Christo-Paganism	0%	1	
Baali	Baali	Zaire	38,000	Animism	0%	1	
Babajou	Babajou	Cameroon	500	Animism	0%	1	
Babri	Babri	India	9,700	Hinduism	-1%	1	
**Babur Thali	Bura (Babur)	Nigeria	75,000	Animism	3%	6	80
Baburiwa	Baburiwa	Indonesia	160	Animism	-1%	1	
Bachama	Bachama	Nigeria	20,000	Islam	-1%	1	
**Bachelors in Lagos	Tribal Languages	Nigeria	26,000	Secularism	nr	6	82
Bada	Bada	Nigeria	10,000	Animism	-1%	1	
Badagu in Nilgiri	Badagu	India	104,920	Animism	-1%	1	
Bade	Bade	Nigeria	10,000	Islam	-1%	1	
Badyara	Badyara	Guinea-Bissau	100,000	Islam	0%	1	
Bafut	Bafut	Cameroon	25,000	Animism	0%	1	
Bageikhandi in M.P.	Bageikhandi	India	231,230	Hindu-Animist	-1%	1	
Baghati in H.P.	Baghati	India	3,980	Animism	-1%	1	
Bagirmi	Bagirmi	Chad	40,000	Islam-Animist	-1%	1	
***Bagobo	Bagobo	Philippines	35,000	Christo-Paganism	14%	5	
Bagri	Bagri	Pakistan	20,000	Hinduism	14%	4	
Baguio Area Miners	Ilocano	Philippines	40,000	Nominal Christian	15%	5	81
Bahais in Teheran	Farsi	Iran	45,000	Bahaism	0%	6	82
Baham	Baham	Indonesia	500	Animism	-1%	3	
Baharlu (Kamesh)	Turkish	Iran	7,500	Islam	0%	3	
Bahawalpuri in M.P.	Bahawalpuri	India	640	Animism	-1%	1	
Bahinemo	Bahinemo	Papua New Guinea	325	Animism	-1%	1	
Bai	Bai	Sudan	2,500	Islam	0%	1	

183

NAME	COUNTRY	LANGUAGE	GROUP SIZE	PRIMARY RELIGION	% CHR	V	VOL U.P.
Baibai	Papua New Guinea	Baibai	315	Animism	0%	1	
Baiga in Bihar	India	Baiga	11,110	Animism	-1%	1	
Baining	Papua New Guinea	Baining	4,500	Animism	-1%	1	
Bajania	Pakistan	Gujarati Dialect	20,000	Hinduism	1%	6	79
Bajau, Indonesian	Indonesia	Bajau, Indonesian	50,000	Islam	-1%	2	
Bajau, Land	Malaysia	Bajau, Indonesian	90,000	Islam-Animist	-1%	1	
Baka	Cameroon	Baka	15,000	Animism	-0%	1	
Bakairi	Brazil	Bakairi	2,600	Animism	-1%	1	
Bakhtiaris	Iran	Bakhtiaris	300	Animism	-1%	1	
**Bakuba	Zaire	Tshiluba	590,000	Islam	0%	5	80
Bakwe	Ivory Coast	Bakwe	75,000	Animism	14%	5	
**Bakwele	Congo	Bakwele	5,060	Islam-Animist	-1%	1	
**Balangao	Philippines	Balangao	8,000	Animism	0%	1	
Balangaw	Philippines	Balangaw	4,500	Christo-Paganism	3%	4	
Balanta	Senegal	Balanta	5,000	Animism	-1%	1	
Balantak	Indonesia	Balantak	49,200	not reported	nr	3	
Balante	Guinea-Bissau	Balanta	125,000	Islam-Animist	-1%	3	
Bali	Nigeria	Bali	100,000	Animism	-1%	1	
Bali-Vitu	Papua New Guinea	Bali-Vitu	1,000	Islam-Animist	7%	4	
Balinese	Indonesia	Balinese	6,660	Animism	-1%	4	
Balkars	Soviet Russia	Balkar	2,000,000	Hindu-Animism	-1%	1	
Balmiki	Pakistan	Hindustani	60,000	Islam	1%	5	
Balong	Cameroon	Duala	20,000	Hinduism	0%	1	
Balti in Jammu	India	Balti	4,500	Hinduism	1%	5	
Baluchi	Iran	Baluchi	40,140	Islam	1%	5	
Bam	Papua New Guinea	Bam	1,100,000	Animism	-1%	1	
Bambara	Ivory Coast	Bambara	600	Islam	0%	6	80
Bambara	Mali	Bambara	1,000,000	Animism	-1%	1	
Bambuka	Nigeria	Bambuka	1,000,000	Islam-Animist	1%	5	
Bamougoun-Bamenjou	Cameroon	Bamougoun-Bamenjou	31,000	Islam	0%	1	
Bamum	Cameroon	Bamum	7,000	Islam	nr	1	
**Banai	Bangladesh	Bengali	2,000	not reported	1%	4	
***Banaro	Papua New Guinea	Banaro	2,500	Buddhist-Animist	5%	4	
Bandawa-Minda	Nigeria	Bandawa-Minda	10,000	Animism	-1%	1	
Bandi	Liberia	Bandi	32,000	Islam	6%	4	
Bandjoun	Cameroon	Bandjoun	60,000	Animism	6%	4	
Banen	Cameroon	Banen	28,000	Animism	0%	1	
Banga	Nigeria	Banga	8,000	Islam	0%	1	
Bangangte	Cameroon	Local Dialects	475,000	Unknown	-1%	1	
Bangaru in Punjab	India	Bangri	4,000,000	Hindu-Animism	-1%	1	
Bangba	Zaire	Bangba	29,000	Animism	0%	1	
Banggai	Indonesia	Banggai	200,000	Islam	1%	1	

People	Country	Name	Population	Religion	%		Year
Baniwa	Brazil	Baniwa	2,440	Animism	-1%	1	
Banoni	Papua New Guinea	Banoni	1,000	Animism	-1%	1	
Bantuanon	Philippines	Bantuanon	50,000	Christo-Paganism	-1%	1	
***Banyarwanda	Rwanda	Kinyarwanda	4,000,000	Animism	6%	5	
Banyum	Senegal	Banyum	9,000	Islam-Animist	0%	1	
Banyun	Guinea-Bissau	Banyun	15,000	Animism	6%	4	
***Baoule	Ivory Coast	Baule	1,200,000	Animism	9%	4	
Barabaig	Tanzania	Tatoga	49,000	Animism	2%	5	79
Barai	Papua New Guinea	Barai	1,500	Animism	-1%	1	
Barambu	Sudan	Barambu	46,000	Islam	-0%	1	
Barasano	Colombia	Barasano	400	Animism	-1%	1	
Barasano, Northern	Colombia	Barasano, Northern	450	Animism	3%	5	
Barasano, Southern	Colombia	Janena	400	Animism	2%	4	
Barau	Indonesia	Barau	150	Animism	-1%	1	
*Barbers in Tokyo	Japan	Japanese	220,000	Buddhism	1%	6	82
Bare'e	Indonesia	Bare'e	325,000	Animism	-1%	1	
Bareli in Madhya Pradesh	India	Bareli	230,030	Hinduism	-1%	1	
Bari	Sudan	Bari	340,000	Islam	0%	1	
Bariai	Papua New Guinea	Bariai	1,500	Animism	-1%	1	
*Bariba	Benin	Bariba	400,000	Islam	4%	6	80
Bariba	Nigeria	Bariba	55,000	Islam-Animist	-1%	1	
Bariji	Papua New Guinea	Bariji	260	Animism	-1%	1	
Barim	Papua New Guinea	Barim	600	Animism	-1%	1	
Barok	Papua New Guinea	Barok	1,425	Animism	-1%	1	
Baruga	Papua New Guinea	Baruga	1,050	Animism	-1%	1	
Baruya	Papua New Guinea	Baruya	4,400	Animism	0%	1	
Basaa	Cameroon	Basaa	170,000	Unknown	12%	4	
Basakomo	Nigeria	not reported	60,000	Animism	0%	1	
Basari	Guinea	Basari	3,500	Animism	0%	3	
	Senegal	Gasari	8,000	Animism	0%	1	
Basari	Senegal	Basari	8,000	Animism	10%	5	
Bashar	Nigeria	Bashar	20,000	Animism	-1%	1	
Bashgali	Afghanistan	Bashgali	10,000	Islam	-1%	1	
Bashkir	Soviet Russia	Tatar	1,200,000	Islam	0%	5	80
Basila	Togo	Basila	4,750	Islam-Animist	0%	1	
Basketo	Ethiopia	Basketo	9,000	Animism	-1%	1	
***Basotho, Mountain	Lesotho	Southern Sesotho	70,000	Animism	8%	6	79
*Bassa	Liberia	Bassa	200,000	Animism	11%	5	
**Bassa	Nigeria	Bassa	100,000	Animism	8%	5	
Bata	Nigeria	Bata	26,400	Islam-Animist	-1%	1	
*Batak, Angkola	Indonesia	Batak, Angkola	nr	Islam	6%	6	80
Batak, Karo	Indonesia	Batak, Karo	400,000	Animism	-1%	1	

185

NAME	COUNTRY	LANGUAGE	GROUP SIZE	PRIMARY RELIGION	% CHR	V	VOL U.P.
Batak, Palawan	Philippines	Batak, Palawan	390	Christo-Paganism	-1%	1	
Batak, Simalungun	Indonesia	Batak, Simalungun	800,000	Animism	-1%	1	
Batak, Toba	Indonesia	Batak, Toba	1,600,000	Animism	-1%	1	
Batanga-Ngolo	Cameroon	Batanga-Ngolo	9,000	Animism	-1%	1	
**Batangeno	Philippines	Tagalog	nr	Nominal Christian	7%	4	
Bateg	Malaysia	Bateg	400	Animism	0%	2	
Bathudi in Bihar	India	Bathudi	73,890	Hinduism	-1%	1	
Batsi	Soviet Russia	Batsi	3,000	Unknown	0%	1	
Batu	Nigeria	Batu	25,000	Islam	0%	1	
Bau	Papua New Guinea	Bau	1,790	Animism	-1%	1	
Baushi	Nigeria	Baushi	2,650	Islam	-1%	1	
Bauwaki	Papua New Guinea	Bauwaki	380	Animism	-1%	1	
Bawm	Bangladesh	Bawm	7,000	Islam	-1%	1	
Bayats	Iran	Bayat	nr	Islam	0%	3	
Bayot	Gambia	Bayot	4,000	Islam-Animist	-1%	1	
	Guinea-Bissau	Bayot	3,000	Islam-Animist	-1%	1	
	Senegal	Bayot	4,000	Islam-Animist	0%	1	
Bazigar in Gujarat	India	Bazigar	100	Animism	-1%	1	
Bebeli	Papua New Guinea	Bebeli	600	Animism	-1%	1	
Bediya in Bihar	India	Bediya	32,200	Animism	-1%	1	
Bedoanas	Indonesia	Bedoanas	250	Animism	-1%	1	
Beja	Ethiopia	Beja	39,000	Islam	-1%	1	
	Sudan	Beja	91,000	Islam	0%	1	
Bekwarra	Nigeria	Bekwarra	34,000	Animism	-1%	1	
Bembe	Zaire	Bembe	50,000	Animism	0%	1	
Bembi	Papua New Guinea	Bembi	360	Animism	0%	1	
Bena	Tanzania	Bena	150,000	Animism	0%	1	
Benabena	Papua New Guinea	Benabena	14,000	Animism	-1%	1	
Bencho	Ethiopia	Bencho	5,000	Animism	-1%	1	
Bende	Tanzania	Bende	9,000	Animism	-1%	1	
Bene	Cameroon	Bene	60,000	Animism	0%	1	
Benga	Gabon	Benga	nr	Animism	0%	1	
Bengali	Bangladesh	Bengali	80,000,000	Islam	-1%	6	80
Bengalis in London	United Kingdom	Bengali	15,000	Islam	0%	5	82
Berba	Benin	Berba	44,000	Animism	0%	1	
Berik	Indonesia	Berik	800	Animism	-1%	1	
Berom	Nigeria	Berom	116,000	Animism	0%	1	
Besisi	Malaysia	Besisi	7,000	Animism	0%	2	
*Bete	India	Bete	2,960	Animism	-1%	1	
Bethen	Ivory Coast	Bethen	300,000	Animism	-1%	1	
Betsinga	Cameroon	Betsinga	10,000	Animism	0%	1	
Bette-Bende	Nigeria	Bette-Bende	10,000	Animism	0%	1	

Name	Alt.	Country	Population	Religion	%	
Bhakta	Bhakta	India	55,150	Hindu-Animist	-1%	1
Bharia in Madhya Pradesh	Bharia	India	5,380	Animism	-1%	1
Bhatneri	Bhatneri	India	190	Islam	-1%	1
Bhattri	Bhattri	India	103,770	Hindu-Animist	-1%	1
**Bhil	Marwari	Pakistan	800,000	Hinduism	-1%	6
*Bhilala	Bhilala	India	246,720	Hindu-Animist	-1%	1
**Bhils	Dangi	India	806,000	Animism	-1%	6 79
*Bhojpuri	Bhojpuri	Nepal	806,480	Hinduism	-1%	4
Bhoyari in Maharashtra	Bhoyari	India	5,390	Hindu-Animist	-1%	1
Bhuiya in Bihar	Bhuiya	India	4,430	Animism	-1%	1
Bhumij in Assam	Bhumij	India	48,240	Hindu-Animist	-1%	1
Bhunjia in Madhya Pradesh	Bhunjia	India	5,240	Hindu-Animist	-1%	1
Bhutias	Sharchagpakha	Bhutan	780,000	Buddhism	-1%	6
Biafada	Biatada	Guinea-Bissau	15,000	Animism	6%	4
Biak	Biak	Indonesia	40,000	Animism	-1%	1
Biaka	Biaka	Papua New Guinea	400	Animism	-1%	1
Biangai	Biangai	Papua New Guinea	1,100	Animism	-1%	1
Bibling	Bibling	Papua New Guinea	1,500	Animism	-1%	5 81
**Bidayuh of Sarawak	Biatah	Malaysia	110,000	Christo-Paganism	0%	2
Biduanda	Biduanda	Malaysia	4,000	Animism	-1%	1
Bidyogo	Bidyogo	Guinea-Bissau	10,000	Islam-Animist	8%	4
**Bijogo	Bidyogo	Guinea-Bissau	25,000	Animism	8%	4
Bijori in Bihar	Bijori	India	2,390	Hindu-Animist	-1%	1
Biksi	Biksi	Indonesia	200	Animism	-1%	1
Bilala	Bilala	Chad	42,000	Islam-Animist	-1%	1
**Bilan	Bilaan	Philippines	75,000	Animism	-1%	5
Bile	Bile	Nigeria	1,000	Islam-Animist	-1%	1
Bilen	Bilen	Ethiopia	32,000	Islam	-1%	1
Biliau	Biliau	Papua New Guinea	620	Animism	-1%	5
Bimanese	Bima	Indonesia	300,000	Islam	-1%	5
Bimin	Bimin	Papua New Guinea	400	Animism	-1%	1
Bimoba	Bimoba	Ghana	49,800	Islam-Animist	-1%	1
	Bimoba	Togo	70,000	Islam-Animist	-1%	1
Binahari	Binahari	Papua New Guinea	770	Animism	-1%	1
Binandere	Binandere	Papua New Guinea	3,000	Animism	-1%	1
Binawa	Binawa	Nigeria	2,000	Islam	-1%	1
Bine	Bine	Papua New Guinea	2,000	Animism	-1%	1
Binga	Binga	Sudan	1,000	Islam	0%	1
Bingkokak	Bingkokak	Indonesia	150,000	Islam	-1%	1
Binjhwari in Bihar	Binjhwari	India	48,800	Hindu-Animist	-1%	1
Binji	Binji	Zaire	64,000	Animism	0%	1
Binumarien	Binumarien	Papua New Guinea	190	Animism	-1%	1
***Bipim	Bipim	Indonesia	450	Christo-Paganism	5%	4

NAME	COUNTRY	LANGUAGE	GROUP SIZE	PRIMARY RELIGION	% CHR	V	VOL U.P.
Bira	Indonesia	Bira	75,000	Islam-Animist	-1%	1	
	Zaire	Bira	35,000	Animism	-1%	1	
Birhor in Bihar	India	Birhor	590	Hindu-Animist	-1%	1	
Birifor	Ghana	Birifor	40,000	Animism	3%	5	
	Upper Volta	Birifor	50,000	Islam-Animist	-1%	1	
Bisa	Zambia	Bisa	83,000	Animism	-0%	1	
Bisaya	Malaysia	Bisaya	2,800	Animism	nr	6	81
Bisis	Papua New Guinea	Bisis	355	Animism	0%	1	
Bitara	Papua New Guinea	Bitara	100	Animism	0%	1	
Bitare	Cameroon	Bitare	50,000	Islam-Animist	0%	1	
	Nigeria	Bitare	3,000	Islam	-1%	1	
Biti	Sudan	Biti	280	Islam	0%	1	
Biyom	Papua New Guinea	Biyom	400	Animism	0%	1	
**Black Caribs, Belize	Belize	Moreno	10,000	Christo-Paganism	1%	6	79
**Black Caribs, Guatemala	Guatemala	Moreno	1,500	Christo-Paganism	1%	5	
**Black Caribs, Honduras	Honduras	Moreno	20,000	Christo-Paganism	1%	5	
Blacks in Soweto	South Africa	Tribal Languages	1,250,000	Secularism	16%	6	82
Boanaki	Papua New Guinea	Boanaki	1,700	Animism	-1%	1	
Bobe	Cameroon	Bobe	600	Animism	0%	1	
Bobo Fing	Mali	Bobo Fing	3,000	Animism	-1%	1	
Bobo Wule	Mali	Bobo Wule	366,000	Animism	-1%	1	
Bodo in Assam	India	Bodo	509,010	Animism	-1%	1	
**Bodo Kachari	India	Bodo	610,000	Hindu-Animist	2%	4	
Boghom	Nigeria	Boghom	50,000	Animism	-1%	1	
Bohutu	Papua New Guinea	Bohutu	1,065	Animism	-1%	1	
Boikin	Papua New Guinea	Boikin	31,000	Animism	-1%	1	
**Boko	Benin	Boko (Busa)	40,000	Animism	2%	4	
Bokyi	Cameroon	Bokyi	87,000	Animism	-1%	1	
	Nigeria	Bokyi	87,000	Animism	-1%	1	
Bola	Papua New Guinea	Bola	4,600	Animism	-1%	1	
Bole	Nigeria	Bole	32,000	Islam	-1%	1	
***Bolinao	Philippines	Bolinao	26,000	Nominal Christian	19%	4	
Bolon	Upper Volta	Bolon	4,000	Islam-Animist	-1%	1	
Bolondo	Zaire	Bolondo	1,000	Animism	0%	1	
Bom	Papua New Guinea	Bom	1,130	Animism	-1%	1	
	Zaire	Boma	15,000	Animism	-1%	1	
Bomboko	Cameroon	Bomboko	2,500	Animism	0%	1	
Bomou	Chad	Bomou	15,000	Islam-Animist	-1%	1	
Bondei	Tanzania	Bondei	30,000	Islam	0%	1	
Bondo in Orissa	India	Bondo	2,370	Hinduism	-1%	1	
Bonerif	Indonesia	Bonerif	100	Hinduism	-1%	1	
Bonggo	Indonesia	Bonggo	430	Animism	-1%	1	
Bongili	Congo	Bongili	4,000	Animism	0%	1	

Name	Country	Language	Population	Primary Religion	%	Vol	Ref
Bongo	Sudan	Bongo	2,400	Islam	0%	1	
Bongu	Papua New Guinea	Bongu	415	Animism	-1%	1	
Bonkeng-Pendia	Cameroon	Bonkeng-Pendia	1,500	Animism	0%	1	
Bonkiman	Papua New Guinea	Bonkiman	250	Animism	1%	5	81
**Bontoc, Central	Philippines	Bontoc, Central	20,000	Animism	4%	5	
**Bontoc, Southern	Philippines	Southern Bontoc	12,000	Christo-Paganism	0%	1	
Bor Gok	Sudan	Bor Gok	5,800	Islam	-1%	1	
Bora	Colombia	Bora	400	Animism	-1%	1	
Borai	Indonesia	Borai	1,000	Animism	-1%	1	
Boran	Ethiopia	Boran	132,000	Islam-Animist	3%	5	
**Boran	Kenya	Boran	37,000	Islam-Animist	0%	3	
Boran	Kenya	Boran	40,000	Islam-Animist	1%	5	
*Bororo	Brazil	Bororo	500	Animism	0%	1	
Bosavi	Papua New Guinea	Bosavi	350	Animism	-1%	1	
Bosilewa	Papua New Guinea	Bosilewa	350	Animism	-1%	1	
Bosngun	Papua New Guinea	Bosngun	715	Animism	-1%	6	80
*Bosnian	Yugoslavia	Serbo-Croation	1,740,000	Islam	-1%	1	
Botlikh	Soviet Russia	Botlikh	3,500	Unknown	0%	4	
Bousansi	Upper Volta	Bisa	140,000	Islam-Animist	-1%	1	
Bovir-Ahmadi	Iran	Lori	110,000	Islam	-1%	4	
Bowili	Togo	Bowili	3,300	Islam-Animist	-1%	1	
Boya	Sudan	Boya	15,000	Animism	0%	5	
Bozo	Mali	Bozo	nr	Animism	-1%	1	
Brahui	Pakistan	Brahui	745,000	Islam	1%	6	79
Braj in Uttar Pradesh	India	Braj	6,000,000	Animism	-1%	1	
Brao	Laos	Brao	18,000	Animism	0%	1	
Brat	Indonesia	Brat	20,000	Animism	0%	2	
Breri	Papua New Guinea	Breri	25,720	Animism	0%	3	
Bruneis	Malaysia	Bruneis	20,000	Animism	-1%	1	
Bua	Chad	Bua	150,000	Islam	-1%	1	
Buang, Central	Indonesia	Buang, Central	6,100	Animism	0%	1	
Buang, Mangga	Papua New Guinea	Buang, Mangga	2,500	Animism	-1%	1	
Bube	Equatorial Guinea	Bube	20,000	Animism	0%	4	
Budibud	Papua New Guinea	Budibud	170	Animism	0%	1	
Budu	Zaire	Budu	83,000	Animism	-1%	4	
Budug	Soviet Russia	Budug	2,000	Unknown	-1%	1	
Budugum	Cameroon	Masa	10,000	Animism	0%	4	
Buduma	Nigeria	Buduma	80,000	Islam	1%	6	80
Bugis	Indonesia	Bugis	3,500,000	Islam-Animist	-1%	1	
Bugiere	Panama	Bugiere	2,000	Christo-Paganism	0%	1	
Bugombe	Zaire	Bugombe	12,000	Animism	-1%	1	
Buhid	Philippines	Buhid	6,000	Christo-Paganism	-1%	1	

NAME	COUNTRY	LANGUAGE	GROUP SIZE	PRIMARY RELIGION	% CHR	V	VOL U.P.
Builsa	Ghana	Buli	97,000	Animism	-1%	4	
Buin	Papua New Guinea	Buin	9,000	Animism	-1%	1	
Buja	Zaire	Buja	200,000	Animism	0%	1	
Buka-Khwe	Botswana	Local dialects	9,000	Animism	0%	1	
Bukaua	Papua New Guinea	Bukaua	5,000	Animism	0%	1	
**Bukidnon	Philippines	Manobo, Binukid	100,000	Animism	15%	5	
Buli	Indonesia	Buli	1,000	Islam-Animist	-1%	1	
	Zaire	Buli	60,000	Islam-Animist	0%	1	
Bulia	Zaire	Bulia	45,000	Animism	0%	1	
Bullom, Northern	Sierra Leone	Bullom, Northern	167,000	Islam-Animist	-1%	1	
Bullom, Southern	Sierra Leone	Bullom, Southern	40,000	Islam-Animist	-1%	1	
Bulu	Papua New Guinea	Bulu	200	Animism	-0%	1	
Buna	Papua New Guinea	Buna	935	Animism	0%	1	
Bunabun	Indonesia	Bunabun	500	Animism	-1%	1	
Bunak	Indonesia	Bunak	50,000	Animism	-1%	1	
Bunama	Papua New Guinea	Bunama	5,000	Animism	-1%	1	
Bunann in Kashmir	India	Bunan	2,000	Animism	-1%	1	
Bungku	Indonesia	Bungku	180,000	Animism	-1%	1	
Bunu	Nigeria	Bunu	150,000	Animism	-1%	4	
Bura	Cameroon	Bura	100,000	Animism	-1%	1	
Burak	Nigeria	Burak	2,000	Islam	-1%	1	
Buraka-Gbanziri	Congo	Buraka-Gbanziri	2,000	Animism	0%	1	
Buriat	China	Buriat	26,500	Traditional Chinese	-1%	1	
	Soviet Russia	Buriat	315,000	Buddhist-Animist	-1%	1	
Burig	China	Burig	148,000	Traditional Chinese	-1%	1	
Burig in Kashmir	India	Burig	132,200	Animism	-1%	1	
Burji	Ethiopia	Burji	20,000	Animism	-1%	1	
Buru	Indonesia	Buru	6,000	Animism	-1%	1	
Burum	Papua New Guinea	Burum	3,200	Animism	-1%	1	
Burun	Sudan	Burun	5,000	Islam	0%	1	
Burungi	Tanzania	Burungi	20,000	Animism	7%	4	
**Bus Drivers, South Korea	Korea, Republic of	Korean	26,000	Unknown	8%	6	82
**Bus Girls in Seoul	Korea, Republic of	Korean	15,000	Secularism	8%	6	80
Busa	Nigeria	Busa (Bokobarn Akiba)	50,000	Islam	1%	6	
	Papua New Guinea	Busa	230	Animism	0%	1	
Busami	Indonesia	Busami	350	Animism	-1%	1	
**Busanse	Ghana	Bisa (Busanga)	50,000	Animism	2%	5	
Bushmen (Heikum)	Namibia	Heikum	16,000	Animism	6%	6	
*Bushmen (Hiechware)	Zimbabwe	Kwe-Etshari	1,600	Animism	6%	6	
*Bushmen (Kung)	Namibia	Xu	10,000	Animism	6%	6	79
Bushmen in Botswana	Botswana	Buka-khwe	30,000	Animism	7%	4	
Bushoong	Zaire	Bushoong	100,000	Animism	-1%	1	
Bussa	Ethiopia	Bussa	1,000	Animism	-1%	1	

Name	Country	People	Population	Religion	%	
Butawa	Nigeria	Buta	20,000	Islam	0%	5
Butung	Indonesia	Butung	200,000	Islam-Animist	-1%	1
Buwid	Philippines	Buwid	16,000	Islam	0%	5 81
Bviri	Sudan	Bviri	140,000	Animism	0%	6 80
Bwa	Upper Volta	Buamu (Bobo Wule)	35,000	Animism	9%	6
Bwaidoga	Papua New Guinea	Bwaidoga	5,380	Animism	-1%	1
Bwisi	Zaire	Bwisi	6,000	Animism	-0%	1
Cacua	Colombia	Cacua	150	Animism	-1%	1
Caiwa	Brazil	Caiwa	7,000	Animism	-1%	1
Cakchiquel, Central	Guatemala	Cakchiquel, Central	300,000	Christo-Paganism	-1%	1
Caluyanhon	Philippines	Caluyanhon	30,000	Christo-Paganism	-1%	1
*Cambodians	Thailand	Northern Kamer	1,000,000	Buddhist-Animist	-1%	5
Campa	Peru	Campa	5,000	Animism	-1%	1
Camsa	Colombia	Camsa	2,000	Animism	-1%	1
Candoshi	Peru	Candoshi	3,000	Animism	-1%	1
Canela	Brazil	Canela	1,400	Animism	-1%	1
Capanahua	Peru	Capanahua	500	Animism	-1%	1
Cape Malays in Cape Town	South Africa	Afrikaans	150,000	Islam	7%	6 82
Carapana	Colombia	Carapana	200	Animism	-1%	1
Cashibo	Peru	Cashibo	1,500	Animism	-1%	1
*Casiguranin	Philippines	Casiguranin	10,000	Nominal Christian	17%	4
*Casual Laborers-Atlanta	United States of America	English	1,500	Secularism	nr	5 82
Cayapa	Ecuador	Cayapa	3,000	Animism	-1%	1
***Cebu, Middle-Class	Philippines	Cebuano	500,000	Christo-Paganism	12%	4
*Central Thailand Farmers	Thailand	Thai	5,000,000	Buddhist-Animist	1%	5 81
Cewa	Zambia	Cewa	200,000	Animism	-0%	1
Ch'iang	China	Ch'iang	77,000	Traditional Chinese	-1%	1
**Ch'ol Sabanilla	Mexico	Tila Chol	20,000	Christo-Paganism	5%	4
**Ch'ol Tila	Mexico	Tila Chol	38,000	Christo-Paganism	5%	5
Chacobo	Bolivia	Chacobo	250	Animism	-1%	1
Chagga	Tanzania	Chagga	800,000	Animism	-0%	1
Chaghatai	Afghanistan	Chaghatai	300,000	Islam	-1%	1
Chakfem-Mushere	Nigeria	Chakfem-Mushere	5,000	Animism	-1%	5 81
*Chakmas of Mizoram	India	Chakma	20,000	Buddhist-Animist	1%	5
Chakossi in Ghana	Ghana	Chakossi	31,000	Animism	1%	5
Chakossi in Togo	Togo	Chakossi	22,000	Animism	3%	4
Chala	Ghana	Chala	1,000	Islam-Animist	-1%	1
*Cham (Western)	Kampuchea, Democratic	Cham	45,000	Hindu-Animist	0%	6 80
Cham	Viet Nam	Cham	90,000	Islam	-1%	1
Chamacoco, Bahia Negra	Paraguay	Chamacoco, Bahia Negra	1,000	Animism	-0%	1
Chamalin	Soviet Russia	Chamalin	5,000	Unknown	-1%	1
Chamari in Madhya Pradesh	India	Chamari	5,320	Hindu-Animist	-1%	1

NAME	COUNTRY	LANGUAGE	GROUP SIZE	PRIMARY RELIGION	% CHR	V	VOL U.P.
Chamba Daka	Nigeria	Chamba Daka	66,000	Islam-Animist	-1%	1	
Chamba Leko	Nigeria	Chamba Leko	30,000	Islam-Animist	-1%	1	
Chambri	Papua New Guinea	Chambri	935	Animism	0%	1	
Chameali in H.P.	India	Chameali	52,970	Hindu-Animist	-1%	1	
Chami	Colombia	Chami	3,000	Animism	-1%	1	
Chamicuro	Peru	Chamicuro	150	Animism	-1%	1	
Chamorro	Turks and Caicos Islands	Chamorro		Animism	-1%	1	
Chamula	Mexico	Tzotzil (Chamula)	15,000	Christo-Paganism	10%	4	
*Chang-Pa of Kashmir	India	Tibetan Dialect	50,000	Christo-Paganism	1%	6	79
Chara	Ethiopia	Chara	7,000	Buddhist-Animist	0%	5	81
Chatino, Nopala	Mexico	Chatino, Nopala	1,000	Christo-Paganism	-1%	1	
Chatino, Panixtlahuaca	Mexico	Chatino, Panixtlahuaca	7,500	Christo-Paganism	-1%	1	
Chatino, Tataltepec	Mexico	Chatino, Tataltepec	4,500	Christo-Paganism	-1%	1	
Chatino, Yaitepec	Mexico	Spanish	2,000	Christo-Paganism	-1%	1	
Chatino, Zacatepec	Mexico	Chatino, Zacatepec	2,000	Christo-Paganism	-1%	1	
Chatino, Zenzontepec	Mexico	Chatino, Zenzontepec	500	Christo-Paganism	0%	1	
Chaungtha	Burma	Chaungtha	4,000	Buddhist-Animist	0%	1	
Chawai	Nigeria	Chawai	34,600	Animism	-1%	1	
**Chayahuita	Peru	Chayawita	30,000	Christo-Paganism	11%	4	
Chenapian	Papua New Guinea	Chenapian	6,000	Animism	0%	1	
Chenchu in Andhra Pradesh	India	Chenchu	150	Hindu-Animist	-1%	1	
Chero in Bihar	India	Chero	17,610	Animism	-1%	1	
Cherkess	Soviet Russia	Cherkess	40,000	Islam	0%	1	
**Chicanos in Denver	United States of America	Spanish	28,370	Nominal Christian	-1%	5	82
Chiga	Uganda	Chiga	121,000	Animism	nr	1	
Chik-Barik in Bihar	India	Chik-Barik	272,000	Animism	0%	1	
Chin	China	Chin	30,040	Traditional Chinese	-1%	1	
Chin, Asho	Burma	Chin, Asho	95,500	Buddhist-Animist	-1%	1	
Chin, Falam	Burma	Chin, Falam	11,000	Buddhist-Animist	-1%	1	
Chin, Haka	Burma	Chin, Haka	92,000	Buddhist-Animist	-1%	1	
Chin, Khumi	Burma	Chin, Khumi	85,000	Buddhist-Animist	-1%	1	
Chin, Ngawn	Burma	Chin, Ngawn	30,000	Buddhist-Animist	-1%	1	
Chin, Tiddim	Burma	Chin, Tiddim	5,000	Buddhist-Animist	-1%	1	
Chinanteco, Tepinapa	Mexico	Chinanteco, Tepinapa	38,000	Christo-Paganism	-1%	1	
Chinanteco, Ayotzintepec	Mexico	Chinanteco, Ayotzintepec	3,000	Christo-Paganism	0%	1	
Chinanteco, Chiltepec	Mexico	Chinanteco, Chiltepec	2,000	Christo-Paganism	0%	1	
Chinanteco, Comaltepec	Mexico	Chinanteco, Comaltepec	3,000	Christo-Paganism	0%	1	
Chinanteco, Lalana	Mexico	Chinanteco, Lalana	1,500	Christo-Paganism	-1%	1	
Chinanteco, Lealao	Mexico	Chinanteco, Lealao	10,000	Christo-Paganism	-1%	1	
Chinanteco, Ojitlan	Mexico	Chinanteco, Ojitlan	5,000	Christo-Paganism	-1%	1	
Chinanteco, Palantla	Mexico	Chinanteco, Palantla	10,000	Christo-Paganism	-1%	1	
Chinanteco, Quiotepec	Mexico	Chinanteco, Quiotepec	10,600	Christo-Paganism	-1%	1	
Chinanteco, Sochiapan	Mexico	Chinanteco, Sochiapan	7,000	Christo-Paganism	-1%	1	

Name	Country	Language	Population	Religion	%
Chinanteco, Tepetotutla	Mexico	Chinanteco, Tepetotutla	1,000	Christo-Paganism	-1%
Chinanteco, Usila	Mexico	Chinanteco, Usila	5,000	Christo-Paganism	-1%
Chinbok	Burma	Chinbok	21,000	Buddhist-Animist	-1%
Chinese Businessmen	Hong Kong	Cantonese	10,000	Traditional Chinese	8%
Chinese Factory Workers	Hong Kong	Cantonese	500,000	Traditional Chinese	2%
Chinese Fishermen	Malaysia	Hokkien	4,000	Traditional Chinese	0%
**Chinese Hakka of Taiwan	Taiwan	Hakka	1,750,000	Traditional Chinese	1%
*Chinese in Amsterdam	Netherlands	Cantonese	15,000	Unknown	1%
**Chinese in Australia	Australia	Cantonese	30,000	Traditional Chinese	8%
*Chinese in Austria	Austria	Mandarin	1,000	Traditional Chinese	5%
**Chinese in Boston	United States of America	Mandarin	20,000	Secularism	4%
**Chinese in Brazil	Brazil	Hakka	45,000	Traditional Chinese	8%
Chinese in Burma	Burma	Mandarin and dialects	600,000	Traditional Chinese	4%
Chinese in Costa Rica	Costa Rica	Cantonese	5,000	Unknown	2%
*Chinese in Holland	Netherlands	Mandarin	35,000	Unknown	1%
**Chinese in Hong Kong	Hong Kong	Cantonese	4,135,000	Traditional Chinese	1%
**Chinese in Indonesia	Indonesia	Indonesian	3,600,000	Traditional Chinese	6%
*Chinese in Japan	Japan	Mandarin	50,000	Traditional Chinese	1%
*Chinese in Korea	Korea, Republic of	Mandarin	20,000	Secularism	5%
*Chinese in Laos	Laos	Mandarin	25,000	Traditional Chinese	1%
*Chinese in Malaysia	Malaysia	Chinese dialects	3,555,879	Traditional Chinese	8%
*Chinese in New Zealand	New Zealand	Cantonese	12,500	Traditional Chinese	4%
*Chinese in Panama	Panama	Spanish	2,500	Traditional Chinese	4%
Chinese in Puerto Rico	Puerto Rico	Hakka	200	Traditional Chinese	1%
**Chinese in Sabah	Malaysia	Mandarin and dialects	180,000	Traditional Chinese	0%
**Chinese in Sarawak	Malaysia	Hakka	330,000	Traditional Chinese	10%
*Chinese in Saudi Arabia	Saudi Arabia	Arabic	20,000	Islam	7%
*Chinese in South Africa	South Africa	Cantonese	11,470,000	Traditional Chinese	0%
*Chinese in Taiwan	Taiwan	Taiwanese (Minnan, Amoy)	3,600,000	Traditional Chinese	9%
*Chinese in Thailand	Thailand	Hakka	105,000	Buddhism	2%
*Chinese in United Kingdom	United Kingdom	Mandarin	550,000	Traditional Chinese	2%
**Chinese in United States	United States of America	Mandarin	80,000	Traditional Chinese	3%
*Chinese in Vancouver B.C.	Canada	Cantonese		Traditional Chinese	9%
*Chinese in West Germany	German Federal Rep.	Mandarin		Secularism	6%
*Chinese Mainlanders	Taiwan	Mandarin	2,010,200	Secularism	2%
Chinese Merchants	Ghana	Chinese dialects	40	Unknown	8%
Chinese Muslims	Taiwan	Mandarin	45,000	Islam	0%
*Chinese of W. Malaysia	Malaysia	Cantonese	3,500,000	Traditional Chinese	-1%
*Chinese Refugees in Macau	Macau	Cantonese	100,000	Traditional Chinese	4%
**Chinese Refugees, France	France	Tien-Chiu	100,000	Traditional Chinese	1%
*Chinese Restaurant Wrkrs.	France	Won Chow	50,000	Traditional Chinese	2%
*Chinese Stud., Australia	Australia	Chinese Dialects	5,500	Secularism	2%
**Chinese Students Glasgow	United Kingdom	Mandarin	1,000	Traditional Chinese	15%

NAME	COUNTRY	LANGUAGE	GROUP SIZE	PRIMARY RELIGION	% CHR	V	VOL U.P.
Chinese Villagers	Hong Kong	Cantonese	500,000	Traditional Chinese	1%	3	
Chinga	Cameroon	Chinga	12,600	Animism	0%	1	
Chinga	Cameroon	Chinga	12,600	Animism	0%	1	
Chingp'o	China	Chingp'o	101,850	Traditional Chinese	1%	1	
Chip	Nigeria	Chip	6,000	Animism	-1%	1	
Chipaya	Bolivia	Chipaya	850	Animism	-1%	1	
Chiquitano	Bolivia	Chiquitano	20,000	Animism	-1%	1	
**Chiriguano	Argentina	Guarani (Bolivian)	15,000	Animism	8%	5	
Chitralis	Pakistan	Khuwar	120,000	Islam	0%	6	79
Chocho	Mexico	Spanish	2,500	Christo-Paganism	0%	1	
Chodhari in Gujarat	India	Chodhari	135,980	Hindu-Animist	-1%	1	
Chokobo	Nigeria	Chokobo	425	Animism	-1%	1	
Chokwe	Zambia	Chokwe	25,000	Animism	0%	5	
Chokwe (Lunda)	Angola	Chokwe	400,000	Animism	9%	5	
Chola Naickans	India	Canarese	400,100	Animism	0%	3	
Chopi	Mozambique	Chopi	400,000	Animism	-1%	1	
Chorote	Argentina	Chorote	500	Animism	-1%	1	
Chorote	Paraguay	Chorote	nr	Animism	-1%	1	
Chorti	Guatemala	Chorti	25,000	Animism	-1%	1	
**Chrau	Viet Nam	Jro	15,000	Animism	14%	4	
Chuabo	Mozambique	Chwabo	250,000	Animism	9%	4	
Chuang	China	Chuang	12,000,000	Animism	0%	5	81
Chuave	Papua New Guinea	Chuave	20,000	Animism	-1%	1	
Chuj	Guatemala	Chuj	15,000	Animism	-1%	1	
Chuj of San Mateo Ixtatan	Guatemala	Chuj, San Mateo Ixtatan	17,000	Animism	12%	5	
Chuj, San Mateo Ixtatan	Mexico	Chuj, San Mateo Ixtatan	3,000	Christo-Paganism	-1%	1	
Chukot	Soviet Russia	Chukot	14,000	Unknown	0%	1	
Chulupe	Paraguay	Chulupe	8,000	Christo-Paganism	-1%	1	
Chungchia	China	Chungchia	1,500,000	Traditional Chinese	-1%	1	
Churahi in H.P.	India	Churahi	34,670	Hindu-Animist	-1%	1	
Chwang	Brazil	Chwang	7,785,410	Traditional Chinese	-1%	1	
Cinta Larga	Brazil	Cinta Larga	500	Animism	-1%	1	
Circassian	Turkey	Circassian	113,370	Islam	-1%	1	
Circassians in Amman	Jordan	Arabic	17,000	Islam	0%	5	82
Cirebon	Indonesia	Javanese, Tjirebon	2,500,000	Islam-Animist	-1%	1	
**Citak	Indonesia	Citak (Asmat)	6,500	Animism	-1%	5	
Citak	Indonesia	Citak	6,000	Animism	-1%	5	
Cocama	Peru	Cocama	18,900	Animism	0%	1	
Cocopa	Mexico	Cocopa		Christo-Paganism	-1%	1	
Cofan	Colombia	Cofan	900	Animism	-1%	1	
Cogui	Colombia	Cogui	250	Animism	-1%	1	
*Coloureds in Eersterust	South Africa	Afrikaans	4,000	Secularism	15%	6	82
*Comorians	Comoros	Comorian (Shingazidja)	20,000	Islam	-1%	1	
*Comorians	Comoros	Comorian (Shingazidja)	300,000	Islam	1%	6	79

Name	Country	Language	Population	Religion	% Chr.
***Copacabana Apt. Dwellers	Brazil	Portuguese	400,000	Nominal Christian	-1% 4
Cora	Mexico	Cora	8,000	Christo-Paganism	-1% 4
**Coreguaje	Colombia	Coreguaje	500	Animism	-1% 1
Coreguaje	Colombia	Coreguaje	500	Animism	-1% 1 [79]
Cubeo	Colombia	Cubeo	2,000	Animism	-1% 1
Cuiba	Colombia	Cuiba	2,000	Animism	-1% 1
Cuicateco, Tepeuxila	Mexico	Cuicateco, Tepeuxila	10,000	Christo-Paganism	-1% 1
Cuicateco, Teutila	Mexico	Cuicateco, Teutila	6,000	Christo-Paganism	-1% 1
Cujareno	Peru	Cujareno	800	Animism	-1% 1
Culina	Brazil	Culina	800	Animism	-1% 1
*Cuna	Colombia	Cuna	600	Animism	-1% 5
Cuna	Colombia	Cuna	600	Animism	7% 5
Curipaco	Colombia	Curipaco	2,500	Animism	-1% 1
Cuyonon	Philippines	Cuyonon	49,000	Christo-Paganism	-1% 1
Daba	Cameroon	Daba	31,000	Animism	-1% 1
Daba	Cameroon	Daba	31,000	Animism	-1% 1
Dabra	Indonesia	Dabra	5,500	Animism	-1% 1
Dadibi	Papua New Guinea	Dadibi	2,300	Animism	-1% 1
Dadiya	Nigeria	Dadiya	5,500	Islam	-1% 1
Daga	Papua New Guinea	Daga	30,000	Animism	-1% 1
Dagada	Indonesia	Dagada	200,000	Animism	-1% 4
Dagari	Ghana	Dagari	150,000	Islam-Animist	-1% 4
Dagari	Upper Volta	Dagari	350,000	Islam-Animist	-1% 1
*Dagomba	Ghana	Dagbanli	22,600	Traditional Chinese	-1% 1
Dagur	China	Dagur	920	Animism	-1% 1
Dahating	Papua New Guinea	Dahating	10,200	Buddhist-Animist	-1% 1
Dai	Burma	Dai	225	Islam	0% 1
Dair	Sudan	Dair	27,000	Islam-Animist	-1% 1
Daju of Dar Dadju	Chad	Daju of Dar Dadju	12,000	Animism	0% 1
Daju of Dar Fur	Sudan	Daju of Dar Sila	33,000	Islam-Animist	0% 1
Daju of Dar Sila	Chad	Daju	6,000	Islam	0% 4
Daju of West Kordofan	Sudan	Dakanci	10,000	Animism	3% 4
*Daka	Nigeria	Dami	1,100	Animism	2% 5
Dami	Papua New Guinea	Dan	270,000	Animism	2% 5
***Dan	Liberia	Dan	94,000	Islam-Animist	2% 5 [82]
Dan	Ivory Coast	Japanese	2,500,000	Secularism	-1% 1
*Danchi Dwellers in Tokyo	Japan	Dangaleat	50,000	Islam-Animist	-1% 1 [79]
Dangaleat	Chad	Dani, Grand Valley	70,000	Animism	2% 5
*Dani, Baliem	Indonesia	Burmese	70,100	Buddhism	3% 6
Danu	Burma	Daonda	100	Animism	0% 2
Daonda	Papua New Guinea	Dargin	231,100	Islam	0% 1
Dargin	Soviet Russia	Dass	8,830	Islam-Animist	-1% 1
Dass	Nigeria				

195

NAME	COUNTRY	LANGUAGE	GROUP SIZE	PRIMARY RELIGION	% CHR	V	VOL U.P.
Dathanik	Ethiopia	Dathanik	18,000	Animism	-1%	1	
Davaweno	Philippines	Davaweno	13,000	Christo-Paganism	-1%	1	
Dawawa	Papua New Guinea	Dawawa	1,700	Animism	-1%	1	
Dawoodi Muslims	India	Gujarati	225,000	Islam	0%	4	
Day	Central African Republic	Day	nr	Animism	-1%	1	
Daza	Chad	Dazaga	159,000	Islam	0%	5	
Dead-End Kids - Amsterdam	Netherlands	Dutch	30,000	Secularism	0%	6	82
Deccani Muslims	India	Dakhni (Urdu)	nr	Islam	0%	5	
Deccani Muslims-Hyderabad	India	Dakhni	500,000	Islam	-1%	6	82
Dedua	Papua New Guinea	Dedua	4,400	Animism	0%	1	
Degema	Nigeria	Degema	10,000	Animism	-1%	1	
Degenan	Papua New Guinea	Degenan	500	Animism	-1%	1	
Dem	Indonesia	Demen	2,000	Animism	-1%	1	
Demta	Indonesia	Demta	840	Animism	-1%	1	
Dendi	Benin	Dendi	40,000	Islam	0%	3	
Dengese	Zaire	Dengese	4,000	Animism	0%	1	
Deno	Nigeria	Deno	14,000	Islam	-1%	1	
Deori in Assam	India	Deori	14,940	Animism	-1%	1	
Dera	Nigeria	Dera	20,000	Islam	-1%	1	
Desano	Brazil	Desano	1,040	Animism	-1%	1	
*Deviant Youth in Taipei	Taiwan	Taiwanese	80,000	Folk Religion	nr	5	82
Dewein	Liberia	De	5,000	Islam	1%	4	
Dghwede	Cameroon	Dghwede	13,000	Animism	-1%	1	
*Dghwede	Cameroon	Dghwede	13,000	Animism	-1%	1	
Dhaiso	Tanzania	Zighvana(Dghwede)	12,000	Animism	-1%	5	
Dhanka in Gujarat	India	Dhaiso	13,000	Animism	-1%	1	
Dhanwar in Madhya Pradesh	India	Dhanka	10,230	Animism	-1%	1	
*Dhodias	India	Dhanwar	21,140	Animism	-1%	1	
Dhurwa	India	Dhodia Dialects	300,000	Hindu-Animist	1%	4	
Dia	Papua New Guinea	Parji	20,000	Hindu-Animist	0%	4	
Dida	Ivory Coast	Dia	1,850	Animism	-1%	1	
**Dida	Ivory Coast	Dida	115,000	Islam-Animist	-1%	1	
Didinga	Sudan	Dida	120,000	African Independent	7%	4	
	Sudan	Didinga	30,000	Animism	-1%	4	
Didoi	Soviet Russia	Didinga	3,000	Islam	-1%	1	
Digo	Kenya	Didoi	7,000	Unknown	0%	4	
	Tanzania	Digo	168,000	Islam	0%	1	
Dimasa in Cachar	India	Digo	30,000	Islam	0%	4	
Dime	Ethiopia	Dimasa	37,900	Animism	-1%	1	
Dimir	Papua New Guinea	Dime	2,000	Animism	-1%	1	
Dinka	Sudan	Dimir	1,270	Animism	4%	5	
Dinka, Agar	Sudan	Dinka, Agar	1,940,000	Islam	0%	1	

Name	Country	People/Language	Population	Religion	%Chr / Vol / Yr
Diodio	Papua New Guinea	Diodio	1,200	Animism	-1% 1
Diola	Guinea-Bissau	Diola	15,000	Islam	3% 5 80
	Senegal	Diola	266,000	Islam-Animist	-1% 1
Dirim	Nigeria	Dirim	11,000	Islam-Animist	-1% 1
Dirya	Nigeria	Dirya	3,750	Islam	0% 6 80
Divehi	Maldives	Divehi	120,000	Islam	-1% 1
Djuka	Surinam	Djuka	8,000	Christo-Paganism	0% 1
Dobu	Papua New Guinea	Dobu	8,000	Animism	0% 6 81
Doe	Tanzania	Doe	2,000	Animism	-1% 1
*Dog-Pa of Ladakh	India	Shrina	2,000	Animism	10% 6 79
Doga	Papua New Guinea	Doga		Animism	0% 1
Doghosie	Upper Volta	Doghosie	7,900	Islam-Animist	0% 1
*Dogon	Mali	Dogon	312,000	Animism	7% 6 4
Dogoro	Papua New Guinea	Dogoro	120	Animism	-1% 1
Dolgans	Soviet Russia	Dolgan	4,900	Unknown	-1% 1
Dom	Papua New Guinea	Dom	8,860	Animism	0% 1
Dompago	Benin	Dompago	19,000	Animism	0% 1
Domu	Papua New Guinea	Domu	480	Animism	12% 5
Domung	Papua New Guinea	Domung	850	Animism	-1% 1
Dongjoi	Sudan	Dongjoi	9,000	Islam	-1% 5
Dongo	Sudan	Dongo	100	Islam	-1% 4
	Zaire	Dongo	5,000	Animism	-1% 1
**Doohwaayo	Cameroon	Doohyaayo	24,320	Animism	-1% 1
Dorlin in Andhra Pradesh	India	Dorli	22,000	Hindu-Animist	
Dorobo	Kenya	Nandi	3,000	Animism	
	Tanzania	Hadza	840	Animism	
Doromu	Papua New Guinea	Doromu	3,000	Animism	
Dorze	Ethiopia	Dorze	300	Animism	
Doura	Papua New Guinea	Doura		Animism	
*Drug Addicts in Sao Paulo	Brazil	Portuguese	200,000	Nominal Christian	
Druzes	Israel	Arabic	33,000	Folk Religion	
Duau	Papua New Guinea	Duau		Animism	nr 5 82
**Dubla	India	Gujarati	202,218	Hindu-Animist	0% 6 79
Dubu	Indonesia	Dubu	130	Animism	4% 4
Duguir	Nigeria	Duguri	12,000	Islam	-1% 1
Duguza	Nigeria	Duguza	2,000	Islam	-1% 1
**Duka	Nigeria	Dukanci	10,000	Animism	-1% 5
Duma	Gabon	Duka	10,000	Animism	0% 1
*Dumagat , Casiguran	Philippines	Dumagat	1,000	Animism	3% 6 81
Duna	Papua New Guinea	Duna	11,000	Animism	-1% 1
Dungan	Soviet Russia	Dungan	39,000	Islam	-0% 1
Duru	Cameroon	Duru	20,000	Animism	-1% 4
Dusun	Malaysia	Kadazan	160,000	Animism	nr 6 81

NAME	COUNTRY	LANGUAGE	GROUP SIZE	PRIMARY RELIGION	% CHR	V	VOL U.P.
Duvele	Indonesia	Duvele	500	Animism	-1%	1	
Dyan	Upper Volta	Dyan	8,000	Islam-Animist	0%	1	
Dyerma	Niger	Dyerma	1,000,000	Islam-Animist	1%	6	80
	Nigeria	Dyerma	50,000	Islam	-1%	1	
Dyola	Gambia	Dyerma	216,000	Islam-Animist	-1%	1	
	Guinea-Bissau	Dyola	nr	Islam-Animist	-1%	1	
	Senegal	Dyola	nr	Islam-Animist	0%	1	
Ebira	Nigeria	Ebira	325,000	Islam-Animist	-1%	1	
Ebriē	Ivory Coast	Ebrie	50,000	Islam-Animist	-1%	1	
Edawapi	Papua New Guinea	Edawapi	3,800	Animism	0%	1	
Edo	Nigeria	Edo	430,000	Animism	-1%	1	
Efik	Nigeria	Efik	26,300	Animism	-1%	1	
Efutop	Nigeria	Efutop	10,000	Animism	-1%	1	
Eggon	Nigeria	Eggon	80,000	Animism	12%	5	
Eivo	Papua New Guinea	Eivo	1,120	Animism	-1%	1	
Ejagham	Nigeria	Ejagham	100,000	Animism	-1%	1	
Ekagi	Indonesia	Ekagi	100,000	Animism	-1%	1	
Ekajuk	Nigeria	Ekajuk	15,000	Animism	-1%	1	
Eket	Nigeria	Eket	22,000	Animism	-1%	1	
Ekpeye	Nigeria	Ekpeye	30,000	Animism	-1%	1	
El Molo	Kenya	Samburu	1,000	Animism	3%	4	
Eleme	Nigeria	Eleme	16,000	Animism	-1%	1	
Elkei	Papua New Guinea	Elkei	1,400	Animism	-1%	1	
Emai-Iuleha-Ora	Nigeria	Emai-Iuleha-Ora	48,000	Animism	-1%	1	
Embera, Northern	Colombia	Embera	2,000	Animism	-1%	1	
Emerum	Papua New Guinea	Emerum	460	Animism	-1%	1	
Emira	Papua New Guinea	Emira	3,650	Animism	-1%	1	
Emumu	Indonesia	Emumu	1,100	Animism	-1%	1	
Endangen	Papua New Guinea	Endangen	450	Animism	0%	1	
Enga	Papua New Guinea	Enga	110,000	Animism	-1%	1	
Engenni	Nigeria	Engenni	10,000	Animism	-1%	1	
Enya	Zaire	Enya	7,000	Animism	0%	1	
Eotile	Ivory Coast	Eotile	4,000	Islam-Animist	-1%	1	
Epie	Nigeria	Epie	12,000	Animism	-1%	1	
Erokwanas	Indonesia	Erokwanas	250	Animism	-1%	1	
Esan	Nigeria	Esan	200,000	Animism	-1%	1	
Eton	Cameroon	Eton	112,000	Animism	0%	1	
	Cameroon	Eton	112,000	Animism	-1%	1	
Etulo	Nigeria	Etulo	2,900	Animism	-1%	1	
Evant	Nigeria	Evant	5,000	Animism	-1%	1	
Evenki	China	Evenki	7,200	Traditional Chinese	-1%	1	
Evenks	Soviet Russia	Evenk	25,000	Buddhist-Animist	0%	1	
Ewage-Notu	Papua New Guinea	Ewage-Notu	10,000	Animism	-1%	1	

Name	Country	Alternate Name	Population	Religion	%		
Ewenkis	China	Altaic	10,000	Animism	0%	5	81
**Ex-Mental Patients in NYC	United States of America	Spanish	20,000	Secularism	nr	5	82
*Expatriates in Riyadh	Saudi Arabia	English	2,000	Secularism	0%	5	82
Fa D'Ambu	Equatorial Guinea	Fa D'Ambu	40,000	Unknown	0%	1	
*Factory Workers	Hong Kong	Cantonese	415	Animism	5%	6	
Fagululu	Papua New Guinea	Fagululu	2,500	Animism	-1%	1	
Faiwol	Papua New Guinea	Faiwol	15,000	Animism	1%	1	
**Fakai	Nigeria	Faka	30,000	Animism	7%	7	79
**Falasha	Ethiopia	Agau	50,000	Judaism	1%	1	
Fali	Cameroon	Fali	50,000	Islam	1%	1	
Fali	Cameroon	Fali	25,000	Islam	2%	5	
**Fali	Nigeria	Fali	24,988,740	Animism	1%	4	
Farmers of Japan	Japan	Japanese	1,600	Traditional Japanese	1%	1	
Fas	Papua New Guinea	Fas	850	Animism	1%	5	82
Fasu	Papua New Guinea	Fasu	600,000	Animism	1%	1	
*Favelados-Rio de Janeiro	Brazil	Portuguese	400	Christo-Paganism	0%	1	
Finungwan	Papua New Guinea	Finungwan	78,000	Animism	2%	4	
Fipa	Tanzania	Fipa	150,000	Animism	-1%	1	
Fishing Village People	Taiwan	Amoy	230	Traditional Chinese	1%	1	
Foau	Indonesia	Foau	2,585	Animism	1%	1	
Foi	Papua New Guinea	Foi	800	Animism	1%	1	
Foran	Indonesia	Foran	9,770	Animism	1%	4	
Fordat	Indonesia	Fordat	16,000	Animism	1%	5	
Fore	Papua New Guinea	Fore	230,000	Animism	0%	5	
Fra-Fra	Ghana	Fra-Fra	1,500,000	Animism	1%	1	
Fula	Guinea	Fula	250,000	Islam	1%	1	
Fula	Sierra Leone	Fula	250,000	Islam	1%	1	
Fula, Cunda	Upper Volta	Fula	70,200	Islam-Animist	0%	1	
Fula, Macina	Gambia	Fula, Macina	50,000	Islam-Animist	0%	1	
Fula, Peuhala	Mali	Fula, Peuhala	450,000	Animism	1%	4	
*Fulah	Mali	Fulani	300,000	Animism	1%	5	79
*Fulani	Upper Volta	Fulani	70,000	Islam	0%	1	
Fulani	Benin	Fulani	250,000	Islam-Animist	1%	1	
*Fulbe	Cameroon	Fulani	5,500	Islam-Animist	0%	1	
Fuliro	Ghana	Fuliro	56,000	Islam-Animist	-1%	1	
Fulnio	Zaire	Fulnio	1,500	Animism	0%	1	
Fungom, Northern	Brazil	Fungom, Northern	15,000	Animism	0%	1	
Fungom, Northern	Cameroon	Fungom, Northern	15,000	Animism	0%	1	
Fungor	Cameroon	Fungor	4,500	Islam	0%	1	
Furu	Sudan	Furu	5,000	Animism	0%	1	
Fuyuge	Zaire	Fuyuge	13,000	Animism	-1%	1	
Fyam	Papua New Guinea	Fyam	14,000	Animism	-1%	1	

NAME	COUNTRY	LANGUAGE	GROUP SIZE	PRIMARY RELIGION	% CHR	V	VOL U.P.
Fyer	Nigeria	Fyer	3,000	Animism	-1%	1	
Ga-dang	Philippines	Ga-Dang	5,500	Animism	-1%	5	
*Gabbra	Ethiopia	Gabrinja	nr	Folk Religion	-1%	4	
Gabbra	Kenya	Galla	12,000	Folk Religion	-1%	4	
Gabri	Chad	Gabri	20,000	Islam-Animist	-1%	1	
Gadaban in Andhra Pradesh	India	Gadaba	20,410	Hindu-Animist	-1%	1	
Gaddi in Himachal Pradesh	India	Gaddi	70,220	Hindu-Animist	-1%	1	
Gade	Nigeria	Gade	25,000	Animism	-1%	4	
Gadsup	Papua New Guinea	Gadsup	7,000	Animism	-1%	1	
Gaguzes	Soviet Russia	Gaguaz	157,000	Christo-Paganism	-1%	1	
**Gagre	Pakistan	Punjabi	40,000	Animism	-1%	4	
Gagu	Ivory Coast	Gagou	25,000	Animism	-1%	1	
Gahuku	Papua New Guinea	Gahuku	8,390	Animism	-1%	4	
Gaikundi	Papua New Guinea	Gaikundi	700	Animism	-1%	1	
Gaina	Papua New Guinea	Gaina	1,130	Animism	-1%	1	
Gal	Papua New Guinea	Gal	210	Animism	-1%	1	
Galambi	Nigeria	Galambi	1,000	Islam	-1%	1	
Galeshis	Iran	Galeshi	2,000	Islam	0%	3	
*Galla (Bale)	Ethiopia	Galla	750,000	Islam-Animist	7%	5	
Galla of Bucho	Ethiopia	Gallinya (Oromo)	1,500	Christo-Paganism	-1%	3	
Galla, Harar	Ethiopia	Gallinya	1,305,400	Islam	-1%	5	
Galler	Laos	Galler	50,000	Animism	-1%	1	
Galong in Assam	India	Galong	36,860	Hindu-Animist	-1%	1	
Gambai	Chad	Gambai	200,000	Islam-Animist	-1%	1	
Gamei	Papua New Guinea	Gamei	930	Animism	-1%	1	
Gamti in Gujarat	India	Gamti	136,210	Hindu-Animist	-1%	1	
Gan	Upper Volta	Gan	4,000	Islam-Animist	-1%	1	
Gane	Indonesia	Gane	1,500	Islam-Animist	-1%	1	
Gangam	Togo	Gangam	16,000	Islam-Animist	0%	1	
Ganglau	Papua New Guinea	Ganglau	200	Animism	-1%	1	
Gangte in Assam	India	Gangte	6,030	Hindu-Animist	-1%	1	
Garuh	Papua New Guinea	Garuh	1,730	Animism	-1%	1	
Garus	Papua New Guinea	Garus	2,100	Animism	-1%	1	
Garuwahi	Papua New Guinea	Garuwahi	225	Animism	-1%	1	
Gawar-Bati	Afghanistan	Gawar-Bati	8,000	Islam	-1%	1	
Gawri in Andhra Pradesh	India	Gawari	21,100	Hindu-Animist	-1%	1	
Gawwada	Ethiopia	Gawwada	4,000	Animism	-1%	1	
Gayo	Indonesia	Gayo	200,000	Islam-Animist	0%	4	80
Gays in San Francisco	United States of America	English	150,000	Secularism	0%	6	82
Gbande	Guinea	Bandi	66,000	Animism	3%	4	
Gbari	Nigeria	Gbari	500,000	Animism	2%	6	80
Gbaya	Nigeria	Gbaya	350,000	Islam	-1%	1	
Gbaya-Ndogo	Sudan	Gbaya-Ndogo	1,800	Islam	-1%	1	

Gbazantche	Gbazantche	Benin	9,000	Islam	0% 3
Gberi	Gberi	Sudan	600	Islam	0% 1
Gedaged	Gedaged	Papua New Guinea	2,765	Animism	-1% 1
Gedeo	Gedeo	Ethiopia	250,000	Animism	-1% 1
Geishas in Osaka	Japanese	Japan	nr	Secularism	-0% 5 82
Geji	Geji	Nigeria	2,650	Islam	-1% 1
Genagane	Genagane	Papua New Guinea	1,165	Animism	-1% 1
Gende	Gende	Papua New Guinea	8,000	Animism	-1% 1
Gera	Gera	Nigeria	13,300	Islam	-1% 1
Geruma	Geruma	Nigeria	4,700	Islam	-1% 1
Gesa	Gesa	Indonesia	4,200	Animism	-1% 1
Gheko	Gheko	Burma	4,000	Buddhist-Animist	4% 5
**Ghimeera	Gimira	Ethiopia	50,000	Animism	4% 5
Ghol	Ghol	Sudan	2,000	Islam	-1% 1
Ghotuo	Ghotuo	Nigeria	9,000	Animism	-0% 1
Ghulfan	Ghulfan	Sudan	3,300	Islam	-1% 1
Gidar	Gidar	Cameroon	50,000	Animism	-1% 1
	Gidar	Cameroon	50,000	Animism	-1% 1
	Gidar	Chad	50,000	Islam-Animist	-1% 1
Gidicho	Gidicho	Ethiopia	500	Animism	-1% 1
Gidra	Gidra	Papua New Guinea	1,600	Animism	-1% 1
Gilakis	Gilaki	Iran	1,950,000	Islam	0% 4
Gilyak	Gilyak	Soviet Russia	4,400	Unknown	0% 1
Gimi	Gimi	Papua New Guinea	18,000	Animism	0% 1
Ginuman	Ginuman	Papua New Guinea	775	Animism	-1% 1
Gio	Dan (Yacouba)	Liberia	92,000	Animism	5% 5
Gira	Gira	Papua New Guinea	400	Animism	-1% 1
Girawa	Girawa	Papua New Guinea	3,820	Animism	-1% 1
Giri	Giri	Papua New Guinea	1,540	Animism	-1% 1
Giryama	Giryama	Kenya	335,900	Animism	-1% 1
Gisei	Masa	Cameroon	10,000	Animism	9% 4
Gisiga	Gisiga	Cameroon	30,000	Animism	-1% 4
Gitua	Gitua	Papua New Guinea	450	Animism	11% 4
Gizra	Gizra	Papua New Guinea	600	Animism	-1% 1
**Glavda	Glavda	Nigeria	19,000	Animism	-0% 1
Gobasi	Gobasi	Papua New Guinea	1,000	Animism	4% 5
Gobato	Gobato	Ethiopia	22,000	Animism	0% 1
Gobeze	Gobeze	Ethiopia	20,000	Animism	-1% 1
**Godie	Godie	Ivory Coast	80,000	Animism	-1% 1
Goemai	Goemai	Nigeria	280,000	Animism	12% 4
Gogo	Gogo	Tanzania	10,000	Animism	-0% 1
Gogodala	Gogodala	Papua New Guinea	54,000	Animism	-1% 1
Gokana	Gokana	Nigeria		Animism	-1% 1

NAME	COUNTRY	LANGUAGE	GROUP SIZE	PRIMARY RELIGION	% CHR	V	VOL. U.P.
Gola	Liberia	Gola	47,000	Islam-Animist	-1%	1	
	Sierra Leone	Mende	1,400	Islam-Animist	0%	1	
Golo	Chad	Golo	3,400	Islam-Animist	-1%	1	
*Gonds	India	Gondi	4,000,000	Animism	1%	5	
Gonja	Ghana	Gonja	108,000	Islam-Animist	2%	4	
*Gorkha	India	Napali	180,000	Hinduism	0%	4	
Goroa	Tanzania	Goroa	500,000	Animism	0%	1	
Gorontalo	Indonesia	Gorontalo	3,000	Islam	-1%	1	
Gosha	Kenya	Gosha	2,000	Islam	0%	3	
Goudari	Iran	Goudari	25,000	Islam-Animist	0%	1	
Gouin-Turka	Upper Volta	Gouin-Turka	300,000	Islam-Animist	-1%	1	
Goulai	Chad	Goulai	200,000	Animism	5%	4	
Gourency	Upper Volta	Gourendi	300,000	Animism	4%	4	
**Gouro	Ivory Coast	Gouro	5,000	Animism	4%	4	
Gouwar	Cameroon	Gouwar	5,000	Animism	0%	1	
Government officials	Thailand	Thai	100,000	Buddhism	0%	1	
Grasia in Gujarat	India	Grasia	27,160	Hindu-Animist	0%	3	
Grunshi	Ghana	Grunshi	65,000	Animism	8%	4	
Gu	Liberia	Grebo Dialects	200,000	Animism	-1%	4	
	Benin	not reported	173,000	Animism	-1%	1	
Guaiaqui	Paraguay	Guaiaqui	350	Animism	-1%	1	
Guajajara	Brazil	Guajajara	5,000	Animism	-1%	1	
*Guajibo	Colombia	Guajibo	15,000	Animism	-1%	1	
*Guajiro	Colombia	Guajiro	60,000	Animism	12%	5	
Guambiano	Colombia	Guambiano	9,000	Animism	-1%	1	
Guana	Paraguay	Guana	3,000	Animism	0%	1	
*Guanano	Colombia	Guanano	800	Christo-Paganism	1%	4	79
***Guarani	Bolivia	Guarani	15,000	Animism	10%	6	79
Guarayu	Bolivia	Guarayu	5,000	Christo-Paganism	1%	5	
Guarojio	Mexico	Guarojio	5,000	Christo-Paganism	-1%	1	
Guayabero	Colombia	Guayabero	700	Animism	-1%	1	
Guayabevo	Colombia	Guayabero	600	Animism	8%	5	
Gude	Cameroon	Gude	40,000	Animism	1%	4	
	Nigeria	Gude	400,000	Animism	-1%	1	
Gudu	Nigeria	Gudu	1,200	Animism	-1%	1	
Guduf	Nigeria	Guduf	21,300	Animism	1%	1	
Guere	Ivory Coast	Guere	117,370	Islam-Animist	-1%	1	
Gugu-Yalanji	Australia	Gugu-Yalanji	5,400	Animism	1%	4	
Guhu-Samane	Papua New Guinea	Guhu-Samane	4,000	Animism	-1%	1	
Gujarati	United Kingdom	Gujarati	300,000	Hinduism	1%	6	81
Gujars of Kashmir	India	Gujari	150,000	Islam-Animist	0%	5	81

Name	Country	Language/Dialect	Population	Religion	%		
Gujuri	Afghanistan	Gujuri	10,000	Islam	-1%	1	
Gula	Chad	Gula	2,500	Islam-Animist	-1%	1	
Gulfe	Cameroon	Gulfe	36,000	Animism	0%	1	
Gulfe	Cameroon	Gulfe	36,000	Animism	-1%	1	
Gumasi	Papua New Guinea	Gumasi	250	Animism	-1%	1	
Gumine	Papua New Guinea	Gumine	24,715	Animism	-1%	1	
Gumuz	Ethiopia	Gumuz	53,000	Animism	-1%	1	
Gumuz	Sudan	Gumuz	40,000	Islam	0%	1	
Gurage	Ethiopia	Gurage Dialects	750,000	Islam-Animist	3%	6	80
Gure-Kahugu	Nigeria	Gure-Kahugu	5,000	Islam	-1%	1	
Gurensi	Ghana	Gurenne	250,000	Animism	1%	4	
Gurma	Upper Volta	Gurma	250,000	Islam-Animist	-1%	1	
Gurung	Nepal	Gurung	172,000	Hinduism	0%	5	
Guruntum-Mbaaru	Nigeria	Guruntum-Mbaaru	10,000	Islam	-1%	1	
Gusap	Papua New Guinea	Gusap	400	Animism	-1%	1	
Guwot	Papua New Guinea	Guwot	1,000	Animism	-1%	1	
Gwa	Ivory Coast	Gwa	8,300	Islam-Animist	-1%	1	
Gwandara	Nigeria	Gwandara	25,000	Animism	-1%	5	
Gwari Matai	Nigeria	Gwari Matai	200,000	Islam	-1%	1	
Gwedena	Papua New Guinea	Gwedena	2,400	Animism	-1%	1	
Gwere	Uganda	Gwere	162,000	Animism	-1%	1	
Gypsies	Soviet Russia	not reported	175,000	Christo-Paganism	3%	6	
Gypsies in Jerusalem	Israel	Romany Dialect	300	Folk Religion	0%	5	82
Gypsies in Spain	Spain	Rom	200,000	Islam	3%	6	79
Gypsies in Yugoslavia	Yugoslavia	Romany (Serbian Kaldnash)	800,000	Islam	17%	4	
Ha	Tanzania	Ha	286,000	Animism	0%	1	
Hadiyya	Ethiopia	Hadiyya	700,000	Animism	-1%	3	
**Hadrami	Yemen, Democratic	Arabic	151,000	Islam	-1%	1	
Hahon	Papua New Guinea	Hahon	1,300	Animism	-1%	1	
**Hajong	Bangladesh	Bengali	17,000	Hindu-Animist	1%	5	
Halbi in Madhya Pradesh	India	Tribal dialects	20,000	Animism	3%	5	
***Halam in Tripura	India	Halbi	349,260	Hindu-Animist	-1%	1	
Halia	Papua New Guinea	Halia	13,200	Animism	-1%	1	
Hallam	Burma	Hallam	11,000	Buddhist-Animist	-1%	1	
Hamtai	Papua New Guinea	Hamtai	32,200	Animism	-1%	1	
Hangaza	Tanzania	Hangaza	54,000	Animism	0%	1	
Hani	China	Hani	138,000	Traditional Chinese	-1%	1	
Hanonoo	Philippines	Hanonoo	6,000	Christo-Paganism	-1%	1	
Harari	Ethiopia	Harari	13,000	Islam	-1%	1	
Harauti in Rajasthan	India	Harauti	334,380	Hindu-Animist	-1%	1	
Hatsa	Tanzania	Hatsa	2,000	Animism	0%	1	
*Havasupai	United States of America	English	300	Unknown	3%	4	
Havu	Zaire	Havu	262,000	Animism	0%	1	

NAME	COUNTRY	LANGUAGE	GROUP SIZE	PRIMARY RELIGION	% CHR	V	VOL U.P.
Havunese	Indonesia	Havunese	40,000	Animism	-1%	1	
Haya	Tanzania	Haya	276,000	Animism	0%	1	
**Hazara in Kabul	Afghanistan	Hazaragi	300,000	Islam	0%	6	82
Hehe	Tanzania	Hehe	192,000	Animism	0%	1	
Heiban	Sudan	Heiban	25,000	Islam	-1%	1	
Helong	Indonesia	Helong	5,000	Animism	-1%	1	
Herero	Botswana	Herero	10,000	Animism	0%	1	
	Namibia	Dhimba	40,000	Animism	-1%	1	
Heso	Zaire	Heso	6,000	Animism	0%	1	
**Hewa	Papua New Guinea	Hewa	1,500	Animism	5%	6	79
Hezareh	Iran	Hezara'i	nr	Islam	0%	3	
**High School Students	Hong Kong	Cantonese	453,000	Traditional Chinese	7%	4	
***Higi	Nigeria	Higi	150,000	Animism	7%	5	
Hixkaryana	Brazil	Hixkaryana	150	Animism	-1%	1	
Hkun	Burma	Shan	20,000	Buddhism	0%	2	
Ho in Bihar	India	Ho	749,800	Hindu-Animist	-1%	1	
Hohodene	Brazil	Hohodene	1,000	Animism	-1%	1	
Holiya in Madhya Pradesh	India	Holiya	3,090	Hindu-Animist	-1%	1	
Holoholo	Tanzania	Holoholo	5,000	Animism	0%	1	
Holu	Angola	Holu	12,000	Animism	0%	1	
Hopi	United States of America	Hopi	6,000	Animism	4%	5	
Hote	Papua New Guinea	Hote	2,500	Animism	4%	5	
**Hotel Workers in Manila	Philippines	Pilipino	11,000	Nominal Christian	13%	5	81
Hrangkhol	Burma	Hrangkhol	8,500	Buddhist-Animist	-1%	1	
Huachipaire	Peru	Huachipaire	215	Animism	-1%	1	
Huambisa	Peru	Huambisa	5,000	Animism	-1%	1	
Huasteco	Mexico	Huasteco	80,000	Christo-Paganism	-1%	1	
**Huave	Mexico	Huave	18,000	Christo-Paganism	5%	5	
Hui	China	Hui-hui-yu	5,200,000	Islam	0%	6	80
Huichol	Mexico	Huichol	8,000	Christo-Paganism	-1%	1	
**Huila	Angola	Huila	200,000	Animism	1%	4	
Huitoto, Meneca	Colombia	Huitoto, Meneca	600	Animism	-1%	1	
Huitoto, Murui	Peru	Huitoto, Murui	800	Animism	-1%	1	
Hukwe	Angola	Hukwe	9,000	Animism	3%	4	
Hula	Papua New Guinea	Hula	3,000	Animism	-1%	1	
Huli	Papua New Guinea	Huli	54,000	Animism	-1%	1	
Humene	Papua New Guinea	Humene	440	Animism	-1%	1	
Hunde	Zaire	Hunde	33,500	Animism	0%	1	
Hunjara	Papua New Guinea	Hunjara	4,300	Animism	0%	1	
**Hunzakut	Pakistan	Burushaski	10,150	Islam	0%	6	79
Hupda Maku	Colombia	Hupda Maku	150	Animism	-1%	1	
Hwana	Nigeria	Hwana	20,000	Islam	-1%	1	
Hwela-Numu	Ivory Coast	Hwela-Numu	50,000	Islam-Animist	-1%	1	

Name	Country	Language	Religion	Population	%		
Hyam	Nigeria	Hyam	Islam	60,000	-1%	1	
Iatmul	Papua New Guinea	Iatmul	Animism	8,000	-1%	1	
Ibaji	Nigeria	Ibaji	Animism	20,000	-1%	4	
**Iban	Malaysia	Iban	Animism	30,000	nr	6	81
Ibanag	Philippines	Ibanag	Animism	319	-1%	1	
*Ibataan	Philippines	Ibataan	Christo-Paganism	500	0%	4	
Ibibio	Nigeria	Ibibio	Animism	2,000,000	-1%	1	
Ica	Colombia	Ica	Animism	3,000	-2%	5	
Icen	Nigeria	Icen	Islam-Animist	7,000	-1%	1	
Idi	Papua New Guinea	Idi	Animism	900	-0%	1	
Idoma	Nigeria	Idoma	Animism	300,000	-1%	1	
Idoma, North	Nigeria	Idoma, North	Animism	56,000	-1%	1	
Ifugao, Antipolo	Philippines	Keley-i	Animism	5,000	6%	5	
*Ifugao	Philippines	Ifugao	Animism	95,000	6%	5	
**Ifugao (Kalangoya)	Philippines	Kalangoya	Animism	35,000	5%	4	
Ifugao in Cababuyan	Philippines	Ifugao	Animism	4,000	14%	4	
Ifugao, Amband	Philippines	Ifugao, Amband	Animism	15,000	-1%	1	
Ifugao, Kiangan	Philippines	Ifugao, Kiangan	Animism	25,000	-1%	1	
Ifumu	Congo	Ifumu	Animism	200	-0%	1	
Igala	Nigeria	Igala	Animism	350,000	-1%	1	80
Igbirra	Nigeria	Igbirra	Islam-Animist	400,000	14%	6	
Igede	Nigeria	Igede	Animism	70,000	-1%	1	
Ignaciano	Bolivia	Ignaciano	Animism	5,000	-1%	1	
Igora	Papua New Guinea	Igora	Animism	880	-1%	1	
Igorot	Philippines	Igorot	Animism	20,000	-1%	1	
Iha	Indonesia	Iha	Animism	5,500	-1%	1	
Ihceve	Nigeria	Icheve	Animism	5,000	-1%	1	
Ijo, Central-Western	Nigeria	Ijo	Animism	338,700	-1%	1	
Ijo, Northeast	Nigeria	Ijo	Animism	395,300	-1%	1	
Ijo, Northeast Central	Nigeria	Ijo	Animism	8,400	-1%	1	
Ikalahan	Philippines	Ikalahan	Animism	40,000	0%	nr	6
Ikizu	Tanzania	Swahili	Animism	9,000	0%	1	
Ikobi-Mena	Papua New Guinea	Ikobi-Mena	Islam	650	-1%	1	
Ikulu	Nigeria	Ikulu	Islam	6,000	-1%	1	
Ikundun	Papua New Guinea	Ikundun	Animism	880	-1%	1	
Ikwere	Nigeria	Ikwere	Animism	200,000	-0%	1	
Ila	Zambia	Ila	Animism	39,000	-0%	1	
Ilongot	Philippines	Ilongot	Islam	7,640	-0%	3	
Inallu	Iran	Afshari	Animism	5,000	-1%	1	
Inanwatan	Indonesia	Inanwatan	Islam	1,100	0%	1	82
**Indian Tamils - Colombo	Sri Lanka	Tamil	Hindu-Animist	nr	6%	5	82
Indians in Dubai	United Arab Emirates	Malayalam	Hinduism	24,000	6%	5	
Indians in Fiji	Fiji	Hindustani	Hinduism	265,000	2%	6	79

NAME	COUNTRY	LANGUAGE	GROUP SIZE	PRIMARY RELIGION	% CHR	V	VOL U.P.
*Indians In Rhodesia	Zimbabwe	Gujarati	9,600	Hinduism	9%	4	
**Indians, East	Trinidad and Tobago	English with Hindi	400,000	Hinduism	5%	6	79
Indinogosima	Papua New Guinea	Indinogosima	3,450	Animism	0%	1	
Indust.Workers Yongdungpo	Korea, Republic of	Korean	140,000	Folk Religion	6%	4	
*Industrial Workers	Taiwan	Taiwanese (Hoklo)	500,000	Secularism	2%	5	81
*Industry Laborers-Japan	Japan	Japanese	21,000,000	Traditional Japanese	1%	4	
Inga	Colombia	Inga	6,000	Christo-Paganism	0%	5	
Ingassana	Sudan	Tabi	35,000	Animism	0%	1	
Ingushes	Soviet Russia	Ingush	158,000	Islam	1%	4	
*Inland Sea Island Peoples	Japan	Japanese	1,000,000	Traditional Japanese	1%	4	
Insinai	Philippines	Insinai	10,000	Animism	2%	4	
*Int'l Stud., Los Banos	Philippines	Vietnamese	nr	Islam	-1%	1	
Intha	Burma	Intha	80,200	Buddhist-Animist	-1%	1	
Ipiko	Papua New Guinea	Ipiko	6,000	Animism	-1%	1	
Ipili	Papua New Guinea	Ipili	150	Animism	-1%	1	
Iquito	Peru	Spanish	4,000	Animism	-1%	1	
Irahutu	Indonesia	Irahutu	218,000	Animism	11%	4	
Iraqw	Tanzania	Iraqw	103,000	Animism	-1%	4	
Iravas in Kerala	India	English	3,700,000	Hinduism	1%	4	
Iraya	Philippines	Iraya	6,000	Christo-Paganism	-1%	1	
Iresim	Indonesia	Iresim	100	Animism	-1%	1	
Iria	Indonesia	Iria	850	Animism	-1%	1	
Irigwe	Nigeria	Irigwe	15,000	Animism	-1%	1	
**Irulas in Kerala	India	Irula	10,000	Hinduism	0%	4	
Irumu	Papua New Guinea	Irumu	1,800	Animism	-1%	1	
Isanzu	Tanzania	Isanzu	12,000	Animism	0%	1	
Isebe	Papua New Guinea	Isebe	770	Animism	-1%	1	
Isekiri	Nigeria	Isekiri	33,000	Animism	-1%	1	
**Ishans	Nigeria	Esan	25,000	Nominal Christian	16%	5	
Isneg, Dibagat-Kabugao	Philippines	Isneg, Dibagat-Kabugao	10,000	Animism	-1%	1	
Isneg, Karagawan	Philippines	Isneg, Karagawan	8,000	Animism	-1%	1	
Isoko	Nigeria	Isoko	20,000	Animism	-1%	1	
Itawit	Philippines	Itawit	15,000	Christo-Paganism	-1%	1	
Itelmen	Soviet Russia	Itelmen	1,300	Unknown	0%	1	
Itik	Indonesia	Itik	100	Animism	-1%	1	
Itneg, Adasen	Philippines	Itneg, Adasen	4,000	Christo-Paganism	-1%	1	
Itneg, Binongan	Philippines	Itneg, Binongan	7,500	Christo-Paganism	-1%	1	
Itneg, Masadiit	Philippines	Itneg, Masadiit	7,500	Christo-Paganism	-1%	1	
Itonama	Bolivia	Itonama	110	Animism	-1%	1	
Ivbie North-Okpela-Atte	Nigeria	Ivbie North-Okpela-Atte	20,000	Christo-Paganism	-1%	1	
Iwa	Zambia	Iwa	15,000	Animism	0%	1	
*Iwaidja	Austria	Iwaidja	15,150	Animism	1%	4	

Name	Country	Language	Population	Religion	%	Code	Yr
Iwal	Papua New Guinea	Iwal	1,500	Animism	-1%	1	
Iwam	Papua New Guinea	Iwam	2,000	Animism	-1%	1	
Iwam, Sepik	Papua New Guinea	Iwam, Sepik	3,500	Animism	-1%	1	
Iwur	Indonesia	Iwur	1,000	Animism	0%	1	
Ixil	Guatemala	Cuyolbal	45,000	Christo-Paganism	1%	4	
Iyon	Cameroon	Iyon	4,000	Animism	0%	1	
	Cameroon	Iyon	4,000	Animism	0%	1	
	Nigeria	Iyon	2,000	Animism	-1%	1	
Izarek	Nigeria	Izarek	30,000	Animism	-1%	1	
Izhor	Soviet Russia	Izhor	1,100	Unknown	-0%	1	
**Izi	Nigeria	Izi	200,000	Animism	11%	4	
Jaba	Nigeria	Jaba	60,000	Animism	-1%	4	
Jabem	Papua New Guinea	Jabem	2,900	Animism	-1%	1	
Jacalteco	Guatemala	Jacalteco	12,000	Animism	-1%	1	
Jagannathi in A.P.	India	Jagannathi	1,310	Hindu-Animist	1%	4	
Jains	India	Hindi	2,000,000	Jain	1%	5	80
Jama Mapun	Philippines	Cagayan	15,000	Islam-Animist	-0%	1	
**Jamaican Elite	Jamaica	Jamaican Patois	800,000	Secularism	0%	1	
Jamamadi	Brazil	Jamamadi	1,200	Animism	-0%	3	
Jambi	Indonesia	Indonesian	850,000	Islam-Animist	-1%	1	
Jamden	Indonesia	Jamden	14,330	Animism	-1%	1	
Jamshidis	Iran	Jamshidi	1,000	Islam	-0%	3	
Janjero	Ethiopia	Janjero	1,000	Animism	-1%	1	
Janjo	Nigeria	Janjo	6,100	Animism	-0%	1	
Japanese in Brazil	Brazil	Japanese	750,000	Buddhism	8%	8	79
Japanese in Korea	Korea, Republic of	Japanese	5,000	Traditional Japanese	1%	3	
*Japanese Students In USA	United States of America	Japanese	nr	Secularism	1%	4	
Jaqaru	Peru	Jaqaru	2,000	Animism	-1%	1	
Jara	Nigeria	Jara	40,000	Islam	6%	5	
**Jarawa	Nigeria	Jaranchi	150,000	Animism	-1%	1	
Jatapu in Andhra Pradesh	India	Jatapu	36,450	Hindu-Animist	-1%	1	
Jati	Afghanistan	Jati	1,000	Islam	-1%	1	
Jaunsari in Uttar Pradesh	India	Jaunsari	56,560	Hindu-Animist	2%	6	79
**Javanese (rural)	Indonesia	Javanese	60,000,000	Islam-Animist	5%	5	
**Javanese of Central Java	Indonesia	Javanese	20,000,000	Islam-Animist	7%	4	
**Javanese of Pejompongan	Indonesia	Bahasa Jawa	5,000	Islam	-1%	4	
Jebero	Peru	Spanish	3,000	Animism	-1%	1	
*Jeepney Drivers in Manila	Philippines	Pilipino	20,000	Nominal Christian	nr	5	81
	Philippines	Pilipino	20,000	Nominal Christian	nr	5	81
Jemez Pueblo	United States of America	Tewa (Jemez)	1,800	Christo-Paganism	5%	4	
Jeng	Laos	Jeng	500	Animism	0%	4	
Jera	Nigeria	Jera	23,000	Islam	-1%	1	
Jerawa	Nigeria	not reported	70,000	Animism	-1%	4	

NAME	COUNTRY	LANGUAGE	GROUP SIZE	PRIMARY RELIGION	% CHR	V	VOL U.P.
*Jewish Imgrnts.-American	Israel	Hebrew	25,797	Judaism	0%	3	
*Jewish Imgrnts.-Argentine	Israel	Hebrew	17,686	Judaism	0%	3	
*Jewish Imgrnts.-Australia	Israel	Hebrew	1,257	Judaism	0%	3	
*Jewish Imgrnts.-Brazilian	Israel	Hebrew	4,005	Judaism	0%	3	
*Jewish Imgrnts.-Mexican	Israel	Hebrew	1,065	Judaism	0%	3	
*Jewish Imgrnts.-Uruguayan	Israel	Hebrew	2,720	Judaism	0%	3	
*Jewish Immigrants, Other	Israel	Hebrew	5,520	Judaism	0%	3	
Jews in Venice	Italy	Italian	650	Judaism	0%	5	82
Jews of Iran	Iran	Farsi	93,000	Judaism	1%	4	
Jews of Montreal	Canada	English	120,000	Judaism	1%	5	
Jews, Sephardic	Canada	French	26,000	Judaism	1%	3	
Jharia in Orissa	India	Jharia	2,060	Hinduism	-1%	5	
*Jibu	Nigeria	Jibu, Jibanci	20,000	Animism	1%	5	
Jiji	Tanzania	Jiji	3,000	Animism	0%	1	
Jimajima	Papua New Guinea	Jimajima	540	Animism	-1%	1	
Jimbin	Nigeria	Jimbin	1,500	Islam	0%	1	
**Jimini	Ivory Coast	Jimini	42,000	Islam	14%	5	
Jinja	Tanzania	Jinja	66,000	Animism	0%	1	
Jinuos	China	Tibeto-Burman	10,000	Animism	0%	5	81
Jita	Tanzania	Jita	71,000	Animism	0%	1	
**Jivaro (Achuara)	Venezuela	Jivaro	27,000	Christo-Paganism	6%	4	
*Jiye	Sudan	Jiye (Karamojong)	7,000	Animism	0%	5	
Jiye	Uganda	Jiye	34,000	Animism	-1%	4	
Jongor	Chad	Jongor	16,000	Islam-Animist	1%	1	
Juang in Orissa	India	Juang	12,170	Hinduism	-1%	2	
Juhai	Malaysia	Juhai	400	Animism	0%	2	
Jukun	Nigeria	not reported	20,000	Animism	1%	4	
Jyarung	China	Jyarung	70,000	Traditional Chinese	10%	5	
**K'anjobal of San Miguel	Guatemala	K'anjobal	18,000	Ancestor Worship	2%	3	
Ka'mis	Papua New Guinea	Waffa Dialect	50	Christo-Paganism	-1%	1	
Kaagan	Philippines	Kaagan	20,000	Christo-Paganism	0%	1	
Kaalong	Cameroon	Kaalong	50,000	Animism	0%	1	
Kaalong	Cameroon	Kaalong	50,000	Animism	0%	1	
Kaba	Central African Republic	Kaba	11,000	Animism	0%	1	
Kaba Dunjo	Central African Republic	Kaba Dunjo	17,000	Animism	1%	1	
Kabadi	Papua New Guinea	Kabadi	1,500	Animism	-1%	1	
Kabixi	Brazil	Kabixi	100	Animism	-1%	1	
Kabre	Benin	Kabre		Animism	-1%	1	
Kabre	Togo	Kabre	35,000	Animism	0%	1	
Kabyle	Algeria	Kabyle	273,000	Islam	9%	6	79
Kachama	Ethiopia	Kachama	1,000,000	Animism	1%	6	
Kachchi in Andhra Pradesh	India	Kachchi	470,990	Hinduism	-1%	1	
Kachin in Shan State	Burma	Burmese	80,000	Buddhism	-0%	2	

Name	Alternate / Detail	Country	Population	Religion	Index
Kadaklan-Barlig Bontoc	Kadaklan-Barlig Bontoc	Philippines	4,000	Animism	-1% 1
Kadar in Andhra Pradesh	Kadar	India	800	Hindu-Animism	-1% 1
Kadara	Kadara	Nigeria	40,000	Animism	9% 5
Kadazans	Kadazans	Malaysia	110,000	Animism	-1% 2
Kadiweu	Kadiweu	Brazil	550	Animism	-1% 1
Kadugli	Kadugli	Sudan	19,000	Islam	0% 1
Kae Sung Natives in Seoul	Korean	Korea, Republic of	20,000	Buddhism	1% 5 82
Kaeti	Kaeti	Indonesia	4,000	Animism	1% 5
**Kaffa	Kaffenya (Kefa)	Ethiopia	320,000	Christo-Paganism	-1% 1
**Kafirs	Kafiristani (Bashgali)	Pakistan	3,000	Animism	2% 6 80
Kagoma	Kagoma	Nigeria	6,250	Islam	-1% 6 79
Kagoro	Logoro (Bambara)	Mali	30,000	Animism	-1% 1
Kagulu	Kagulu	Tanzania	59,000	Animism	-1% 4
Kahluri in Andamans	Kahluri	India	66,190	Hindu-Animist	0% 1
Kaian	Kaian	Papua New Guinea	230	Animism	-1% 1
Kaibu	Kaibu	Nigeria	650	Islam	0% 1
Kaiep	Kaiep	Papua New Guinea	300	Animism	0% 1
Kaikadi in Maharashtra	Kaikadi	India	11,850	Hindu-Animist	-1% 1
Kaili	Kaili	Indonesia	300,000	Animism	-1% 1
Kaingang	Kaingang	Brazil	7,000	Christo-Paganism	-1% 1
Kairi	Kairi	Papua New Guinea	650	Animism	0% 1
Kairiru	Kairiru	Papua New Guinea	2,800	Animism	-1% 1
Kaiwai	Kaiwai	Indonesia	600	Animism	-1% 1
Kajang	Kajang	Indonesia	50,000	Animism	-1% 1
Kaka	Kaka	Cameroon	2,000	Animism	-0% 1
Kaka	Kaka	Cameroon	2,000	Animism	0% 1
Kaka	Kaka	Central African Republic	37,000	Animism	-1% 1
Kakoa	Kakoa	Nigeria	2,000	Islam	
Kakuna-Mamusi	Kakuna-Mamusi	Papua New Guinea	6,870	Animism	
Kakwa	Kakwa	Papua New Guinea	2,900	Animism	
Kakwa	Kakwa	Sudan	84,000	Islam	
Kakwa	Kakwa	Uganda	573,000	Animism	
**Kalagan	Kalagan	Zaire	19,000	Animism	-0% 1
*Kalanga	ChiKalanga	Botswana	150,000	Animism	0% 1
Kalanga	Kalanga	Zimbabwe	87,000	Animism	1% 5
Kaliko	Kaliko	Zaire	18,000	Animism	2% 5
Kalinga, Kalagua	Kalinga, Kalagua	Philippines	3,600	Animism	-1% 1
Kalinga, Limus-Linan	Kalinga, Limus-Linan	Philippines	20,000	Animism	0% 1
Kalinga, Quinaang	Kalinga, Quinaang	Philippines	21,000	Animism	-1% 1
*Kalinga, Southern	Kalinga, Sumadel-Tinglayan	Philippines	11,000	Animism	-1% 1
**Kalinga, Tanudan	Kalinga	Philippines	5,700	Nominal Christian	4% 5
**Kalinga,Northern	Kalinga	Philippines	20,000	Christo-Paganism	3% 5 81

NAME	COUNTRY	LANGUAGE	GROUP SIZE	PRIMARY RELIGION	% CHR	v	VOL U.P.
Kalmytz	China	Kalmytz	70,000	Traditional Chinese	-1%	1	
	Soviet Russia	Kalmytz	137,000	Buddhism	0%	1	
Kalokalo	Papua New Guinea	Kalokalo	720	Animism	-1%	1	
Kam	China	Kam	825,320	Traditional Chinese	-1%	1	
Kamano	Papua New Guinea	Kam	47,000	Animism	-1%	1	
Kamantan	Nigeria	Kadara	5,000	Animism	-1%	4	
Kamar in Madhya Pradesh	India	Kamar	10,110	Hindu-Animist	-1%	1	
Kamayura	Brazil	Kamayura	110	Animism	-1%	1	
*Kambari	Nigeria	Kambarci	100,000	Animism	6%	6	80
Kambera	Indonesia	Kambera	200,000	Animism	-1%	1	
Kamberataro	Indonesia	Kamberataro	970	Animism	-1%	1	
	Papua New Guinea	Kamberataro	690	Animism	-1%	1	
Kambot	Papua New Guinea	Kambot	4,380	Animism	0%	1	
Kami	Tanzania	Kami	180,000	Animism	-1%	1	
Kamkam	Cameroon	Kamkam	800	Animism	0%	1	
	Cameroon	Kamkam	800	Animism	0%	1	
Kamnum	Papua New Guinea	Kamnum	400	Animism	-1%	1	
Kamo	Nigeria	Kamo	3,000	Islam	-1%	1	
Kamoro	Indonesia	Kamoro	8,000	Animism	-1%	1	
Kampung Baru	Indonesia	Kampung Baru	400	Animism	-1%	1	
Kamtuk-Gresi	Indonesia	Kamtuk-Gresi	5,000	Animism	-1%	1	
*Kamuku	Nigeria	Kamuku	20,000	Animism	3%	6	80
Kana	Nigeria	Kana	90,000	Animism	-1%	1	
Kanauri in Uttar Pradesh	India	Kanauri	28,500	Hindu-Buddhist	-1%	1	
Kandas	Papua New Guinea	Kandas	480	Animism	-1%	1	
Kanembu	Chad	Kanembu	2,250	Islam-Animist	-1%	1	
	Niger	Kanembu	1,500	Islam-Animist	0%	1	
Kanga	Sudan	Kanga	6,400	Islam	-1%	1	
Kanikkaran in Kerala	India	Kanikkaran	10,000	Hindu-Animism	-1%	1	
Kaningra	Papua New Guinea	Kaningra	330	Animism	-1%	1	
Kanite	Papua New Guinea	Kanite	16,000	Animism	-1%	1	
Kanjari in Andhra Pradesh	India	Kanjari	55,390	Hindu-Animist	-1%	1	
**Kankanay, Central	Philippines	Kankanay	40,000	Animism	2%	5	
Kankanay, Northern	Philippines	Northern Kankanay	40,000	Animism	2%	5	
Kanu	Zaire	Kanu	3,500	Animism	0%	1	
Kanum	Papua New Guinea	Kanum	320	Animism	-1%	1	
	Indonesia	Kanum	320	Animism	0%	1	
Kanuri	Nigeria	Kanuri	3,000,600	Islam	1%	6	80
	Nigeria	Kanuri Dialects		Islam	-1%	1	
Kao	Ethiopia	Karo	600	Animism	-1%	1	
Kaonde	Zaire	Kaonde	20,000	Animism	-1%	1	
	Zambia	Kaonde	116,000	Animism	0%	1	
Kapin	Papua New Guinea	Kapin	1,700	Animism	-1%	1	
Kapore	Papua New Guinea	Kapore	600	Animism	0%	1	

Name	Alternate Name	Country	Population	Religion	%
Kapori	Kapori	Indonesia	60	Animism	-1% 1
Kapriman	Kapriman	Papua New Guinea	1,165	Animism	-1% 1
Kapuchin	Kapuchin	Soviet Russia	2,500	Unknown	0% 1
Kara	Kara	Papua New Guinea	2,255	Animism	-1% 1
		Tanzania	32,000	Animism	0% 4
*Karaboro	Karaboro	Upper Volta	40,000	Animism	1% 4
Karachay	Karachay-Balkan	Soviet Russia	173,000	Islam-Animist	0% 5
Karagas	Karagas	Soviet Russia	600	Unknown	0% 1
Karaim	Karaim	Soviet Russia	1,000	Unknown	0% 1
Karakalpak	Karakalpak	Soviet Russia	277,000	Islam	0% 6 80
	Karakalpak		236,000	Unknown	0% 6
Karam	Karam	Papua New Guinea	11,000	Animism	-1% 1
Karanga	Karanga	Chad	57,200	Islam-Animist	-1% 1
Karangi	Karangi	Papua New Guinea	200	Animism	-1% 1
Karas	Karas	Indonesia	200	Animism	-1% 1
Karatin	Karatin	Soviet Russia	6,000	Unknown	-1% 1
**Karbis	Mikir	India	300,000	Hindu-Animist	5% 5
Kare	Kare	Papua New Guinea	340	Animism	-1% 1
Karekare	Karekare	Nigeria	39,000	Islam	1% 1
Karen	Sgaw Karen	Thailand	80,000	Animism	1% 6 79
Karen, Pwo	Pwo Karen	Thailand	40,000	Animism	1% 5
Kari	Kari	Central African Republic	4,000	Animism	0% 1
	Kari	Chad	40,000	Islam-Animist	-1% 1
		Zaire	1,000	Animism	0% 1
Karipuna Creole	Karipuna Creole	Brazil	500	Animism	-1% 1
Karipuna Do Guapore	Karipuna Do Guapore	Brazil	150	Animism	-1% 1
Kariya	Kariya	Nigeria	2,200	Islam	-1% 1
Karkar	Karkar	Papua New Guinea	1,200	Animism	-1% 1
Karko	Karko	Sudan	2,200	Islam	0% 1
Karmali in Dihar	Karmali	India	69,620	Hindu-Animist	-1% 1
Karon Dori	Karon Dori	Indonesia	5,000	Animism	1% 6 79
Karon Pantai	Karon Pantai	Indonesia	2,500	Animism	-1% 1
Karre	Karre	Central African Republic	40,000	Animism	0% 1
Karua	Karua	Papua New Guinea	850	Animism	-1% 1
Kasanga	Kasanga	Guinea-Bissau	420	Islam-Animist	0% 1
Kasele	Kasele	Togo	20,000	Islam-Animist	0% 1
Kasem	Kasem	Upper Volta	28,000	Islam-Animist	0% 1
**Kasena	Kasem	Ghana	70,000	Animism	11% 4
**Kashmiri Muslims	Kashmiri	India	3,060,000	Islam	0% 5
Kasseng	Kasseng	Laos	15,000	Animism	-1% 1
Kasua	Kasua	Papua New Guinea	1,200	Animism	-1% 1
Kasuweri	Kasuweri	Indonesia	1,200	Animism	-1% 1
Katab	Katab	Nigeria	32,370	Islam	-1% 1

NAME	COUNTRY	LANGUAGE	GROUP SIZE	PRIMARY RELIGION	% CHR	V	VOL U.P.
Katakari in Gujarat	India	Katakari	4,950	Hindu-Animist	-1%	1	
Katcha	Sudan	Katcha	6,000	Islam	0%	1	
Kate	Papua New Guinea	Kate	5,600	Animism	-1%	1	
Kati, Northern	Indonesia	Kati, Northern	8,000	Animism	-1%	1	
Kati, Southern	Indonesia	Kati, Southern	4,000	Animism	-1%	1	
Katiati	Papua New Guinea	Katiati	2,300	Animism	-1%	1	
Katla	Sudan	Katla	8,700	Islam	0%	1	
Katukina, Panoan	Brazil	Katukina, Panoan	180	Animism	-1%	1	
Kaugat	Indonesia	Kaugat	1,000	Animism	-1%	1	
Kaugel	Papua New Guinea	Kaugel	35,000	Animism	-1%	1	
**Kaur	Indonesia	Kaur	50,000	Islam-Animist	0%	3	
Kaure	Indonesia	Kaure	800	Animism	-1%	1	
Kavwol	Indonesia	Kavwol	500	Animism	-1%	1	
Kaw	Burma	Kaw	30,000	Animism	0%	2	
Kawar in Madhya Pradesh	India	Kawar	33,770	Hindu-Animist	-1%	1	
Kawe	Indonesia	Kawe	300	Animism	-1%	1	
Kayabi	Brazil	Kayabi	300	Animism	-1%	1	
Kayagar	Indonesia	Kayagar	9,000	Animism	8%	4	
Kayan	Burma	Padaung	18,000	Animism	0%	2	
	Malaysia	Kayan	12,000	Animism	0%	3	
Kayapo	Brazil	Kayapo	600	Animism	0%	4	
Kaygir	Indonesia	Kaygir	4,000	Animism	-1%	1	
Kayupulau	Indonesia	Kayupulau	570	Animism	-1%	1	
Kazakhs	China	Kazakh	700,000	Islam-Animist	0%	6	81
	Iran	Kazakhi	3,000	Islam	0%	5	80
Kebu	Togo	Kebu	20,000	Islam-Animist	-1%	1	
Kebumtamp	Bhutan	Kebumtamp	400,000	Buddhist-Animist	-1%	2	
Kedayanas	Malaysia	Kedayanas	2,890	Animism	-1%	1	
Keer in Madhya Pradesh	India	Keer	30,000	Hindu-Animist	-1%	1	
Kei	Indonesia	Kei	6,000	Animism	-1%	1	
Keiga Jirru	Sudan	Keiga Jirru	1,400	Islam	0%	1	
**KekChi	Guatemala	Kekchi	270,000	Christo-Paganism	3%	4	
Kela	Papua New Guinea	Kela	1,500	Animism	-1%	1	
	Zaire	Kela	100,000	Animism	0%	1	
Kelabit	Malaysia	Kelabit	17,000	Animism	nr	6	81
Kelao	China	Kelao	23,000	Traditional Chinese	-1%	1	
Kele	Gabon	Kele	15,000	Animism	-1%	1	
Kemak	Indonesia	Kemak	50,000	Animism	-1%	1	
Kembata	Ethiopia	Kembata	250,000	Animism	-1%	1	
Kemok	Malaysia	Kemok	400	Animism	0%	2	
Kenati	Papua New Guinea	Kenati	600	Animism	-1%	1	

Name	Alternate	Country	Population	Religion	
Kendari	Kendari	Indonesia	500,000	Islam-Animist	-1% 1
Kenga	Kenga	Chad	25,000	Islam-Animist	-1% 1
Kenyah	Kenyah	Indonesia	37,500	Animism	-1% 1
Keopara	Keopara	Papua New Guinea	16,420	Animism	-1% 1
*Kepas	Kewa	Papua New Guinea	5,000	Animism	-1% 3
Kera	Kera	Cameroon	15,000	Animism	-1% 1
	Kera	Cameroon	15,000	Animism	-1% 1
	Kera	Chad	5,000	Islam-Animist	-1% 4
Kerewe	Kikerewe	Tanzania	35,000	Animism	-1% 1
Kerewo	Kerewo	Papua New Guinea	2,200	Animism	-1% 1
Keriaka	Keriaka	Papua New Guinea	990	Animism	-1% 1
Kerinchi	Kerinchi	Indonesia	170,000	Islam-Animist	-0% 1
Ket	Ket	Soviet Russia	1,200	Unknown	-0% 1
Kewa, East	Kewa, East	Papua New Guinea	20,000	Animism	-1% 1
Kewa, South	Kewa, South	Papua New Guinea	5,000	Animism	-1% 1
Kewa, West	Kewa, West	Papua New Guinea	20,000	Animism	-1% 1
Khakas	Khakas	Soviet Russia	67,000	Unknown	-0% 1
Khalaj	Khalaj	Iran	20,000	Islam	-1% 1
Khalka	Khalka	China	68,000	Traditional Chinese	-1% 1
Kham	Kham	China	11,400	Traditional Chinese	-1% 1
Khamti in Assam	Khamti	India	300	Hindu-Buddhist	-0% 4
*Khamu	Khamu	Thailand	6,300	Animism	-1% 5
Khana	Khana	Nigeria	90,000	Unknown	-1% 5
Khandesi	Khandesi	India	14,700	Hindu-Animist	-0% 1
Khanti	Khanti	Soviet Russia	21,000	Unknown	-0% 1
Kharia in Bihar	Kharia	India	88,900	Hindu-Animist	-1% 1
Khasi in Assam	Khasi	India	384,010	Hinduism	-1% 1
Khasonke	Khasonke	Mali	71,500	Islam	-0% 1
Khinalug	Khinalug	Soviet Russia	1,500	Unknown	-0% 1
Khirwar in Madhya Pradesh	Khirwar	India	34,250	Hindu-Animist	-1% 1
**Khmer Refugees	Cambodia	Thailand	15,000	Buddhist-Animist	-1% 4
Khojas, Agha Khani	Gujarati	India	175,000	Islam	-0% 4
Khowar	Khowar	India	6,960	Hindu-Animist	-0% 1
Khvarshin	Khvarshin	Soviet Russia	1,800	Unknown	-1% 1
Kiari	Kiari	Papua New Guinea	1,180	Animism	-1% 1
Kibet	Kibet	Chad	22,000	Islam-Animist	-1% 1
Kibiri	Kibiri	Papua New Guinea	1,100	Animism	-1% 1
Kichepo	Kichepo	Sudan	16,000	Animism	-0% 3
Kikapoo	Kikapoo	Mexico	5,001	Christo-Paganism	-1% 1
Kilba	Kilba	Nigeria	80,000	Islam	-1% 1
Kilmera	Kilmera	Papua New Guinea	1,880	Animism	-0% 1
Kim	Kim	Central African Republic	5,000	Animism	-1% 1
	Kim	Chad	5,000	Islam-Animist	-1% 1

NAME	COUNTRY	LANGUAGE	GROUP SIZE	PRIMARY RELIGION	% CHR	VOL V	U.P.
Kimaghama	Indonesia	Kimaghama	3,000	Animism	-1%	1	
Kimbu	Tanzania	Kimbu	15,000	Animism	0%	1	
*Kimyal	Indonesia	Kimyal	7,000	Animism	2%	4	
Kinalakna	Papua New Guinea	Kinalakna	220	Animism	-1%	1	
Kinaray-A	Philippines	Kinaray-A	288,000	Christo-Paganism	-1%	1	
Kinga	Tanzania	Kinga	57,000	Animism	0%	1	
Kirghiz	Afghanistan	Kirghiz	45,000	Islam	-1%	1	
Kirgiz	China	Kirgiz	90,000	Islam	0%	5	
Kirgiz	Soviet Russia	Kirgiz	1,700,000	Islam-Animist	0%	6	80
Kirifi	Nigeria	Krifi	14,000	Islam	-1%	1	
Kiriwina	Papua New Guinea	Kiriwina	14,000	Animism	-1%	1	
Kis	Papua New Guinea	Kis	215	Animism	-1%	1	
Kisan in Bihar	India	Kisan	73,850	Hindu-Animist	-1%	1	
Kisankasa	Tanzania	Kisankasa	3,600	Animism	0%	1	
Kishanganjia in Bihar	India	Kishanganjia	56,920	Hindu-Animist	-1%	1	
Kishtwari in Jammu	India	Kishtwari	12,170	Hindu-Animist	-1%	1	
Kisi	Tanzania	Kisi	3,600	Animism	-1%	1	
Kissi	Guinea	Kissi	266,000	Animism	0%	1	
*Kissi	Liberia	Kissi	35,000	Animism	2%	4	
Kissi, Southern	Sierra Leone	Kissi, Southern	48,000	Animism	3%	4	
Kita	Sierra Leone	Kissi, Southern	58,000	Islam-Animist	12%	4	
Kiwai, Northeast	Mali	not reported	150,000	Islam	-1%	1	
Kiwai, Southern	Papua New Guinea	Kiwai, Northeast	3,700	Animism	2%	3	
Kiwai, Wabuda	Papua New Guinea	Kiwai, Southern	9,700	Animism	-1%	1	
Klaoh	Papua New Guinea	Kiwai, Wabuda	1,700	Animism	-1%	1	
Koalib	Liberia	Klaoh	81,000	Islam-Animist	0%	1	
Kobiana	Sudan	Koalib (Nuba)	320,300	Islam-Animist	6%	6	79
Kobon	Guinea	Kobiana		Animism	0%	1	
**Koch	Papua New Guinea	Kobon	6,800	Islam-Animist	6%	6	
Kodi in Bihar	Bangladesh	Bengali	35,400	Hindu-Animist	1%	5	
Kodi	India	Kodi	14,140	Hindu-Animist	1%	5	
Koenoem	Indonesia	Kodi	25,000	Animism	-1%	1	
Kofyar	Nigeria	Koenoem	3,000	Animism	-1%	1	
**Kohli, Kutchi	Nigeria	Kofyar	40,000	Animism	1%	1	
**Kohli, Tharadari	Pakistan	Gujarati, Koli	50,000	Hinduism	4%	4	
**Kohli, Wadiara	Pakistan	Gujarati, Koli	40,000	Hinduism	1%	5	
**Kohlis, Parkari	Pakistan	Gujarati, Koli	40,000	Hindu-Animist	1%	5	
Kohoroxitari	Brazil	Gujarati, Koli	100,000	Hinduism	5%	4	
Kohumono	Nigeria	Kohoroxitari	620	Animism	-1%	1	
Koiari, Grass	Papua New Guinea	Kohumono	11,870	Animism	-1%	1	
Koiari, Mountain	Papua New Guinea	Koiari, Grass	1,800	Animism	-1%	1	
Koita	Papua New Guinea	Koiari, Mountain	1,700	Animism	-1%	1	
		Koita	2,300	Animism	-1%	1	

Kokant	Kokant	Burma	50,000 Buddhist-Animist	0% 2
Koke	Koke	Chad	1,000 Islam-Animist	-1% 1
Kol	Kol	Papua New Guinea	1,900 Animism	-1% 1
Kol in Assam	Kol	India	82,900 Hindu-Animist	-1% 5
*Kolam	Kolami	India	60,000 Hindu-Animist	1% 5
Kolbila	Kolbila	Cameroon	1,000 Islam-Animist	1% 1
Kole	Kole	Cameroon	300 Animism	0% 1
	Kole	Cameroon	300 Animism	0% 1
Koliku	Koliku	Papua New Guinea	300 Animism	-1% 1
Kolom	Kolom	Papua New Guinea	120 Animism	-1% 1
Kom in Manipur	Kom	India	6,970 Hindu-Animist	-1% 1
Koma	Koma	Cameroon	15,000 Animism	0% 1
	Koma	Cameroon	15,000 Animism	0% 1
	Koma	Ghana	1,000 Animism	0% 5
	Koma	Nigeria	15,000 Animism	-1% 1
Koma, Central	Koma, Central	Sudan	3,000 Islam	-0% 1
Komba	Kombio	Papua New Guinea	10,500 Animism	-1% 1
Kombio	Komba	Papua New Guinea	2,150 Animism	0% 3
Komering	Komering	Indonesia	400,000 Islam-Animist	1% 1
Komi-Permyat	Komi-Permyat	Soviet Russia	153,000 Christo-Paganism	-1% 1
Komi-Zyrian	Komi-Zyrian	Soviet Russia	322,000 Christo-Paganism	-1% 1
*Komo	Komo	Ethiopia	20,000 Animism	1% 4
Komono	Komono	Upper Volta	6,000 Islam-Animist	-0% 1
Komutu	Komutu	Papua New Guinea	500 Animism	-1% 1
Konabem	Konabem	Cameroon	3,000 Animism	0% 1
	Konabem	Cameroon	3,000 Animism	0% 1
***Kond	Kui	India	900,000 Animism	3% 5
Konda-Dora in A.P.	Konda-Dora	India	15,650 Hindu-Animist	-1% 1
Koneraw	Koneraw	Indonesia	300 Animism	-1% 1
Kongo	Kongo	Angola	756,000 Unknown	-0% 1
Konkani in Gujarat	Konkani	India	1,522,680 Hindu-Animist	9% 5
Konkomba	Konkomba	India	175,000 Animism	1% 4
*Konkomba	Kom Komba	Togo	25,000 Animism	-1% 5
Kono	Kono	Nigeria	1,550 Islam	1% 1
**Kono	Kono	Sierra Leone	133,000 Animism	5% 5
Konomala	Konomala	Papua New Guinea	600 Animism	-1% 1
Konongo	Konongo	Tanzania	20,000 Animism	-0% 1
Konso	Konso	Ethiopia	30,000 Animism	1% 5
Konyagi	Konyagi	Guinea	85,000 Islam-Animist	0% 1
Koraga in Kerala	Koraga	India	1,500 Hindu-Animist	-0% 1
Korak	Korak	Papua New Guinea	170 Animism	-1% 1
**Koranko	Kuranko (Maninka)	Sierra Leone	103,000 Islam-Animist	-1% 5
Korape	Korape	Papua New Guinea	4,200 Animism	-1% 1

215

NAME	LANGUAGE	COUNTRY	GROUP SIZE	PRIMARY RELIGION	% CHR	V	VOL U.P.
Korapun	Korapun	Indonesia	4,000	Animism	-1%	1	
**Korean Prisoners	Korean	Korea, Republic of	45,000	Secularism	10%	4	
***Koreans in Germany	Korean	German Federal Rep.	10,000	Unknown	4%	4	
*Koreans in Manchuria	Korean	China	3,000,000	Buddhism	nr	5	81
*Koreans of Japan	Korean	Japan	600,000	Folk Religion	6%	5	
*Korku in Madhya Pradesh	Korku	India	250,000	Animism	1%	5	
Koro	Koro	Nigeria	35,000	Animism	1%	5	
Koroma	Koroma	Sudan	30,000	Animism	1%	3	
Korop	Korop	Cameroon	10,000	Animism	0%	1	
	Korop	Cameroon	10,000	Animism	0%	1	
	Korop	Nigeria	10,000	Animism	0%	1	
Korwa in Bihar	Korwa	India	14,250	Hindu-Animist	-1%	1	
Koryak	Koryak	Soviet Russia	7,500	Unknown	0%	1	
Kosorong	Kosorong	Papua New Guinea	1,350	Animism	-1%	1	
Kota	Kota	Gabon	nr	Animism	-1%	1	
Kota in Tamil Nadu	Kota	India	860	Hindu-Animist	-1%	1	
Kotia in Andhra Pradesh	Kotia	India	15,000	Hindu-Animist	-1%	1	
Kotogut	Kotogut	Indonesia	1,000	Animism	-1%	1	
Kotoko	Kotoko	Cameroon	31,000	Animism	0%	1	
	Kotoko	Cameroon	31,000	Animism	-1%	3	
Kotokoli	Kotokoli	Chad	31,000	Islam-Animist	0%	1	
	Kotokoli	Benin	75,000	Islam	0%	4	
Kotopo	Kotopo	Togo	150,000	Islam-Animist	0%	5	
Kotta	Kota	Cameroon	10,000	Animism	-1%	1	
Kouya	Kouya	Ivory Coast	5,690	Islam-Animist	0%	1	
Kovai	Kovai	Papua New Guinea	2,800	Animism	-1%	1	
	Kove	Papua New Guinea	3,000	Animism	0%	1	
**Kowaao	Kowaao	Liberia	7,000	Animism	0%	1	
Koya in Andhra Pradesh	Koya	India	211,880	Hindu-Animist	3%	4	
Koyra	Koyra	Ethiopia	5,000	Animism	-1%	1	
Kpa	Kpa	Cameroon	17,000	Animism	-1%	1	
	Kpa	Cameroon	17,000	Animism	0%	1	
Kpelle	Kpelle	Guinea	250,000	Islam-Animist	0%	1	
	Kpelle	Liberia	200,000	Animism	6%	5	
Kposo	Kposo	Togo	250,000	Islam-Animist	0%	1	
Krachi	Krachi	Ghana	45,000	Animism	0%	1	
*Krahn	Guere	Ivory Coast	21,800	Islam-Animist	0%	1	
***Krahn	Krahn	Liberia	250,000	Animism	3%	4	
Kreen-Akakore	Kreen-Akakore	Brazil	90	Animism	7%	4	
Krim	Mende	Sierra Leone	3,400	Islam-Animist	-1%	1	
Krio	Krio	Gambia	3,000	Islam-Animist	-1%	1	
Krisa	Krisa	Papua New Guinea	485	Animism	0%	1	

Name	Group	Country	Population	Religion	%	
Laamang	Laamang	Nigeria	40,000	Islam	-1%	1
Labans	Labaani	India	nr	Hindu-Buddhist	-0%	3
Labbai	Tamil	India	1,203,340	Hindu-Buddhist	-1%	5
Labhani in Andhra Pradesh	Labhani	India	1,500	Hinduism	10%	4
*Labourers of Jhoparpatti	Marathi	India	800	Animism	-1%	1
Labu	Labu	Papua New Guinea	200	Christo-Paganism	-1%	1
Lacandon	Lacandon	Mexico	56,740	Hindu-Buddhist	-1%	1
Ladakhi in Jammu	Ladakhi	India	7,300	Judaism	-1%	1
Ladinos	Ladinos	Lebanon	1,840	Animism	-1%	1
Laewomba	Laewomba	Papua New Guinea	2,000	Islam	0%	1
Lafofa	Lafofa	Sudan	18,000	Buddhism	-1%	4
**Lahaulis in Punjab	Lahouli	India	40,000	Animism	0%	2
Lahu	Lahu	India	22,500	Animism	7%	81
*Lahu	Lahu	Burma	1,600	Traditional Chinese	7%	5
Lahul	Lahul	Thailand	10,000	Animism	-0%	4
Laka	Laka	China	40,000	Animism	-1%	1
	Laka	Cameroon	40,000	Islam-Animist	-1%	1
	Lakal	Central African Republic	6,000	Traditional Chinese	-1%	1
	Laka	Chad	86,000	Islam	-0%	1
	Lakian	China	500	Islam	-1%	1
Lakians	Lakka	Soviet Russia	125,000	Animism	-0%	1
Lakka	Lala	Nigeria	30,000	Hindu-Buddhist	-0%	1
Lala	Lalia	Zambia	10,650	Buddhist-Animist	-1%	1
Lalung in Assam	Lalung	Zaire	3,000	Animism	-1%	1
Lama	Lamba	India	29,000	Animism	3%	4
Lamba	Lamba	Burma	80,000	Animism	-1%	1
	Lamba	Benin	89,000	Animism	-0%	1
	Lamba	Togo	1,300,000	Animism	nr	81
	Lambadi	Zaire	18,600	Animism	-1%	5
**Lambadi in Andhra Pradesh	Lambi	Zambia	7,000	Animism	-0%	1
Lambi	Lambya	India	2,000	Islam	-1%	1
Lambya	Lambya	Cameroon	1,000	Animism	-1%	1
	Lamogai	Malawi	1,500,000	Islam-Animist	-0%	80
Lame	Komering	Tanzania	4,000	Islam-Animist	0%	5
Lamogai	Landoma	Nigeria	5,000	Islam-Animist	0%	1
Lampung	Landoma	Papua New Guinea	95,000	Animism	0%	1
Landoma	Langi	Indonesia	8,000	Animism	0%	3
	Lango	Guinea	560,000	Animism	-1%	1
Langi	Lango	Guinea-Bissau	400	Animism	0%	3
*Lango	Lanoh	Tanzania	1,908,600	Buddhism	1%	79
Lango	Lao	Ethiopia				
Lanoh		Uganda				
*Lao		Malaysia				
		Laos				

NAME	LANGUAGE	COUNTRY	GROUP SIZE	PRIMARY RELIGION	% CHR	V	VOL. U.P.
Krobou	Aro006u	Ivory Coast	3,400	Islam-Animist	-1%	1	
Krongo	Krongo	Sudan	121,000	Animism	1%	4	
Krumen	Krumen	Ivory Coast	17,000	Animism	2%	4	
Kryz	Kryz	Soviet Russia	6,000	Unknown	0%	1	
Kuatinema	Asurini	Brazil	70	Animism	0%	5	
Kube	Kube	Papua New Guinea	4,000	Animism	-1%	1	
Kubu	Local dialects	Indonesia	25,000	Animism	1%	6	80
	Kubu	Indonesia	6,000	Islam-Animist	1%	6	81
Kuda-Chamo	Kuda-Chamo	Nigeria	4,000	Islam	nr	6	
*Kudisai Vagh Makkal	Tamil	India	1,000,000	Hinduism	-1%	1	
Kudiya	Kudiya	India	100	Hindu-Animism	2%	3	
Kugbo	Kugbo	Nigeria	2,000	Animism	-1%	1	
*Kui	Kui	Thailand	160,000	Buddhist-Animist	-1%	5	
Kuikuro	Kuikuro	Brazil	120	Animism	-1%	1	
Kuka	Kuka	Chad	38,000	Islam-Animist	-1%	1	
Kukele	Kukele	Nigeria	31,700	Animism	-1%	1	
*Kuknas	Kukni	India	125,000	Hindu-Animist	-1%	4	
Kukuwy	Kukuya	Papua New Guinea	1,230	Animism	-1%	1	
Kukwa	Kukwa	Congo	11,000	Animism	0%	1	
Kulango	Kulango	Ivory Coast	60,000	Animism	3%	4	
Kulele	Kulele	Ivory Coast	15,000	Islam-Animist	-1%	1	
Kulere	Kulere	Nigeria	8,000	Animism	-1%	1	
Kullo	Kullo	Ethiopia	82,000	Islam-Animist	-1%	1	
**Kuluis in Himachal Prades	Kului	India	200,000	Hinduism	1%	5	81
Kulung	Kulung	Nigeria	15,000	Islam-Animist	-1%	1	
Kumai	Kumai	Papua New Guinea	3,940	Animism	0%	1	
Kuman	Kumam	Uganda	100,000	Animism	0%	1	
Kuman	Kuman	Papua New Guinea	66,000	Animism	-1%	1	
Kumauni in Assam	Kumdauron	India	1,234,940	Hindu-Animist	-1%	1	
Kumdauron	Kumdauron	Papua New Guinea	400	Animism	-1%	1	
Kumu	Kumu	Zaire	60,000	Animism	-1%	1	
Kumukio	Kumukio	Papua New Guinea	300	Animism	-1%	1	
Kunama	Kunama	Ethiopia	70,000	Islam	-1%	1	
Kunante	Kunante	Guinea-Bissau	6,000	Islam-Animist	-1%	1	
Kunda	Kunda	Mozambique	60,000	Animism	0%	1	
	Kunda	Zambia	21,000	Animism	0%	1	
	Kunda	Zambia	8,000	Animism	0%	1	
	Kunda	Zimbabwe	40,000	Animism	0%	1	
Kuni	Kuni	Papua New Guinea	2,400	Animism	-1%	1	
**Kunimaipa	Kunimaipa	Papua New Guinea	9,000	Christo-Paganism	6%	5	
Kunua	Kunua	Papua New Guinea	1,340	Animism	-1%	1	
Kuot	Kuot	Papua New Guinea	900	Animism	-1%	1	
Kupia in Andhra Pradesh	Kupia	India	4,000	Hindu-Animist	-1%	1	

People	Country	Language	Population	Religion	%		
Kupsabiny	Uganda	Kupsabiny	60,000	Animism	0%	1	
Kurada	Papua New Guinea	Kurada	935	Animism	-1%	1	
Kurds in Iran	Iran	Kurdish Dialects	2,000,000	Islam	1%	6	80
Kurds in Kuwait	Kuwait	Kurdish	1,145,000	Islam	0%	3	
*Kurds of Turkey	Turkey	Kurdish (Kirmancho)	1,900,000	Islam	-1%	6	79
Kurfei	Niger	Hausa	50,000	Animism	-1%	4	
Kuria	Tanzania	Kuria	75,000	Animism	-1%	5	81
Kurichiya in Kerala	India	Kurichiya	12,130	Hindu-Animist	-1%	1	
Kuruba in Tamil Nadu	India	Kuruba	7,900	Hindu-Animist	-1%	1	
Kurudu	Indonesia	Kurudu	7,100	Animism	-1%	1	
Kurumba	Upper Volta	Kurumba	86,000	Islam-Animist	-1%	1	
Kurux in Bihar	India	Kurux	1,240,400	Hindu-Animist	-1%	1	
**Kusaasi	Ghana	Kusaal	150,000	Animism	3%	5	
Kushi	Nigeria	Kushi	4,000	Islam	-1%	1	
Kusu	Zaire	Kusu	26,000	Animism	-0%	1	
Kuteb	Nigeria	Kuteb	26,400	Islam	-1%	1	
Kutin	Cameroon	Kutin	17,000	Animism	-0%	1	
Kutu	Tanzania	Kutu	2,950	Animism	-0%	1	
Kuturmi	Nigeria	Kuturmi		Islam	-1%	1	
Kuvi in Orissa	India	Kuvi	190,000	Hindu-Animist	-1%	1	
Kuwaa	Liberia	Kuwaa	5,500	Islam-Animist	-1%	1	
Kuzamani	Nigeria	Kuzamani	1,000	Islam	-1%	1	
Kvanadin	Soviet Russia	Kvanadin	5,500	Unknown	-1%	1	
Kwa	Nigeria	Kwa	1,000	Islam	-1%	1	
Kwadi	Angola	Kwadi	15,000	Animism	0%	1	
Kwakum	Cameroon	Kwakum	3,000	Animism	-1%	1	
Kwale	Papua New Guinea	Kwale	720	Animism	-1%	1	
Kwambi	Namibia	Kwambi	30,000	Animism	-1%	1	
Kwanga	Papua New Guinea	Kwanga	5,110	Animism	-1%	1	
Kwangali	Angola	Kwangali	25,000	Animism	-1%	1	
Kwansu	Indonesia	Kwansu	350	Animism	-0%	1	
Kwanyama	Angola	Kwanyama	100,000	Animism	-1%	1	
Kwanyama	Namibia	Kwanyama	150,000	Animism	0%	1	
Kwaya	Tanzania	Kwaya	35,000	Animism	-0%	1	
Kwe-etshori	Botswana	Kwe-etshori	3,000	Animism	-1%	1	
Kwe-Etshori	Zimbabwe	Kwe-Etshori	1,800	Animism	-0%	1	
Kwerba	Indonesia	Kwerba	2,000	Animism	10%	5	
Kwere	Tanzania	Kwere	63,000	Animism	-1%	1	
Kwese	Zaire	Kwese	60,000	Animism	-1%	1	
Kwesten	Indonesia	Kwesten	2,480	Animism	-0%	1	
Kwoma	Papua New Guinea	Kwoma	2,235	Animism	-1%	1	
Kwomtari	Papua New Guinea	Kwomtari	780	Animism	-1%	1	
Kyibaku	Nigeria	Kyibaku	20,000	Islam	-1%	1	

NAME	COUNTRY	LANGUAGE	GROUP SIZE	PRIMARY RELIGION	% CHR	V	VOL U.P.
*Lao Refugees	Thailand	Lao	20,000	Buddhist-Animist	-1%	4	
Lara	Indonesia	Lara	12,000	Animism	-1%	1	
Laro	Sudan	Laro	3,000	Islam	0%	1	
Laru	Nigeria	Laru	1,000	Islam	-1%	1	
Latdwalam	Indonesia	Latdwalam	860	Animism	-1%	1	
Lati	China	Lati	450	Traditional Chinese	-1%	1	
Laudje	Indonesia	Laudje	125,000	Animism	-1%	1	
Lavatbura-Lamusong	Papua New Guinea	Lavatbura-Lamusong	1,300	Animism	-1%	1	
Lavongai	Papua New Guinea	Lavongai	9,365	Animism	-1%	1	
Lawa, Eastern	Thailand	Lawa	2,500	Buddhist-Animist	-1%	5	81
Lawa, Mountain	Thailand	Tibeto-Burman Dialect	10,000	Buddhist-Animist	4%	5	
Lebgo	Nigeria	Lebgo	30,000	Animism	-1%	5	
Lebong	Indonesia	Redjang-Lebong	nr	Islam	0%	5	
Leco	Bolivia	Leco	200	Animism	-1%	1	
Lega	Zaire	Lega	150,000	Animism	-1%	1	
Lele	Upper Volta	Lele	30,000	Islam-Animist	-1%	1	
	Chad	Lele	61,000	Islam-Animist	-1%	1	
Lelemi	Ghana	Lelemi	26,000	Animism	-1%	1	
Lendu	Zaire	Lendu	14,900	Islam-Animist	0%	1	
Lengua, Northern	Paraguay	Lengua, Northern	250,000	Animism	0%	1	
Lenje	Zambia	Lenje	95,000	Animism	-1%	1	
**Lepcha	Sikkim	Lepcha	79,000	Animism	0%	1	
**Lepers of Cen. Thailand	Thailand	Thai	18,000	Hindu-Buddhist	10%	4	
**Lepers of N.E. Thailand	Thailand	Northeast Thai	28,000	Buddhist-Animist	1%	6	81
Leron	Papua New Guinea	Leron	390,000	Buddhism	1%	4	
Lese	Zaire	Lese	500	Animism	-1%	1	
Letti	Indonesia	Letti	20,000	Animism	0%	1	
Li	China	Li	6,000	Traditional Chinese	-1%	1	
Libyans	Libya	Arabic	1,000,000	Islam	-1%	1	
Ligbi	Ghana	Ligbi	2,300,000	Islam	0%	3	
	Ivory Coast	Ligbi	6,000	Islam	0%	5	
Liguri	Sudan	Liguri	20,000	Islam-Animist	-1%	4	
Lihir	Papua New Guinea	Lihir	2,000	Animism	0%	1	
Liko	Zaire	Liko	4,790	Animism	0%	1	
Lima	Zambia	Lima	26,000	Animism	0%	1	
Limba	Sierra Leone	Limba	12,000	Animism	4%	4	
Lionese	Indonesia	Lio	233,000	Christo-Paganism	4%	4	
*Lisu	China	Tibeto-Burman	470,000	Animism	-1%	5	81
Lisu	Thailand	Lisu	12,500	Animism	0%	4	
Liv	Soviet Russia	Liv	1,500	Unknown	6%	1	
Lo	Nigeria	Lo	2,000	Animism	-1%	1	
Lobi	Ivory Coast	Lobi	40,000	Animism	1%	4	

		Country	Population	Religion	%		
Lodhi in Bihar	Lodhi	India	44,070	Hindu-Animist	-1%	1	
Logba	Logba	Ghana	3,200	Islam-Animist	0%	1	
Logo	Logo	Zaire	54,000	Animism	1%	4	
Lohar	Gujarati Dialect	Pakistan	nr	Hinduism	0%	1	
Lohiki	Lohiki	Papua New Guinea	850	Animism	0%	3	
**Loho Loho	Kolaka	Indonesia	10,000	Animism	nr	5	81
Loinang	Loinang	Indonesia	100,000	Animism	1%	4	
Loko	Loko	Guinea	16,000	Islam-Animist	1%	4	
	Loko	Sierra Leone	80,000	Animism	1%	4	
	Loko	Sierra Leone	60,700	Islam-Animist	-1%	1	
*Lokoro	Lokoro	Sudan	22,000	Christo-Paganism	5%	4	
Lolo	Yi	China	4,800,000	Animism	0%	5	81
Loma	Loma	Guinea	4,180,000	Animism	0%	5	
	Loma	Liberia	60,000	Animism	3%	4	
Lombi	Lombi	Zaire	8,100	Animism	12%	4	
Lombo	Lombo	Zaire	10,000	Animism	0%	1	
Lomwe	not reported	Mozambique	1,000,000	Animism	9%	4	
Longuda	Longuda	Nigeria	32,000	Islam	-1%	1	
Lore	Lore	Indonesia	140,000	Animism	-1%	1	
Lori	Lori	Sudan	1,000	Islam	0%	1	
Lors	Luri	Iran	600,000	Islam	0%	5	80
Lotsu-Piri	Lotsu-Piri	Nigeria	2,000	Islam	-1%	1	
**Lotuka	Latuka	Sudan	150,000	Other	-1%	5	
Lou-Baluan-Pam	Lou-Baluan-Pam	Papua New Guinea	1,280	Animism	6%	5	
Loven	Loven	Laos	25,000	Buddhist-Animist	-1%	1	
Lozi	Lozi	Zambia	215,000	Animism	1%	5	81
	Lozi	Zimbabwe	8,100	Animism	0%	1	
Lu	Lu	China	400,000	Buddhist-Animist	0%	1	
Luac	Luac	Sudan	700	Islam	-1%	1	
Luano	Luano	Zambia	4,000	Animism	0%	1	
Lubang Islanders	Pilipino	Philippines	18,000	Christo-Paganism	0%	5	81
Lubu	Lubu	Indonesia	1,000,000	Islam	-1%	1	
Luchazi	Luchazi	Angola	60,000	Animism	-1%	1	
	Luchazi	Zambia	34,000	Animism	-1%	1	
Lue	Lue	Cameroon	4,000	Animism	12%	5	
Lugbara	Lugbara	Uganda	260,000	Unknown	1%	1	
	Lugbara	Zaire	350,000	Animism	0%	1	
Lugitama	Lugitama	Papua New Guinea	520	Animism	-1%	1	
Luimbi	Luimbi	Angola	20,000	Animism	0%	1	
Lukep	Lukep	Papua New Guinea	600	Animism	-1%	1	
Lumbu	Lumbu	Gabon	12,000	Animism	-1%	1	
Luna	Luna	Zaire	50,000	Animism	-1%	1	
Lunda	Lunda	Angola	50,000	Animism	-1%	1	

NAME	COUNTRY	LANGUAGE	GROUP SIZE	PRIMARY RELIGION	% CHR	V	VOL U.P.
Lunda, Ndembu	Zambia	Lunda, Ndembu	102,000	not reported	nr		1
Lundu	Cameroon	Lundu	24,000	Animism	0%		1
Lungu	Nigeria	Lungu	10,000	Animism	-1%		4
Luo	Tanzania	Luo	1,522,000	Animism	-1%		1
Lushai in Assam	India	Lushai	270,310	Hindu-Animist	-1%		1
Luwu	Indonesia	Luwu	500,000	Islam	-1%		1
Luyana	Angola	Luyana	3,500	Animism	0%		1
Lwalu	Zambia	Luyana	50,000	Animism	0%		1
Lwena	Zaire	Lwalu	21,000	Animism	0%		1
Lwo	Angola	Lwena	90,000	Animism	-1%		1
Ma	Sudan	Lwo	20,000	Islam	0%		1
Maanyan	Zaire	Ma	4,700	Animism	0%		1
**Maasai	Indonesia	Maanyan	15,000	Animism	-1%		1
Maba	Kenya	Masai	100,000	Animism	5%	6	79
Maban-Jumjum	Chad	Maba	56,000	Islam-Animist	-1%		1
Maca	Sudan	Maban-Jumjum	9,000	Islam	0%		1
Machiguenga	Sudan	Maca	20,000	Islam	-1%		1
Macu	Paraguay	Machiguenga	600	Animism	-1%		1
Macuna	Peru	Macu	10,000	Animism	-1%		3
**Macuxi	Colombia	Macuna	1,000	Animism	-1%		1
Madak	Colombia	Macuxi	1,300	Animism	5%	5	3
Madda	Brazil	Madak	6,000	Animism	0%		1
Madi	Papua New Guinea	Madda	2,690	Animism	-1%		1
Madik	Nigeria	Madi	30,000	Animism	0%		1
Madurese	Sudan	Madik	6,000	Islam	-1%		1
**Magar	Uganda	Madurese	114,000	Animism	-1%		1
Maghi	Indonesia	Magar	1,000	Animism	-1%	6	79
Magori	Nepal	Maghi	7,000,000	Islam	-1%		1
Maguindano	Burma	Magori	300,000	Hindu-Animist	-1%		1
***Maguzawa	Papua New Guinea	Maguindano	309,200	Buddhist-Animist	1%	6	80
Mahali in Assam	Philippines	Hausa	700,000	Islam	1%	6	79
*Mahrah	Nigeria	Mahali	100,000	Islam	-1%		1
Mahri	India	Local dialects	14,300	Hindu-Animist	0%		3
Mai	Yemen, Democratic	Mahri	50,000	Islam	0%		1
Mailu	Oman	Mai	50,000	Animism	-1%		1
Maiongong	Papua New Guinea	Mailu	210	Animism	1%		1
Mairasi	Papua New Guinea	Maiongong	4,700	Animism	-1%		3
Maisan	Brazil	Mairasi	86	Animism	-1%		1
Maithili	Indonesia	Maisan	1,000	Animism	-1%		1
Maiwa	Papua New Guinea	Maithili	1,800	Hindu-Animist	0%		4
	Nepal	Maithili	1,000,000	Hindu-Animist	0%		4
	Papua New Guinea	Maiwa	1,300	Animism	-1%		1

Majhwar in Madhya Pradesh	India	Majhwar	27,960	Hindu-Animist	-1%	1	
Maji	Ethiopia	Maji	15,000	Animism	-1%	4	
Majingai-ngama	Central African Republic	Majingai-ngama	47,000	Animism	-1%	1	
Majingai-Ngama	Chad	Majingai-Ngama	47,000	Islam-Animist	-1%	1	
Maka	Cameroon	Maka	51,000	Animism	0%	1	
Makarim	Papua New Guinea	Makarim	1,500	Animism	0%	1	
Makasai	Indonesia	Makasai	70,000	Animism	-1%	1	
Makere	Uganda	Makere	17,500	Animism	0%	1	
Makian, West	Indonesia	Makian, West	12,000	Animism	-1%	1	
Maklew	Indonesia	Maklew	120	Animism	-1%	1	
Makonde	Tanzania	not reported	550,000	Islam	6%	5	
Makua	Mozambique	Makua	1,200,000	Animism	10%	4	
Malakkaras of Kerela	India	Malamutha	1,000	Hindu-Animist	0%	5	81
Malalamai	Papua New Guinea	Malalamai	340	Animism	-1%	1	
Malankuravan in Kerala	India	Malankuravan	5,000	Hindu-Animist	-1%	1	
Malapandaram in Kerala	India	Malapandaram	500	Hindu-Animist	-1%	1	
Malappanackers	India	Malappanackan	1,000	Animism	0%	4	
Malaryan in Kerala	India	Malaryan	5,000	Hindu-Animist	-1%	1	
Malas	Papua New Guinea	Malas	190	Animism	-1%	1	
Malasanga	Papua New Guinea	Malasanga	400	Animism	-1%	1	
Malavedan in Kerala	India	Malavedan	2,000	Hinduism	-1%	1	
*Malayalars	India	Malayalam	nr	Animism	0%	4	
Malayo	Colombia	Malayo	1,000	Animism	6%	4	
Malays of Singapore	Singapore	Malay	300,000	Islam	1%	6	79
Male	Ethiopia	Male	12,000	Animism	-1%	1	
Malek	Papua New Guinea	Malek	1,200	Animism	0%	1	
Maleu	Papua New Guinea	Maleu	4,000	Animism	-1%	1	
Mali in Andhra Pradesh	India	Mali	970	Hindu-Animist	-1%	1	
Malila	Tanzania	Malila	175,000	Animism	0%	1	
Malki in Bihar	India	Malki	88,650	Hindu-Animist	-1%	1	
Malon	Papua New Guinea	Malon	3,330	Animism	0%	1	
Malpaharia in Assam	India	Malpaharia	9,080	Hindu-Animist	-1%	1	
Malvi in Madhya Pradesh	India	Malvi	644,030	Hindu-Animist	-1%	1	
**Mam Indian	Guatemala	Mam	470,000	Christo-Paganism	7%	5	
Mama	Nigeria	Mama	20,000	Animism	-1%	1	
Mamaa	Papua New Guinea	Mamaa	200	Animism	-1%	1	
**Mamanua	Philippines	Minamanwa	1,000	Christo-Paganism	3%	6	81
Mamasani	Iran	Luri	110,000	Islam	0%	4	
Mambai	Indonesia	Mambai	80,000	Animism	-1%	1	
Mambila	Cameroon	Mambila	40,000	Animism	-1%	4	
Mambwe-Lungu	Tanzania	Mambwe-Lungu	16,000	Animism	0%	1	
	Zambia	Mambwe-Lungu	121,000	Animism	-1%	1	
Mamprusi	Ghana	not reported	80,000	Animism	-1%	4	

NAME	COUNTRY	LANGUAGE	GROUP SIZE	PRIMARY RELIGION	% CHR	V	VOL U.P.
Mamvu-Efe	Ghana	Mampruli	90,600	Islam-Animist	-1%	1	
Mancang	Zaire	Mamvu-Efe	40,000	Animism	0%	1	
Manchu	Senegal	Mankang	35,200	not reported	nr	3	
Manda	China	Manchu	200,000	Traditional Chinese	-1%	5	81
Mandar	Tanzania	Manda	10,000	Animism	0%	1	
Mandara	Indonesia	Mandar	302,000	Islam	0%	1	
Mandaya	Nigeria	Mandara	19,300	Islam	-1%	1	
Mandaya, Mansaka	Philippines	Mandaya	3,000	Animism	-1%	1	
Mander	Philippines	Mandaya, Mansaka	35,400	Animism	-1%	1	
Manding	Indonesia	Mander	100	Animism	-1%	1	
Mandingo	Senegal	Malinke, Senegalese	208,400	not reported	nr	3	
Mandyak	Liberia	Mandingo	30,000	Islam	1%	6	79
Manem	Gambia	Mandyak	85,300	Islam-Animist	-1%	1	
Mangbai	Indonesia	Manem	400	Animism	-1%	1	
Mangbutu	Chad	Mangbai	2,000	Islam-Animist	-1%	1	
Manggarai Muslims	Indonesia	Mangbutu	8,000	Animism	0%	1	
Mangisa	Cameroon	Manggarai	25,000	Islam	0%	5	81
Mangs in Maharashtra	India	Mangisa	14,000	Animism	0%	1	
*Mangyan	Philippines	Marathi	nr	Hinduism	0%	3	
*Manikion	Indonesia	Various Dialects	60,000	Animism	-1%	5	
Maninka	Guinea-Bissau	Sough	8,000	Animism	6%	5	
	Sierra Leone	Maninka	65,000	Islam-Animist	0%	5	
Manjack	Senegal	Maninka	64,200	Islam-Animist	0%	1	
*Manjaco	Guinea-Bissau	Mandyako	44,200	not reported	nr	3	
Mankanya	Guinea-Bissau	Mandyale	80,000	Animism	7%	8	
	Senegal	Mankanya	35,000	Islam-Animist	0%	1	
Manna-Dora in A.P.	India	Manna-Dora	8,480	Hindu-Animist	0%	1	
Mannan in Kerala	India	Mannan	4,980	Hindu-Animist	-1%	1	
Mano	Liberia	Mano	65,000	Animism	4%	4	
Manobo, Agusan	Philippines	Manobo, Agusan	15,000	Animism	-1%	1	
Manobo, Ata	Philippines	Manobo, Ata	7,000	Animism	-1%	1	
Manobo, Binokid	Philippines	Manobo, Binokid	40,550	Animism	-1%	1	
*Manobo, Cotabato	Philippines	Cotabato Manobo	10,000	Animism	1%	4	
Manobo, Dibabawon	Philippines	Manobo, Dibabawon	1,790	Animism	-1%	1	
*Manobo, Ilianen	Philippines	Ilianen Manobo	5,000	Animism	3%	5	
Manobo, Obo	Philippines	Manobo, Obo	4,000	Animism	-1%	1	
*Manobo, Salug	Philippines	Manobo, Tigwa	4,000	Animism	4%	5	
Manobo, Sarangani	Philippines	Manobo, Sarangani	15,000	Animism	4%	5	
Manobo, Tagabawa	Philippines	Manobo, Tagabawa	9,900	Animism	-1%	1	
*Manobo, Tigwa	Philippines	Manobo, Tigwa	4,000	Animism	1%	1	
*Manobo, Western Bukidnon	Philippines	Manobo, Binokid	12,000	Animism	3%	5	
Manobos, Pulangi	Philippines	Manobo, Pulangi	5,000	Animism	1%	4	

*Mansaka	Philippines	25,000	Christo-Paganism	10% 5
Mansi	Soviet Russia	7,700	Unknown	0% 2
Mantera	Malaysia	4,000	Animism	0% 1
Mantion	Indonesia	12,000	Animism	-1% 1
Manu Park Panoan	Peru	200	Animism	-1% 1
Manyika	Zimbabwe	350,000	Animism	-1% 1
Mao, Northern	Ethiopia	13,000	Animism	-1% 1
Maou	Ivory Coast	80,000	Islam-Animist	-1% 1
Mapoyo	Venezuela	200	Animism	0% 1
Mappillas	India	4,500,000	Islam	-1% 5
Mapuche	Chile	300,000	Christo-Paganism	1% 5
Maquiritari	Venezuela	5,000	Animism	-1% 1
Mara in Assam	India	11,870	Hindu-Animist	-1% 1
Maranao	Philippines	500,000	Islam	2% 6
Maranao, Lanad	Philippines	500,000	Islam-Animist	-1% 1
Mararit	Chad	42,000	Islam-Animist	-1% 1
Marau	Indonesia	1,000	Animism	-1% 1
Marba	Chad	30,000	Islam-Animist	-1% 1
Marghi Central	Nigeria	135,000	Islam	-1% 1
Mari	Soviet Russia	599,000	Christo-Paganism	-1% 1
Maria in Andhra Pradesh	India	78,500	Hindu-Animist	-1% 1
Marind	Indonesia	7,000	Animism	-1% 1
Marind, Bian	Indonesia	900	Animism	-0% 1
Marka	Upper Volta	39,000	Islam	0% 1
Marubo	Brazil	400	Animism	-1% 1
Marwari in Gujarat	India	6,807,650	Hindu-Animist	6% 4
Masa	Chad	80,000	Animism	-1% 1
Masaba	Uganda	110,000	Animism	0% 1
Masakin	Sudan	16,000	Islam	-0% 1
Masalit	Chad	73,500	Islam-Animist	-0% 1
	Sudan	27,000	Islam	0% 1
	Arabic			
Majangiir	Ethiopia	7,000	Animism	1% 5
*Masengo	Indonesia	250,000	Islam	-1% 1
Masenrempulu	Zambia	21,000	Animism	0% 1
Mashi	Chad	23,000	Islam-Animist	-1% 1
Massalat	Argentina	10,000	Animism	-1% 1
Mataco	Cameroon	140,000	Animism	2% 4
Matakam	Nigeria	2,000	Islam	-1% 1
Matakam	Surinam	1,000	Animism	0% 1
Matawari	Indonesia	550	Animism	-1% 1
Matbat	Tanzania	58,000	Animism	0% 5
Matengo	India	200,000	Hinduism	2% 5
***Matharis	Brazil	100	Animism	-1% 1
Matipuhy-Nahukua				

79

225

NAME	COUNTRY	LANGUAGE	GROUP SIZE	PRIMARY RELIGION	% CHR	V	VOL U.P.
Matlatzinca, Atzingo	Mexico	Matlatzinca, Atzingo	1,700	Christo-Paganism	0%	4	
Matumbi	Tanzania	Matumbi	72,000	Islam	8%	4	
Maure	Mali	Maure	58,000	Islam-Animist	0%	3	
Maures	Senegal	Arabic	57,000	Islam	0%	4	
Mauri	Niger	Hausa	100,000	Animism	1%	4	
Maviha	Mozambique	Maviha	70,000	Animism	0%	5	
**Mawchi	India	Mawchi	300,000	Hindu-Animist	3%	1	
Mawes	Indonesia	Mawes	690	Animism	1%	1	
Maxakali	Brazil	Maxakali	400	Animism	0%	1	
Mayo	Mexico	Mayo	30,000	Christo-Paganism	1%	1	
Mayoruna	Peru	Mayoruna	1,000	Animism	1%	4	
**Mazahua	Mexico	Mazahua	150,000	Christo-Paganism	6%	4	
Mazandaranis	Iran	Mazandarani	1,620,000	Islam	0%	4	
Mba	Zaire	Mba	12,000	Animism	0%	1	
Mbaama	Gabon	Mbaama	73,000	Animism	1%	1	
Mbai	Central African Republic	Mbai	200,000	Islam-Animist	0%	1	
Mbala	Zaire	Mbala	2,000	Animism	0%	1	
Mbangwe	Zaire	Mbangwe	81,000	Animism	0%	1	
Mbanja	Central African Republic	Mbanja	15,000	Animism	0%	1	
Mbati	Nigeria	Mbati	14,300	Animism	1%	1	
Mbe	Gabon	Mbe	45,000	Animism	0%	1	
Mbede	Cameroon	Mbede	25,000	Animism	0%	1	
Mbembe	Nigeria	Mbembe	2,900	Animism	1%	1	
Mbembe (Tigong)	Cameroon	Mbembe	nr	Animism	0%	1	
Mbimu	Cameroon	Mbimu	22,500	Animism	0%	1	
Mbo	Zaire	Mbo	2,000	Animism	1%	1	
Mboi	Nigeria	Mboi	3,200	Islam	1%	1	
Mbole	Zaire	Mbole	100,000	Animism	0%	1	
Mbugwe	Tanzania	Mbugwe	8,000	Animism	0%	4	
Mbukushu	Angola	Kusso	6,900	Animism	6%	1	
Mbula-Bwazza	Nigeria	Mbula-Bwazza	7,900	Islam	1%	1	
Mbum	Chad	Mbum	20,000	Islam-Animist	1%	1	
Mbunda	Angola	Mbunda	59,000	Animism	0%	1	
Mbunga	Tanzania	Mbunga	10,000	Animism	1%	1	
Mbwela	Angola	Mbwela	100,000	Animism	0%	1	
Me'en	Ethiopia	Me'en	38,000	Animism	1%	1	
Meax	Indonesia	Meax	10,000	Animism	1%	4	
Meban	Sudan	Maban-Jumjum	130,000	Animism	1%	4	
**Meghwar	Pakistan	Marwari	100,000	Hinduism	1%	6	79
**Meitei	India	Manipuri	700,000	Hinduism	1%	6	79
**Mejah	India	Mejah	5,500	Animism	1%	4	

Name	Country	Group / Language	Religion	Population	% Xn	C	Yr
Meje	Uganda	Meje	Animism	13,200	0%	1	
Mekwei	Indonesia	Mekwei	Animism	1,200	-1%	1	
*Melanau of Sarawak	Malaysia	Melanau	Islam-Animist	61,000	1%	6	80
Mende	Liberia	Mende	Animism	5,000	13%	5	
Mende	Sierra Leone	Mende	Animism	600,000	-1%	1	
Menemo-Mogamo	Cameroon	Menemo-Mogamo	Animism	35,000	0%	2	
Menka	Cameroon	Menka	Animism	10,000	0%	5	
Menri	Malaysia	Menri	Animism	400	9%	5	
**Meo	Thailand	Meo	Animism	29,173	0%	5	80
Meos of Rajasthan	India	Rajasthani	Islam	500,000	-1%	1	
Mesengo	Ethiopia	Mesengo	Islam-Animist	28,000	-1%	1	
Mesme	Chad	Mesme	Islam-Animist	28,000	-1%	1	
Mesmedje	Chad	Mesmedje	Islam-Animist	11,000	-1%	1	
***Mestizos in La Paz	Bolivia	Spanish	Christo-Paganism	400,000	4%	5	82
Miao	China	Miao	Animism	2,800,000	-1%	4	
**Middle Class-Mexico City	Mexico	Spanish	Nominal Christian	nr	nr	5	82
Miching	India	Miching	Islam	259,551	0%	4	
Midob	Sudan	Midob	Islam	1,800	-1%	6	81
Mien	China	Mien	Animism	740,000	-1%	1	
Migili	Nigeria	Migili	Animism	10,000	15%	3	
**Military Personnel	Ecuador	Spanish	Nominal Christian	80,000	-1%	1	
Mimi	Chad	Mimi	Islam-Animist	15,000	3%	5	
*Mimika	Indonesia	Mimika	Christo-Paganism	10,000	-1%	6	80
Mina in Madhya Pradesh	India	Mina	Hindu-Animist	764,850	0%	6	
Minangkabau	Indonesia	Minangkabau	Islam	5,000,000	0%	1	
Minduumo	Gabon	Minduumo	Animism	4,000	-1%	4	
Mingat	Soviet Russia	Mingat	Unknown	4,000	0%	4	
Minianka	Mali	Suppire	Animism	300,000	-1%	1	
Mirdha in Orissa	India	Mirdha	Hindu-Animist	5,820	-1%	4	
Miri	Sudan	Miri	Islam	8,000	-1%	1	
Mirung	Bangladesh	Mirung	Animism	12,000	1%	1	
Mishmi in Assam	India	Mishmi	Hindu-Animist	5,230	-1%	1	
Miskito	Nicaragua	Miskito	Christo-Paganism	20,000	-1%	1	
**Mixes	Mexico	Mixe	Christo-Paganism	60,000	2%	5	
Mixteco, Amoltepec	Mexico	Mixteco, Amoltepec	Christo-Paganism	6,000	0%	1	
Mixteco, Apoala	Mexico	Mixteco, Apoala	Christo-Paganism	6,000	-1%	1	
Mixteco, Central Puebla	Mexico	Spanish	Christo-Paganism	3,000	-0%	1	
Mixteco, Eastern	Mexico	Mixteco, Eastern	Christo-Paganism	15,000	-1%	1	
Mixteco, Eastern Putla	Mexico	Mixteco, Eastern Putla	Christo-Paganism	7,000	0%	1	
Mixteco, Huajuapan	Mexico	Mixteco, Huajuapan	Christo-Paganism	3,000	0%	1	
Mixteco, Silacayoapan	Mexico	Mixteco, Silacayoapan	Christo-Paganism	15,000	-1%	1	
Mixteco, Southern Puebla	Mexico	Mixteco, Southern Puebla	Christo-Paganism	12,000	-1%	1	
Mixteco, Southern Putla	Mexico	Mixteco, Southern Putla	Christo-Paganism	2,500	0%	1	

NAME	COUNTRY	LANGUAGE	GROUP SIZE	PRIMARY RELIGION	% CHR	V	VOL U.P.
Mixteco, Tututepec	Mexico	Mixteco, Tututepec	2,000	Christo-Paganism	0%	1	
Mixteco, Yosondua	Mexico	Mixteco, Yosondua	15,000	Christo-Paganism	-1%	1	
*Mixteco,San Juan Mixtepic	Mexico	Mixteco	15,000	Christo-Paganism	-1%	1	
Miya	Nigeria	Miya	5,200	Animism	-1%	5	
Mo	Ghana	Mo (Degha)	13,000	Animism	-1%	5	
	Ivory Coast	Mo	800	Islam-Animist	-1%	4	
Moba	Ghana	Bimoba	80,000	Animism	-8%	4	
	Togo	Bimoba	70,000	Animism	-1%	4	
Mober	Nigeria	Mober	44,800	Islam	4%	4	
***Mocha	Ethiopia	Mocha	170,000	Islam	4%	4	
Modo	Sudan	Modo	1,700	Islam	0%	1	
Mofu	Cameroon	Mofu	33,000	Animism	-1%	1	
Mogholi	Afghanistan	Mogholi	2,000	Islam-Animist	-1%	1	
Mogum	Chad	Mogum	6,000	Animism	-1%	1	
Moi	Indonesia	Moi	4,000	Animism	-1%	1	
Moken	Burma	Moken	5,000	Animism	-1%	6	79
Moken of Thailand	Thailand	Local dialects	3,000	Animism	-1%	1	
*Mokole	Benin	Mokole	7,000	Animism	0%	3	
*Molbog	Philippines	Molbog	5,000	Islam-Animist	0%	7	
Molof	Indonesia	Molof	200	Animism	-1%	1	
Mombum	Indonesia	Mombum	250	Animism	-1%	1	
Momoguns	Malaysia	Momoguns	110,000	Animism	-1%	2	
Mon	Burma	Mon	350,000	Buddhist-Animist	-1%	5	81
Mona	Ivory Coast	Mona	5,570	Islam-Animist	-1%	1	
Mongondow	Indonesia	Mongondow	400,000	Animism	-1%	5	81
Mongour	China	Mongour	50,000	Traditional Chinese	-1%	1	
Moni	Indonesia	Moni	20,000	Animism	-1%	1	
Monjombo	Central African Republic	Monjombo	11,000	Animism	0%	1	
Mono	Zaire	Mono	30,000	Animism	0%	3	
Monpa	India	Monpa	22,000	Buddhist-Animist	0%	1	
Montol	Nigeria	Montol	20,000	Islam	-1%	6	79
Moor & Malays	Sri Lanka	Tamil	895,322	Islam	0%	5	
Moors in Mauritania	Mauritania	Arabic (Hassani)	1,000,000	Islam	15%	5	
**Mopan Maya	Belize	Mopan Maya	4,000	Christo-Paganism	15%	5	
	Guatemala	Mopan Maya	2,000	Christo-Paganism	15%	5	
Moqaddam	Iran	Moqaddam	1,000	Islam	0%	3	
Mor	Indonesia	Mor	1,000	Animism	-1%	1	
Moreb	Sudan	Moreb	560	Animism	-1%	1	
Mori	Indonesia	Mori	200,000	Islam	0%	5	81
Moru	Ivory Coast	Moru	10,000	Islam-Animist	-1%	1	
	Sudan	Moru	23,000	Animism	-1%	1	
Morunahua	Peru	Morunahua	150	Animism	-1%	1	
Morwap	Indonesia	Morwap	300	Animism	-1%	1	

People	Country	Language	Population	Religion	%		
Mosi	Tanzania	Mosi	240,000	Animism	0%	1	
Mossi	Upper Volta	Mole	3,300,000	Animism	7%	6	80
Motilon	Colombia	Motilon	2,000	Animism	-1%	1	
	Venezuela	Motilon	3,000	Animism	-1%	1	
Movima	Bolivia	Movima	1,000	Animism	0%	1	
Mpoto	Malawi	Mpoto	22,000	Animism	0%	1	
	Tanzania	Mpoto	36,000	Animism	1%	5	
Mru	Bangladesh	Murung	50,000	Animism	5%	4	
Mualthuam	India	Mualthuam	2,000	Islam-Animist	-1%	1	
Mubi	Chad	Mubi	36,150	Animism	nr	1	
Muinane	Colombia	Muinane	3,000	not reported	-1%	1	
Mulimba	Cameroon	Mulimba	15,690	Hindu-Animist	-1%	5	
Multani in Punjab	India	Multani	10,000	Islam	-1%	1	
Mumbake	Nigeria	Mumbake					
Mumuye	Nigeria	Mumuye	200,000	Animism	-1%	1	
Mun	Burma	Mun	10,000	Buddhist-Animist	-1%	1	
Muna	Indonesia	Muna	200,000	Islam-Animist	-1%	1	
Mundang	Chad	Mundang	100,000	Islam-Animist	-1%	1	
Mundari in Assam	India	Mundari	770,920	Hindu-Animist	0%	4	
**Mundas in Bihar	India	Munda	25,000	Animism	0%	1	
Mundu	Zaire	Mundu	5,000	Animism	-1%	1	
Munduruku	Brazil	Munduruku	2,000	Animism	-1%	1	
Mungaka	Cameroon	Mungaka	14,000	Animism	-1%	1	
Munggui	Indonesia	Munggui	650	Islam	1%	4	
Munji-Yidgha	Afghanistan	Munji-Yidgha	14,000	Animism	-1%	1	
Mura-Piraha	Brazil	Mura-Piraha	110	Animism	-1%	1	
Muria in Andhra Pradesh	India	Muria	12,900	Hindu-Animist	1%	4	
Murle	Sudan	Murle	40,000	Animism	1%	4	
*Murngin (Wulamba)	Australia	Dhuwal	3,500	Animism	-1%	1	
Mursi	Ethiopia	Mursi	6,000	Animism	1%	4	
Murut	Malaysia	Murut	37,500	Animism	-1%	1	
Musei	Chad	Musei	60,000	Islam-Animist	-1%	3	
Musgu	Chad	Musgu	75,000	Islam-Animist	-1%	1	
Musi	Indonesia	Indonesian	400,000	Islam-Animist	-1%	3	
Muslim Community of Bawku	Ghana	Hausa, Ghana	20,000	Islam	0%	3	
Muslim Gypsies in Skoplje	Yugoslavia	Romany Dialects	23,000	Islam	0%	5	82
**Muslim Immigrants in U.K.	United Kingdom	not reported	500,000	Islam	-1%	4	
Muslim Malays	Malaysia	Bahasa Malaysia	5,500,000	Islam	-1%	6	80
Muslims (West Nile Dist.)	Uganda	Lugbara	45,000	Islam	1%	6	79
Muslims in U.A.E.	United Arab Emirates	Arabic	202,000	Islam	1%	1	
Muslims of Jordan	Jordan	Arabic	1,000,000	Islam	-1%	1	
Muthuvan in A.P.	India	Muthuvan	7,000	Hindu-Animist	-1%	1	
Mutu	Venezuela	Spanish	300	Christo-Paganism	0%	1	

NAME	COUNTRY	LANGUAGE	GROUP SIZE	PRIMARY RELIGION	% CHR	V	VOL U.P.
Muwasi in Madhya Pradesh	India	Muwasi	21,120	Hindu-Animist	-1%	1	
Mwanga	Tanzania	Mwanga	27,000	Animism	0%	1	
Mwera	Tanzania	Mwera	110,000	Animism	0%	1	
Myaung-Ze	Burma	Myaung-Ze	7,000	Animism	0%	2	
Nabi	Indonesia	Nabi	550	Animism	-1%	1	
Nadeb Maku	Brazil	Nadeb Maku	200	Animism	-1%	1	
**Nafaara	Ghana	Mafaara	40,000	Animism	15%	6	79
Nafar	Iran	Turkish	3,500	Islam	0%	3	
Nafri	Indonesia	Nafri	1,630	Animism	-1%	1	
Naga, Kalyokengnyu	India	Naga, Kalyokengnyu	14,410	Hindu-Animist	-1%	1	
Naga, Mao	India	Naga, Mao	19,970	Hindu-Buddhist	-1%	1	
Naga, Nruanghmei	India	Naga, Nruanghmei	48,600	Hindu-Buddhist	-1%	1	
Naga, Sangtam	India	Naga, Sangtam	20,000	Hindu-Buddhist	-1%	1	
Naga, Sema	India	Naga, Sema	65,230	Unknown	-1%	1	
Naga, Tangkhul	India	Naga, Tangkhul	58,170	Hindu-Buddhist	-1%	1	
Naga, Wancho	India	Naga, Wancho	28,650	Hindu-Buddhist	-1%	1	
Nagar in Madhya Pradesh	India	Nagar	7,090	Hindu-Animist	-1%	1	
Nahsi	China	Nahsi	155,750	Traditional Chinese	-1%	1	
*Nahua, North Pueblo	Mexico	Nahua	3,600	Christo-Paganism	9%	4	
Naka	Sudan	Naka	3,600	Islam	0%	1	
Naltya	Indonesia	Naltya	7,000	Animism	-1%	1	
Nalu	Guinea	Nalu	10,000	Islam-Animist	0%	1	
Nama	Namibia	Nama	10,000	Animism	-1%	1	
	South Africa	Nama	15,000	Animism	-1%	1	
Nambikuara	Brazil	Nambikuara	400	Animism	3%	5	
**Nambya	Zimbabwe	Nambya	40,000	Animism	8%	5	
Namshi	Cameroon	Namshi	30,000	Animism	1%	4	
Nanai	China	Nanai	1,000	Traditional Chinese	-1%	1	
	Soviet Russia	Nanai	12,400	Unknown	0%	1	
Nancere	Chad	Nancere	35,000	Islam-Animist	-1%	1	
Nandi	Nigeria	Nandi	310,000	Animism	-1%	1	
Nandu-Tari	Ethiopia	Nandu-Tari	4,000	Islam	-1%	1	
Nao	Togo	Nao	5,000	Animism	-1%	1	
Naoudem	Ethiopia	Naoudem	90,000	Islam-Animist	-1%	1	
Nara	Nigeria	Nara	25,000	Islam-Animist	-1%	1	
Naraguta	Tanzania	Naraguta	3,000	Animism	-1%	1	
Nata	Togo	Nata	9,500	Animism	0%	1	
Natemba	Upper Volta	Natemba	17,000	Islam-Animist	0%	1	
Natioro	Ghana	Natioro	1,100	Animism	1%	5	
Nawuri	Ghana	Nawuri	10,000	Islam-Animist	7%	5	
Nchimburu	Ghana	Nchumburu	7,000	Animism	0%	1	
Nchumbulu	Ghana	Nchumbulu	1,000	Islam-Animist	0%	1	
Nchumunu	Ghana	Nchumunu	8,000	Islam-Animist	0%	1	

Name	Country	Language	Population	Religion	%	Code
Ndaaka	Zaire	Ndaaka	4,700	Animism	0%	1
Ndali	Tanzania	Ndali	57,000	Animism	0%	1
Ndam	Central African Republic	Ndam	670	Animism	0%	1
Ndamba	Tanzania	Ndamba	19,000	Animism	0%	1
Ndaonese	Indonesia	Ndao	2,160	Animism	-1%	1
Ndau	Zimbabwe	Ndau	178,000	Animism	-1%	1
Nde-Nsele-Nta	Nigeria	Nde-Nsele-Nta	10,000	Animism	-1%	1
**Ndebele	Zimbabwe	Sindebele / Ndebele	1,000,000	Animism	7%	6 79
Ndengereko	Tanzania	Ndengereko	53,000	Animism	0%	1
Ndjem	Cameroon	Ndjem	25,000	Animism	-1%	1
Ndo	Zaire	Ndo	13,000	Animism	-1%	1
Ndoe	Nigeria	Ndoe	3,000	Animism	-1%	1
Ndogo	Central African Republic	Ndogo	3,000	Animism	0%	1
	Sudan	Ndogo	3,500	not reported	nr	1
Ndom	Indonesia	Ndom	450	Animism	-1%	1
Ndomde	Tanzania	Ndomde	12,000	Animism	0%	1
Ndoolo	Zaire	Ndoolo	5,000	Animism	0%	1
Ndop-Bamessing	Cameroon	Ndop-Bamessing	17,000	Animism	0%	1
Ndoro	Cameroon	Ndoro	10,000	Animism	6%	5
**Ndoro	Nigeria	Ndoro	10,000	Animism	-1%	1
Nduga	Indonesia	Nduga	2,500	Animism	0%	1
Ndunga	Zaire	Ndunga	1,000	Islam-Animist	1%	4
Ndunpa Duupa	Cameroon	Ndunpa Duupa	29,000	Unknown	0%	1
Nentsy	Soviet Russia	Nentsy	90,000	Hinduism	12%	4
**Nepalese in India	India	Nepali	6,060,758	Hinduism	3%	5 82
*Nepali	Nepal	Nepali	100,000	Hinduism	-1%	5
Newar in Kathmandu	Nepal	Newari	500,000	Hindu-Buddhist	0%	3
*Newari	Nepal	Newari	5,000	Buddhism	0%	3
Neyo	Ivory Coast	Nevo	5,000	Animism	-1%	1
Ngada	Indonesia	Ngada	40,000	Christo-Paganism	-1%	1
Ngalik, North	Indonesia	Ngalik, North	35,000	Animism	-1%	1
Ngalik, Southern	Indonesia	Ngalik, Southern	5,000	Animism	8%	4
Ngalum	Indonesia	Ngalum	10,000	Animism	0%	1
**Ngamo	Nigeria	Ngamo	18,000	Animism	0%	1
Nganasan	Soviet Russia	Nganasan	1,000	Unknown	0%	1
Ngando	Central African Republic	Ngando	2,000	Animism	0%	1
	Zaire	Ngando	121,000	Animism	0%	1
Ngasa	Tanzania	Ngasa	1,000	Animism	0%	1
Ngayaba	Cameroon	Ngayaba	1,000	Animism	-1%	1
Ngbaka	Zaire	Ngbaka	700,000	Animism	-1%	1
Ngbaka Ma'bo	Central African Republic	Ngbaka Ma'bo	17,000	Animism	0%	1
	Zaire	Ngbaka Ma'bo	17,000	Animism	0%	1
Ngbandi	Zaire	Ngbandi	137,000	Animism	0%	1

NAME	LANGUAGE	COUNTRY	GROUP SIZE	PRIMARY RELIGION	% CHR	V	VOL U.P.
Ngbee	Ngbee	Zaire	30,000	Animism	0%		1
Ngemba	Ngemba	Cameroon	33,500	Animism	-1%		1
*Ngen	Ngen	Ivory Coast	20,000	Animism	2%		4
Ngeq	Ngeq	Laos	50,000	Animism	5%		5
Ngere	not reported	Ivory Coast	150,000	Animism	-1%		4
Ngi	Ngi	Cameroon	10,000	Animism	0%		1
Ngindo	Ngindo	Tanzania	85,000	Animism	0%		1
Nginyukwur	Nginyukwur	Sudan	3,800	Islam	0%		1
Ngirere	Ngirere	Sudan	4,200	Islam	0%		1
Ngiri	Ngiri	Zaire	6,000	Animism	0%		1
Ngizim	Ngizim	Nigeria	39,200	Islam	-1%		1
Ngok	Ngok	Sudan	21,000	Islam	0%		1
**Ngombe	Ngombe	Zaire	5,000	Animism	3%		5
Ngoni	Ngoni	Tanzania	85,000	Animism	0%		1
	Ngoni	Zambia	257,000	Animism	0%		1
Ngulu	Ngulu	Malawi	476,000	Animism	0%		1
	Ngulu	Tanzania	12,800	Animism	-1%		1
Ngumba	Ngumba	Cameroon	10,000	Animism	0%		1
Ngumbi	Ngumbi	Equatorial Guinea	4,000	Animism	0%		1
Ngunduna	Ngunduna	Sudan	9,000	Animism	0%		1
Nguqwurang	Nguqwurang	Sudan	8,000	Islam	0%		1
Ngurimi	Ngurimi	Tanzania	11,800	Animism	0%		1
Nguu	Nguu	Tanzania	46,000	Animism	0%		1
	Ngwo	Cameroon	10,000	Islam	0%		1
Ngwoi	Ngwoi	Nigeria	1,000	Animism	-1%		1
Nharon	Nharon	Botswana	3,000	Animism	0%		1
Nhengatu	Nhengatu	Brazil	3,000	Animism	-1%		1
Nias	Nias	Indonesia	230,000	Animism	-1%		1
Nielim	Nielim	Chad	2,000	Islam-Animist	-1%		1
Nihali in Madhya Pradesh	Nihali	India	1,170	Hindu-Animist	0%		1
Nilamba	Nilamba	Tanzania	210,400	Animism	-1%		1
Nimadi in Madhya Pradesh	Nimadi	India	794,250	Hindu-Buddhist	-1%		1
Nimboran	Nimboran	Indonesia	3,500	Animism	0%		1
Ninam	Ninam	Brazil	470	Animism	-1%		1
*Ningerum	Ningerum	Papua New Guinea	3,000	Animism	-1%		4
Ninggrum	Ninggrum	Indonesia	3,500	Animism	-1%		1
Ninzam	Ninzam	Nigeria	35,000	Islam	-1%		1
Nisa	Nisa	Indonesia	250	Animism	0%		1
Nivkhi	Nivkhi	Soviet Russia	4,400	Unknown	-1%		1
Njadu	Njadu	Indonesia	9,000	Animism	-1%		1
Njalgulgule	Njalgulgule	Sudan	900	Islam	0%		1
Nkem-Nkum	Nkem-Nkum	Nigeria	16,700	Animism	-1%		1
Nkom	Nkom	Cameroon	30,000	Animism	0%		1

Name	Country	Language	Population	Religion	%	Scale	Yr
Nkonya	Ghana	Nkonya	17,000	Islam-Animist	0%	1	
*Nkoya	Zambia	Shinkoya	nr	Animism	5%	4	
Nkutu	Zaire	Nkutu	40,000	Animism	-1%	1	
***Nocte	India	Nocte	19,400	Animism	0%	3	
Nohu	Cameroon	Nohu	6,500	Animism	-1%	1	
Norra	Burma	Norra	10,000	Buddhist-Animist	-1%	6	80
North Africans in Belgium	Belgium	Arabic	90,000	Islam	-1%	1	
Northern Cagayan Negrito	Philippines	Northern Cagayan Negrito	1,200	Christo-Paganism	-3%	4	
Nosu	China	Nosu	556,000	Traditional Chinese	-1%	1	
*Nouni	Upper Volta	Nouni	50,000	Animism	0%	1	
Nsenga	Zambia	Nsenga	191,000	Animism	-1%	1	
Nsenga	Zimbabwe	Nsenga	16,100	Animism	-1%	1	
Nso	Cameroon	Nso	100,000	Animism	0%	1	
Nsongo	Angola	Nsongo	15,000	Animism	-1%	1	
Ntomba	Zaire	Ntomba	50,000	Animism	0%	1	
Ntrubo	Ghana	Ntrubo	4,600	Animism	-1%	5	
Ntrubo	Togo	Ntrubo	3,000	Islam-Animist	-1%	6	79
Ntrubs	Ghana	Ntrubo	5,000	Animism	-1%	1	
*Nuer	Ethiopia	Nuer	70,000	Animism	-1%	1	
Nuer	Sudan	Nuer	844,000	Animism	<1%	1	
Numana-Nunku-Gwantu	Nigeria	Numana-Nunku-Gwantu	15,000	Islam	2%	5	80
Nung	China	Nung	100,000	Traditional Chinese	-1%	5	82
Nungu	Nigeria	Nungu	25,000	Animism	3%	5	
Nunuma	Upper Volta	Nunuma	43,000	Islam-Animist	2%	4	
**Nupe	Nigeria	Nupe	600,000	Islam	0%	1	
Nuristani	Afghanistan	Local dialects	67,000	Islam	0%	1	
Nurses in St. Louis	United States of America	English	3,200	Secularism	9%	6	80
**Nyabwa	Ivory Coast	Nyabwa	35,000	Animism	0%	1	
Nyaheun	Laos	Nyaheun	15,000	Animism	-1%	1	
Nyakyusa	Malawi	Nyakyusa	34,000	Animism	0%	1	
Nyakyusa	Tanzania	Nyakyusa	193,000	Animism	0%	1	
Nyambo	Tanzania	Nyambo	4,000	Animism	-1%	1	
Nyamusa	Sudan	Nyamusa	1,200	Islam	0%	1	
Nyamwezi	Tanzania	Nyamwezi	590,000	Animism	-1%	3	
Nyaneka	Angola	Nyaneka	40,000	Animism	0%	1	
Nyang	Cameroon	Nyang	10,000	Animism	-1%	1	
Nyanga-Li	Zaire	Nyanga-Li	25,000	Animism	0%	1	
Nyangbo	Ghana	Nyangbo	3,000	Islam-Animist	0%	1	
Nyanja	Zimbabwe	Nyanja	252,000	Animism	-1%	1	
*Nyankole	Uganda	Nyankole	810,000	Animism	0%	1	
*Nyantruku	Benin	Aledjo	4,000	Animism	-1%	3	
Nyarueng	Sudan	Nyarueng	2,000	Islam	0%	1	
Nyemba	Angola	Nyemba	100,000	Animism	-1%	1	

NAME	COUNTRY	LANGUAGE	GROUP SIZE	PRIMARY RELIGION	% CHR	V	VOL U.P.
Nyiha	Tanzania	Nyiha	64,000	Animism	0%		1
Nyoro	Zambia	Nyiha	59,000	Animism	0%		1
Nyuli	Uganda	Nyoro	620,000	Animism	-1%		1
Nyungwe	Uganda	Nyuli	140,000	Animism	0%		1
Nyzatom	Mozambique	Nyungwe	700,000	Animism	-1%		1
Nzakara	Sudan	Toposa, Donyiro	80,000	Animism	-1%		3
Nzanyi	Central African Republic	Nzakara	3,000	Animism	0%		1
Nzebi	Nigeria	Nzanyi	14,000	Islam	-1%		1
Nzema	Congo	Nzebi	40,000	Animism	0%		1
	Ghana	Nzema	275,000	Islam-Animist	-1%		1
O'ung	Ivory Coast	Nzema	24,080	Islam-Animist	-1%		1
Obanliku	Angola	O'ung	5,000	Animism	0%		1
Obolo	Nigeria	Obanliku	19,800	Animism	-1%		1
Ocaina	Nigeria	Obolo	70,000	Animism	-1%		1
Od	Peru	Ocaina	250	Animism	-1%		1
Odual	Pakistan	Odki	40,000	Hinduism	-1%		4
Odut	Nigeria	Odual	9,000	Animism	-1%		1
Ogan	Nigeria	Odut	9,700	Animism	0%		1
Ogbia	Indonesia	Ong	200,000	Islam-Animist	-0%		3
Oi	Nigeria	Ogbia	22,000	Animism	-1%		1
Oirat	Laos	Oi	10,000	Animism	-1%		5
Ojhi in Madhya Pradesh	China	Oirat	60,000	Traditional Chinese	-1%		1
Okobo	India	Ojhi	1,070	Hindu-Animist	-1%		1
Okpamheri	Nigeria	Okobo	11,200	Animism	-1%		1
Ollari in Orissa	Nigeria	Okpamheri	30,000	Animism	-1%		1
Olulumo-Ikom	India	Ollari	800	Hindu-Animist	-1%		1
Ong in Andamans	Nigeria	Olulumo-Ikom	9,250	Animism	-1%		1
Onin	India	Ong	200	Animism	-1%		1
Orang Kanak	Indonesia	Onin	600	Animism	-1%		1
Orang Laut	Malaysia	Orang Kanak	4,000	Animism	0%		2
Orang Ulu	Malaysia	Orang Laut	4,000	Animism	0%		2
Orejon	Malaysia	Orang Ulu	4,000	Animism	0%		2
Oring	Peru	Orejon	300	Animism	-1%		1
Ormu	Nigeria	Oring	25,000	Animism	-1%		1
Oroch	Indonesia	Ormu	750	Animism	-1%		1
Orok	Soviet Russia	Oroch	1,100	Unknown	0%		1
Oron	Soviet Russia	Orok	400	Unknown	0%		1
Oronchon	Nigeria	Oron	48,300	Animism	-1%		1
Oso	China	Oronchon	2,400	Traditional Chinese	-1%		1
Ot Danum	Cameroon	Oso	25,000	Animism	0%		1
Otank	Indonesia	Ot Danum	30,000	Animism	-1%		1
Otomi, Eastern	Nigeria	Otank	3,000	Animism	-1%		1
	Mexico	Otomi, Eastern					

Name	Country	Reference Name	Population	Religion	%	Code	Ref
Otomi, Mezquital	Mexico	Otomi, Mezquital	100,000	Christo-Paganism	-1%	1	
Otomi, Northwestern	Mexico	Otomi, Northwestern	40,000	Christo-Paganism	-0%	1	
Otomi, Southeastern	Mexico	Otomi, Southeastern	1,500	Christo-Paganism	0%	1	
Otomi, State of Mexico	Mexico	Otomi	70,000	Christo-Paganism	-1%	1	
Otomi, Tenango	Mexico	Otomi, Tenango	10,000	Christo-Paganism	-1%	1	
Otomi, Texcatepec	Mexico	Otomi, Texcatepec	8,000	Christo-Paganism	-0%	1	
Otoro	Sudan	Otoro	28,000	Islam	1%	1	
Ouaddai	Chad	Maba	320,000	Islam	-1%	4	
Oubi	Ivory Coast	Oubi	1,340	Islam-Animist	-1%	1	
Oyampipuku	Brazil	Oyampipuku	100	Animism	-1%	1	
Oyda	Ethiopia	Oyda	3,000	Animism	-1%	1	
Pacu	Brazil	Tucano	120	Animism	-1%	1	
***Paez	Colombia	Paez	40,000	Christo-Paganism	-1%	5	
Pahari Garhwali in U.P.	India	Pahari Garhwali	1,277,150	Hindu-Animist	-1%	5	81
Pai	China	Yi	1,000,000	Buddhist-Animist	-1%	5	79
Pai	Nigeria	Pai	2,000	Animism	-1%	1	
Paipai	Mexico	Spanish	27,520	Christo-Paganism	-0%	1	
Paite in Assam	India	Paite, Northern	5,800	Hindu-Animist	-1%	4	
Paiute, Northern	United States of America	Paiute, Northern	800	Peyote Religion	3%	4	
Pakaasnovos	Brazil	Pakaasnovos	3,000	Animism	3%	4	
***Pakabeti of Equator	Zaire	Pakabeti	50,000	Animism	-1%	5	
*Pala'wan	Philippines	Pala'wan	10,000	Islam-Animist	-1%	5	81
Palara	Ivory Coast	Palara	150,000	Buddhism	-1%	5	79
Palaung	Burma	Palaung	3,000	Animism	-1%	1	
Palawano, Central	Philippines	Palawano, Central	3,000	Animism	-1%	1	
Palembang	Indonesia	Palembang	500,000	Islam	-1%	1	
Palenquero	Colombia	Spanish	3,000	Animism	-1%	1	
Palikur	Brazil	Palikur	500	Animism	-1%	1	
Paloc	Sudan	Paloc	13,500	Islam	0%	1	
Pambia	Central African Republic	Pambia	2,000	Animism	-1%	1	
Pame, Central Chichimeca	Mexico	Pame, Central Chichimeca	2,500	Christo-Paganism	-1%	1	
Pame, Chichimeca-Jonaz	Mexico	Spanish	1,200	Christo-Paganism	-0%	1	
Pame, Northern	Mexico	Pame, Northern	20,000	Christo-Paganism	0%	1	
Pana	Central African Republic	Pana	1,200	Animism	-1%	1	
Panare	Venezuela	Panare	1,000	Animism	0%	1	
Pande	Congo	Pande	1,000	Animism	0%	1	
Pangwa	Tanzania	Pangwa	26,500	Animism	0%	1	
Panika	India	Panika	1,200	Animism	0%	1	
**Paniyan of Kerela	India	Paniyan	30,690	Hindu-Animist	-1%	5	81
Pankararu	Brazil	Portuguese	6,330	Animism	-1%	1	
Pankhu	Bangladesh	Pankhu	630	Islam	-1%	1	
Pantu	Indonesia	Pantu	9,000	Animism	-1%	1	

235

NAME	COUNTRY	LANGUAGE	GROUP SIZE	PRIMARY RELIGION	% CHR	V	VOL U.P.
Pao	Burma	Pao	100,000	Buddhism	0%	2	
Pao in Madhya Pradesh	India	Pao	15,860	Hindu-Buddhist	-1%	1	
Paongan	China	Paongan	8,000	Traditional Chinese	-1%	1	
Pape	Cameroon	Pape	1,000	Animism	0%	1	
Papel	Guinea-Bissau	Papel	36,300	Islam-Animist	-1%	1	
Papuma	Indonesia	Papuma	700	Animism	-1%	1	
Parakanan	Brazil	Parakanan	500	Animism	-1%	1	
Paranan	Philippines	Paranan	6,000	Christo-Paganism	-1%	1	
Pardhan in Andhra Pradesh	India	Pardhan	450	Hindu-Animist	-1%	1	
Pare	Tanzania	Pare	99,000	Animism	0%	1	
Parengi in Orissa	India	Parengi	3,000	Hindu-Animism	-1%	1	
Paresi	Brazil	Paresi	350	Animism	-1%	1	
Parintintin	Brazil	Parintintin	200	Animism	-1%	1	
*Parsees	India	Gujarati	120,000	Secularism	-1%	5	81
*Parsis in Bombay	India	Parsi	80,000	Zoroastrianism	0%	6	82
Pashayi	Afghanistan	Pashayi	96,000	Islam-Animist	-1%	1	
Pashtuns	Iran	Pashtu	3,000	Islam	0%	6	80
Patamona	Guyana	Patamona	1,000	Christo-Paganism	-1%	1	
Patelia in Gujarat	India	Patelia	23,210	Hindu-Animist	-1%	1	
Pato Tapuia	Brazil	Pato Tapuia	140	Animism	-1%	1	
Paumari	Brazil	Paumari	250	Animism	-1%	1	
Paya	Honduras	Spanish	300	Animism	-1%	1	
Penan, Western	Malaysia	Penan	2,600	Animism	nr	6	81
Pende	Zaire	Pende	200,000	Animism	0%	1	
Pengo in Orissa	India	Pengo	1,250	Hindu-Animist	-1%	1	
Pension Students-Madrid	Spain	Italian	1,500	Secularism	nr	5	82
Peri	Zaire	Peri	40,000	Animism	0%	1	
Pero	Nigeria	Pero	20,000	Islam	0%	1	
Persians of Iran	Iran	Persian	2,000,000	Islam	-1%	6	80
Phu Thai	Laos	Phu Thai	100,000	Buddhist-Animist	1%	5	
Piapoco	Colombia	Piapoco	3,000	Animism	-1%	1	
Piaroa	Venezuela	Piaroa	12,000	Animism	-1%	1	
**Pila	Benin	Pila	50,000	Animism	-1%	4	
Pilaga	Argentina	Pilaga	4,000	Animism	-1%	1	
Pima Bajo	Mexico	Pima Bajo	1,000	Christo-Paganism	0%	1	
Pimbwe	Tanzania	Pimbwe	13,000	Animism	0%	1	
Piratapuyo	Brazil	Tucano	800	Animism	-1%	1	
Piro	Peru	Maniteneri	2,500	Animism	-1%	1	
Pisa	Indonesia	Pisa	3,500	Animism	-1%	1	
Pishagchi	Iran	Pishagchi	1,000	Islam	0%	3	
Pitu Uluna Salu	Indonesia	Pitu Uluna Salu	175,000	Animism	-1%	1	
Piya	Nigeria	Piya	2,500	Islam	-1%	1	

Name	Country	Language	Population	Religion	%	
**Plantation Workers	Papua New Guinea	Local dialects	5,000	Christo-Paganism	6%	5
Pnar in Assam	India	Pnar	82,500	Hindu-Animist	-1%	1
Pocomchi, Eastern	Guatemala	Pocomchi, Eastern	20,000	Christo-Paganism	-1%	1
Pocomchi, Western	Guatemala	Pocomchi, Western	25,000	Christo-Paganism	-1%	1
Podokwo	Cameroon	Podokwo	25,000	Animism	-1%	4
Podzo	Mozambique	Podzo	45,000	Animism	0%	1
Pogolo	Tanzania	Pogolo	65,000	Animism	0%	1
Poke	Zaire	Poke	46,000	Animism	0%	1
Pokot	Uganda	Pokot	170,000	Animism	-1%	1
Pol	Congo	Pol	2,000	Animism	0%	1
Polci	Nigeria	Polci	6,150	Islam	-1%	1
Pom	Indonesia	Pom	1,700	Animism	-1%	1
Pongu	Nigeria	Pongu	3,680	Islam	-1%	1
Poouch in Kashmir	India	Poochi	500,000	Islam	0%	4
Popoloca, Ahuatempan	Mexico	Spanish	6,000	Christo-Paganism	0%	1
Popoloca, Coyotepec	Mexico	Spanish	500	Christo-Paganism	0%	1
Popoloca, Eastern	Mexico	Popoloca, Eastern	2,000	Christo-Paganism	-1%	1
Popoloca, Northern	Mexico	Popoloca, Northern	6,000	Christo-Paganism	-1%	1
Popoloca, Southern	Mexico	Spanish	1,000	Christo-Paganism	0%	1
Popoloca, Western	Mexico	Popoloca, Western	8,000	Christo-Paganism	-1%	1
Popoloca, Oluta	Mexico	Spanish	200	Christo-Paganism	0%	1
Popoloca, Sayula	Mexico	Popoloca, Sayula	6,000	Christo-Paganism	0%	1
Popoloca, Sierra	Mexico	Popoloca, Sierra	18,000	Christo-Paganism	-1%	1
Popoloca, Texistepec	Mexico	Spanish	2,000	Christo-Paganism	0%	1
Porohanon	Philippines	Porohanon	23,000	Animism	-1%	1
**Portuguese in France	France	Portuguese	150,000	Secularism	10%	4
Prang	Ghana	Prang	5,000	Islam-Animist	-1%	1
***Prasuni	Afghanistan	Prasuni	2,000	Islam	-1%	1
**Prisoners in Antananarivo	Madagascar	Malagasy	10,000	Folk Religion	2%	82
**Pro Hockey Players	United States of America	English	560	Secularism	5%	82
Pu-I	China	Pu-I	1,311,020	Traditional Chinese	6%	6
Puguli	Upper Volta	Puguli	5,000	Islam-Animist	-0%	1
Puku-Geeri-Keri-Wipsi	Nigeria	Puku-Geeri-Keri-Wipsi	15,000	Islam	-1%	1
Pular	Senegal	Fouta Toro	281,000	Islam	nr	3
Punjabis	Pakistan	Punjabi	49,000,000	Islam	2%	80
Punu	China	Punu	220,000	Traditional Chinese	8%	80
Punu	Congo	Punu	46,000	Animism	0%	1
Puragi	Indonesia	Puragi	900	Animism	-1%	1
Purig-Pa of Kashmir	India	Purig-Skad	nr	Islam	-1%	5
Purum	Burma	Purum	300	Buddhist-Animist	-1%	81
**Puyuma	Taiwan	Puyuma	7,300	Christo-Paganism	nr	5
Pye	Ivory Coast	Pye	6,120	Islam-Animist	-1%	81
Pygmy (Binga)	Burundi	Local dialects	30,000	Animism	6%	5

NAME	COUNTRY	LANGUAGE	GROUP SIZE	PRIMARY RELIGION	% CHR	V	VOL U.P.
*Pygmy (Mbuti)	Central African Republic	Local dialects	2,000	Animism	0%	4	
*Pygmy (Mbuti)	Zaire	local languages	40,000	Animism	-1%	8	79
Pyu	Indonesia	Pyu	100	Animism	-1%	3	
Qajars	Iran	Qajar	3,000	Islam	0%	3	
Qarai	Iran	Qara'i	2,000	Islam	0%	5	80
Qaragozlu	Iran	Qaragozlu	350,000	Islam	0%	5	
Qashqa'i	Iran	Qashqa'i	5,000	Islam	-1%	4	
Quaiquer	Colombia	Quaiquer	340	Animism	1%	1	
Quarequena	Brazil	Tucano	1,000,000	Animism	4%	4	
**Quechua	Bolivia	Quechua	3,000,000	Christo-Paganism	2%	5	
**Quechua, Huanco	Peru	Quechua, Huancayo	275,000	Christo-Paganism	6%	5	79
**Quiche	Guatemala	Quiche	500,000	Christo-Paganism	5%	6	79
**Quichua	Ecuador	Quichua	2,000,000	Christo-Paganism	6%	5	
Rabha in Assam	India	Rabha	10,000	Hindu-Animist	4%	4	
Rabinal-Achi	Guatemala	Rabinal Achi	21,000	Christo-Paganism	3%	4	
**Racetrack Residents	United States of America	English	50,000	Secularism	6%	5	79
Rai	Nepal	Rai	232,000	Hindu-Buddhist	6%	3	
*Rai, Danuwar	India	Danuwar Rai	12,000	Hindu-Animist	0%	3	
Rajasthani Muslims-Jaipur	India	Jaipuri	3,500	Islam	0%	6	82
Rajbansi	Nepal	Rajbansi	15,000	Hindu-Animist	0%	3	
Ralte	Burma	Ralte	17,000	Buddhist-Animist	-1%	4	
*Ramkamhaeng Un. Students	Thailand	Thai	200,000	Buddhism	-1%	1	
Ratahan	Indonesia	Ratahan	150,000	Animism	-1%	5	
Rataning	Chad	Rataning	10,000	Islam-Animist	-1%	5	
*Rava in Assam	India	Rava	45,000	Hinduism	1%	3	
Rawang	China	Rawang	60,000	Traditional Chinese	-1%	6	80
Redjang	Indonesia	Rejang	300,000	Islam-Animist	-1%	5	
Rendille	Kenya	Rendille	20,000	Islam-Animist	0%	3	
Reshe	Nigeria	Reshe	30,000	Animism	-1%	3	
Reshiat	Ethiopia	not reported	10,000	Animism	-1%	1	
Reyesano	Bolivia	Reyesano	1,000	Animism	-1%	1	
Riang in Assam	India	Riang	74,930	Hindu-Buddhist	-1%	1	
Riang-Lang	Burma	Riang-Lang	20,000	Buddhist-Animist	-1%	1	
Riantana	Indonesia	Riantana	1,100	Animism	-1%	1	
Rikbaktsa	Brazil	Rikbaktsa	200	Animism	-1%	1	
Romany	Turkey	Romany	20,000	Folk Religion	0%	1	
Ronga	Mozambique	Ronga	400,000	Animism	0%	1	
Ronga	South Africa	Ronga	600,000	Animism	0%	1	
Ruihi	Tanzania	Ruihi	71,000	Animism	0%	1	
Rukuba	Nigeria	not reported	50,000	Islam	-1%	1	
Rumaya	Nigeria	Rumaya	1,800	Islam	-1%	1	
Runga	Central African Republic	Runga	13,000	Animism	0%	1	

Language	Country	Population	Religion	
Rungi	Chad	13,000	Islam-Animist	-1% 1
Rungwa	Tanzania	95,000	Animism	0% 1
Ruruma	Tanzania	5,000	Animism	-1% 1
Rusha	Nigeria	2,200	Islam	0% 1
Rut	Tanzania	54,000	Animism	-1% 1
Rutul	Sudan	515	Islam	0% 1
Rwamba	Soviet Russia	12,000	Islam	0% 1
	Uganda	60,000	Animism	0% 1
	Zaire	48,000	Animism	0% 1
*Ryukyuan	Japan	1,000,000	Traditional Japanese	4% 4
Saamia	Uganda	124,000	Animism	0% 1
Saams	Soviet Russia	1,900	Unknown	0% 1
Sabra	Kenya	18,000	Animism	15% 3
Saberi	Indonesia	1,500	Animism	-1% 1
Sadan in Andamans	India	807,180	Hindu-Animist	-1% 1
Sadang	Indonesia	50,000	Animism	-1% 1
Safaliba	Ghana	2,500	Islam-Animist	-1% 1
Safwa	Tanzania	102,000	Animism	3% 4
Sagala	Tanzania	20,000	Animism	0% 1
**Saguye	Kenya	30,000	Islam	1% 3
Saija	Colombia	2,500	Animism	0% 1
Saisiat	Taiwan	2,900	Animism	-1% 1
**Saiva Vellala	India	1,500,000	Hinduism	nr 5 81
Sakata	Zaire	75,000	Animism	2% 4
Sakuye	Kenya	8,000	Islam-Animist	-1% 1
Sala	Zambia	11,000	Animism	0% 3
Salampasu	Zaire	60,000	Animism	0% 1
Salar	China	31,000	Traditional Chinese	-1% 1
Saliba	Colombia	900	Animism	-1% 1
Sama Bangingi	Philippines	70,000	Islam-Animist	-1% 6 80
Sama Pangutaran	Philippines	15,000	Islam	-1% 6 80
Sama, Mapun	Philippines	20,000	Animism	-1% 1
Sama, Siasi	Philippines	100,000	Islam-Animist	-1% 1
Sama, Sibuku	Philippines	11,000	Islam-Animist	-1% 1
Sama-Badjaw	Philippines	120,000	Islam-Animist	-1% 5 79
Samarkena	Indonesia	750	Animism	-1% 1
Samburu	Kenya	60,500	Animism	3% 4
Samo, Northern	Mali	50,000	Animism	0% 1
*Samo-Kubo	Upper Volta	70,000	Islam-Animist	-1% 1
Samogho	Papua New Guinea	1,500	Animism	-1% 4
San	Mali	10,000	Animism	0% 1
Sanapana	Namibia	6,000	Animism	0% 1
	Paraguay	4,000	Animism	0% 1

239

NAME	COUNTRY	LANGUAGE	GROUP SIZE	PRIMARY RELIGION	% CHR	V	VOL U.P.
Sandawe	Tanzania	Sandawe	38,000	Animism	0%	1	
Sanga	Nigeria	Sanga	5,000	Islam	-1%	1	
Sanga	Zaire	Sanga	35,000	Animism	0%	1	
Sangil	Philippines	Sangil	7,500	Islam	-1%	5	
Sangir	Indonesia	Sangir	145,000	Animism	-1%	1	
Sangke	Indonesia	Sangke	250	Animism	-1%	1	
Sangu	Gabon	Sangu	18,000	Animism	-1%	1	
Sangu	Tanzania	Sangu	30,000	Animism	-0%	1	
Santa	China	Santa	155,500	Traditional Chinese	-1%	4	
**Santhali	Nepal	Santhali	nr	Animism	3%	4	
Santrokofi	Ghana	Sele	5,000	Islam-Animist	0%	1	
*Sanuma	Brazil	Sanuma	326	Animism	-1%	3	
Sanuma	Venezuela	Sanuma	4,000	Animism	-1%	1	
Sanza	Zaire	Sanza	15,000	Animism	-0%	1	
Sapo	Liberia	Sapo	30,000	Animism	12%	4	
Sarakole	Senegal	Soninke	67,600	Islam	0%	6	80
Saramaccan	Surinam	Saramaccan	20,000	Christo-Paganism	-1%	1	
Sarwa	Chad	Sarwa	400	Islam-Animist	-1%	1	
Sasak	Indonesia	Sasak	1,600,000	Islam-Animist	-1%	6	80
Sasanis	Iran	Sasani	1,000	Islam	0%	3	
Sasaru-Enwan Igwe	Nigeria	Sasaru-Enwan Igwe	3,780	Animism	-1%	1	
Satere	Brazil	Satere	3,000	Animism	-1%	1	
Satnamis in M.P.	India	Chhattisgarhi	30,000	Animism	2%	4	
Sau	Afghanistan	Sau	1,000	Islam	-1%	1	
Sause	Indonesia	Sause	500	Animism	-1%	1	
**Save	Benin	Save (Yoruba)	15,000	Animism	16%	5	
**Sawi	Indonesia	Sawi	2,800	Animism	-1%	4	
Saya	Nigeria	Saya	50,000	Islam	-1%	1	
Sayyids	Yemen, Arab Republic	Arabic	nr	Islam	-1%	1	
Secoya	Ecuador	Secoya	400	Animism	-1%	1	
Sekar	Indonesia	Sekar	450	Animism	-1%	1	
Sekayu	Indonesia	Indonesian	200,000	Islam-Animist	-0%	3	
Seko	Indonesia	Seko	275,000	Animism	-1%	1	
Sekpele	Ghana	Sekpele	11,000	Islam-Animist	0%	1	
**Selakau of Sarawak	Malaysia	Selakau	5,300	Animism	7%	4	
Selkup	Soviet Russia	Selkup	4,300	Unknown	0%	1	
Semelai	Malaysia	Semelai	3,000	Animism	0%	2	
Sempan	Indonesia	Sempan	2,000	Animism	-1%	1	
Sena	Malawi	Sena	115,000	Animism	0%	1	
Sena	Mozambique	Sena	85,000	Animism	0%	1	
Senggi	Indonesia	Senggi	120	Animism	-1%	1	
**Senoi	Malaysia	Native Senoi	337,400	Animism	2%	5	81
Sentani	Indonesia	Sentani	10,000	Animism	-1%	1	

Name	Alt. Name	Country	Population	Religion	% Chr.	Sc.	Yr.
Senthang	Senthang	Burma	10,000	Buddhist-Animist	-1%	1	
Senufo	Senari	Ivory Coast	300,000	Animism	2%	6	80
**Serawai	Serawai (Pasemah)	Indonesia	60,000	Islam-Animist	1%	5	81
Sere	Sere	Sudan	3,500	Islam	1%	5	
Serere	Serere	Senegal	700,000	Animism	9%	6	79
Serere-Non	Serere-Non	Senegal	70,000	Islam-Animist	0%	1	
Serere-Sine	Serere-Sine	Senegal	315,400	Islam-Animist	-1%	1	
Seri	Seri	Mexico	1,400	Christo-Paganism	-1%	1	
Serui-Laut	Serui-Laut	Indonesia	400	Animism	-1%	1	
Seuci	Tucano	Brazil		Animism	-1%	1	
Seychellois	Creole	Seychelles	51,000	Secularism	10%	4	
Sha	Sha	Nigeria	500	Animism	-1%	1	
Shahsavans	Azerbaijani (Shahsavani)	Iran	180,000	Islam	8%	6	80
Shambala	Shambala	Tanzania	152,000	Animism	0%	2	
Shan	Shan	Burma	800,000	Buddhism	-1%	4	
Shan	Shan	Thailand	300,000	Buddhist-Animist	0%	4	
Shan Chinese	Shan	Burma	20,000	Buddhist-Animist	0%	4	
Shanga	Shanga	Nigeria	5,000	Animism	1%	5	
***Shankilla (Kazza)	Shankilla (Kazza)	Ethiopia	20,000	Christo-Paganism	-1%	1	
Sharanahua	Sharanahua	Peru	1,500	Animism	0%	1	
Sharchagpakha	Sharchagpakha	Bhutan	400,000	Buddhist-Animist	-1%	1	
Shatt	Shatt	Sudan	9,000	Islam	-1%	1	
Shawiya	Shawiya	Algeria	150,000	Islam	-1%	1	
Sheko	Sheko	Ethiopia	23,000	Animism	0%	3	
*Sherpa	Sherpa	Nepal	20,000	Buddhism	-1%	1	
*Shihu	Shihu	United Arab Emirates	10,000	Islam	-1%	1	
Shilha	Shilha	Morocco	3,000,000	Islam-Animist	-1%	1	
Shilluk	Shilluk	Sudan	1,110,000	Islam	-1%	1	
Shina	Shina	Afghanistan	50,000	Islam-Animist	-1%	1	
Shinasha	Shinasha	Ethiopia	4,000	Animism	5%	3	
Shipibo	Shipibo	Peru	15,240	Animism	0%	5	
**Shirishana	Shirishana	Brazil	2,000,000	Animism	-1%	4	
**Shluh Berbers	Tashilhait	Morocco	16,000	Islam-Animist	0%	1	
Shor	Shor	Soviet Russia	200,000	Unknown	-1%	1	
*Shourastra in Tamil Nadu	Shourastra	India	400	Hinduism	-1%	1	
Shua	Shua	Botswana	3,000	Animism	0%	1	
Shughni	Shughni	Afghanistan	100,000	Islam	-1%	1	
Shuwa Arabic	Shuwa Arabic	Nigeria	2,800	Islam	-1%	1	
Shwai	Shwai	Sudan	3,000	Islam	-1%	1	
Siagha-Yenimu	Siagha-Yenimu	Indonesia		Animism	-1%	1	
Sibo	Sibo	China	21,000	Traditional Chinese	-1%	1	
Sidamo	Sidamo	Ethiopia	857,000	Islam-Animist	-1%	1	
Sikanese	Sikka	Indonesia	100,000	Animism	-1%	1	

NAME	COUNTRY	LANGUAGE	GROUP SIZE	PRIMARY RELIGION	% CHR	VOL V	VOL U.P.
Sikhule	Indonesia	Sikhule	20,000	Animism	-1%	1	
Sikkimese	India	Sikkimese	36,580	Hindu-Buddhist	-1%	1	
Simaa	Zambia	Simaa	40,000	Animism	0%	1	
Sindhi Muslims in Karachi	Pakistan	Sindhi	350,000	Islam-Animist	0%	6	82
*Sindhis of India	India	Sindhi	3,000,000	Hinduism	1%	5	
Sinhalese	Sri Lanka	Sinhala	9,146,679	Buddhism	6%	5	
Siona	Colombia	Siona	250	Animism	-1%	1	
Sira	Gabon	Sira	17,000	Animism	0%	1	
Siri	Nigeria	Siri	2,000	Islam	-1%	1	
Siriano	Colombia	Siriano	600	Animism	-1%	1	
Siriono	Bolivia	Siriono	500	Animism	-1%	1	
**Sisaala	Ghana	Isaalin	60,000	Animism	1%	4	
Sisala	Upper Volta	Sisaala	4,000	Islam-Animist	0%	1	
Siwu	Ghana	Siwu	4,500	Islam-Animist	0%	1	
*Slum Dwellers of Bangkok	Thailand	Thai	45,000	Buddhism	-1%	4	
So	Cameroon	So	6,000	Animism	-1%	1	
*So	Laos	So	15,000	Animism	1%	5	81
Sobei	Thailand	Sobei	8,000	Animism	-1%	1	
Sochi	Indonesia	Sochi	1,400	Animism	1%	3	
	Pakistan	Sindhi	nr	Hinduism	1%	3	
Soga	Uganda	Soga	780,000	Animism	0%	1	
Soka Gakkai Believers	Japan	Japanese	6,500,000	Buddhism	0%	5	81
Soli	Zambia	Soli	32,000	Animism	0%	3	
Solorese Muslims	Indonesia	Solor	131,000	Islam	0%	1	
*Somahai	Indonesia	Somagai	3,000	Animism	-1%	1	
Somahai	Indonesia	Somahai	1,500	Animism	1%	5	81
Somali	Ethiopia	Somali	1,000,000	Islam	1%	5	
	Somalia	Somali	2,500,000	Islam	1%	5	
Somali, Ajuran	Kenya	Somali (Ajuran)	25,374	Islam	1%	5	79
Somali, Degodia	Kenya	Somali	68,667	Islam	1%	6	79
Somali, Gurreh	Kenya	Somali	54,165	Islam	1%	5	
Somali, Ogadenya	Kenya	Somali	99,129	Islam	1%	5	
**Somba	Benin	Somba (Detammari)	60,000	Animism	1%	4	
Somrai	Central African Republic	Somrai	50,000	Animism	0%	1	
	Chad	Somrai	50,000	Islam-Animist	-1%	1	
Sondwari in M.P.	India	Sondwari	31,490	Hindu-Animist	-1%	1	
Songe	Zaire	Songe	500,000	Animism	0%	1	
Songhai	Mali	Songhai	125,100	Animism	-1%	1	
	Niger	Songhai	93,000	Islam-Animist	-1%	1	
	Upper Volta	Songhai	35,000	Islam-Animist	-1%	1	
Songomeno	Zaire	Songomeno	40,000	Animism	0%	1	
Songoora	Zaire	Songoora	1,300	Animism	0%	1	
Soninke	Gambia	Soninke	10,000	Islam	-1%	1	

People	(Language)	Country	Population	Religion	%		
	Soninke	Mali	283,000	Islam	0%	1	
	Soninke	Mauritania	22,000	Islam	0%	1	
Sonjo	Sonjo	Tanzania	7,400	Animism	5%	5	
Sopi	Sopi	Sudan	1,600	Islam	0%	1	
Sora in Orissa	Sora	India	221,710	Hinduism	0%	3	
Soruba	Soruba	Benin	5,000	Animism	0%	3	
Sowanda	Sowanda	Indonesia	1,100	Animism	1%	3	
Spiritists	Portuguese	Brazil	9,000,000	Folk Religion	1%	3	79
Street Vendors in Saigon	Vietnamese	Viet Nam	nr	Buddhist-Animist	nr	5	82
Students in Cuiaba	Portuguese	Brazil	20,000	Secularism	1%	3	
Su	Su	Cameroon	500	Animism	-1%	1	
Suba	Suba	Tanzania	17,000	Animism	0%	1	
**Subanen (Tuboy)	Subanen, Tuboy	Philippines	20,000	Animism	2%	5	
**Subanen, Sindangan	Subanun	Philippines	80,000	Animism	-1%	6	80
Subanun, Lapuyan	Subanun, Lapuyan	Philippines	25,000	Islam-Animist	0%	1	
Subi	Subi	Tanzania	74,000	Animism	4%	4	
**Suena	Suena	Papua New Guinea	2,000	Christo-Paganism	0%	4	
Suga	Suga	Cameroon	10,000	Animism	-1%	5	
**Sugut	Dusun	Malaysia	10,000	Animism	8%	5	
Sui	Sui	China	160,310	Traditional Chinese	0%	1	
Suk	not reported	Kenya	133,200	Animism	-1%	1	
Suku	Suku	Zaire	74,000	Animism	-1%	5	
Sukur	Sukur	Nigeria	10,000	Islam	-1%	1	
Sulung	Sulung	India	nr	Hindu-Buddhist	0%	1	
Sumba	Sumba	Indonesia	400,000	Christo-Paganism	0%	1	
Sumbawa	Sumbawa	Indonesia	114,000	Islam	-1%	6	80
Sumbwa	Sumbwa	Tanzania	64,000	Animism	-1%	1	
Sumu	Sumu	Nicaragua	2,000	Christo-Paganism	-1%	1	
**Sundanese	Sundanese	Indonesia	20,000,000	Islam-Animist	1%	4	
Sungor	Sungor	Chad	39,000	Islam-Animist	7%	4	
Suppire	Suppire	Mali	300,000	Animism	-1%	1	
Sura	Sura	Nigeria	40,000	Animism	-1%	1	
**Suri	Suri	Ethiopia	30,000	Animism	0%	1	
**Suriguenos	Surigueno	Philippines	23,950	Secularism	0%	1	
Surubu	Surubu	Nigeria	1,950	Islam	-1%	4	
Surui	Surui	Brazil	250	Animism	-1%	1	
Susu	Susu	Guinea-Bissau	2,000	Islam-Animist	-1%	4	
Susu	Susu	Sierra Leone	86,500	Islam-Animist	-1%	4	
Svan	Svan	Soviet Russia	35,000	Unknown	0%	1	
Swaga	Swaga	Zaire	121,000	Animism	0%	1	
Swaka	Swaka	Zambia	33,000	Animism	0%	1	
Swatis	Swati	Pakistan	600,000	Islam	0%	6	79
**Swazi	siSwati	South Africa	500,000	Animism	17%	5	

NAME	COUNTRY	LANGUAGE	GROUP SIZE	PRIMARY RELIGION	% CHR	V	VOL U.P.
**T'boli	Philippines	Tboli	150,000	Animism	3%	5	81
T'in	Thailand	T'in	25,000	Animism	-1%	5	81
Ta-Oi	Laos	Ta-Oi	15,000	Animism	-1%	5	
Tabasaran	Soviet Russia	Tabasaran	55,000	Islam	0%	1	
Tabi	Sudan	Tabi	10,000	Animism	0%	1	
Tacana	Bolivia	Tacana	3,500	Animism	-1%	1	
Tadjio	Indonesia	Tadjio	100,000	Animism	-1%	1	
Tadyawan	Philippines	Tadyawan	1,000	Animism	-1%	1	
Tafi	Togo	Tafi	1,000	Islam-Animist	0%	1	
Tagal	Malaysia	Tagal	19,000	Animism	nr	6	81
**Tagbanwa, Aborlan	Philippines	Tagbanwa	10,000	Animism	1%	5	
Tagbanwa, Kalamian	Philippines	Tagbanwa, Kalamian	25,000	Christo-Paganism	0%	3	
***Tagin	India	Tagin	25,000	Animism	0%	3	
Tagwana	Ivory Coast	Tagwana	43,000	Islam-Animist	-1%	1	
Tahit	Indonesia	Tehit	6,000	Animism	-1%	1	
Taikat	Indonesia	Taikat	600	Animism	-1%	1	
Taiwan-Chinese Un. Stud.	Taiwan	Mandarin	308,800	Secularism	nr	6	
Tajik	Afghanistan	Pamiri	3,600,000	Islam	0%	5	80
	Iran	Dari	15,000	Islam	0%	5	
	Soviet Russia	Persian (Tajiki)	2,500,000	Islam	0%	5	
Takankar	India	Takankar	10,960	Hindu-Animist	-1%	1	
Takemba	Benin	Takemba	10,000	Animism	0%	1	
Takestani	Iran	Takestani	220,000	Islam	-1%	1	
Tal	Nigeria	Tal	10,000	Islam	-1%	3	
Talish	Iran	Talish	20,000	Islam	-0%	3	
*Talo	Indonesia	Talo	90,000	Islam-Animist	1%	3	
Talodi	Sudan	Talodi	1,200	Islam	-0%	1	
Tama	Chad	Tama	60,000	Islam-Animist	-1%	1	
Tamagario	Indonesia	Tamagario	3,500	Islam-Animist	-1%	1	
Taman	Burma	Taman	10,000	Buddhist-Animist	-1%	3	
*Tamang in Bihar	Nepal	Tamang	nr	Hindu-Buddhist	nr	3	
Tamaria in Bihar	India	Tamaria	5,050	Hindu-Buddhist	-1%	1	
Tamazight	Morocco	Tamazight	1,800,000	Islam-Animist	-0%	1	
Tambas	Nigeria	Tambas	3,000	Animism	-0%	1	
Tambo	Zambia	Tambo	7,000	Animism	0%	1	
Tamil (Ceylonese)	Sri Lanka	Tamil	1,415,567	Hinduism	5%	5	
*Tamil in Yellagiri Hills	India	Tamil	3,500	Hinduism	2%	5	
**Tamil Laborers in Bombay	India	Tamil	3,000	Hinduism	-1%	5	82
Tamil Muslims in Madras	India	Tamil	50,000	Islam	0%	6	82
***Tamil Plantation Workers	Malaysia	Tamil	137,150	Hinduism	4%	5	
*Tamils (Indian)	Malaysia	Tamil	600,000	Hinduism	7%	5	
**Tamils (Indian)	Sri Lanka	Tamil	1,195,368	Hinduism	5%	4	79
Tampulma	Ghana	Tampulensi	8,000	Animism	2%	5	

Name	Country	People/Language	Population	Religion	%	Code
Tana	Central African Republic	Tana	35,000	Animism	0%	1
Tana	Chad	Tana	35,000	Islam-Animist	-1%	1
Tanahmerah	Indonesia	Tanahmerah	3,200	Animism	nr	3
Tandanke	Senegal	Tandanke	1,000	not reported	-1%	1
Tandia	Indonesia	Tandia	350	Animism	-1%	1
Tangale	Nigeria	Tangale	100,000	Islam	-1%	3
Tangchangya	Bangladesh	Tangchangya	8,310	Islam	0%	3
**Tangsa	India	Tangsa	10,700	Animism	-1%	1
Taninuca-Retuama	Colombia	Tanimuca-Retuama	300	Animism	0%	4
Tao't Bato	Philippines	not reported	150	Animism	-1%	1
Taori-Kei	Indonesia	Taori-Kei	140	Animism	-1%	1
Tara	Indonesia	Tara	125,000	Animism	0%	1
Tarahumara, Northern	Mexico	Tarahumara, Northern	500	Christo-Paganism	-1%	1
Tarahumara, Rocoroibo	Mexico	Tarahumara, Rocoroibo	12,000	Christo-Paganism	-1%	1
Tarahumara, Samachique	Mexico	Tarahumara, Samachique	40,000	Christo-Paganism	0%	1
Taram	Cameroon	Taram	3,000	Animism	-1%	1
Tarasco	Mexico	Tarasco	60,000	Christo-Paganism	-1%	1
Targum	Israel	Targum	5,000	Judaism	-1%	1
Tarof	Indonesia	Tarof	600	Animism	-1%	1
Tarok	Nigeria	Tarok	60,000	Animism	-1%	1
Tarpia	Indonesia	Tarpia	560	Animism	-1%	1
Tat	Soviet Russia	Tat	17,000	Islam	0%	1
Tatars	Soviet Russia	Tatar dialects	6,000,000	Islam	-1%	6 80
Tatoga	Tanzania	Tatoga	22,000	Animism	-1%	1
**Tatuyo	Colombia	Tatuyo	300	Animism	-1%	5
Taucouleur	Senegal	Tancouleur	464,700	Islam	0%	5 80
Taungyo	Burma	Taungyo	159,200	Buddhist-Animist	-1%	1
Taungyoe	Burma	Burmese	18,000	Buddhism	-1%	2
Taurap	Indonesia	Taurap	160	Animism	-1%	1
Tausug	Philippines	Tausug	500,000	Islam	0%	1
Tawr	Burma	Tawr	700	Buddhist-Animist	-1%	6 80
Tayaku	Benin	Tayaku	10,000	Animism	-1%	1
Tchang	Cameroon	Tchang	100,000	Animism	0%	1
Teda	Chad	Teda	10,000	Islam	0%	6 80
Teda	Libya	Teda	16,000	Islam	-1%	1
*Teenbu	Ivory Coast	Lorhon	120,000	Islam-Animist	-1%	4
Tegali	Sudan	Tegali	5,000	Islam	0%	1
Teimuri	Iran	Teimuri	16,000	Islam	0%	3
Teimurtash	Iran	Teimurtash	10,000	Islam	0%	3
Teke, Eastern	Zaire	Teke, Eastern	71,000	Animism	0%	1
Teke, Northern	Congo	Teke, Northern	24,000	Animism	-1%	1
Teke, Southwestern	Congo	Teke, Southwestern	32,000	Animism	-1%	1

NAME	COUNTRY	LANGUAGE	GROUP SIZE	PRIMARY RELIGION	% CHR	V	VOL U.P.
Tem	Togo	Kotokoli	100,000	Islam	5%	4	
Tembe	Brazil	Tembe	250	Animism	-1%	1	
Tembo	Zaire	Tembo	30,000	Animism	-1%	1	
Temein	Sudan	Temein	2,300	Islam	0%	1	
Temira	Malaysia	Temira	7,000	Animism	0%	2	
**Temne	Sierra Leone	Temne	1,000,000	Animism	6%	6	80
Tengger	Indonesia	Tenggerese	400,000	Hindu-Animist	1%	5	
*Tense	Ivory Coast	Teen	5,000	Animism	-1%	5	
Tepehua, Huehuetla	Mexico	Tepehua, Huehuetla	2,000	Christo-Paganism	-1%	1	
Tepehua, Pisa Flores	Mexico	Tepehua, Pisa Flores	2,500	Christo-Paganism	-0%	1	
Tepehua, Veracruz	Mexico	Tepehua, Veracruz	900	Christo-Paganism	-1%	1	
Tepehua, Northern	Mexico	Tepehua, Northern	5,000	Christo-Paganism	-1%	1	
Tepehuan, Southeastern	Mexico	Tepehuan, Southeastern	8,000	Christo-Paganism	-1%	1	
Tepehuan, Southwestern	Mexico	Tepehuan, Southwestern	6,000	Christo-Paganism	-1%	1	
Tepeth	Uganda	Tepeth	4,000	Animism	0%	1	
Tepo	Ivory Coast	Tepo	20,000	Islam-Animism	-1%	1	
Tera	Nigeria	Tera	46,000	Islam	-1%	1	
Terena	Brazil	Terena	5,000	Animism	-1%	1	
**Teribe	Panama	Teribe	1,000	Christo-Paganism	15%	5	
Ternatans	Indonesia	Ternate	42,000	Islam	-1%	5	
*Tertiary Level Youth	Iran	Persian	nr	Islam	1%	4	
**Teso	Kenya	Luteso	110,000	Animism	8%	5	
Teso	Uganda	Teso	830,000	Animism	1%	1	
Thado in Assam	India	Thado	42,340	Hindu-Buddhist	-1%	1	
Thai Islam (Malay)	Thailand	Mala, Pattani	1,700,000	Islam-Animist	1%	6	80
*Thai Islam (Thai)	Thailand	Thai, Southern	6,000,000	Buddhist-Animist	0%	4	
Thai Northern	Thailand	North Thai Dialect	6,000,000	Buddhist-Animist	1%	4	
Thai of Bangkok	Thailand	Thai, Central	4,500,000	Buddhist-Animist	1%	4	
*Thai University Students	Thailand	Thai	nr	Buddhism	nr	5	81
Thai, North East	Thailand	N.E. Thai	15,500,000	Buddhist-Animist	1%	4	
Thai, Southern	Thailand	Southern Thai	4,000,000	Buddhist-Animist	1%	4	
Thai-Ney	Burma	Shan	5,000	Buddhist-Animist	0%	2	
Thakur	India	Thakur	99,000	Hindu-Animist	1%	1	
Thar in Bihar	India	Thar	8,790	Hindu-Animist	-1%	1	
Tharu	Nepal	Bhojpuri	495,000	Hinduism	-1%	5	
Thoi	Sudan	Thoi	400	Islam	0%	1	
Thuri	Sudan	Thuri	154,000	Islam	0%	4	
*Tibetan Refugees	India	Tibetan	nr	Buddhism	1%	4	
Tibetans	China	Tibetan	3,000,000	Buddhism	-1%	5	
Tibetans in Bhutan	Bhutan	Tibetan	5,000	Buddhism	1%	4	
Ticuna	Brazil	Ticuna	8,000	Animism	-1%	1	
Tidorese	Indonesia	Tidore	26,000	Islam-Animist	-1%	1	
Tiefo	Upper Volta	Tiefo	6,500	Islam-Animist	0%	1	

Name (cross-reference)	Entry	Country	Population	Religion	%	Code
Tiene	Tiene	Zaire	24,500	Animism	-1%	1
Tigon	Tigon	Cameroon	25,000	Animism	-1%	4
Tikar	Tikar	Cameroon	12,500	Animism	-1%	1
Timorese	Timorese	Indonesia	300,000	Animism	-1%	1
Tindin	Tat	Soviet Russia	5,000	Unknown	0%	1
Tippera	Tippera	Bangladesh	38,000	Islam	-1%	1
Tira	Tira	Sudan	10,200	Islam	-1%	1
Tirma	Tirma	Sudan	8,500	Islam	0%	1
Tiro	Tiro	Indonesia	75,000	Animism	-1%	1
Tiruray	Tiruray	Philippines	30,000	Animism	-1%	1
Tlapaneco, Malinaltepec	Tlapaneco, Malinaltepec	Mexico	40,000	Christo-Paganism	-1%	1
Toala	Toala	Indonesia	100	Animism	-1%	1
Toba	Toba	Argentina	15,000	Animism	-1%	1
Toda in Tamil Nadu	Toda	India	770	Hindu-Animist	-1%	1
*Tofi	Tofi	Benin	33,000	Animism	3%	4
Togbo	Togbo	Zaire	5,500	Animism	0%	1
Tojolabal	Tojolabal	Mexico		Christo-Paganism	-1%	1
Tokkaru in Tamil Nadu	Tokkaru	India	1,298,860	Hindu-Animist	-1%	1
Tol	Tol	Honduras	200	Animism	-1%	1
Tombulu	Tombulu	Indonesia	40,000	Animism	-1%	1
Tomini	Tomini	Indonesia	50,000	Animism	-1%	1
Tondanou	Tondanou	Indonesia	35,000	Animism	0%	1
Tonga	Tonga	Botswana	6,000	Animism	-1%	1
Tonga	Tonga	Malawi	62,200	Animism	-1%	1
Tonga	Tonga	Mozambique	10,000	Animism	-1%	1
*Tonga	ChiTonga	Zimbabwe	90,000	Animism	2%	5
Tonga, Gwembe Valley	ChiTonga	Zambia	86,000	Animism	2%	7 79
Tongwe	Tongwe	Tanzania	8,000	Animism	0%	1
Tonsea	Tonsea	Indonesia	90,000	Animism	-1%	1
Tontemboa	Tontemboa	Indonesia	140,000	Animism	-1%	4
*Topotha	Toposa	Sudan	60,000	Animism	2%	4
Toraja, Southern	Tae'	Indonesia	250,000	Animism	nr	5 81
Totis	Gondi	India	nr	Hinduism	0%	3
Totonaco, Northern	Totonaco, Northern	Mexico	15,000	Christo-Paganism	-1%	1
Totonaco, Oxumatlan	Totonaco, Oxumatlan	Mexico	1,300	Christo-Paganism	0%	1
Totonaco, Papantla	Totonaco, Papantla	Mexico	50,000	Christo-Paganism	-1%	1
Totonaco, Sierra	Totonaco, Sierra	Mexico	100,000	Christo-Paganism	-1%	1
Totonaco, Yecuatla	Spanish	Mexico	500	Christo-Paganism	0%	1
*Toussian	Toussian	Upper Volta	20,000	Islam	8%	4
Towei	Towei	Indonesia	120	Animism	-1%	1
Trepo	Trepo	Ivory Coast	3,400	Islam-Animist	-1%	1
Trio	Trio	Surinam	800	Animism	-1%	1
Trique, San Juan Copala	Trique, San Juan Copala	Mexico	8,000	Christo-Paganism	-1%	1

NAME	COUNTRY	LANGUAGE	GROUP SIZE	PRIMARY RELIGION	% CHR	V	VOL U.P.
Tsaangi	Congo	Tsaangi	10,000	not reported	nr	1	
**Tsachila	Ecuador	Colorado	1,100	Christo-Paganism	8%	5	
Tsakhur	Soviet Russia	Tsakhur	11,000	Islam	0%	1	
Tsamai	Ethiopia	Tsamai	7,000	Animism	-1%	1	
Tsimane	Bolivia	Tsimane	5,500	Animism	-1%	1	
Tsogo	Gabon	Tsogo	15,000	Animism	0%	1	
Tsonga	Mozambique	Tsonga	1,500,000	Animism	-1%	5	81
Tsou	Taiwan	Tsou	4,100	Animism	-1%	5	
Tswa	Mozambique	Tswa	200,000	Animism	0%	1	
	Zimbabwe	Tswa	300,000	Animism	0%	1	
Tswana	Namibia	Tswana	11,300	Animism	-1%	1	
	Zimbabwe	Tswana	30,000	Animism	-1%	1	
Tuareg	Niger	Tamachek	200,000	Islam	-1%	6	79
Tubar	Mexico	Tubar	100	Christo-Paganism	0%	1	
Tucano	Brazil	Tucano	2,000	Animism	-1%	1	
Tugara	India	Tugara	43,680	Hindu-Animist	-1%	1	
Tukude	Indonesia	Tukude	45,000	Christo-Paganism	-1%	1	
Tula	Nigeria	Tula	19,000	Islam	-1%	1	
Tulishi	Sudan	Tulishi	8,700	Islam	-1%	1	
Tumale	Sudan	Tumale	1,100	Islam	0%	1	
Tumawo	Indonesia	Tumawo	350	Animism	-1%	1	
Tumma	Sudan	Tumma	5,200	Islam	0%	1	
Tumtum	Sudan	Tumtum	7,300	Islam	0%	1	
Tunebo, Cobaria	Colombia	Tunebo, Cobaria	2,000	Animism	-1%	1	
Tung-Chia	China	Tung	1,100,000	Animism	0%	5	81
Tunya	Central African Republic	Tunya	800	Islam-Animist	0%	1	
	Chad	Tunya	800	Animism	-1%	1	
Tupuri	Cameroon	Tupuri	70,000	Animism	-1%	1	
	Chad	Tupuri	60,000	Islam-Animist	-1%	1	
Tura	Ivory Coast	Tura	19,230	Islam-Animist	-1%	1	
**Turkana Fishing Community	Kenya	Turkana	20,000	Animism	4%	5	
Turkana Immigrant Workers	Kenya	Turkana	224,000	Animism	4%	5	79
Turkish Workers	German Federal Rep.	Turkish	1,200,000	Islam	1%	6	79
Turkish Immigrant Workers	Belgium	Kurdish	60,000	Islam	1%	6	80
Turkomans	Iran	Turkomani	550,000	Islam	0%	6	80
Turks in Basel	Switzerland	Kurdish	3,000	Islam	nr	6	82
Turks, Anatolian	Turkey	Turkish, Osmanli	31,000,000	Islam	-1%	6	
Turkwam	Nigeria	Turkwam	6,800	Islam	-1%	1	
Turu	Indonesia	Turu	800	Animism	-1%	1	
	Tanzania	Nyaturu	316,000	Animism	10%	4	
Tuvinian	Soviet Russia	Tuvin	139,000	Buddhist-Animist	0%	1	
Tuyuca	Brazil	Tuyuca	500	Animism	-1%	1	
Twi	Sudan	Twi	8,800	Islam	0%	1	

Name	Language	Country	Population	Religion	%	№	Year
Tzeltal, Bachajon	Tzeltal, Bachajon	Mexico	20,000	Christo-Paganism	-1%	1	
Tzeltal, Highland	Tzeltal, Highland	Mexico	25,000	Christo-Paganism	-1%	1	
Tzotzil, Chenalho	Tzotzil, Chenalho	Mexico	16,000	Christo-Paganism	-1%	1	
Tzotzil, Huistan	Tzotzil, Huistan	Mexico	11,000	Christo-Paganism	-1%	1	
Tzutujil	Tzutujil	Guatemala	5,000	Christo-Paganism	-1%	1	
Udegeis	Udegeis	Soviet Russia	1,500	Unknown	0%	1	
Udin	Udin	Soviet Russia	3,700	Unknown	0%	1	
Udmurt	Udmurt	Soviet Russia	704,000	Animism	9%	4	
Uduk	Uduk	Sudan	7,000	Animism	0%	1	
Uhunduni	Uhunduni	Indonesia	14,000	Animism	-1%	1	
Uighur	Uighur	Afghanistan	3,000	Islam	0%	5	80
Uigur	Uigur	China	4,800,000	Islam	-1%	1	
Ukaan	Ukaan	Nigeria	18,000	Animism	-1%	1	
Ukpe-Bayobiri	Ukpe-Bayobiri	Nigeria	12,000	Animism	-1%	1	
Ukwuani-Aboh	Ukwuani-Aboh	Nigeria	150,000	Animism	-1%	1	
Ulchi	Ulchi	Soviet Russia	2,400	Unknown	0%	4	
Ulithi-Mall	Ulithi	Turks and Caicos Islands	2,000	Christo-Paganism	-1%	1	
Ullatan in Kerala	Ullatan	India	1,500	Hindu-Animism	0%	1	
Umm Dorein	Umm Dorein	Sudan	460	Islam	0%	1	
Umm Gabralla	Umm Gabralla	Sudan	9,000	Islam	1%	4	
**Univ. Students of Japan	Japanese	Japan	2,000,000	Traditional Japanese	2%	6	82
*Universitarios - Rosario	Spanish	Argentina	10,000	Nominal Christian	2%	6	79
*University Students	French	France	800,000	Secularism	10%	6	79
	German	German Federal Rep.	850,000	Secularism	-1%	1	
Urali in Kerala	Urali	India	1,080	Hindu-Animist	11%	5	
Urarina	Urarina	Peru	3,500	Animism	-1%	1	
**Urban Mestizos	Spanish	Ecuador	600,000	Nominal Christian	-1%	1	
Urhobo	Urhobo	Nigeria	340,000	Animism	-1%	1	
Uria	Uria	Indonesia	1,200	Animism	-1%	1	
Uruangnirin	Uruangnirin	Indonesia	250	Animism	-1%	1	
Urubu	Urubu	Brazil	500	Animism	-1%	1	
Urupa	Urupa	Brazil	250	Animism	-1%	1	
Uspanteco	Uspanteco	Guatemala	15,000	Animism	-1%	1	
Utugwang	Utugwang	Nigeria	12,000	Animism	-1%	1	
Uvbie	Uvbie	Nigeria	6,000	Animism	-1%	1	
**Uzbeks	Uzbeki, Turkic	Afghanistan	1,000,000	Islam-Animist	0%	6	79
Uzekwe	Uzekwe	Nigeria	5,000	Animism	-1%	1	
Vagala	Vagala	Ghana	3,000	Animism	1%	4	
Vagari	Gujarati Dialect	Pakistan	30,000	Hinduism	1%	5	
Vagla	Vagla	Ghana	6,000	Islam-Animist	-1%	1	
*Vai	Vai	Liberia	30,000	Islam	1%	6	80
Vai	Vai	Sierra Leone	2,800	Islam-Animist	0%	1	
Vaikino	Vaikino	Indonesia	14,000	Animism	-1%	1	

NAME	COUNTRY	LANGUAGE	GROUP SIZE	PRIMARY RELIGION	% CHR	V	VOL U.P.
Vaiphei in Assam	India	Vaiphei	12,210	Hindu-Buddhist	-1%		1
Vale	Central African Republic	Vale	1,400	Animism	0%		1
Venda	Zimbabwe	Venda	38,000	Animism	0%		1
Veps	Soviet Russia	Veps	16,000	Unknown	0%		1
Vere	Cameroon	Vere	20,000	Animism	0%		1
***Vere	Nigeria	Vere	20,000	Animism	9%	5	
Vidunda	Tanzania	Vidunda	11,000	Animism	0%		1
Vietnamese	Laos	Vietnamese	20,000	Buddhism	1%		4
**Vietnamese in the USA	United States of America	Vietnamese	261	Buddhism	7%		4
**Vietnamese Refugees	Australia	Vietnamese	140,000	Folk Religion	7%		4
Vige	Upper Volta	Vige	7,800	Buddhism	4%		4
Vinza	Tanzania	Vinza	3,500	Islam-Animist	0%		1
Vishavan in Kerala	India	Vishavan	4,000	Animism	0%		1
**Vohras of Yavatmal	India	Gujarati	10,000	Hindu-Animist	-1%		4
Voko	Cameroon	Woko	1,000	Islam	0%		1
Vute	Nigeria	Vute	1,000	Islam-Animist	-1%		4
Wa	Burma	Wa	1,000	Animism	-1%		1
	China	Wa	50,000	Animism	0%		2
Wabo	Indonesia	Wabo	900	Traditional Chinese	-1%		1
Waddar in Andhra Pradesh	India	Waddar	35,900	Animism	-1%		1
Wagdi in Rajasthan	India	Wagdi	756,790	Hindu-Animist	-1%		1
Waimiri	Brazil	Waimiri	1,000	Hindu-Animist	-1%		1
Waiwai	Brazil	Waiwai	1,000	Animism	-1%		1
	Guyana	Waiwai	1,000	Christo-Paganism	-1%		1
Waja	Nigeria	Waja	30,000	Islam	-1%		1
**Wajita	Tanzania	Kijita	65,000	Animism	1%		4
Wala	Ghana	Wali	60,000	Animism	2%		5
Walamo	Ethiopia	Walamo	908,000	Animism	-1%		1
Wambon	Indonesia	Wanchoo	2,000	Animism	-1%		3
***Wanchoo	India	Wanchoo	nr	Animism	0%		1
Wanda	Tanzania	Wanda	8,000	Animism	0%		1
Wandamen	Indonesia	Wandamen	4,000	Animism	-1%		1
Wandji	Gabon	Wandji	6,000	Animism	-0%		1
Wanggom	Indonesia	Wanggom	1,000	Animism	-1%		1
Wanji	Tanzania	Wanji	19,000	Animism	-0%		1
Wano	Indonesia	Wano	1,700	Animism	0%		1
Wapishana	Brazil	Wapishana	1,500	Animism	-1%		1
	Guyana	Wapishana	4,000	Christo-Paganism	-1%		1
Wara	Venezuela	Wara	20,000	Animism	-1%		1
Warao	Upper Volta	Wapishana	2,200	Islam-Animist	-1%		1
Ware	Venezuela	Warao	15,000	Animism	-0%		1
	Mali	Ware	2,000	Animism	0%		1

Name	Country	Population	Religion	%
Warembori	Indonesia	350	Animism	-1% 1
Waris	Indonesia	1,480	Animism	-1% 1
*Warjawa	Nigeria	70,000	Animism	-1% 4
Warkay-Bipim	Indonesia	250	Animism	-1% 1
Waropen	Indonesia	6,000	Animism	-1% 1
Wasi	Tanzania	13,000	Animism	0% 1
Watchi	Togo	1,000,000	Animism	5% 4
Waura	Brazil	120	Animism	-1% 1
Wayana	Surinam	600	Animism	-1% 1
*Wazinza	Tanzania	2,000	Animism	7% 4
Weda	Indonesia	900	Islam	-1% 1
Wetawit	Ethiopia	28,000	Animism	-1% 1
Wewewa	Indonesia	55,000	Animism	-1% 1
Widekum	Cameroon	10,000	Animism	-1% 1
**Wimbum	Cameroon	50,000	Animism	1% 5
Win	Upper Volta	20,000	Islam-Animist	-1% 1
Winji-Winji	Benin	5,000	Islam	-1% 3
Wobe	Ivory Coast	40,000	Animism	12% 4
Wodani	Indonesia	3,000	Animism	-1% 1
Woi	Indonesia	1,300	Animism	-1% 1
Woleat	Turks and Caicos Islands	1,000	Christo-Paganism	-1% 4
Wolio	Indonesia	25,000	Islam-Animist	-1% 1
Wolof	Senegal	1,500,000	Islam-Animist	1% 6 80
Wolof, Gambian	Gambia	64,800	Islam-Animist	1% 8
Wom	Nigeria	10,000	Islam-Animist	-1% 1
*Women Laborers	Taiwan	1,200,000	Traditional Chinese	2% 4
Wongo	Zaire	8,000	Animism	2% 4
Woro	Sudan	400	Islam	0% 1
Wumbvu	Gabon	103	Animism	0% 1
Wungu	Tanzania	8,000	Animism	0% 1
Xavante	Brazil	2,000	Animism	-1% 1
Xerente	Brazil	500	Animism	-1% 1
Xokleng	Brazil	250	Animism	-1% 1
Xu	Namibia	8,000	Animism	-1% 1
Yafi	Indonesia	180	Animism	-1% 1
Yaghan	Chile	50	Christo-Paganism	0% 1
Yagnobi	Soviet Russia	2,000	Unknown	0% 1
Yagua	Peru	4,000	Animism	0% 1
Yahadian	Indonesia	700	Animism	-1% 1
Yaka	Zaire	200,000	Animism	-1% 1
Yakan	Philippines	97,000	Islam-Animist	1% 6 80
Yakoma	Central African Republic	5,300	Animism	0% 1
*Yala	Nigeria	60,000	Animism	6% 4

NAME	COUNTRY	LANGUAGE	GROUP SIZE	PRIMARY RELIGION	% CHR	V	VOL U.P.
*Yalunka	Sierra Leone	Yalunka	25,000	Islam-Animist	-1%	6	80
Yaly	Indonesia	Yaly	12,000	Animism	-1%	1	
Yambasa	Cameroon	Yambasa	26,000	Animism	-1%	1	
Yaminahua	Peru	Yaminahua	1,200	Animism	-1%	1	
Yanadi in Andhra Pradesh	India	Yanadi	205,380	Hindu-Animist	-1%	1	
Yandang	Nigeria	Yandang	10,000	Islam-Animist	-1%	1	
Yanga	Togo	Yanga	nr	Islam-Animist	-0%	1	
Yangbye	Burma	Yangbye	326,650	Buddhist-Animist	-1%	1	
*Yanomamo in Brazil	Brazil	Yanomam (Waica)	3,000	Animism	-1%	6	79
Yanomamo in Venezuela	Venezuela	Shamatali	nr	Animism	5%	5	
Yans	Zaire	Yans	nr	Animism	0%	1	
*Yanyula	Australia	Yanyula (Yanjula)	nr	Animism	9%	4	
Chiyao	Malawi	Chiyao	165,000	Other	2%	4	
**Yao	Mozambique	Yao	600,000	Islam-Animist	12%	5	
**Yao	Thailand	Yao (Mien Wa)	220,000	Islam	2%	6	79
*Yao Refugees from Laos	Thailand	Yao	19,867	Animism	2%	6	
Yaoure	Ivory Coast	Yaoure	7,000	Animism	4%	4	
Yaqui	Mexico	Yaqui	14,000	Christo-Paganism	-1%	4	
Yaruro	Venezuela	Yaruro	5,000	Animism	-1%	5	
Yasing	Cameroon	Yasing	25,000	Animism	0%	1	
Yaur	Indonesia	Yaur	350	Animism	-1%	1	
Yava	Indonesia	Yava	4,500	Animism	-1%	1	
Yazgulyam	Soviet Russia	Yazgulyam	2,000	Unknown	0%	1	
**Yei	Botswana	Yei	10,000	Animism	4%	5	
Yei	Indonesia	Yei	1,000	Animism	-1%	1	
Yela	Zaire	Yela	33,000	Animism	-0%	1	
Yellow Uighur	China	Yellow Uighur	4,000	Traditional Chinese	-1%	1	
Yelmek	Indonesia	Yelmek	400	Animism	-1%	1	
Yemenis	Yemen, Arab Republic	Arabic (Eastern)	5,600,000	Islam	-1%	5	79
Yerava in Karnataka	India	Yerava	10,870	Hindu-Animist	-1%	1	
Yeretuar	Indonesia	Yeretuar	250	Animism	-1%	1	
Yerukala in A.P.	India	Yerukala	67,550	Hindu-Animist	-1%	1	
Yeskwa	Nigeria	Yeskwa	13,000	Islam	-1%	1	
Yidinit	Ethiopia	Yidinit	600	Animism	-1%	1	
Yin-Kyar	Burma	Shan Dialects	2,000	Animism	0%	2	
Yin-Nett	Burma	Shan Dialects	2,000	Animism	0%	2	
Yinchia	Burma	Yinchia	4,000	Buddhist-Animist	-1%	4	
Yinga	Cameroon	Yinga	300	Animism	1%	4	
Yoabu	Benin	Yoabu	8,000	Animism	0%	1	
Yogad	Philippines	Yogad	7,000	Animism	-1%	1	
Yonggom	Indonesia	Yonggom	2,000	Animism	-1%	1	
Yoruk	Turkey	Turkish (Danubian)	600,000	Islam	0%	5	
Yos	Burma	Yos	4,500	Buddhist-Animist	-1%	1	

Name	Country	People/Language	Population	Religion			
Yotafa	Indonesia	Yotafa	2,460	Animism	-1%	1	
Yuana	Venezuela	Yuana	300	Animism	-1%	1	
Yucateco	Guatemala	Yucateco	3,000	Animism	-1%	1	
	Mexico	Yucateco	500,000	Christo-Paganism	-1%	1	
*Yucuna	Colombia	Yucuna	500	Christo-Paganism	1%	5	
Yukagirs	Soviet Russia	Yukagir	nr	Unknown	0%	1	
Yukpa	Colombia	Yukpa	2,500	Animism	-1%	1	
	Venezuela	Yukpa	3,000	Animism	0%	1	
Yuku	China	Yuku	4,000	Traditional Chinese	-1%	1	
Yulu	Sudan	Yulu	1,500	Islam	-0%	1	
Yungur	Nigeria	Yungur	44,300	Islam	-1%	1	
Yuracare	Bolivia	Yuracare	2,500	Animism	-1%	1	
Yurak	Soviet Russia	Yurak	29,000	Unknown	0%	1	
Yuruti	Colombia	Yuruti	150	Animism	-1%	1	
Zaghawa	Chad	Zaghawa	61,000	Islam-Animist	-1%	1	
	Libya	Zaghawa	nr	Islam	nr	1	
	Sudan	Zaghawa	nr	Islam	nr	1	
Zanaki	Tanzania	Zanaki	23,000	Animism	-1%	1	
Zande	Zaire	Zande	467,000	Animism	-1%	1	
Zangskari in Kashmir	India	Zangskari	5,000	Hindu-Animist	-1%	1	
Zaramo	Tanzania	Zaramo	296,000	Islam-Animist	2%	5	
**Zaranda Hill Peoples	Nigeria	local languages	10,000	Animism	2%	4	
Zari	Nigeria	Zari	3,950	Islam	-1%	1	
Zayse	Ethiopia	Zayse	21,000	Animism	nr	6	81
Zemi Naga of Assam	India	Jeme	16,000	Animism	0%	1	
Zenaga	Mauritania	Zenaga	16,000	Islam	-1%	1	
Zigwa	Tanzania	Zigwa	112,000	Animism	0%	1	
Zilmamu	Ethiopia	Zilmamu	3,000	Animism	-1%	1	
Zimba	Zaire	Zimba	50,000	Animism	0%	1	
Zinacantecos	Mexico	Tzotzil, Chenalho	10,000	Christo-Paganism	1%	7	79
Zoliang	India	Naga, Zoliang	50,000	Animism	0%	3	
Zome	Burma	Zome	30,000	Buddhist-Animist	-1%	1	
Zome in Manipur	India	Zome	30,000	Hindu-Buddhist	-1%	1	
Zoque, Chimalapa	Mexico	Zoque, Chimalapa	6,000	Christo-Paganism	-1%	1	
Zoque, Copainala	Mexico	Zoque, Copainala	10,000	Christo-Paganism	-1%	1	
Zoque, Francisco Leon	Mexico	Zoque, Francisco Leon	12,000	Christo-Paganism	-1%	1	
Zoque, Tabasco	Mexico	Zoque, Tabasco	400	Christo-Paganism	-1%	1	
Zowla	Ghana	Ewe	800,000	Animism	2%	5	
Zulu	Malawi	Zulu	37,500	Animism	-1%	1	
Zuni	United States of America	Zuni	6,000	Animism	1%	4	

Index by
Receptivity

INDEX BY RECEPTIVITY

This index lists groups by their reported attitude toward the gospel. The judgment of receptivity or resistance to the gospel is a subjective and difficult question. Oftentimes what appears to be resistance to the gospel turns out to be a rejection of the Western or foreign cultural trappings with which the gospel is offered. Or perhaps it is a resistance to the agents who bear witness because they come from a country or people not respected by those who are being asked to hear the gospel. Nonetheless, this index gives the considered judgment of those who have reported these unreached peoples. Within each category (very receptive, receptive, indifferent, reluctant, very reluctant, and unknown) peoples are listed alphabetically by group name. Their country or location is also listed.

VERY RECEPTIVE

Adi, India
Akhdam, Yemen, Arab Republic
Azteca, Mexico (79)
Bagobo, Philippines
Banaro, Papua New Guinea
Banyarwanda, Rwanda
Baoule, Ivory Coast
Basotho, Mountain, Lesotho (79)
Bipim, Indonesia
Bolinao, Philippines
Cebu, Middle-Class, Philippines
Ch'ol Sabanilla, Mexico
Citak, Indonesia
Copacabana Apt. Dwellers, Brazil
Dan, Ivory Coast
Godie, Ivory Coast
Guarani, Bolivia (79)
Halam in Tripura, India
Higi, Nigeria
Irulas in Kerala, India
Kond, India
Koreans in Germany, German Federal
  Rep.
Krahn, Liberia
Maguzawa, Nigeria (79)
Matharis, India
Mestizos in La Paz, Bolivia (82)
Mocha, Ethiopia
Nocte, India
Paez, Colombia
Pakabeti of Equator, Zaire
Prasuni, Afghanistan
Shankilla (Kazza), Ethiopia
Tagin, India
Tamil Plantation Workers, Malaysia
Vere, Nigeria

RECEPTIVE

Adja, Benin
Afo, Nigeria (80)
African Students in Cairo, Egypt
Ahl-i-Haqq in Iran, Iran (79)
Akha, Thailand (79)
Ampeeli, Papua New Guinea
Apartment Residents-Seoul, Korea,
  Republic of
Apatani in Assam, India
Apayao, Philippines
Arabs in New Orleans, United States
  of America (82)
Auberge Crowd in Geneva,
  Switzerland (82)
Aymara, Bolivia
Azerbaijani, Afghanistan
Babur Thali, Nigeria (80)
Bachelors in Lagos, Nigeria (82)
Bakuba, Zaire
Balangao, Philippines
Banai, Bangladesh
Bassa, Nigeria

Batangeno, Philippines
Bhil, Pakistan
Bhils, India (79)
Bidayuh of Sarawak, Malaysia (81)
Bijogo, Guinea-Bissau
Bilan, Philippines
Black Caribs, Belize, Belize (79)
Black Caribs, Guatemala, Guatemala
Black Caribs, Honduras, Honduras
Bodo Kachari, India
Boko, Benin
Bontoc, Central, Philippines (81)
Bontoc, Southern, Philippines
Boran, Kenya
Bukidnon, Philippines
Bus Drivers, South Korea, Korea,
  Republic of
Bus Girls in Seoul, Korea, Republic
  of (82)
Busanse, Ghana
Chayahuita, Peru
Chicanos in Denver, United States
  of America (82)
Chinese Hakka of Taiwan, Taiwan
  (79)
Chinese in Australia, Australia
Chinese in Boston, United States of
  America (82)
Chinese in Brazil, Brazil
Chinese in Hong Kong, Hong Kong
Chinese in Indonesia, Indonesia
Chinese in Panama, Panama
Chinese in Sabah, Malaysia
Chinese in Sarawak, Malaysia
Chinese in United Kingdom, United
  Kingdom
Chinese in United States, United
  States of America
Chinese in Vancouver B.C., Canada
Chinese Refugees, France, France
  (79)
Chinese Stud., Australia, Australia
Chinese Students Glasgow, United
  Kingdom
Chiriguano, Argentina
Chrau, Viet Nam
Coreguaje, Colombia
Dagomba, Ghana
Dhodias, India
Dida, Ivory Coast
Doohwaayo, Cameroon
Dubla, India
Duka, Nigeria
Ex-Mental Patients in NYC, United
  States of America (82)
Fakai, Nigeria
Falasha, Ethiopia (79)
Fali, Nigeria
Gagre, Pakistan
Ghimeera, Ethiopia
Glavda, Nigeria
Gouro, Ivory Coast
Grebo, Liberia
Hadrami, Yemen, Democratic
Hajong, Bangladesh
Hazara in Kabul, Afghanistan (82)
Hewa, Papua New Guinea (79)
High School Students, Hong Kong
Hotel Workers in Manila,
  Philippines (81)

REGISTRY OF THE UNREACHED

Huave, Mexico
Huila, Angola
Hunzakut, Pakistan (79)
Iban, Malaysia (81)
Ifugao (Kalangoya), Philippines
Indian Tamils - Colombo, Sri Lanka
(82)
Indians, East, Trinidad and Tobago
(79)
Ishans, Nigeria
Izi, Nigeria
Jamaican Elite, Jamaica
Japanese Students In USA, United
States of America
Jarawa, Nigeria
Javanese (rural), Indonesia (79)
Javanese of Central Java, Indonesia
Javanese of Pejompongan, Indonesia
Jimini, Ivory Coast
Jivaro (Achuara), Venezuela
K'anjobal of San Miguel, Guatemala
Kafirs, Pakistan (79)
Kalagan, Philippines
Kalinga, Tanudan, Philippines
Kalinga,Northern, Philippines (81)
Kankanay, Central, Philippines
Karbis, India
Kasena, Ghana
Kashmiri Muslims, India (79)
Kaur, Indonesia
Kekchi, Guatemala
Khmer Refugees, Thailand
Koch, Bangladesh
Kohli, Kutchi, Pakistan
Kohli, Tharadari, Pakistan
Kohli, Wadiara, Pakistan
Kohlis, Parkari, Pakistan
Kolam, India
Kono, Sierra Leone
Koranko, Sierra Leone
Korean Prisoners, Korea, Republic
of
Kowaao, Liberia
Kuluis in Himachal Prades, India
(81)
Kunimaipa, Papua New Guinea
Kusaasi, Ghana
Lahaulis in Punjab, India
Lambadi in Andhra Pradesh, India
(81)
Lepcha, Sikkim
Lepers of Cen. Thailand, Thailand
(81)
Lepers of N.E. Thailand, Thailand
Loho Loho, Indonesia
Lotuka, Sudan
Maasai, Kenya (79)
Macuxi, Brazil
Magar, Nepal
Mam Indian, Guatemala
Mamanua, Philippines (81)
Mangyan, Philippines
Manikion, Indonesia
Manjaco, Guinea-Bissau
Manobo, Cotabato, Philippines
Manobo, Salug, Philippines
Manobo, Tigwa, Philippines
Manobo, Western Bukidnon,
Philippines

Mansaka, Philippines
Mawchis, India
Mazahua, Mexico
Meghwar, Pakistan (79)
Mejah, India
Melanau of Sarawak, Malaysia (80)
Meo, Thailand
Miching, India
Middle Class-Mexico City, Mexico
(82)
Military Personnel, Ecuador
Mixes, Mexico
Mopan Maya, Guatemala
Mopan Maya, Belize
Mundas in Bihar, India
Muslim Immigrants in U.K., United
Kingdom
Nafaara, Ghana (79)
Nambya, Zimbabwe
Ndebele, Zimbabwe (79)
Ndoro, Nigeria
Nepalese in India, India
Ngamo, Nigeria
Ngombe, Zaire
Nupe, Nigeria
Nyabwa, Ivory Coast
Paniyan of Kerela, India (81)
Pila, Benin
Plantation Workers, Papua New
Guinea
Portuguese in France, France
Pro Hockey Players, United States
of America (82)
Puyuma, Taiwan (81)
Quechua, Peru
Quechua, Bolivia
Quechua, Huanco, Peru
Quiche, Guatemala (79)
Quichua, Ecuador
Racetrack Residents, United States
of America (79)
Saguye, Kenya
Saiva Vellala, India
Santhali, Nepal
Save, Benin
Sawi, Indonesia
Selakau of Sarawak, Malaysia
Senoi, Malaysia (81)
Serawai, Indonesia (81)
Shihu, United Arab Emirates
Shirishana, Brazil
Shluh Berbers, Morocco
Sisaala, Ghana
Somba, Benin
Subanen (Tuboy), Philippines
Subanen, Sindangan, Philippines
(80)
Suena, Papua New Guinea
Sugut, Malaysia
Sundanese, Indonesia (80)
Suri, Ethiopia
Suriguenos, Philippines
Swazi, South Africa
T'boli, Philippines (81)
Tagbanwa, Aborlan, Philippines
Tamil Laborers in Bombay, India
(82)
Tamils (Indian), Sri Lanka (79)
Tangsa, India

Tatuyo, Colombia
Temne, Sierra Leone (80)
Teribe, Panama
Teso, Kenya
Tsachila, Ecuador
Turkana Fishing Community, Kenya
 (79)
Univ. Students of Japan, Japan
Urban Mestizos, Ecuador
Uzbeks, Afghanistan (79)
Vietnamese in the USA, United
 States of America
Vietnamese Refugees, Thailand
Vietnamese Refugees, Australia
Vohras of Yavatmal, India
Wajita, Tanzania
Wanchoo, India
Wimbum, Cameroon
Yala, Nigeria
Yao, Thailand (79)
Yao, Malawi
Yei, Botswana
Zaranda Hill Peoples, Nigeria

INDIFFERENT

Afawa, Nigeria (80)
Alars, India
Alawites, Syria (79)
Albanian Muslims, Albania (80)
Albanians in Yugoslavia, Yugoslavia
Americans in Geneva, Switzerland
Ami, Taiwan (81)
Anatolian Turks-Istanbul, Turkey
 (82)
Arnatas, India
Asmat, Indonesia (79)
Ata of Davao, Philippines
Atta, Philippines
Atye, Ivory Coast
Barbers in Tokyo, Japan (82)
Bariba, Benin (80)
Bassa, Liberia
Batak, Angkola, Indonesia (80)
Bete, Ivory Coast
Bhojpuri, Nepal
Bororo, Brazil
Bosnian, Yugoslavia (80)
Bushmen (Hiechware), Zimbabwe
Bushmen (Kung), Namibia (79)
Cambodians, Thailand
Casiguranin, Philippines
Casual Laborers-Atlanta, United
 States of America (82)
Central Thailand Farmers, Thailand
 (81)
Chakmas of Mizoram, India (81)
Cham (Western), Kampuchea,
 Democratic (80)
Chang-Pa of Kashmir, India (81)
Chinese in Amsterdam, Netherlands
Chinese in Austria, Austria
Chinese in·Holland, Netherlands
Chinese in Japan, Japan
Chinese in Korea, Korea, Republic
 of

Chinese in Laos, Laos
Chinese in Malaysia, Malaysia
Chinese in New Zealand, New Zealand
Chinese in South Africa, South
 Africa
Chinese in Taiwan, Taiwan
Chinese in Thailand, Thailand
Chinese in West Germany, German
 Federal Rep.
Chinese Mainlanders, Taiwan
Chinese of W. Malaysia, Malaysia
Chinese Refugees in Macau, Macau
 (81)
Chinese Restaurant Wrkrs., France
Coloureds in Eersterust, South
 Africa (82)
Comorians, Comoros (79)
Cuna, Colombia (79)
Daka, Nigeria
Danchi Dwellers in Tokyo, Japan
 (82)
Dani, Baliem, Indonesia (79)
Deviant Youth in Taipei, Taiwan
 (82)
Dewein, Liberia
Dghwede, Nigeria
Dog-Pa of Ladakh, India (81)
Dogon, Mali (79)
Drug Addicts in Sao Paulo, Brazil
 (82)
Dumagat , Casiguran, Philippines
 (81)
Expatriates in Riyadh, Saudi Arabia
 (82)
Factory Workers, Hong Kong
Favelados-Rio de Janeiro, Brazil
 (82)
Fulani, Benin
Fulbe, Ghana
Gabbra, Ethiopia
Galla (Bale), Ethiopia
Gonds, India
Gorkha, India
Guajiro, Colombia
Guanano, Colombia (79)
Gypsies in Spain, Spain (79)
Havasupai, United States of America
Ibataan, Philippines
Ifugao, Philippines
Indians In Rhodesia, Zimbabwe
Industrial Workers, Taiwan (81)
Industry Laborers-Japan, Japan
Inland Sea Island Peoples, Japan
Int'l Stud., Los Banos, Philippines
Iwaidja, Austria
Japanese in Korea, Korea, Republic
 of
Jeepney Drivers in Manila,
 Philippines (81)
Jeepney Drivers in Manila,
 Philippines (81)
Jewish Imgrnts.-American, Israel
Jewish Imgrnts.-Argentine, Israel
Jewish Imgrnts.-Australia, Israel
Jewish Imgrnts.-Brazilian, Israel
Jewish Imgrnts.-Mexican, Israel
Jewish Imgrnts.-Uruguayan, Israel
Jewish Immigrants, Other, Israel
Jibu, Nigeria

259

Jiye, Sudan
Kaffa, Ethiopia (80)
Kalanga, Botswana
Kalinga, Southern, Philippines
Kambari, Nigeria (80)
Kamuku, Nigeria (80)
Karaboro, Upper Volta
Kepas, Papua New Guinea
Khamu, Thailand
Kimyal, Indonesia
Kissi, Sierra Leone
Kissi, Liberia
Komo, Ethiopia
Konkomba, Togo
Koreans of Japan, Japan
Korku in Madhya Pradesh, India
Krahn, Ivory Coast
Kudisai Vagh Makkal, India
Kui, Thailand
Kuknas, India
Kurds of Turkey, Turkey (79)
Labourers of Jhoparpatti, India
Lahu, Thailand (81)
Lango, Ethiopia
Lao, Laos (79)
Lao Refugees, Thailand
Lisu, Thailand
Lokoro, Sudan
Mahrah, Yemen, Democratic
Malayalars, India
Manobo, Ilianen, Philippines
Masengo, Ethiopia
Meitei, India (79)
Mimika, Indonesia
Mixteco,San Juan Mixtepic, Mexico
Mokole, Benin
Molbog, Philippines
Murngin (Wulamba), Australia
Nahua, North Pueblo, Mexico
Nepali, Nepal
Newari, Nepal
Ngen, Ivory Coast
Ningerum, Papua New Guinea
Nkoya, Zambia
Nouni, Upper Volta
Nuer, Ethiopia
Nuer, Sudan (79)
Nyantruku, Benin
Pala'wan, Philippines (81)
Parsees, India (81)
Parsis in Bombay, India (82)
Prisoners in Antananarivo,
  Madagascar (82)
Pygmy (Mbuti), Zaire (79)
Rai, Danuwar, Nepal
Ramkamhaeng Un. Students, Thailand
Rava in Assam, India
Ryukyuan, Japan
Samo-Kubo, Papua New Guinea
Sanuma, Brazil
Sherpa, Nepal
Shourastra in Tamil Nadu, India
Sindhis of India, India
Slum Dwellers of Bangkok, Thailand
So, Thailand (81)
Somahai, Indonesia
Talo, Indonesia
Tamang, Nepal
Tamil in Yellagiri Hills, India

Tamils (Indian), Malaysia
Teenbu, Ivory Coast
Tense, Ivory Coast
Tertiary Level Youth, Iran
Thai Islam (Thai), Thailand
Thai University Students, Thailand
  (81)
Tibetan Refugees, India
Tibetans, China
Tofi, Benin
Tonga, Zimbabwe
Topotha, Sudan
Toussian, Upper Volta
Universitarios - Rosario, Argentina
  (82)
University Students, France (79)
University Students, German Federal
  Rep. (79)
Vai, Liberia (80)
Warjawa, Nigeria
Wazinza, Tanzania
Women Laborers, Taiwan
Yalunka, Sierra Leone (80)
Yanomamo in Brazil, Brazil (79)
Yanyula, Australia
Yao Refugees from Laos, Thailand
Yucuna, Colombia

RELUCTANT

Aborigines in Brisbane, Australia
  (82)
Afar, Ethiopia (79)
Ahmadis in Lahore, Pakistan (82)
Alaba, Ethiopia
Alago, Nigeria
Arabs in Morocco, Morocco
Arabs of Khuzestan, Iran
Barasano, Southern, Colombia
Bengalis in London, United Kingdom
  (82)
Busa, Nigeria (80)
Butawa, Nigeria
Bwa, Upper Volta (80)
Cape Malays in Cape Town, South
  Africa (82)
Chinese Fishermen, Malaysia
Chitralis, Pakistan (79)
Chola Naickans, India
Chuj of San Mateo Ixtatan,
  Guatemala
Circassians in Amman, Jordan (82)
Dead-End Kids - Amsterdam,
  Netherlands (82)
Deccani Muslims-Hyderabad, India
  (82)
Digo, Kenya
Druzes, Israel (79)
Farmers of Japan, Japan
Fishing Village People, Taiwan
Fra-Fra, Ghana
Fulani, Cameroon (79)
Ga-Dang, Philippines
Galla, Harar, Ethiopia
Gilakis, Iran

Gourency, Upper Volta
Government officials, Thailand
Guarayu, Bolivia
Gujarati, United Kingdom
Gujars of Kashmir, India (81)
Gujars of Kashmir, India (81)
Gypsies in Jerusalem, Israel (82)
Hopi, United States of America
Ica, Colombia
Ifugao in Cababuyan, Philippines
Igbira, Nigeria (80)
Indians in Fiji, Fiji (79)
Indust.Workers Yongdungpo, Korea,
  Republic of
Iravas in Kerala, India
Ixil, Guatemala
Jama Mapun, Philippines (80)
Japanese in Brazil, Brazil (79)
Jews of Iran, Iran
Jews of Montreal, Canada
Jews, Sephardic, Canada
Kankanay, Northern, Philippines
Karen, Pwo, Thailand
Kayagar, Indonesia
Kerewe, Tanzania
Komering, Indonesia
Kotokoli, Benin
Krumen, Ivory Coast
Lamba, Togo
Lawa, Eastern, Thailand (81)
Lawa, Mountain, Thailand
Lubang Islanders, Philippines (81)
Maithili, Nepal
Malappanackers, India
Malays of Singapore, Singapore (79)
Mappillas, India
Mapuche, Chile
Mazandaranis, Iran
Miya, Nigeria
Moken, Burma (79)
Moken of Thailand, Thailand
Monpa, India
Mru, Bangladesh
Mualthuam, India
Musi, Indonesia
Muslim Gypsies in Skoplje,
  Yugoslavia (82)
Nambikuara, Brazil
Nurses in St. Louis, United States
  of America (82)
Ogan, Indonesia
Palaung, Burma (79)
Pension Students-Madrid, Spain (82)
Poouch in Kashmir, India
Purig-Pa of Kashmir, India (81)
Rabinal-Achi, Guatemala
Rajasthani Muslims-Jaipur, India
  (82)
Rajbansi, Nepal
Sabbra, Kenya
Sama Bangingi, Philippines (80)
Sama Pangutaran, Philippines (80)
Sama-Badjaw, Philippines (79)
Sangil, Philippines
Satnamis in M.P., India
Sayyids, Yemen, Arab Republic
Senufo, Ivory Coast (80)
Sindhi Muslims in Karachi, Pakistan
  (82)

Sinhalese, Sri Lanka
Solorese Muslims, Indonesia (81)
Somali, Ajuran, Kenya (79)
Somali, Degodia, Kenya
Somali, Gurreh, Kenya
Somali, Ogadenya, Kenya
Street Vendors in Saigon, Viet Nam
  (82)
Swatis, Pakistan (79)
T'in, Thailand (81)
Tagbanwa, Kalamian, Philippines
Tamil (Ceylonese), Sri Lanka
Tengger, Indonesia
Thai Northern, Thailand
Thai of Bangkok, Thailand
Thai, North East, Thailand
Thai, Southern, Thailand
Tibetans in Bhutan, Bhutan (81)
Tonga, Gwembe Valley, Zambia (79)
Turkana, Kenya
Turkish Immigrant Workers, German
  Federal Rep. (79)
Watchi, Togo
Winji-Winji, Benin
Woleat, Turks and Caicos Islands
Yakan, Philippines (80)
Yanomamo in Venezuela, Venezuela
Zowla, Ghana
Zuni, United States of America

VERY RELUCTANT

Achehnese, Indonesia (80)
Algerian (Arabs), Algeria (80)
Arab Immigrants in Bangui, Central
  African Republic (82)
Arawa, Nigeria
Azerbaijani Turks, Iran (80)
Balinese, Indonesia
Baluchi, Iran (80)
Bhutias, Bhutan
Bugis, Indonesia (80)
Chamula, Mexico (79)
Dawoodi Muslims, India
Dendi, Benin
Divehi, Maldives (80)
Fula, Guinea
Fula, Sierra Leone
Fulah, Upper Volta
Gays in San Francisco, United
  States of America (82)
Guaiaqui, Paraguay
Gugu-Yalanji, Australia
Gwandara, Nigeria
Jains, India
Jemez Pueblo, United States of
  America
Kabyle, Algeria (79)
Kae Sung Natives in Seoul, Korea,
  Republic of (82)
Khojas, Agha Khani, India
Kotta, India
Kreen-Akakore, Brazil
Kurds in Iran, Iran (80)
Libyans, Libya

Macu, Colombia
Madurese, Indonesia (79)
Maguindano, Philippines (80)
Malakkaras of Kerela, India (81)
Malayo, Colombia
Mandingo, Liberia (79)
Maranao, Philippines (79)
Maures, Senegal
Minangkabau, Indonesia (80)
Mirung, Bangladesh
Moor Malays, Sri Lanka (79)
Mumuyē, Nigeria
Muslim Malays, Malaysia (80)
Muslims (West Nile Dist.), Uganda
Muslims in U.A.E., United Arab
  Emirates (79)
Muslims of Jordan, Jordan
North Africans in Belgium, Belgium
  (80)
Ouaddai, Chad
Paiute, Northern, United States of
  America
Redjang, Indonesia (80)
Shan, Thailand
Soka Gakkai Believers, Japan
Somali, Ethiopia
Somali, Somalia (79)
Spiritists, Brazil (79)
Tausug, Philippines (80)
Tem, Togo
Tepehuan, Southwestern, Mexico
Thai Islam (Malay), Thailand (80)
Tuareg, Niger (79)
Turkomans, Iran (80)
Turks in Basel, Switzerland (82)
Turks, Anatolian, Turkey
Ulithi-Mall, Turks and Caicos
  Islands
Wolof, Senegal (80)
Yaoure, Ivory Coast
Yaquis, Mexico
Yemenis, Yemen, Arab Republic (79)
Zemi Naga of Assam, India (81)
Zinacantecos, Mexico (79)

NOT REPORTED

"Au"ei, Botswana
Abaknon, Philippines
Abanyom, Nigeria
Abau, Indonesia
Abau, Papua New Guinea
Abazin, Soviet Russia
Abe, Ivory Coast
Abialang, Sudan
Abidji, Ivory Coast
Abie, Papua New Guinea
Abkhaz, Turkey
Abkhaz, Soviet Russia
Abong, Nigeria
Abou Charib, Chad
Abu Leila, Sudan
Abua, Nigeria
Abujmaria in M.P., India
Abulas, Papua New Guinea

Abure, Ivory Coast
Ach'ang, China
Achagua, Colombia
Acheron, Sudan
Achi, Cubulco, Guatemala
Achi, Rabinal, Guatemala
Achipa, Nigeria
Achode, Ghana
Acholi, Uganda
Achual, Peru
Adamawa, Cameroon
Adele, Togo
Adhola, Uganda
Adiyan in Kerala, India
Adjora, Papua New Guinea
Adygei, Soviet Russia
Adyukru, Ivory Coast
Aeka, Papua New Guinea
Aeta, Philippines
Afitti, Sudan
Afshars, Iran
Agajanis, Iran
Agarabi, Papua New Guinea
Agariya in Bihar, India
Age, Cameroon
Aghem, Cameroon
Aghu, Indonesia
Agob, Papua New Guinea
Agoi, Nigeria
Aguacateco, Guatemala
Aguaruna, Peru
Agul, Soviet Russia
Agutaynon, Philippines
Agwagwune, Nigeria
Ahir in Maharashtra, India
Ahlo, Togo
Aibondeni, Indonesia
Aiku, Papua New Guinea
Aikwakai, Indonesia
Aimol in Assam, India
Aiome, Papua New Guinea
Aion, Papua New Guinea
Airo-Sumaghaghe, Indonesia
Airoran, Indonesia
Aja, Sudan
Ajmeri in Rajasthan, India
Aka, India
Akan, Brong, Ivory Coast
Akawaio, Guyana
Ake, Nigeria
Akhavakh, Soviet Russia
Akpa-Yache, Nigeria
Akpafu, Ghana
Akrukay, Papua New Guinea
Aladian, Ivory Coast
Alak, Laos
Alamblak, Papua New Guinea
Alangan, Philippines
Alas, Indonesia
Alatil, Papua New Guinea
Alauagat, Papua New Guinea
Alege, Nigeria
Algerian Arabs in France, France
Alor, Kolana, Indonesia (81)
Alur, Zaire
Alutor, Soviet Russia
Ama, Papua New Guinea
Amahuaca, Peru
Amaimon, Papua New Guinea

Amanab, Indonesia
Amanab, Papua New Guinea
Amar, Ethiopia
Amarakaeri, Peru
Amasi, Cameroon
Ambai, Indonesia
Ambasi, Papua New Guinea
Amber, Indonesia
Amberbaken, Indonesia
Ambo, Zambia
Ambonese, Netherlands
Ambonese, Indonesia
Amo, Nigeria
Amsterdam Boat Dwellers,
  Netherlands
Amto, Papua New Guinea
Amuesha, Peru
Amuzgo, Guerrero, Mexico
Amuzgo, Oaxaca, Mexico
Ana, Togo
Anaang, Nigeria
Anal in Manipur, India
Andarum, Papua New Guinea
Andha in Andhra Pradesh, India
Andi, Soviet Russia
Andoque, Colombia
Anem, Papua New Guinea
Anga in Bihar, India
Angaataha, Papua New Guinea
Angal Heneng, South, Papua New
  Guinea
Angal Heneng, West, Papua New
  Guinea
Angal, East, Papua New Guinea
Angas, Nigeria
Angaua, Papua New Guinea
Anggor, Papua New Guinea
Angoram, Papua New Guinea
Animere, Togo
Ankave, Papua New Guinea
Ankwe, Nigeria
Anor, Papua New Guinea
Ansus, Indonesia
Anuak, Ethiopia
Anuak, Sudan
Anuki, Papua New Guinea
Anyanga, Togo
Apalai, Brazil
Apinaye, Brazil
Apurina, Brazil
Ara, Indonesia
Arab-Jabbari (Kamesh), Iran
Arab-Shaibani (Kamesh), Iran
Arabela, Peru
Arafundi, Papua New Guinea
Aranadan in Tamil Nadu, India
Arandai, Indonesia
Arapaco, Brazil
Arapesh, Bumbita, Papua New Guinea
Arapesh, Mountain, Papua New Guinea
Arapesh, Muhiang, Papua New Guinea
Arawak, Guyana
Arawe, Papua New Guinea
Arbore, Ethiopia
Archin, Soviet Russia
Arecuna, Venezuela
Argobba, Ethiopia
Arguni, Indonesia
Arifama-Miniafia, Papua New Guinea

Arigibi, Papua New Guinea
Arinua, Papua New Guinea
Arop, Papua New Guinea
Aruop, Papua New Guinea
Arusha, Tanzania
Arutani, Venezuela
Arya in Andhra Pradesh, India
Asaro, Papua New Guinea
Asat, Papua New Guinea
Asienara, Indonesia
Assamese, Bangladesh
Assumbo, Cameroon
Asu, Tanzania
Asuri in Bihar, India
Ata, Papua New Guinea
Aten, Nigeria
Ati, Philippines
Atoc, Sudan
Atruahi, Brazil
Attie, Ivory Coast
Atuot, Sudan
Au, Papua New Guinea
Aunalei, Papua New Guinea
Auyana, Papua New Guinea
Avatime, Ghana
Avikam, Ivory Coast
Avukaya, Sudan
Awa, Papua New Guinea
Awar, Papua New Guinea
Awara, Papua New Guinea
Awin, Papua New Guinea
Awngi, Ethiopia
Awutu, Ghana
Awyi, Indonesia
Awyu, Indonesia
Ayana, Kenya
Aymara, Carangas, Chile
Ayoreo, Paraguay
Ayu, Nigeria
Azera, Papua New Guinea
Baali, Zaire
Babajou, Cameroon
Babri, India
Baburiwa, Indonesia
Bachama, Nigeria
Bada, Nigeria
Badagu in Nilgiri, India
Bade, Nigeria
Badyara, Guinea-Bissau
Bafut, Cameroon
Bagelkhandi in M.P., India
Baghati in H.P., India
Bagirmi, Chad
Bagri, Pakistan
Baguio Area Miners, Philippines
  (81)
Bahais in Teheran, Iran (82)
Baham, Indonesia
Baharlu (Kamesh), Iran
Bahawalpuri in M.P., India
Bahinemo, Papua New Guinea
Bai, Sudan
Baibai, Papua New Guinea
Baiga in Bihar, India
Baining, Papua New Guinea
Bajania, Pakistan (79)
Bajau, Indonesian, Indonesia
Bajau, Land, Malaysia
Baka, Cameroon

263

Baka, Zaire
Bakairi, Brazil
Bakhtiaris, Iran (80)
Bakwe, Ivory Coast
Bakwele, Congo
Balangaw, Philippines
Balanta, Senegal
Balantak, Indonesia
Balante, Guinea-Bissau
Bali, Nigeria
Bali-Vitu, Papua New Guinea
Balkars, Soviet Russia
Balmiki, Pakistan
Balong, Cameroon
Balti in Jammu, India
Bam, Papua New Guinea
Bambara, Mali
Bambara, Ivory Coast
Bambuka, Nigeria
Bamougoun-Bamenjou, Cameroon
Bamum, Cameroon
Bandawa-Minda, Nigeria
Bandi, Liberia
Bandjoun, Cameroon
Banen, Cameroon
Banga, Nigeria
Bangangte, Cameroon
Bangaru in Punjab, India
Bangba, Zaire
Banggai, Indonesia
Baniwa, Brazil
Banoni, Papua New Guinea
Bantuanon, Philippines
Banyum, Senegal
Banyun, Guinea-Bissau
Barabaig, Tanzania (79)
Barai, Papua New Guinea
Barambu, Sudan
Barasano, Colombia
Barasano, Northern, Colombia
Barau, Indonesia
Bare'e, Indonesia
Bareli in Madhya Pradesh, India
Bari, Sudan
Bariai, Papua New Guinea
Bariba, Nigeria
Bariji, Papua New Guinea
Barim, Papua New Guinea
Barok, Papua New Guinea
Baruga, Papua New Guinea
Baruya, Papua New Guinea
Basaa, Cameroon
Basakomo, Nigeria
Basari, Togo
Basari, Senegal
Basari, Guinea
Basari, Senegal
Bashar, Nigeria
Bashgali, Afghanistan
Bashkir, Soviet Russia (80)
Basila, Togo
Basketo, Ethiopia
Bata, Nigeria
Batak, Karo, Indonesia
Batak, Palawan, Philippines
Batak, Simalungun, Indonesia
Batak, Toba, Indonesia
Batanga-Ngolo, Cameroon
Bateg, Malaysia

Bathudi in Bihar, India
Batsi, Soviet Russia
Batu, Nigeria
Bau, Papua New Guinea
Baushi, Nigeria
Bauwaki, Papua New Guinea
Bawm, Bangladesh
Bayats, Iran
Bayot, Gambia
Bayot, Guinea-Bissau
Bayot, Senegal
Bazigar in Gujarat, India
Bebeli, Papua New Guinea
Bediya in Bihar, India
Bedoanas, Indonesia
Beja, Ethiopia
Beja, Sudan
Bekwarra, Nigeria
Bembe, Zaire
Bembi, Papua New Guinea
Bena, Tanzania
Benabena, Papua New Guinea
Bencho, Ethiopia
Bende, Tanzania
Bene, Cameroon
Benga, Gabon
Bengali, Bangladesh (80)
Berba, Benin
Berik, Indonesia
Berom, Nigeria
Besisi, Malaysia
Bete, India
Bethen, Cameroon
Betsinga, Cameroon
Bette-Bende, Nigeria
Bhakta, India
Bharia in Madhya Pradesh, India
Bhatneri, India
Bhattri, India
Bhilala, India
Bhoyari in Maharashtra, India
Bhuiya in Bihar, India
Bhumij in Assam, India
Bhunjia in Madhya Pradesh, India
Biafada, Guinea-Bissau
Biak, Indonesia
Biaka, Papua New Guinea
Biangai, Papua New Guinea
Bibling, Papua New Guinea
Biduanda, Malaysia
Bidyogo, Guinea-Bissau
Bijori in Bihar, India
Biksi, Indonesia
Bilala, Chad
Bile, Nigeria
Bilen, Ethiopia
Biliau, Papua New Guinea
Bimanese, Indonesia
Bimin, Papua New Guinea
Bimoba, Ghana
Bimoba, Togo
Binahari, Papua New Guinea
Binandere, Papua New Guinea
Binawa, Nigeria
Bine, Papua New Guinea
Binga, Sudan
Bingkokak, Indonesia
Binjhwari in Bihar, India
Binji, Zaire

Binumarien, Papua New Guinea
Bira, Indonesia
Bira, Zaire
Birhor in Bihar, India
Birifor, Ghana
Birifor, Upper Volta
Bisa, Zambia
Bisaya, Malaysia (81)
Bisis, Papua New Guinea
Bitara, Papua New Guinea
Bitare, Nigeria
Bitare, Cameroon
Biti, Sudan
Biyom, Papua New Guinea
Boanaki, Papua New Guinea
Bobe, Cameroon
Bobo Fing, Mali
Bobo Wule, Mali
Bodo in Assam, India
Boghom, Nigeria
Bohutu, Papua New Guinea
Boikin, Papua New Guinea
Bokyi, Nigeria
Bokyi, Cameroon
Bola, Papua New Guinea
Bole, Nigeria
Bolon, Upper Volta
Bolondo, Zaire
Bom, Papua New Guinea
Boma, Zaire
Bomboko, Cameroon
Bomou, Chad
Bondei, Tanzania
Bondo in Orissa, India
Bonerif, Indonesia
Bonggo, Indonesia
Bongili, Congo
Bongo, Sudan
Bongu, Papua New Guinea
Bonkeng-Pendia, Cameroon
Bonkiman, Papua New Guinea
Bor Gok, Sudan
Bora, Colombia
Borai, Indonesia
Boran, Ethiopia
Boran, Kenya
Bosavi, Papua New Guinea
Bosilewa, Papua New Guinea
Bosngun, Papua New Guinea
Botlikh, Soviet Russia
Bousansi, Upper Volta
Bovir-Ahmadi, Iran
Bowili, Togo
Boya, Sudan
Bozo, Mali
Brahui, Pakistan
Braj in Uttar Pradesh, India
Brao, Laos (79)
Brat, Indonesia
Breri, Papua New Guinea
Bruneis, Malaysia
Bua, Chad
Bual, Indonesia
Buang, Central, Papua New Guinea
Buang, Mangga, Papua New Guinea
Bube, Equatorial Guinea
Budibud, Papua New Guinea
Budu, Zaire

Budug, Soviet Russia
Budugum, Cameroon
Buduma, Nigeria
Buglere, Panama
Bugombe, Zaire
Buhid, Philippines
Builsa, Ghana
Buin, Papua New Guinea
Buja, Zaire
Buka-khwe, Botswana
Bukaua, Papua New Guinea
Buli, Indonesia
Buli, Upper Volta
Bulia, Zaire
Bullom, Northern, Sierra Leone
Bullom, Southern, Sierra Leone
Bulu, Papua New Guinea
Buna, Papua New Guinea
Bunabun, Papua New Guinea
Bunak, Indonesia
Bunama, Papua New Guinea
Bunann in Kashmir, India
Bungku, Indonesia
Bunu, Nigeria
Bura, Cameroon
Burak, Nigeria
Buraka-Gbanziri, Congo
Buriat, China
Buriat, Soviet Russia
Burig, China
Burig in Kashmir, India
Burji, Ethiopia
Buru, Indonesia
Burum, Papua New Guinea
Burun, Sudan
Burungi, Tanzania
Busa, Papua New Guinea
Busami, Indonesia
Bushmen (Heikum), Namibia
Bushmen in Botswana, Botswana
Bushoong, Zaire
Bussa, Ethiopia
Butung, Indonesia
Buwid, Philippines (81)
Bviri, Sudan
Bwa, Zaire
Bwaidoga, Papua New Guinea
Bwisi, Zaire
Cacua, Colombia
Caiwa, Brazil
Cakchiquel, Central, Guatemala
Caluyanhon, Philippines
Campa, Peru
Camsa, Colombia
Candoshi, Peru
Canela, Brazil
Capanahua, Peru
Carapana, Colombia
Cashibo, Peru
Cayapa, Ecuador
Cewa, Zambia
Ch'iang, China
Ch'ol Tila, Mexico
Chacobo, Bolivia
Chagga, Tanzania
Chaghatai, Afghanistan
Chakfem-Mushere, Nigeria
Chakossi in Ghana, Ghana
Chakossi in Togo, Togo

Chala, Ghana
Cham, Viet Nam
Chamacoco, Bahia Negra, Paraguay
Chamalin, Soviet Russia
Chamari in Madhya Pradesh, India
Chamba Daka, Nigeria
Chamba Leko, Nigeria
Chambri, Papua New Guinea
Chameali in H.P., India
Chami, Colombia
Chamicuro, Peru
Chamorro, Turks and Caicos Islands
Chara, Ethiopia
Chatino, Nopala, Mexico
Chatino, Panixtlahuaca, Mexico
Chatino, Tataltepec, Mexico
Chatino, Yaitepec, Mexico
Chatino, Zacatepec, Mexico
Chatino, Zenzontepec, Mexico
Chaungtha, Burma
Chawai, Nigeria
Chenapian, Papua New Guinea
Chenchu in Andhra Pradesh, India
Cherkess, Soviet Russia
Chero in Bihar, India
Chiga, Uganda
Chik-Barik in Bihar, India
Chin, China
Chin, Asho, Burma
Chin, Falam, Burma
Chin, Haka, Burma
Chin, Khumi, Burma
Chin, Ngawn, Burma
Chin, Tiddim, Burma
Chinanteco, Tepinapa, Mexico
Chinanteco, Ayotzintepec, Mexico
Chinanteco, Chiltepec, Mexico
Chinanteco, Comaltepec, Mexico
Chinanteco, Lalana, Mexico
Chinanteco, Lealao, Mexico
Chinanteco, Ojitlan, Mexico
Chinanteco, Palantla, Mexico
Chinanteco, Quiotepec, Mexico
Chinanteco, Sochiapan, Mexico
Chinanteco, Tepetotutla, Mexico
Chinanteco, Usila, Mexico
Chinbok, Burma
Chinese Businessmen, Hong Kong (81)
Chinese Factory Workers, Hong Kong
Chinese in Burma, Burma
Chinese in Costa Rica, Costa Rica
Chinese in Puerto Rico, Puerto Rico
Chinese in Saudi Arabia, Saudi
    Arabia
Chinese Merchants, Ghana
Chinese Muslims, Taiwan (81)
Chinese Villagers, Hong Kong
Chinga, Cameroon
Chinga, Cameroon
Chingp'o, China
Chip, Nigeria
Chipaya, Bolivia
Chiquitano, Bolivia
Chocho, Mexico
Chodhari in Gujarat, India
Chokobo, Nigeria
Chokwe, Zambia
Chokwe (Lunda), Angola
Chopi, Mozambique

Chorote, Argentina
Chorote, Paraguay
Chorti, Guatemala
Chuabo, Mozambique
Chuang, China (81)
Chuave, Papua New Guinea
Chuj, Guatemala
Chuj, San Mateo Ixtatan, Mexico
Chukot, Soviet Russia
Chulupe, Paraguay
Chungchia, China
Churahi in H.P., India
Chwang, China
Cinta Larga, Brazil
Circassian, Turkey
Cirebon, Indonesia
Citak, Indonesia
Cocama, Peru
Cocopa, Mexico
Cofan, Colombia
Cogui, Colombia
Cora, Mexico
Coreguaje, Colombia
Cubeo, Colombia
Cuiba, Colombia
Cuicateco, Tepeuxila, Mexico
Cuicateco, Teutila, Mexico
Cujareno, Peru
Culina, Brazil
Cuna, Colombia
Curipaco, Colombia
Cuyonon, Philippines
Daba, Cameroon
Daba, Cameroon
Dabra, Indonesia
Dadibi, Papua New Guinea
Dadiya, Nigeria
Daga, Papua New Guinea
Dagada, Indonesia
Dagari, Ghana
Dagari, Upper Volta
Dagur, China
Dahating, Papua New Guinea
Dai, Burma
Dair, Sudan
Daju of Dar Dadju, Chad
Daju of Dar Fur, Sudan
Daju of Dar Sila, Chad
Daju of West Kordofan, Sudan
Dami, Papua New Guinea
Dan, Liberia
Dangaleat, Chad
Danu, Burma
Daonda, Papua New Guinea
Dargin, Soviet Russia
Dass, Nigeria
Dathanik, Ethiopia
Davaweno, Philippines
Dawawa, Papua New Guinea
Day, Central African Republic
Daza, Chad
Deccani Muslims, India
Dedua, Papua New Guinea
Degema, Nigeria
Degenan, Papua New Guinea
Dem, Indonesia
Demta, Indonesia
Dengese, Zaire
Deno, Nigeria

Deori in Assam, India
Dera, Nigeria
Desano, Brazil
Dghwede, Cameroon
Dghwede, Cameroon
Dhaiso, Tanzania
Dhanka in Gujarat, India
Dhanwar in Madhya Pradesh, India
Dhurwa, India
Dia, Papua New Guinea
Dida, Ivory Coast
Didinga, Sudan
Didinga, Sudan
Didoi, Soviet Russia
Digo, Tanzania
Dimasa in Cachar, India
Dime, Ethiopia
Dimir, Papua New Guinea
Dinka, Sudan
Dinka, Agar, Sudan
Diodio, Papua New Guinea
Diola, Senegal
Diola, Guinea-Bissau (80)
Dirim, Nigeria
Dirya, Nigeria
Djuka, Surinam
Dobu, Papua New Guinea
Doe, Tanzania
Doga, Papua New Guinea
Doghosie, Upper Volta
Dogoro, Papua New Guinea
Dolgans, Soviet Russia
Dom, Papua New Guinea
Dompago, Benin
Domu, Papua New Guinea
Domung, Papua New Guinea
Dongjoi, Sudan
Dongo, Sudan
Dongo, Zaire
Dorlin in Andhra Pradesh, India
Dorobo, Kenya
Dorobo, Tanzania
Doromu, Papua New Guinea
Dorze, Ethiopia
Doura, Papua New Guinea
Duau, Papua New Guinea
Dubu, Indonesia
Duguir, Nigeria
Duguza, Nigeria
Duma, Gabon
Duna, Papua New Guinea
Dungan, Soviet Russia
Duru, Cameroon
Dusun, Malaysia (81)
Duvele, Indonesia
Dyan, Upper Volta
Dyerma, Niger (80)
Dyerma, Nigeria
Dyola, Gambia
Dyola, Guinea-Bissau
Dyola, Senegal
Ebira, Nigeria
Ebrie, Ivory Coast
Edawapi, Papua New Guinea
Edo, Nigeria
Efik, Nigeria
Efutop, Nigeria
Eggon, Nigeria
Eivo, Papua New Guinea

Ejagham, Nigeria
Ekagi, Indonesia
Ekajuk, Nigeria
Eket, Nigeria
Ekpeye, Nigeria
El Molo, Kenya
Eleme, Nigeria
Elkei, Papua New Guinea
Emai-Iuleha-Ora, Nigeria
Embera, Northern, Colombia
Emerum, Papua New Guinea
Emira, Papua New Guinea
Emumu, Indonesia
Endangen, Papua New Guinea
Enga, Papua New Guinea
Engenni, Nigeria
Enya, Zaire
Eotile, Ivory Coast
Epie, Nigeria
Erokwanas, Indonesia
Esan, Nigeria
Eton, Cameroon
Eton, Cameroon
Etulo, Nigeria
Evant, Nigeria
Evenki, China
Evenks, Soviet Russia
Ewage-Notu, Papua New Guinea
Ewenkis, China (81)
Fa D'Ambu, Equatorial Guinea
Fagululu, Papua New Guinea
Faiwol, Papua New Guinea
Fali, Cameroon
Fali, Cameroon
Fas, Papua New Guinea
Fasu, Papua New Guinea
Finungwan, Papua New Guinea
Fipa, Tanzania
Foau, Indonesia
Foi, Papua New Guinea
Foran, Papua New Guinea
Fordat, Indonesia
Fore, Papua New Guinea
Fula, Upper Volta
Fula, Cunda, Gambia
Fula, Macina, Mali
Fula, Peuhala, Mali
Fuliro, Zaire
Fulnio, Brazil
Fungom, Northern, Cameroon
Fungom, Northern, Cameroon
Fungor, Sudan
Furu, Zaire
Fuyuge, Papua New Guinea
Fyam, Nigeria
Fyer, Nigeria
Gabbra, Kenya
Gabri, Chad
Gadaban in Andhra Pradesh, India
Gaddi in Himachal Pradesh, India
Gade, Nigeria
Gadsup, Papua New Guinea
Gagauzes, Soviet Russia
Gagu, Ivory Coast
Gahuku, Papua New Guinea
Gaikundi, Papua New Guinea
Gaina, Papua New Guinea
Gal, Papua New Guinea
Galambi, Nigeria

Galeshis, Iran
Galla of Bucho, Ethiopia
Galler, Laos
Galong in Assam, India
Gambai, Chad
Gamei, Papua New Guinea
Gamti in Gujarat, India
Gan, Upper Volta
Gane, Indonesia
Gangam, Togo
Ganglau, Papua New Guinea
Gangte in Assam, India
Garuh, Papua New Guinea
Garus, Papua New Guinea
Garuwahi, Papua New Guinea
Gawar-Bati, Afghanistan
Gawari in Andhra Pradesh, India
Gawwada, Ethiopia
Gayo, Indonesia (80)
Gbande, Guinea
Gbari, Nigeria (80)
Gbaya, Nigeria
Gbaya-Ndogo, Sudan
Gbazantche, Benin
Gberi, Sudan
Gedaged, Papua New Guinea
Gedeo, Ethiopia
Geishas in Osaka, Japan (82)
Geji, Nigeria
Genagane, Papua New Guinea
Gende, Papua New Guinea
Gera, Nigeria
Geruma, Nigeria
Gesa, Indonesia
Gheko, Burma
Ghol, Sudan
Ghotuo, Nigeria
Ghulfan, Sudan
Gidar, Chad
Gidar, Cameroon
Gidar, Cameroon
Gidicho, Ethiopia
Gidra, Papua New Guinea
Gilyak, Soviet Russia
Gimi, Papua New Guinea
Ginuman, Papua New Guinea
Gio, Liberia
Gira, Papua New Guinea
Girawa, Papua New Guinea
Giri, Papua New Guinea
Giryama, Kenya
Gisei, Cameroon
Gisiga, Cameroon
Gitua, Papua New Guinea
Gizra, Papua New Guinea
Gobasi, Papua New Guinea
Gobato, Ethiopia
Gobeze, Ethiopia
Goemai, Nigeria
Gogo, Tanzania
Gogodala, Papua New Guinea
Gokana, Nigeria
Gola, Liberia
Gola, Sierra Leone
Golo, Chad
Gonja, Ghana
Goroa, Tanzania
Gorontalo, Indonesia
Gosha, Kenya

Goudari, Iran
Gouin-Turka, Upper Volta
Goulai, Chad
Gouwar, Cameroon
Gouwar, Cameroon
Grasia in Gujarat, India
Grunshi, Ghana
Gu, Benin
Guajajara, Brazil
Guajibo, Colombia
Guambiano, Colombia
Guana, Paraguay
Guarojio, Mexico
Guayabero, Colombia
Guayabevo, Colombia
Gude, Cameroon
Gude, Nigeria
Gudu, Nigeria
Guduf, Nigeria
Guere, Ivory Coast
Guhu-Samane, Papua New Guinea
Gujuri, Afghanistan
Gula, Chad
Gulfe, Cameroon
Gulfe, Cameroon
Gumasi, Papua New Guinea
Gumine, Papua New Guinea
Gumuz, Ethiopia
Gumuz, Sudan
Gurage, Ethiopia (80)
Gure-Kahugu, Nigeria
Gurensi, Ghana
Gurma, Upper Volta
Gurung, Nepal
Guruntum-Mbaaru, Nigeria
Gusap, Papua New Guinea
Guwot, Papua New Guinea
Gwa, Ivory Coast
Gwari Matai, Nigeria
Gwedena, Papua New Guinea
Gwere, Uganda
Gypsies, Soviet Russia
Gypsies in Yugoslavia, Yugoslavia
Ha, Tanzania
Hadiyya, Ethiopia
Hahon, Papua New Guinea
Halbi in Madhya Pradesh, India
Halia, Papua New Guinea
Hallam, Burma
Hamtai, Papua New Guinea
Hangaza, Tanzania
Hani, China
Hanonoo, Philippines
Harari, Ethiopia
Harauti in Rajasthan, India
Hatsa, Tanzania
Havu, Zaire
Havunese, Indonesia
Haya, Tanzania
Hehe, Tanzania
Heiban, Sudan
Helong, Indonesia
Herero, Botswana
Herero, Namibia
Heso, Zaire
Hezareh, Iran
Hixkaryana, Brazil
Hkun, Burma
Ho in Bihar, India

Kabadi, Papua New Guinea
Kabixi, Brazil
Kabre, Togo
Kabre, Benin
Kachama, Ethiopia
Kachchi in Andhra Pradesh, India
Kachin in Shan State, Burma
Kadaklan-Barlig Bontoc, Philippines
Kadar in Andhra Pradesh, India
Kadara, Nigeria
Kadazans, Malaysia
Kadiweu, Brazil
Kadugli, Sudan
Kaeti, Indonesia
Kagoma, Nigeria
Kagoro, Mali
Kagulu, Tanzania
Kahluri in Andamans, India
Kaian, Papua New Guinea
Kaibu, Nigeria
Kaiep, Papua New Guinea
Kaikadi in Maharashtra, India
Kaili, Indonesia
Kaingang, Brazil
Kairi, Papua New Guinea
Kairiru, Papua New Guinea
Kaiwai, Indonesia
Kajang, Indonesia
Kaka, Nigeria
Kaka, Central African Republic
Kaka, Cameroon
Kaka, Cameroon
Kakoa, Papua New Guinea
Kakuna-Mamusi, Papua New Guinea
Kakwa, Sudan
Kakwa, Uganda
Kakwa, Zaire
Kalanga, Zimbabwe
Kaliko, Zaire
Kalinga, Kalagua, Philippines
Kalinga, Limus-Linan, Philippines
Kalinga, Quinaang, Philippines
Kalmytz, China
Kalmytz, Soviet Russia
Kalokalo, Papua New Guinea
Kam, China
Kamano, Papua New Guinea
Kamantan, Nigeria
Kamar in Madhya Pradesh, India
Kamayura, Brazil
Kambera, Indonesia
Kamberataro, Indonesia
Kamberataro, Papua New Guinea
Kambot, Papua New Guinea
Kami, Tanzania
Kamkam, Cameroon
Kamkam, Cameroon
Kamnum, Papua New Guinea
Kamo, Nigeria
Kamoro, Indonesia
Kampung Baru, Indonesia
Kamtuk-Gresi, Indonesia
Kana, Nigeria
Kanauri in Uttar Pradesh, India
Kandas, Papua New Guinea
Kanembu, Chad
Kanembu, Niger
Kanga, Sudan
Kanikkaran in Kerala, India

Kaningra, Papua New Guinea
Kanite, Papua New Guinea
Kanjari in Andhra Pradesh, India
Kanu, Zaire
Kanum, Indonesia
Kanum, Papua New Guinea
Kanuri, Nigeria (80)
Kao, Ethiopia
Kaonde, Zaire
Kaonde, Zambia
Kapin, Papua New Guinea
Kapore, Papua New Guinea
Kapori, Indonesia
Kapriman, Papua New Guinea
Kapuchin, Soviet Russia
Kara, Tanzania
Kara, Papua New Guinea
Karachay, Soviet Russia
Karagas, Soviet Russia
Karaim, Soviet Russia
Karakalpak, Soviet Russia (80)
Karakalpak, Soviet Russia
Karam, Papua New Guinea
Karanga, Chad
Karangi, Papua New Guinea
Karas, Indonesia
Karatin, Soviet Russia
Kare, Papua New Guinea
Karekare, Nigeria
Karen, Thailand (79)
Kari, Chad
Kari, Central African Republic
Kari, Zaire
Karipuna Creole, Brazil
Karipuna Do Guapore, Brazil
Kariya, Nigeria
Karkar, Papua New Guinea
Karko, Sudan
Karmali in Dihar, India
Karon Dori, Indonesia
Karon Pantai, Indonesia
Karre, Central African Republic
Karua, Papua New Guinea
Kasanga, Guinea-Bissau
Kasele, Togo
Kasem, Upper Volta
Kasseng, Laos
Kasua, Papua New Guinea
Kasuweri, Indonesia
Katab, Nigeria
Katakari in Gujarat, India
Katcha, Sudan
Kate, Papua New Guinea
Kati, Northern, Indonesia
Kati, Southern, Indonesia
Katiati, Papua New Guinea
Katla, Sudan
Katukina, Panoan, Brazil
Kaugat, Indonesia
Kaugel, Papua New Guinea
Kaure, Indonesia
Kavwol, Indonesia
Kavwol, Papua New Guinea
Kaw, Burma
Kawar in Madhya Pradesh, India
Kawe, Indonesia
Kayabi, Brazil
Kayan, Malaysia
Kayan, Burma

Kayapo, Brazil
Kaygir, Indonesia
Kayupulau, Indonesia
Kazakhs, Iran (80)
Kazakhs, China (81)
Kebu, Togo
Kebumtamp, Bhutan
Kedayanas, Malaysia
Keer in Madhya Pradesh, India
Kei, Indonesia
Keiga, Sudan
Keiga Jirru, Sudan
Kela, Zaire
Kela, Papua New Guinea
Kelabit, Malaysia (81)
Kelao, China
Kele, Gabon
Kemak, Indonesia
Kembata, Ethiopia
Kemok, Malaysia
Kenati, Papua New Guinea
Kendari, Indonesia
Kenga, Chad
Kenyah, Indonesia
Keopara, Papua New Guinea
Kera, Chad
Kera, Cameroon
Kera, Cameroon
Kerewo, Papua New Guinea
Keriaka, Papua New Guinea
Kerinchi, Indonesia
Ket, Soviet Russia
Kewa, East, Papua New Guinea
Kewa, South, Papua New Guinea
Kewa, West, Papua New Guinea
Khakas, Soviet Russia
Khalaj, Iran
Khalka, China
Kham, China
Khamti in Assam, India
Khana, Nigeria
Khandesi, India
Khanti, Soviet Russia
Kharia in Bihar, India
Khasi in Assam, India
Khasonke, Mali
Khinalug, Soviet Russia
Khirwar in Madhya Pradesh, India
Khowar, India
Khvarshin, Soviet Russia
Kiari, Papua New Guinea
Kibet, Chad
Kibiri, Papua New Guinea
Kichepo, Sudan
Kikapoo, Mexico
Kilba, Nigeria
Kilmera, Papua New Guinea
Kim, Chad
Kim, Central African Republic
Kimaghama, Indonesia
Kimbu, Tanzania
Kinalakna, Papua New Guinea
Kinaray-A, Philippines
Kinga, Tanzania
Kirghiz, Afghanistan
Kirgiz, Soviet Russia (80)
Kirgiz, China
Kirifi, Nigeria
Kiriwina, Papua New Guinea

Kis, Papua New Guinea
Kisan in Bihar, India
Kisankasa, Tanzania
Kishanganjia in Bihar, India
Kishtwari in Jammu, India
Kisi, Tanzania
Kissi, Guinea
Kissi, Southern, Sierra Leone
Kita, Mali
Kiwai, Northeast, Papua New Guinea
Kiwai, Southern, Papua New Guinea
Kiwai, Wabuda, Papua New Guinea
Klaoh, Liberia
Koalib, Sudan (79)
Kobiana, Guinea
Kobon, Papua New Guinea
Koda in Bihar, India
Kodi, Indonesia
Koenoem, Nigeria
Kofyar, Nigeria
Kohoroxitari, Brazil
Kohumono, Nigeria
Koiari, Grass, Papua New Guinea
Koiari, Mountain, Papua New Guinea
Koita, Papua New Guinea
Kokant, Burma
Koke, Chad
Kol, Papua New Guinea
Kol in Assam, India
Kolbila, Cameroon
Kole, Cameroon
Kole, Cameroon
Koliku, Papua New Guinea
Kolom, Papua New Guinea
Kom in Manipur, India
Koma, Ghana
Koma, Nigeria
Koma, Cameroon
Koma, Cameroon
Koma, Central, Sudan
Komba, Papua New Guinea
Kombio, Papua New Guinea
Komi-Permyat, Soviet Russia
Komi-Zyrian, Soviet Russia
Komono, Upper Volta
Komutu, Papua New Guinea
Konabem, Cameroon
Konabem, Cameroon
Konda-Dora in A.P., India
Koneraw, Indonesia
Kongo, Angola
Konkani in Gujarat, India
Konkomba, Ghana
Kono, Nigeria
Konomala, Papua New Guinea
Konongo, Tanzania
Konso, Ethiopia
Konyagi, Guinea
Koraga in Kerala, India
Korak, Papua New Guinea
Korape, Papua New Guinea
Korapun, Indonesia
Koreans in Manchuria, China (81)
Koro, Nigeria
Koroma, Sudan
Korop, Nigeria
Korop, Cameroon
Korop, Cameroon
Korwa in Bihar, India

Koryak, Soviet Russia
Kosorong, Papua New Guinea
Kota, Gabon
Kota in Tamil Nadu, India
Kotia in Andhra Pradesh, India
Kotogut, Indonesia
Kotoko, Chad
Kotoko, Cameroon
Kotoko, Cameroon
Kotokoli, Togo
Kotopo, Cameroon
Kouya, Ivory Coast
Kovai, Papua New Guinea
Kove, Papua New Guinea
Koya in Andhra Pradesh, India
Koyra, Ethiopia
Kpa, Cameroon
Kpa, Cameroon
Kpelle, Liberia
Kpelle, Guinea
Kposo, Togo
Krachi, Ghana
Krim, Sierra Leone
Krio, Gambia
Krisa, Papua New Guinea
Krobou, Ivory Coast
Krongo, Sudan
Kryz, Soviet Russia
Kuatinema, Brazil
Kube, Papua New Guinea
Kubu, Indonesia (80)
Kubu, Indonesia (81)
Kuda-Chamo, Nigeria
Kudiya, India
Kugbo, Nigeria
Kuikuro, Brazil
Kuka, Chad
Kukele, Nigeria
Kukuwy, Papua New Guinea
Kukwa, Congo
Kulango, Ivory Coast
Kulele, Ivory Coast
Kulere, Nigeria
Kullo, Ethiopia
Kulung, Nigeria
Kumai, Papua New Guinea
Kumam, Uganda
Kuman, Papua New Guinea
Kumauni in Assam, India
Kumdauron, Papua New Guinea
Kumu, Zaire
Kumukio, Papua New Guinea
Kunama, Ethiopia
Kunante, Guinea-Bissau
Kunda, Mozambique
Kunda, Zimbabwe
Kunda, Zambia
Kunda, Zambia
Kuni, Papua New Guinea
Kunua, Papua New Guinea
Kuot, Papua New Guinea
Kupia in Andhra Pradesh, India
Kupsabiny, Uganda
Kurada, Papua New Guinea
Kurds in Kuwait, Kuwait
Kurfei, Niger
Kuria, Tanzania
Kurichiya in Kerala, India (81)
Kuruba in Tamil Nadu, India

Kurudu, Indonesia
Kurumba, Upper Volta
Kurux in Bihar, India
Kushi, Nigeria
Kusu, Zaire
Kuteb, Nigeria
Kutin, Cameroon
Kutu, Tanzania
Kuturmi, Nigeria
Kuvi in Orissa, India
Kuwaa, Liberia
Kuzamani, Nigeria
Kvanadin, Soviet Russia
Kwa, Nigeria
Kwadi, Angola
Kwakum, Cameroon
Kwale, Papua New Guinea
Kwambi, Namibia
Kwanga, Papua New Guinea
Kwangali, Angola
Kwansu, Indonesia
Kwanyama, Angola
Kwanyama, Namibia
Kwaya, Tanzania
Kwe-etshori, Botswana
Kwe-Etshori, Zimbabwe
Kwerba, Indonesia
Kwere, Tanzania
Kwese, Zaire
Kwesten, Indonesia
Kwoma, Papua New Guinea
Kwomtari, Papua New Guinea
Kyibaku, Nigeria
Laamang, Nigeria
Labans, India
Labbai, India
Labhani in Andhra Pradesh, India
Labu, Papua New Guinea
Lacandon, Mexico
Ladakhi in Jammu, India
Ladinos, Lebanon
Laewomba, Papua New Guinea
Lafofa, Sudan
Lahu, Burma
Lahul, China
Laka, Cameroon
Laka, Chad
Laka, China
Laka, Central African Republic
Lakians, Soviet Russia
Lakka, Nigeria
Lala, Zambia
Lalia, Zaire
Lalung in Assam, India
Lama, Burma
Lamba, Benin
Lamba, Zaire
Lamba, Zambia
Lambi, Cameroon
Lambya, Malawi
Lambya, Tanzania
Lame, Nigeria
Lamogai, Papua New Guinea
Lampung, Indonesia (80)
Landoma, Guinea
Landoma, Guinea-Bissau
Langi, Tanzania
Lango, Uganda
Lanoh, Malaysia

Lara, Indonesia
Laro, Sudan
Laru, Nigeria
Latdwalam, Indonesia
Lati, China
Laudje, Indonesia
Lavatbura-Lamusong, Papua New
  Guinea
Lavongai, Papua New Guinea
Lebgo, Nigeria
Lebong, Indonesia
Leco, Bolivia
Lega, Zaire
Lele, Chad
Lele, Upper Volta
Lele, Zaire
Lelemi, Ghana
Lendu, Zaire
Lengua, Northern, Paraguay
Lenje, Zambia
Leron, Papua New Guinea
Lese, Zaire
Letti, Indonesia
Li, China
Ligbi, Ivory Coast
Ligbi, Ghana
Liguri, Sudan
Lihir, Papua New Guinea
Liko, Zaire
Lima, Zambia
Limba, Sierra Leone
Lionese, Indonesia
Lisu, China (81)
Liv, Soviet Russia
Lo, Nigeria
Lobi, Ivory Coast
Lodhi in Bihar, India
Logba, Ghana
Logo, Zaire
Lohar, Pakistan
Lohiki, Papua New Guinea
Loinang, Indonesia (81)
Loko, Sierra Leone
Loko, Guinea
Loko, Sierra Leone
Lolo, China (81)
Loma, Guinea
Loma, Liberia
Lombi, Zaire
Lombo, Zaire
Lomwe, Mozambique
Longuda, Nigeria
Lore, Indonesia
Lori, Sudan
Lors, Iran (80)
Lotsu-Piri, Nigeria
Lou-Baluan-Pam, Papua New Guinea
Loven, Laos (81)
Lozi, Zimbabwe
Lozi, Zambia
Lu, China
Luac, Sudan
Luano, Zambia
Lubu, Indonesia
Luchazi, Angola
Luchazi, Zambia
Lue, Cameroon
Lugbara, Uganda
Lugbara, Zaire

Lugitama, Papua New Guinea
Luimbi, Angola
Lukep, Papua New Guinea
Lumbu, Gabon
Luna, Zaire
Lunda, Angola
Lunda, Ndembu, Zambia
Lundu, Cameroon
Lungu, Nigeria
Luo, Tanzania
Lushai in Assam, India
Luwu, Indonesia
Luyana, Angola
Luyana, Zambia
Lwalu, Zaire
Lwena, Angola
Lwo, Sudan
Ma, Zaire
Maanyan, Indonesia
Maba, Chad
Maba, Sudan
Maban-Jumjum, Sudan
Maca, Paraguay
Machiguenga, Peru
Macuna, Colombia
Madak, Papua New Guinea
Madda, Nigeria
Madi, Sudan
Madi, Uganda
Madik, Indonesia
Maghi, Burma
Magori, Papua New Guinea
Mahali in Assam, India
Mahri, Oman
Mai, Papua New Guinea
Mailu, Papua New Guinea
Maiongong, Brazil
Mairasi, Indonesia
Maisan, Papua New Guinea
Maiwa, Papua New Guinea
Majhwar in Madhya Pradesh, India
Maji, Ethiopia
Majingai-Ngama, Chad
Majingai-ngama, Central African
  Republic
Maka, Cameroon
Makarim, Papua New Guinea
Makasai, Indonesia
Makere, Uganda
Makian, West, Indonesia
Maklew, Indonesia
Makonde, Tanzania
Makua, Mozambique
Malalamai, Papua New Guinea
Malankuravan in Kerala, India
Malapandaram in Kerala, India
Malaryan in Kerala, India
Malas, Papua New Guinea
Malasanga, Papua New Guinea
Malavedan in Kerala, India
Male, Ethiopia
Malek, Papua New Guinea
Maleu, Papua New Guinea
Mali in Andhra Pradesh, India
Malila, Tanzania
Malki in Bihar, India
Malon, Papua New Guinea
Malpaharia in Assam, India
Malvi in Madhya Pradesh, India

Mama, Nigeria
Mamaa, Papua New Guinea
Mamasani, Iran
Mambai, Indonesia
Mambila, Cameroon
Mambwe-Lungu, Tanzania
Mambwe-Lungu, Zambia
Mamprusi, Ghana
Mamprusi, Ghana
Mamvu-Efe, Zaire
Mancang, Senegal
Manchu, China (81)
Manda, Tanzania
Mandar, Indonesia
Mandara, Nigeria
Mandaya, Philippines
Mandaya, Mansaka, Philippines
Mander, Indonesia
Manding, Senegal
Mandyak, Gambia
Manem, Indonesia
Mangbai, Chad
Mangbutu, Zaire
Manggarai Muslims, Indonesia (81)
Mangisa, Cameroon
Mangs in Maharashtra, India
Maninka, Guinea-Bissau
Maninka, Sierra Leone
Manjack, Senegal
Mankanya, Guinea-Bissau
Mankanya, Senegal
Manna-Dora in A.P., India
Mannan in Kerala, India
Mano, Liberia
Manobo, Agusan, Philippines
Manobo, Ata, Philippines
Manobo, Binokid, Philippines
Manobo, Dibabawon, Philippines
Manobo, Obo, Philippines
Manobo, Sarangani, Philippines
Manobo, Tagabawa, Philippines
Manobos, Pulangi, Philippines
Mansi, Soviet Russia
Mantera, Malaysia
Mantion, Indonesia
Manu Park Panoan, Peru
Manyika, Zimbabwe
Mao, Northern, Ethiopia
Maou, Ivory Coast
Mapoyo, Venezuela
Maquiritari, Venezuela
Mara in Assam, India
Maranao, Lanad, Philippines
Mararit, Chad
Marau, Indonesia
Marba, Chad
Marghi Central, Nigeria
Mari, Soviet Russia
Maria in Andhra Pradesh, India
Marind, Indonesia
Marind, Bian, Indonesia
Marka, Upper Volta
Marubo, Brazil
Marwari in Gujarat, India
Masa, Chad
Masaba, Uganda
Masakin, Sudan
Masalit, Chad
Masalit, Sudan

Masenrempulu, Indonesia
Mashi, Zambia
Massalat, Chad
Mataco, Argentina
Matakam, Cameroon
Matakam, Nigeria
Matawari, Surinam
Matbat, Indonesia
Matengo, Tanzania
Matipuhy-Nahukua, Brazil
Matlatzinca, Atzingo, Mexico
Matumbi, Tanzania
Maure, Mali
Mauri, Niger
Maviha, Mozambique
Mawes, Indonesia
Maxakali, Brazil
Mayo, Mexico
Mayoruna, Peru
Mba, Zaire
Mbaama, Gabon
Mbai, Chad
Mbai, Central African Republic
Mbala, Zaire
Mbangwe, Zaire
Mbanja, Zaire
Mbati, Central African Republic
Mbe, Nigeria
Mbede, Gabon
Mbembe, Cameroon
Mbembe (Tigong), Nigeria
Mbimu, Cameroon
Mbo, Cameroon
Mbo, Zaire
Mboi, Nigeria
Mbole, Zaire
Mbugwe, Tanzania
Mbukushu, Angola
Mbula-Bwazza, Nigeria
Mbum, Chad
Mbunda, Angola
Mbunga, Tanzania
Mbwela, Angola
Me'en, Ethiopia
Meax, Indonesia
Meban, Sudan
Meje, Uganda
Mekwei, Indonesia
Mende, Sierra Leone
Mende, Liberia
Menemo-Mogamo, Cameroon
Menka, Cameroon
Menri, Malaysia
Meos of Rajasthan, India (80)
Mesengo, Ethiopia
Mesme, Chad
Mesmedje, Chad
Miao, China (81)
Midob, Sudan
Mien, China (81)
Migili, Nigeria
Mimi, Chad
Mina in Madhya Pradesh, India
Minduumo, Gabon
Mingat, Soviet Russia
Minianka, Mali
Mirdha in Orissa, India
Miri, Sudan
Mishmi in Assam, India

Miskito, Nicaragua
Mixteco, Amoltepec, Mexico
Mixteco, Apoala, Mexico
Mixteco, Central Puebla, Mexico
Mixteco, Eastern, Mexico
Mixteco, Eastern Putla, Mexico
Mixteco, Huajuapan, Mexico
Mixteco, Silacayoapan, Mexico
Mixteco, Southern Puebla, Mexico
Mixteco, Southern Putla, Mexico
Mixteco, Tututepec, Mexico
Mixteco, Yosondua, Mexico
Mo, Ghana
Mo, Ivory Coast
Moba, Ghana
Moba, Togo
Mober, Nigeria
Modo, Sudan
Mofu, Cameroon
Mogholi, Afghanistan
Mogum, Chad
Moi, Indonesia
Molof, Indonesia
Mombum, Indonesia
Momoguns, Malaysia
Mon, Burma (81)
Mona, Ivory Coast
Mongondow, Indonesia (81)
Mongour, China
Moni, Indonesia
Monjombo, Central African Republic
Mono, Zaire
Montol, Nigeria
Moors in Mauritania, Mauritania
Moqaddam, Iran
Mor, Indonesia
Moreb, Sudan
Mori, Indonesia (81)
Moru, Ivory Coast
Moru, Sudan
Morunahua, Peru
Morwap, Indonesia
Mosi, Tanzania
Mossi, Upper Volta (80)
Motilon, Colombia
Motilon, Venezuela
Movima, Bolivia
Mpoto, Malawi
Mpoto, Tanzania
Mubi, Chad
Muinane, Colombia
Mulimba, Cameroon
Multani in Punjab, India
Mumbake, Nigeria
Mun, Burma
Muna, Indonesia
Mundang, Chad
Mundari in Assam, India
Mundu, Zaire
Munduruku, Brazil
Mungaka, Cameroon
Munggui, Indonesia
Munji-Yidgha, Afghanistan
Mura-Piraha, Brazil
Muria in Andhra Pradesh, India
Murle, Sudan
Mursi, Ethiopia
Murut, Malaysia
Musei, Chad

Musgu, Chad
Muslim Community of Bawku, Ghana
Muthuvan in A.P., India
Mutu, Venezuela
Muwasi in Madhya Pradesh, India
Mwanga, Tanzania
Mwera, Tanzania
Myaung-Ze, Burma
Nabi, Indonesia
Nadeb Maku, Brazil
Nafar, Iran
Nafri, Indonesia
Naga, Kalyokengnyu, India
Naga, Mao, India
Naga, Nruanghmei, India
Naga, Sangtam, India
Naga, Sema, India
Naga, Tangkhul, India
Naga, Wancho, India
Nagar in Madhya Pradesh, India
Nahsi, China
Naka, Sudan
Naltya, Indonesia
Nalu, Guinea
Nama, Namibia
Nama, South Africa
Namshi, Cameroon
Nanai, China
Nanai, Soviet Russia
Nancere, Chad
Nandi, Zaire
Nandu-Tari, Nigeria
Nao, Ethiopia
Naoudem, Togo
Nara, Ethiopia
Naraguta, Nigeria
Nata, Tanzania
Natemba, Togo
Natioro, Upper Volta
Nawuri, Ghana
Nchimburu, Ghana
Nchumbulu, Ghana
Nchumunu, Ghana
Ndaaka, Zaire
Ndali, Tanzania
Ndam, Central African Republic
Ndamba, Tanzania
Ndaonese, Indonesia
Ndau, Zimbabwe
Nde-Nsele-Nta, Nigeria
Ndengereko, Tanzania
Ndjem, Cameroon
Ndo, Zaire
Ndoe, Nigeria
Ndogo, Central African Republic
Ndogo, Sudan
Ndom, Indonesia
Ndomde, Tanzania
Ndoolo, Zaire
Ndop-Bamessing, Cameroon
Ndoro, Cameroon
Nduga, Indonesia
Ndunga, Zaire
Ndunpa Duupa, Cameroon
Nentsy, Soviet Russia
Newar in Kathmandu, Nepal (82)
Neyo, Ivory Coast
Ngada, Indonesia
Ngalik, North, Indonesia

Ngalik, Southern, Indonesia
Ngalum, Indonesia
Nganasan, Soviet Russia
Ngando, Central African Republic
Ngando, Zaire
Ngasa, Tanzania
Ngayaba, Cameroon
Ngbaka, Zaire
Ngbaka Ma'bo, Central African Republic
Ngbaka Ma'bo, Zaire
Ngbandi, Zaire
Ngbee, Zaire
Ngemba, Cameroon
Ngeq, Laos
Ngere, Ivory Coast
Ngi, Cameroon
Ngindo, Tanzania
Nginyukwur, Sudan
Ngirere, Sudan
Ngiri, Zaire
Ngizim, Nigeria
Ngok, Sudan
Ngoni, Tanzania
Ngoni, Zambia
Ngulu, Malawi
Ngulu, Tanzania
Ngumba, Cameroon
Ngumbi, Equatorial Guinea
Ngunduna, Sudan
Nguqwurang, Sudan
Ngurimi, Tanzania
Nguu, Tanzania
Ngwo, Cameroon
Ngwoi, Nigeria
Nharon, Botswana
Nhengatu, Brazil
Nias, Indonesia
Nielim, Chad
Nihali in Madhya Pradesh, India
Nilamba, Tanzania
Nimadi in Madhya Pradesh, India
Nimboran, Indonesia
Ninam, Brazil
Ninggrum, Indonesia
Ninzam, Nigeria
Nisa, Indonesia
Nivkhi, Soviet Russia
Njadu, Indonesia
Njalgulgule, Sudan
Nkem-Nkum, Nigeria
Nkom, Cameroon
Nkonya, Ghana
Nkutu, Zaire
Nohu, Cameroon
Norra, Burma
Northern Cagayan Negrito, Philippines
Nosu, China
Nsenga, Zimbabwe
Nsenga, Zambia
Nso, Cameroon
Nsongo, Angola
Ntomba, Zaire
Ntrubo, Ghana
Ntrubo, Togo
Ntrubs, Ghana
Numana-Nunku-Gwantu, Nigeria
Nung, China

Nungu, Nigeria
Nunuma, Upper Volta
Nuristani, Afghanistan (80)
Nyaheun, Laos
Nyakyusa, Malawi
Nyakyusa, Tanzania
Nyambo, Tanzania
Nyamusa, Sudan
Nyamwezi, Tanzania (80)
Nyaneka, Angola
Nyang, Cameroon
Nyanga-Li, Zaire
Nyangbo, Ghana
Nyanja, Zimbabwe
Nyankole, Uganda
Nyarueng, Sudan
Nyemba, Angola
Nyiha, Tanzania
Nyiha, Zambia
Nyoro, Uganda
Nyuli, Uganda
Nyungwe, Mozambique
Nyzatom, Sudan
Nzakara, Central African Republic
Nzanyi, Nigeria
Nzebi, Congo
Nzema, Ivory Coast
Nzema, Ghana
O'ung, Angola
Obanliku, Nigeria
Obolo, Nigeria
Ocaina, Peru
Od, Pakistan
Odual, Nigeria
Odut, Nigeria
Ogbia, Nigeria
Oi, Laos
Oirat, China
Ojhi in Madhya Pradesh, India
Okobo, Nigeria
Okpamheri, Nigeria
Ollari in Orissa, India
Olulumo-Ikom, Nigeria
Ong in Andamans, India
Onin, Indonesia
Orang Kanak, Malaysia
Orang Laut, Malaysia
Orang Ulu, Malaysia
Orejon, Peru
Oring, Nigeria
Ormu, Indonesia
Oroch, Soviet Russia
Orok, Soviet Russia
Oron, Nigeria
Oronchon, China
Oso, Cameroon
Ot Danum, Indonesia
Otank, Nigeria
Otomi, Eastern, Mexico
Otomi, Mezquital, Mexico
Otomi, Northwestern, Mexico
Otomi, Southeastern, Mexico
Otomi, State of Mexico, Mexico
Otomi, Tenango, Mexico
Otomi, Texcatepec, Mexico
Otoro, Sudan
Oubi, Ivory Coast
Oyampipuku, Brazil
Oyda, Ethiopia

Pacu, Brazil
Pahari Garhwali in U.P., India
Pai, Nigeria
Pai, China (81)
Paipai, Mexico
Paite in Assam, India
Pakaasnovos, Brazil
Palara, Ivory Coast
Palawano, Philippines
Palawano, Central, Philippines
Palembang, Indonesia
Palenquero, Colombia
Palikur, Brazil
Paloc, Sudan
Pambia, Central African Republic
Pame, Central Chichimeca, Mexico
Pame, Chichimeca-Jonaz, Mexico
Pame, Northern, Mexico
Pana, Central African Republic
Panare, Venezuela
Pande, Congo
Pangwa, Tanzania
Panika, India
Pankararu, Brazil
Pankhu, Bangladesh
Pantu, Indonesia
Pao, Burma
Pao in Madhya Pradesh, India
Paongan, China
Pape, Cameroon
Papel, Guinea-Bissau
Papuma, Indonesia
Parakanan, Brazil
Paranan, Philippines
Pardhan in Andhra Pradesh, India
Pare, Tanzania
Parengi in Orissa, India
Paresi, Brazil
Parintintin, Brazil
Pashayi, Afghanistan
Pashtuns, Iran (80)
Patamona, Guyana
Patelia in Gujarat, India
Pato Tapuia, Brazil
Paumari, Brazil
Paya, Honduras
Penan, Western, Malaysia (81)
Pende, Zaire
Pengo in Orissa, India
Peri, Zaire
Pero, Nigeria
Persians of Iran, Iran (80)
Phu Thai, Laos
Piapoco, Colombia
Piaroa, Venezuela
Pilaga, Argentina
Pima Bajo, Mexico
Pimbwe, Tanzania
Piratapuyo, Brazil
Piro, Peru
Pisa, Indonesia
Pishagchi, Iran
Piti, Nigeria
Pitu Uluna Salu, Indonesia
Piya, Nigeria
Pnar in Assam, India
Pocomchi, Eastern, Guatemala
Pocomchi, Western, Guatemala
Podokwo, Cameroon

Podzo, Mozambique
Pogolo, Tanzania
Poke, Zaire
Pokot, Uganda
Pol, Congo
Polci, Nigeria
Pom, Indonesia
Pongu, Nigeria
Popoloca, Ahuatempan, Mexico
Popoloca, Coyotepec, Mexico
Popoloca, Eastern, Mexico
Popoloca, Northern, Mexico
Popoloca, Southern, Mexico
Popoloca, Western, Mexico
Popoluca, Oluta, Mexico
Popoluca, Sayula, Mexico
Popoluca, Sierra, Mexico
Popoluca, Texistepec, Mexico
Porohanon, Philippines
Prang, Ghana
Pu-I, China
Puguli, Upper Volta
Puku-Geeri-Keri-Wipsi, Nigeria
Pular, Senegal
Punjabis, Pakistan (80)
Punu, China
Punu, Congo
Puragi, Indonesia
Purum, Burma
Pye, Ivory Coast
Pygmy (Binga), Burundi
Pygmy (Binga), Central African
  Republic
Pyu, Indonesia
Qajars, Iran
Qara'i, Iran
Qaragozlu, Iran
Qashqa'i, Iran (80)
Quaiquer, Colombia
Quarequena, Brazil
Rabha in Assam, India
Rai, Nepal
Ralte, Burma
Ratahan, Indonesia
Rataning, Chad
Rawang, China
Rendille, Kenya
Reshe, Nigeria
Reshiat, Ethiopia
Reyesano, Bolivia
Riang in Assam, India
Riang-Lang, Burma
Riantana, Indonesia
Rikbaktsa, Brazil
Romany, Turkey
Ronga, Mozambique
Ronga, South Africa
Ruihi, Tanzania
Rukuba, Nigeria
Rumaya, Nigeria
Runga, Chad
Runga, Central African Republic
Rungi, Tanzania
Rungwa, Tanzania
Ruruma, Nigeria
Rusha, Tanzania
Rut, Sudan
Rutul, Soviet Russia
Rwamba, Uganda

277

Rwamba, Zaire
Saamia, Uganda
Saams, Soviet Russia
Saberi, Indonesia
Sadan in Andamans, India
Sadang, Indonesia
Safaliba, Ghana
Safwa, Tanzania
Sagala, Tanzania
Saija, Colombia
Saisiat, Taiwan (81)
Sakata, Zaire
Sakuye, Kenya
Sala, Zambia
Salampasu, Zaire
Salar, China
Saliba, Colombia
Sama, Mapun, Philippines
Sama, Siasi, Philippines
Sama, Sibuku, Philippines
Samarkena, Indonesia
Samburu, Kenya
Samo, Northern, Mali
Samo, Northern, Upper Volta
Samogho, Mali
San, Namibia
Sanapana, Paraguay
Sandawe, Tanzania
Sanga, Nigeria
Sanga, Zaire
Sangir, Indonesia
Sangke, Indonesia
Sangu, Gabon
Sangu, Tanzania
Santa, China
Santrokofi, Ghana
Sanuma, Venezuela
Sanza, Zaire
Sapo, Liberia
Sarakole, Senegal (80)
Saramaccan, Surinam
Sarwa, Chad
Sasak, Indonesia (80)
Sasanis, Iran
Sasaru-Enwan Igwe, Nigeria
Satere, Brazil
Sau, Afghanistan
Sause, Indonesia
Saya, Nigeria
Secoya, Ecuador
Sekar, Indonesia
Sekayu, Indonesia
Seko, Indonesia
Sekpele, Ghana
Selkup, Soviet Russia
Semelai, Malaysia
Sempan, Indonesia
Sena, Malawi
Sena, Mozambique
Senggi, Indonesia
Sentani, Indonesia
Senthang, Burma
Sere, Sudan
Serere, Senegal (79)
Serere-Non, Senegal
Serere-Sine, Senegal
Seri, Mexico
Serui-Laut, Indonesia
Seuci, Brazil

Seychellois, Seychelles
Sha, Nigeria
Shahsavans, Iran (80)
Shambala, Tanzania
Shan, Burma
Shan Chinese, Burma
Shanga, Nigeria
Sharanahua, Peru
Sharchagpakha, Bhutan
Shatt, Sudan
Shawiya, Algeria
Sheko, Ethiopia
Shilha, Morocco
Shilluk, Sudan
Shina, Afghanistan
Shinasha, Ethiopia
Shipibo, Peru
Shor, Soviet Russia
Shua, Botswana
Shughni, Afghanistan
Shuwa Arabic, Nigeria
Shwai, Sudan
Siagha-Yenimu, Indonesia
Sibo, China
Sidamo, Ethiopia
Sikanese, Indonesia
Sikhule, Indonesia
Sikkimese, India
Simaa, Zambia
Siona, Colombia
Sira, Gabon
Siri, Nigeria
Siriano, Colombia
Siriono, Bolivia
Sisala, Upper Volta
Siwu, Ghana
So, Laos
So, Cameroon
Sobei, Indonesia
Sochi, Pakistan
Soga, Uganda
Soli, Zambia
Somahai, Indonesia
Somrai, Chad
Somrai, Central African Republic
Sondwari in M.P., India
Songe, Zaire
Songhai, Mali
Songhai, Niger
Songhai, Upper Volta
Songomeno, Zaire
Songoora, Zaire
Soninke, Gambia
Soninke, Mali
Soninke, Mauritania
Sonjo, Tanzania
Sopi, Sudan
Sora in Orissa, India
Soruba, Benin
Sowanda, Indonesia
Students in Cuiaba, Brazil
Su, Cameroon
Suba, Tanzania
Subanun,Lapuyan, Philippines
Subi, Tanzania
Suga, Cameroon
Sui, China
Suk, Kenya
Suku, Zaire

Sukur, Nigeria
Sulung, India
Sumba, Indonesia
Sumbawa, Indonesia
Sumbwa, Tanzania
Sumu, Nicaragua
Sungor, Chad
Suppire, Mali
Sura, Nigeria
Surubu, Nigeria
Surui, Brazil
Susu, Guinea-Bissau
Susu, Sierra Leone
Svan, Soviet Russia
Swaga, Zaire
Swaka, Zambia
Ta-Oi, Laos
Tabasaran, Soviet Russia
Tabi, Sudan
Tacana, Bolivia
Tadjio, Indonesia
Tadyawan, Philippines
Tafi, Togo
Tagal, Malaysia (81)
Tagwana, Ivory Coast
Tahit, Indonesia
Taikat, Indonesia
Taiwan-Chinese Un. Stud., Taiwan
Tajik, Iran (80)
Tajik, Afghanistan
Tajik, Soviet Russia
Takankar, India
Takemba, Benin
Takestani, Iran
Tal, Nigeria
Talish, Iran
Talodi, Sudan
Tama, Chad
Tamagario, Indonesia
Taman, Burma
Tamaria in Bihar, India
Tamazight, Morocco
Tambas, Nigeria
Tambo, Zambia
Tamil Muslims in Madras, India (82)
Tampulma, Ghana
Tana, Chad
Tana, Central African Republic
Tanahmerah, Indonesia
Tandanke, Senegal
Tandia, Indonesia
Tangale, Nigeria
Tangchangya, Bangladesh
Tanimuca-Retuama, Colombia
Tao't Bato, Philippines
Taori-Kei, Indonesia
Tara, Indonesia
Tarahumara, Northern, Mexico
Tarahumara, Rocoroibo, Mexico
Tarahumara, Samachique, Mexico
Taram, Cameroon
Tarasco, Mexico
Targum, Israel
Tarof, Indonesia
Tarok, Nigeria
Tarpia, Indonesia
Tat, Soviet Russia
Tatars, Soviet Russia (80)
Tatoga, Tanzania

Taucouleur, Senegal (80)
Taungyo, Burma
Taungyoe, Burma
Taurap, Indonesia
Tawr, Burma
Tayaku, Benin
Tchang, Cameroon
Teda, Chad (80)
Teda, Libya
Teda, Niger
Tegali, Sudan
Teimuri, Iran
Teimurtash, Iran
Teke, Eastern, Zaire
Teke, Northern, Congo
Teke, Southwestern, Congo
Tembe, Brazil
Tembo, Zaire
Temein, Sudan
Temira, Malaysia
Tepehua, Huehuetla, Mexico
Tepehua, Pisa Flores, Mexico
Tepehua, Veracruz, Mexico
Tepehuan, Northern, Mexico
Tepehuan, Southeastern, Mexico
Tepeth, Uganda
Tepo, Ivory Coast
Tera, Nigeria
Terena, Brazil
Ternatans, Indonesia
Teso, Uganda
Thado in Assam, India
Thai-Ney, Burma
Thakur, India
Thar in Bihar, India
Tharu, Nepal
Thoi, Sudan
Thuri, Sudan
Ticuna, Brazil
Tidorese, Indonesia
Tiefo, Upper Volta
Tiene, Zaire
Tigon, Cameroon
Tikar, Cameroon
Timorese, Indonesia
Tindin, Soviet Russia
Tippera, Bangladesh
Tira, Sudan
Tirma, Sudan
Tiro, Indonesia
Tiruray, Philippines
Tlapaneco, Malinaltepec, Mexico
Toala, Indonesia
Toba, Argentina
Toda in Tamil Nadu, India
Togbo, Zaire
Tojolabal, Mexico
Tokkaru in Tamil Nadu, India
Tol, Honduras
Tombulu, Indonesia
Tomini, Indonesia
Tondanou, Indonesia
Tonga, Botswana
Tonga, Malawi
Tonga, Mozambique
Tongwe, Tanzania
Tonsea, Indonesia
Tontemboa, Indonesia
Toraja, Southern, Indonesia (81)

REGISTRY OF THE UNREACHED

Totis, India
Totonaco, Northern, Mexico
Totonaco, Oxumatlan, Mexico
Totonaco, Papantla, Mexico
Totonaco, Sierra, Mexico
Totonaco, Yecuatla, Mexico
Towei, Indonesia
Trepo, Ivory Coast
Trio, Surinam
Trique, San Juan Copala, Mexico
Tsaangi, Congo
Tsakhur, Soviet Russia
Tsamai, Ethiopia
Tsimane, Bolivia
Tsogo, Gabon
Tsonga, Mozambique
Tsou, Taiwan (81)
Tswa, Mozambique
Tswa, Zimbabwe
Tswana, Namibia
Tswana, Zimbabwe
Tubar, Mexico
Tucano, Brazil
Tugara, India
Tukude, Indonesia
Tula, Nigeria
Tulishi, Sudan
Tumale, Sudan
Tumawo, Indonesia
Tumma, Sudan
Tumtum, Sudan
Tunebo, Cobaria, Colombia
Tung-Chia, China (81)
Tunya, Chad
Tunya, Central African Republic
Tupuri, Chad
Tupuri, Cameroon
Tura, Ivory Coast
Turkish Workers, Belgium (80)
Turkwam, Nigeria
Turu, Tanzania
Turu, Indonesia
Tuvinian, Soviet Russia
Tuyuca, Brazil
Twi, Sudan
Tzeltal, Bachajon, Mexico
Tzeltal, Highland, Mexico
Tzotzil, Chenalho, Mexico
Tzotzil, Huistan, Mexico
Tzutujil, Guatemala
Udegeis, Soviet Russia
Udin, Soviet Russia
Udmurt, Soviet Russia
Uduk, Sudan
Uhunduni, Indonesia
Uighur, Afghanistan
Uigur, China (80)
Ukaan, Nigeria
Ukpe-Bayobiri, Nigeria
Ukwuani-Aboh, Nigeria
Ulchi, Soviet Russia
Ullatan in Kerala, India
Umm Dorein, Sudan
Umm Gabralla, Sudan
Urali in Kerala, India
Urarina, Peru
Urhobo, Nigeria
Uria, Indonesia
Uruangnirin, Indonesia

Urubu, Brazil
Urupa, Brazil
Uspanteco, Guatemala
Utugwang, Nigeria
Uvbie, Nigeria
Uzekwe, Nigeria
Vagala, Ghana
Vagari, Pakistan
Vagla, Ghana
Vai, Sierra Leone
Vaikino, Indonesia
Vaiphei in Assam, India
Vale, Central African Republic
Venda, Zimbabwe
Veps, Soviet Russia
Vere, Cameroon
Vidunda, Tanzania
Vietnamese, Laos
Vige, Upper Volta
Vinza, Tanzania
Vishavan in Kerala, India
Voko, Cameroon
Vute, Nigeria
Wa, China
Wa, Burma
Wabo, Indonesia
Waddar in Andhra Pradesh, India
Wagdi in Rajasthan, India
Waimiri, Brazil
Waiwai, Brazil
Waiwai, Guyana
Waja, Nigeria
Wala, Ghana
Walamo, Ethiopia
Wambon, Indonesia
Wanda, Tanzania
Wandamen, Indonesia
Wandji, Gabon
Wanggom, Indonesia
Wanji, Tanzania
Wano, Indonesia
Wapishana, Brazil
Wapishana, Guyana
Wapishana, Venezuela
Wara, Upper Volta
Warao, Venezuela
Ware, Mali
Warembori, Indonesia
Waris, Indonesia
Warkay-Bipim, Indonesia
Waropen, Indonesia
Wasi, Tanzania
Waura, Brazil
Wayana, Surinam
Weda, Indonesia
Wetawit, Ethiopia
Wewewa, Indonesia
Widekum, Cameroon
Win, Upper Volta
Wobe, Ivory Coast
Wodani, Indonesia
Woi, Indonesia
Wolio, Indonesia
Wolof, Gambian, Gambia
Wom, Nigeria
Wongo, Zaire
Woro, Sudan
Wumbvu, Gabon
Wungu, Tanzania

Index by
Religion

INDEX BY PRINCIPAL PROFESSED RELIGION

This list indicates predominant professed religion, whether or not a majority of those who profess the religion are active practitioners. Many of the groups have more than one professed religion present, but only the one with the largest percentage of followers is indicated in this section.

AFRICAN INDEPENDENT

**Dida, Ivory Coast

ANCESTOR WORSHIP

**Akha, Thailand (79)
**K'anjobal of San Miguel,
  Guatemala

ANIMISM

"Au"ei, Botswana
Abanyom, Nigeria
Abau, Indonesia
Abau, Papua New Guinea
Abie, Papua New Guinea
Abua, Nigeria
Abulas, Papua New Guinea
Achagua, Colombia
Achi, Cubulco, Guatemala
Achi, Rabinal, Guatemala
Acholi, Uganda
Achual, Peru
Adamawa, Cameroon
Adhola, Uganda
***Adi, India
**Adja, Benin
Adjora, Papua New Guinea
Aeka, Papua New Guinea
*Afawa, Nigeria (80)
**Afo, Nigeria (80)
Agarabi, Papua New Guinea
Age, Cameroon
Aghem, Cameroon
Aghu, Indonesia
Agob, Papua New Guinea
Agoi, Nigeria
Aguacateco, Guatemala
Aguaruna, Peru
Agwagwune, Nigeria
Aibondeni, Indonesia
Aiku, Papua New Guinea
Aikwakai, Indonesia
Aiome, Papua New Guinea
Aion, Papua New Guinea
Airo-Sumaghaghe, Indonesia
Airoran, Indonesia
Aka, India
Ake, Nigeria
Akpa-Yache, Nigeria
Akrukay, Papua New Guinea
Alago, Nigeria
Alak, Laos
Alamblak, Papua New Guinea
Alatil, Papua New Guinea
Alauagat, Papua New Guinea
Alege, Nigeria
Alor, Kolana, Indonesia (81)

Alur, Zaire
Ama, Papua New Guinea
Amahuaca, Peru
Amaimon, Papua New Guinea
Amanab, Indonesia
Amanab, Papua New Guinea
Amar, Ethiopia
Amarakaeri, Peru
Amasi, Cameroon
Ambai, Indonesia
Ambasi, Papua New Guinea
Amber, Indonesia
Amberbaken, Indonesia
Ambo, Zambia
Ambonese, Netherlands
Ambonese, Indonesia
Amo, Nigeria
Amto, Papua New Guinea
Amuesha, Peru
Anaang, Nigeria
Anal in Manipur, India
Andarum, Papua New Guinea
Andha in Andhra Pradesh, India
Andoque, Colombia
Anem, Papua New Guinea
Angaataha, Papua New Guinea
Angal Heneng, South, Papua New
  Guinea
Angal Heneng, West, Papua New
  Guinea
Angal, East, Papua New Guinea
Angas, Nigeria
Angaua, Papua New Guinea
Anggor, Papua New Guinea
Angoram, Papua New Guinea
Ankave, Papua New Guinea
Ankwe, Nigeria
Anor, Papua New Guinea
Ansus, Indonesia
Anuak, Ethiopia
Anuak, Sudan
Anuki, Papua New Guinea
Apalai, Brazil
**Apatani in Assam, India
Apinaye, Brazil
Apurina, Brazil
Arabela, Peru
Arafundi, Papua New Guinea
Arandai, Indonesia
Arapaco, Brazil
Arapesh, Bumbita, Papua New
  Guinea
Arapesh, Mountain, Papua New
  Guinea
Arapesh, Muhiang, Papua New
  Guinea
Arawe, Papua New Guinea
Arbore, Ethiopia
Arecuna, Venezuela
Argobba, Ethiopia
Arguni, Indonesia
Arifama-Miniafia, Papua New
  Guinea
Arigibi, Papua New Guinea
Arinua, Papua New Guinea
*Arnatas, India
Arop, Papua New Guinea
Aruop, Papua New Guinea
Arusha, Tanzania

Arutani, Venezuela
Asaro, Papua New Guinea
Asat, Papua New Guinea
Asienara, Indonesia
*Asmat, Indonesia (79)
Assumbo, Cameroon
Asu, Tanzania
Asuri in Bihar, India
Ata, Papua New Guinea
*Ata of Davao, Philippines
Atruahi, Brazil
*Atta, Philippines
*Atye, Ivory Coast
Au, Papua New Guinea
Aunalei, Papua New Guinea
Auyana, Papua New Guinea
Awa, Papua New Guinea
Awar, Papua New Guinea
Awara, Papua New Guinea
Awin, Papua New Guinea
Awyi, Indonesia
Awyu, Indonesia
**Aymara, Bolivia
Ayoreo, Paraguay
Azera, Papua New Guinea
Baali, Zaire
Babajou, Cameroon
**Babur Thali, Nigeria (80)
Baburiwa, Indonesia
Bada, Nigeria
Badagu in Nilgiri, India
Bafut, Cameroon
Baghati in H.P., India
Baham, Indonesia
Bahawalpuri in M.P., India
Bahinemo, Papua New Guinea
Baibai, Papua New Guinea
Baiga in Bihar, India
Baining, Papua New Guinea
Baka, Cameroon
Baka, Zaire
Bakairi, Brazil
**Bakuba, Zaire
Bakwele, Congo
Balangaw, Philippines
Balante, Guinea-Bissau
Bali-Vitu, Papua New Guinea
Balong, Cameroon
Balti in Jammu, India
Bam, Papua New Guinea
Bamougoun-Bamenjou, Cameroon
***Banaro, Papua New Guinea
Bandi, Liberia
Bandjoun, Cameroon
Banen, Cameroon
Bangba, Zaire
Baniwa, Brazil
Banoni, Papua New Guinea
***Banyarwanda, Rwanda
Banyun, Guinea-Bissau
***Baoule, Ivory Coast
Barabaig, Tanzania (79)
Barai, Papua New Guinea
Barasano, Colombia
Barasano, Northern, Colombia
Barasano, Southern, Colombia
Barau, Indonesia
Bare'e, Indonesia
Bariai, Papua New Guinea

*Bariba, Benin (80)
Bariji, Papua New Guinea
Barim, Papua New Guinea
Barok, Papua New Guinea
Baruga, Papua New Guinea
Baruya, Papua New Guinea
Basakomo, Nigeria
Basari, Togo
Basari, Senegal
Basari, Guinea
Basari, Senegal
Bashar, Nigeria
Basketo, Ethiopia
***Basotho, Mountain, Lesotho (79)
*Bassa, Liberia
**Bassa, Nigeria
Batak, Karo, Indonesia
Batak, Simalungun, Indonesia
Batak, Toba, Indonesia
Batanga-Ngolo, Cameroon
Bateg, Malaysia
Bau, Papua New Guinea
Bauwaki, Papua New Guinea
Bazigar in Gujarat, India
Bebeli, Papua New Guinea
Bediya in Bihar, India
Bedoanas, Indonesia
Bekwarra, Nigeria
Bembe, Zaire
Bembi, Papua New Guinea
Bena, Tanzania
Benabena, Papua New Guinea
Bencho, Ethiopia
Bende, Tanzania
Bene, Cameroon
Benga, Gabon
Berba, Benin
Berik, Indonesia
Berom, Nigeria
Besisi, Malaysia
Bete, India
*Bete, Ivory Coast
Bethen, Cameroon
Betsinga, Cameroon
Bette-Bende, Nigeria
Bharia in Madhya Pradesh, India
**Bhils, India (79)
Bhuiya in Bihar, India
Biafada, Guinea-Bissau
Biak, Indonesia
Biaka, Papua New Guinea
Biangai, Papua New Guinea
Bibling, Papua New Guinea
Biduanda, Malaysia
**Bijogo, Guinea-Bissau
Biksi, Indonesia
**Bilan, Philippines
Biliau, Papua New Guinea
Bimin, Papua New Guinea
Binahari, Papua New Guinea
Binandere, Papua New Guinea
Bine, Papua New Guinea
Binji, Zaire
Binumarien, Papua New Guinea
Bira, Zaire
Birifor, Ghana
Bisa, Zambia
Bisaya, Malaysia (81)
Bisis, Papua New Guinea

Cogui, Colombia
**Coreguaje, Colombia
Coreguaje, Colombia
Cubeo, Colombia
Cuiba, Colombia
Cujareno, Peru
Culina, Brazil
*Cuna, Colombia (79)
Cuna, Colombia
Curipaco, Colombia
Daba, Cameroon
Daba, Cameroon
Dabra, Indonesia
Dadibi, Papua New Guinea
Daga, Papua New Guinea
Dagada, Indonesia
Dagari, Ghana
Dahating, Papua New Guinea
Daju of Dar Fur, Sudan
*Daka, Nigeria
Dami, Papua New Guinea
***Dan, Ivory Coast
*Dani, Baliem, Indonesia (79)
Daonda, Papua New Guinea
Dathanik, Ethiopia
Dawawa, Papua New Guinea
Day, Central African Republic
Dedua, Papua New Guinea
Degema, Nigeria
Degenan, Papua New Guinea
Dem, Indonesia
Demta, Indonesia
Dengese, Zaire
Deori in Assam, India
Desano, Brazil
*Dghwede, Nigeria
Dghwede, Cameroon
Dghwede, Cameroon
Dhaiso, Tanzania
Dhanka in Gujarat, India
Dhanwar in Madhya Pradesh, India
Dia, Papua New Guinea
Didinga, Sudan
Digo, Tanzania
Dimasa in Cachar, India
Dime, Ethiopia
Dimir, Papua New Guinea
Dinka, Sudan
Diodio, Papua New Guinea
Dobu, Papua New Guinea
Doe, Tanzania
*Dog-Pa of Ladakh, India (81)
Doga, Papua New Guinea
*Dogon, Mali (79)
Dogoro, Papua New Guinea
Dom, Papua New Guinea
Dompago, Benin
Domu, Papua New Guinea
Domung, Papua New Guinea
Dongo, Zaire
**Doohwaayo, Cameroon
Dorobo, Kenya
Dorobo, Tanzania
Doromu, Papua New Guinea
Dorze, Ethiopia
Doura, Papua New Guinea
Duau, Papua New Guinea
Dubu, Indonesia
**Duka, Nigeria

Duma, Gabon
*Dumagat , Casiguran, Philippines (81)
Duna, Papua New Guinea
Duru, Cameroon
Dusun, Malaysia (81)
Duvele, Indonesia
Edawapi, Papua New Guinea
Edo, Nigeria
Efik, Nigeria
Efutop, Nigeria
Eggon, Nigeria
Eivo, Papua New Guinea
Ejagham, Nigeria
Ekagi, Indonesia
Ekajuk, Nigeria
Eket, Nigeria
Ekpeye, Nigeria
El Molo, Kenya
Eleme, Nigeria
Elkei, Papua New Guinea
Emai-Iuleha-Ora, Nigeria
Embera, Northern, Colombia
Emerum, Papua New Guinea
Emira, Papua New Guinea
Emumu, Indonesia
Endangen, Papua New Guinea
Enga, Papua New Guinea
Engenni, Nigeria
Enya, Zaire
Epie, Nigeria
Erokwanas, Indonesia
Esan, Nigeria
Eton, Cameroon
Eton, Cameroon
Etulo, Nigeria
Evant, Nigeria
Ewage-Notu, Papua New Guinea
Ewenkis, China (81)
Fa D'Ambu, Equatorial Guinea
Fagululu, Papua New Guinea
Faiwol, Papua New Guinea
**Fakai, Nigeria
**Fali, Nigeria
Fas, Papua New Guinea
Fasu, Papua New Guinea
Finungwan, Papua New Guinea
Fipa, Tanzania
Foau, Indonesia
Foi, Papua New Guinea
Foran, Papua New Guinea
Fordat, Indonesia
Fore, Papua New Guinea
Fra-Fra, Ghana
Fula, Macina, Mali
Fula, Peuhala, Mali
Fuliro, Zaire
Fulnio, Brazil
Fungom, Northern, Cameroon
Fungom, Northern, Cameroon
Furu, Zaire
Fuyuge, Papua New Guinea
Fyam, Nigeria
Fyer, Nigeria
Ga-Dang, Philippines
Gade, Nigeria
Gadsup, Papua New Guinea
**Gagre, Pakistan
Gagu, Ivory Coast

Gahuku, Papua New Guinea
Gaikundi, Papua New Guinea
Gaina, Papua New Guinea
Gal, Papua New Guinea
Galler, Laos
Gamei, Papua New Guinea
Gane, Indonesia
Ganglau, Papua New Guinea
Garuh, Papua New Guinea
Garus, Papua New Guinea
Garuwahi, Papua New Guinea
Gawwada, Ethiopia
Gbande, Guinea
Gbari, Nigeria (80)
Gedaged, Papua New Guinea
Gedeo, Ethiopia
Genagane, Papua New Guinea
Gende, Papua New Guinea
Gesa, Indonesia
**Ghimeera, Ethiopia
Ghotuo, Nigeria
Gidar, Cameroon
Gidar, Cameroon
Gidicho, Ethiopia
Gidra, Papua New Guinea
Gimi, Papua New Guinea
Ginuman, Papua New Guinea
Gio, Liberia
Gira, Papua New Guinea
Girawa, Papua New Guinea
Giri, Papua New Guinea
Giryama, Kenya
Gisei, Cameroon
Gisiga, Cameroon
Gitua, Papua New Guinea
Gizra, Papua New Guinea
**Glavda, Nigeria
Gobasi, Papua New Guinea
Gobato, Ethiopia
Gobeze, Ethiopia
***Godie, Ivory Coast
Goemai, Nigeria
Gogo, Tanzania
Gogodala, Papua New Guinea
Gokana, Nigeria
*Gonds, India
Goroa, Tanzania
Gourency, Upper Volta
**Gouro, Ivory Coast
Gouwar, Cameroon
Gouwar, Cameroon
**Grebo, Liberia
Grunshi, Ghana
Gu, Benin
Guaiaqui, Paraguay
Guajajara, Brazil
Guajibo, Colombia
*Guajiro, Colombia
Guambiano, Colombia
Guana, Paraguay
***Guarani, Bolivia (79)
Guayabero, Colombia
Guayabevo, Colombia
Gude, Cameroon
Gude, Nigeria
Gudu, Nigeria
Guduf, Nigeria
Gugu-Yalanji, Australia
Guhu-Samane, Papua New Guinea

Gulfe, Cameroon
Gulfe, Cameroon
Gumasi, Papua New Guinea
Gumine, Papua New Guinea
Gumuz, Ethiopia
Gurensi, Ghana
Gusap, Papua New Guinea
Guwot, Papua New Guinea
Gwandara, Nigeria
Gwedena, Papua New Guinea
Gwere, Uganda
Ha, Tanzania
Hadiyya, Ethiopia
Hahon, Papua New Guinea
***Halam in Tripura, India
Halia, Papua New Guinea
Hamtai, Papua New Guinea
Hangaza, Tanzania
Hatsa, Tanzania
Havu, Zaire
Havunese, Indonesia
Haya, Tanzania
Hehe, Tanzania
Helong, Indonesia
Herero, Botswana
Herero, Namibia
Heso, Zaire
**Hewa, Papua New Guinea (79)
***Higi, Nigeria
Hixkaryana, Brazil
Hohodene, Brazil
Holoholo, Tanzania
Holu, Angola
Hopi, United States of America
Hote, Papua New Guinea
Huachipaire, Peru
Huambisa, Peru
**Huila, Angola
Huitoto, Meneca, Colombia
Huitoto, Murui, Peru
Hukwe, Angola
Hula, Papua New Guinea
Huli, Papua New Guinea
Humene, Papua New Guinea
Hunde, Zaire
Hunjara, Papua New Guinea
Hupda Maku, Colombia
Iatmul, Papua New Guinea
Ibaji, Nigeria
**Iban, Malaysia (81)
Ibanag, Philippines
Ibibio, Nigeria
Ica, Colombia
Idi, Papua New Guinea
Idoma, Nigeria
Idoma, North, Nigeria
Ifuago, Antipolo, Philippines
*Ifugao, Philippines
**Ifugao (Kalangoya), Philippines
Ifugao in Cababuyan, Philippines
Ifugao, Ambanad, Philippines
Ifugao, Kiangan, Philippines
Ifumu, Congo
Igala, Nigeria
Igede, Nigeria
Ignaciano, Bolivia
Igora, Papua New Guinea
Igorot, Philippines
Iha, Indonesia

REGISTRY OF THE UNREACHED

Ihceve, Nigeria
Ijo, Central-Western, Nigeria
Ijo, Northeast, Nigeria
Ijo, Northeast Central, Nigeria
Ikalahan, Philippines
Ikizu, Tanzania
Ikobi-Mena, Papua New Guinea
Ikundun, Papua New Guinea
Ikwere, Nigeria
Ila, Zambia
Ilongot, Philippines
Inanwatan, Indonesia
Indinogosima, Papua New Guinea
Ingassana, Sudan
Insinai, Philippines
Ipiko, Papua New Guinea
Ipili, Papua New Guinea
Iquito, Peru
Irahutu, Indonesia
Iraqw, Tanzania
Iraqw, Tanzania
Iresim, Indonesia
Iria, Indonesia
Irigwe, Nigeria
Irumu, Papua New Guinea
Isanzu, Tanzania
Isebe, Papua New Guinea
Isekiri, Nigeria
Isneg, Dibagat-Kabugao,
  Philippines
Isneg, Karagawan, Philippines
Isoko, Nigeria
Itik, Indonesia
Itonama, Bolivia
Ivbie North-Okpela-Atte, Nigeria
Iwa, Zambia
*Iwaidja, Austria
Iwal, Papua New Guinea
Iwam, Papua New Guinea
Iwam, Sepik, Papua New Guinea
Iwur, Indonesia
Iyon, Nigeria
Iyon, Cameroon
Iyon, Cameroon
Izarek, Nigeria
**Izi, Nigeria
Jaba, Nigeria
Jabem, Papua New Guinea
Jacalteco, Guatemala
Jamamadi, Brazil
Jamden, Indonesia
Janjero, Ethiopia
Janjo, Nigeria
Jaqaru, Peru
**Jarawa, Nigeria
Jebero, Peru
Jeng, Laos
Jerawa, Nigeria
*Jibu, Nigeria
Jiji, Tanzania
Jimajima, Papua New Guinea
Jinja, Tanzania
Jinuos, China (81)
Jita, Tanzania
Jiye, Uganda
*Jiye, Sudan
Juhai, Malaysia
Jukun, Nigeria
Kaalong, Cameroon

Kaalong, Cameroon
Kaba, Central African Republic
Kaba Dunjo, Central African
  Republic
Kabadi, Papua New Guinea
Kabixi, Brazil
Kabre, Togo
Kabre, Benin
Kachama, Ethiopia
Kadaklan-Barlig Bontoc,
  Philippines
Kadara, Nigeria
Kadazans, Malaysia
Kadiweu, Brazil
Kaeti, Indonesia
**Kafirs, Pakistan (79)
Kagoro, Mali
Kagulu, Tanzania
Kaian, Papua New Guinea
Kaiep, Papua New Guinea
Kaili, Indonesia
Kairi, Papua New Guinea
Kairiru, Papua New Guinea
Kaiwai, Indonesia
Kajang, Indonesia
Kaka, Central African Republic
Kaka, Cameroon
Kaka, Cameroon
Kakoa, Papua New Guinea
Kakuna-Mamusi, Papua New Guinea
Kakwa, Uganda
Kakwa, Zaire
**Kalagan, Philippines
*Kalanga, Botswana
Kalanga, Zimbabwe
Kaliko, Zaire
Kalinga, Kalagua, Philippines
Kalinga, Limus-Linan,
  Philippines
Kalinga, Quinaang, Philippines
*Kalinga, Southern, Philippines
Kalokalo, Papua New Guinea
Kamano, Papua New Guinea
Kamantan, Nigeria
Kamayura, Brazil
*Kambari, Nigeria (80)
Kambera, Indonesia
Kamberataro, Indonesia
Kamberataro, Papua New Guinea
Kambot, Papua New Guinea
Kami, Tanzania
Kamkam, Cameroon
Kamkam, Cameroon
Kamnum, Papua New Guinea
Kamoro, Indonesia
Kampung Baru, Indonesia
Kamtuk-Gresi, Indonesia
*Kamuku, Nigeria (80)
Kana, Nigeria
Kandas, Papua New Guinea
Kaningra, Papua New Guinea
Kanite, Papua New Guinea
**Kankanay, Central, Philippines
Kankanay, Northern, Philippines
Kanu, Zaire
Kanum, Indonesia
Kanum, Papua New Guinea
Kao, Ethiopia
Kaonde, Zaire

Kaonde, Zambia
Kapin, Papua New Guinea
Kapore, Papua New Guinea
Kapori, Indonesia
Kapriman, Papua New Guinea
Kara, Tanzania
Kara, Papua New Guinea
*Karaboro, Upper Volta
Karam, Papua New Guinea
Karangi, Papua New Guinea
Karas, Indonesia
Kare, Papua New Guinea
Karen, Thailand (79)
Karen, Pwo, Thailand
Kari, Central African Republic
Kari, Zaire
Karipuna Creole, Brazil
Karipuna Do Guapore, Brazil
Karkar, Papua New Guinea
Karon Dori, Indonesia
Karon Pantai, Indonesia
Karre, Central African Republic
Karua, Papua New Guinea
**Kasena, Ghana
Kasseng, Laos
Kasua, Papua New Guinea
Kasuweri, Indonesia
Kate, Papua New Guinea
Kati, Northern, Indonesia
Kati, Southern, Indonesia
Katiati, Papua New Guinea
Katukina, Panoan, Brazil
Kaugat, Indonesia
Kaugel, Papua New Guinea
Kaure, Indonesia
Kavwol, Indonesia
Kavwol, Papua New Guinea
Kaw, Burma
Kawe, Indonesia
Kayabi, Brazil
Kayagar, Indonesia
Kayan, Malaysia
Kayan, Burma
Kayapo, Brazil
Kaygir, Indonesia
Kayupulau, Indonesia
Kedayanas, Malaysia
Kei, Indonesia
Kela, Zaire
Kela, Papua New Guinea
Kelabit, Malaysia (81)
Kele, Gabon
Kemak, Indonesia
Kembata, Ethiopia
Kemok, Malaysia
Kenati, Papua New Guinea
Kenyah, Indonesia
Keopara, Papua New Guinea
*Kepas, Papua New Guinea
Kera, Cameroon
Kera, Cameroon
Kerewe, Tanzania
Kerewo, Papua New Guinea
Keriaka, Papua New Guinea
Kewa, East, Papua New Guinea
Kewa, South, Papua New Guinea
Kewa, West, Papua New Guinea
*Khamu, Thailand
Kiari, Papua New Guinea

Kibiri, Papua New Guinea
Kichepo, Sudan
Kilmera, Papua New Guinea
Kim, Central African Republic
Kimaghama, Indonesia
Kimbu, Tanzania
*Kimyal, Indonesia
Kinalakna, Papua New Guinea
Kinga, Tanzania
Kiriwina, Papua New Guinea
Kis, Papua New Guinea
Kisankasa, Tanzania
Kisi, Tanzania
*Kissi, Sierra Leone
Kissi, Guinea
*Kissi, Liberia
Kiwai, Northeast, Papua New
  Guinea
Kiwai, Southern, Papua New
  Guinea
Kiwai, Wabuda, Papua New Guinea
Koalib, Sudan (79)
Kobon, Papua New Guinea
Kodi, Indonesia
Koenoem, Nigeria
Kofyar, Nigeria
Kohoroxitari, Brazil
Kohumono, Nigeria
Koiari, Grass, Papua New Guinea
Koiari, Mountain, Papua New
  Guinea
Koita, Papua New Guinea
Kol, Papua New Guinea
Kole, Cameroon
Kole, Cameroon
Koliku, Papua New Guinea
Kolom, Papua New Guinea
Koma, Ghana
Koma, Nigeria
Koma, Cameroon
Koma, Cameroon
Komba, Papua New Guinea
Kombio, Papua New Guinea
*Komo, Ethiopia
Komutu, Papua New Guinea
Konabem, Cameroon
Konabem, Cameroon
***Kond, India
Koneraw, Indonesia
*Konkomba, Togo
Konkomba, Ghana
**Kono, Sierra Leone
Konomala, Papua New Guinea
Konongo, Tanzania
Konso, Ethiopia
Korak, Papua New Guinea
Korape, Papua New Guinea
Korapun, Indonesia
*Korku in Madhya Pradesh, India
Koro, Nigeria
Koroma, Sudan
Korop, Nigeria
Korop, Cameroon
Korop, Cameroon
Kosorong, Papua New Guinea
Kota, Gabon
Kotogut, Indonesia
Kotoko, Cameroon
Kotoko, Cameroon

Kotopo, Cameroon
Kotta, India
Kovai, Papua New Guinea
Kove, Papua New Guinea
***Kowaao, Liberia
Koyra, Ethiopia
Kpa, Cameroon
Kpa, Cameroon
Kpelle, Liberia
***Krahn, Liberia
*Krahn, Ivory Coast
Kreen-Akakore, Brazil
Krisa, Papua New Guinea
Krongo, Sudan
Krumen, Ivory Coast
Kuatinema, Brazil
Kube, Papua New Guinea
Kubu, Indonesia (80)
Kugbo, Nigeria
Kuikuro, Brazil
Kukele, Nigeria
Kukuwy, Papua New Guinea
Kukwa, Congo
Kulango, Ivory Coast
Kulere, Nigeria
Kumai, Papua New Guinea
Kumam, Uganda
Kuman, Papua New Guinea
Kumdauron, Papua New Guinea
Kumu, Zaire
Kumukio, Papua New Guinea
Kunda, Mozambique
Kunda, Zimbabwe
Kunda, Zambia
Kunda, Zambia
Kuni, Papua New Guinea
Kunua, Papua New Guinea
Kuot, Papua New Guinea
Kupsabiny, Uganda
Kurada, Papua New Guinea
Kurfei, Niger
Kuria, Tanzania
Kurudu, Indonesia
****Kusaasi, Ghana
Kusu, Zaire
Kutin, Cameroon
Kutu, Tanzania
Kwadi, Angola
Kwakum, Cameroon
Kwale, Papua New Guinea
Kwambi, Namibia
Kwanga, Papua New Guinea
Kwangali, Angola
Kwansu, Indonesia
Kwanyama, Angola
Kwanyama, Namibia
Kwaya, Tanzania
Kwe-etshori, Botswana
Kwe-Etshori, Zimbabwe
Kwerba, Indonesia
Kwere, Tanzania
Kwese, Zaire
Kwesten, Indonesia
Kwoma, Papua New Guinea
Kwomtari, Papua New Guinea
Labu, Papua New Guinea
Laewomba, Papua New Guinea
*Lahu, Thailand (81)
Lahu, Burma

Laka, Cameroon
Laka, Central African Republic
Lala, Zambia
Lalia, Zaire
Lamba, Togo
Lamba, Benin
Lamba, Zaire
Lamba, Zambia
****Lambadi in Andhra Pradesh, India
(81)
Lambi, Cameroon
Lambya, Malawi
Lambya, Tanzania
Lamogai, Papua New Guinea
Langi, Tanzania
*Lango, Ethiopia
Lango, Uganda
Lanoh, Malaysia
Lara, Indonesia
Latdwalam, Indonesia
Laudje, Indonesia
Lavatbura-Lamusong, Papua New
Guinea
Lavongai, Papua New Guinea
Lebgo, Nigeria
Leco, Bolivia
Lega, Zaire
Lele, Zaire
Lendu, Zaire
Lengua, Northern, Paraguay
Lenje, Zambia
Leron, Papua New Guinea
Lese, Zaire
Letti, Indonesia
Lihir, Papua New Guinea
Liko, Zaire
Lima, Zambia
Limba, Sierra Leone
*Lisu, Thailand
Lisu, China (81)
Lo, Nigeria
Lobi, Ivory Coast
Logo, Zaire
Lohiki, Papua New Guinea
****Loho Loho, Indonesia
Loinang, Indonesia (81)
Loko, Sierra Leone
Lolo, China (81)
Loma, Guinea
Loma, Liberia
Lombi, Zaire
Lombo, Zaire
Lomwe, Mozambique
Lore, Indonesia
Lou-Baluan-Pam, Papua New Guinea
Lozi, Zimbabwe
Lozi, Zambia
Luano, Zambia
Luchazi, Angola
Luchazi, Zambia
Lue, Cameroon
Lugbara, Zaire
Lugitama, Papua New Guinea
Luimbi, Angola
Lukep, Papua New Guinea
Lumbu, Gabon
Luna, Zaire
Lunda, Angola
Lundu, Cameroon

Menri, Malaysia
**Meo, Thailand
Miao, China (81)
Mien, China (81)
Migili, Nigeria
Minduumo, Gabon
Minianka, Mali
Mirung, Bangladesh
Miya, Nigeria
Mo, Ghana
Moba, Ghana
Moba, Togo
***Mocha, Ethiopia
Mofu, Cameroon
Moi, Indonesia
Moken, Burma (79)
Moken of Thailand, Thailand
*Mokole, Benin
Molof, Indonesia
Mombum, Indonesia
Momoguns, Malaysia
Mongondow, Indonesia (81)
Moni, Indonesia
Monjombo, Central African
   Republic
Mono, Zaire
Mor, Indonesia
Morunahua, Peru
Morwap, Indonesia
Mosi, Tanzania
Mossi, Upper Volta (80)
Motilon, Colombia
Motilon, Venezuela
Movima, Bolivia
Mpoto, Malawi
Mpoto, Tanzania
Mru, Bangladesh
Mualthuam, India
Muinane, Colombia
Mumuye, Nigeria
**Mundas in Bihar, India
Mundu, Zaire
Munduruku, Brazil
Mungaka, Cameroon
Munggui, Indonesia
Mura-Piraha, Brazil
Murle, Sudan
*Murngin (Wulamba), Australia
Mursi, Ethiopia
Murut, Malaysia
Mwanga, Tanzania
Mwera, Tanzania
Myaung-Ze, Burma
Nabi, Indonesia
Nadeb Maku, Brazil
**Nafaara, Ghana (79)
Nafri, Indonesia
Naltya, Indonesia
Nama, Namibia
Nama, South Africa
Nambikuara, Brazil
**Nambya, Zimbabwe
Namshi, Cameroon
Nandi, Zaire
Nao, Ethiopia
Naraguta, Nigeria
Nata, Tanzania
Nawuri, Ghana
Nchimburu, Ghana

Ndaaka, Zaire
Ndali, Tanzania
Ndam, Central African Republic
Ndamba, Tanzania
Ndaonese, Indonesia
Ndau, Zimbabwe
Nde-Nsele-Nta, Nigeria
**Ndebele, Zimbabwe (79)
Ndengereko, Tanzania
Ndjem, Cameroon
Ndo, Zaire
Ndoe, Nigeria
Ndogo, Central African Republic
Ndom, Indonesia
Ndomde, Tanzania
Ndoolo, Zaire
Ndop-Bamessing, Cameroon
**Ndoro, Nigeria
Ndoro, Cameroon
Nduga, Indonesia
Ndunga, Zaire
Neyo, Ivory Coast
Ngalik, North, Indonesia
Ngalik, Southern, Indonesia
Ngalum, Indonesia
**Ngamo, Nigeria
Ngando, Central African Republic
Ngando, Zaire
Ngasa, Tanzania
Ngayaba, Cameroon
Ngbaka, Zaire
Ngbaka Ma'bo, Central African
   Republic
Ngbaka Ma'bo, Zaire
Ngbandi, Zaire
Ngbee, Zaire
Ngemba, Cameroon
*Ngen, Ivory Coast
Ngeq, Laos
Ngere, Ivory Coast
Ngi, Cameroon
Ngindo, Tanzania
Ngiri, Zaire
**Ngombe, Zaire
Ngoni, Tanzania
Ngoni, Zambia
Ngulu, Malawi
Ngulu, Tanzania
Ngumba, Cameroon
Ngumbi, Equatorial Guinea
Ngurimi, Tanzania
Nguu, Tanzania
Ngwo, Cameroon
Nharon, Botswana
Nhengatu, Brazil
Nias, Indonesia
Nilamba, Tanzania
Nimboran, Indonesia
Ninam, Brazil
*Ningerum, Papua New Guinea
Ninggrum, Indonesia
Nisa, Indonesia
Njadu, Indonesia
Nkem-Nkum, Nigeria
Nkom, Cameroon
*Nkoya, Zambia
Nkutu, Zaire
***Nocte, India
Nohu, Cameroon

Salampasu, Zaire
Saliba, Colombia
Sama, Mapun, Philippines
Samarkena, Indonesia
Samburu, Kenya
Samo, Northern, Mali
*Samo-Kubo, Papua New Guinea
Samogho, Mali
San, Namibia
Sanapana, Paraguay
Sandawe, Tanzania
Sanga, Zaire
Sangir, Indonesia
Sangke, Indonesia
Sangu, Gabon
Sangu, Tanzania
**Santhali, Nepal
*Sanuma, Brazil
Sanuma, Venezuela
Sanza, Zaire
Sapo, Liberia
Sasaru-Enwan Igwe, Nigeria
Satere, Brazil
Satnamis in M.P., India
Sause, Indonesia
**Save, Benin
**Sawi, Indonesia
Secoya, Ecuador
Sekar, Indonesia
Seko, Indonesia
*Selakau of Sarawak, Malaysia
Semelai, Malaysia
Sempan, Indonesia
Sena, Malawi
Sena, Mozambique
Senggi, Indonesia
**Senoi, Malaysia (81)
Sentani, Indonesia
Senufo, Ivory Coast (80)
Serere, Senegal (79)
Serui-Laut, Indonesia
Seuci, Brazil
Sha, Nigeria
Shambala, Tanzania
Shanga, Nigeria
Sharanahua, Peru
Sheko, Ethiopia
Shinasha, Ethiopia
Shipibo, Peru
**Shirishana, Brazil
Shua, Botswana
Siagha-Yenimu, Indonesia
Sikanese, Indonesia
Sikhule, Indonesia
Simaa, Zambia
Siona, Colombia
Sira, Gabon
Siriano, Colombia
Siriono, Bolivia
**Sisaala, Ghana
So, Laos
*So, Thailand (81)
So, Cameroon
Sobei, Indonesia
Soga, Uganda
Soli, Zambia
*Somahai, Indonesia
Somahai, Indonesia
**Somba, Benin

Somrai, Central African Republic
Songe, Zaire
Songhai, Mali
Songomeno, Zaire
Songoora, Zaire
Sonjo, Tanzania
Soruba, Benin
Sowanda, Indonesia
Su, Cameroon
Suba, Tanzania
**Subanen (Tuboy), Philippines
**Subanen, Sindangan, Philippines (80)
Subi, Tanzania
Suga, Cameroon
**Sugut, Malaysia
Suk, Kenya
Suku, Zaire
Sumbwa, Tanzania
Suppire, Mali
**Suri, Ethiopia
Surui, Brazil
Swaga, Zaire
Swaka, Zambia
**Swazi, South Africa
**T'boli, Philippines (81)
T'in, Thailand (81)
Ta-Oi, Laos
Tabi, Sudan
Tacana, Bolivia
Tadjio, Indonesia
Tadyawan, Philippines
Tagal, Malaysia (81)
**Tagbanwa, Aborlan, Philippines
***Tagin, India
Tahit, Indonesia
Taikat, Indonesia
Takemba, Benin
Tamagario, Indonesia
Tambas, Nigeria
Tambo, Zambia
Tampulma, Ghana
Tana, Central African Republic
Tanahmerah, Indonesia
Tandia, Indonesia
**Tangsa, India
Tanimuca-Retuama, Colombia
Tao't Bato, Philippines
Taori-Kei, Indonesia
Tara, Indonesia
Taram, Cameroon
Tarof, Indonesia
Tarok, Nigeria
Tarpia, Indonesia
Tatoga, Tanzania
**Tatuyo, Colombia
Taurap, Indonesia
Tayaku, Benin
Tchang, Cameroon
*Teenbu, Ivory Coast
Teke, Eastern, Zaire
Teke, Northern, Congo
Teke, Southwestern, Congo
Tembe, Brazil
Tembo, Zaire
Temira, Malaysia
**Temne, Sierra Leone (80)
*Tense, Ivory Coast
Tepeth, Uganda

Terena, Brazil
Teso, Uganda
**Teso, Kenya
Ticuna, Brazil
Tiene, Zaire
Tigon, Cameroon
Tikar, Cameroon
Timorese, Indonesia
Tiro, Indonesia
Tiruray, Philippines
Toala, Indonesia
Toba, Argentina
*Tofi, Benin
Togbo, Zaire
Tol, Honduras
Tombulu, Indonesia
Tomini, Indonesia
Tondanou, Indonesia
*Tonga, Zimbabwe
Tonga, Botswana
Tonga, Malawi
Tonga, Mozambique
Tonga, Gwembe Valley, Zambia
  (79)
Tongwe, Tanzania
Tonsea, Indonesia
Tontemboa, Indonesia
*Topotha, Sudan
Toraja, Southern, Indonesia (81)
Towei, Indonesia
Trio, Surinam
Tsamai, Ethiopia
Tsimane, Bolivia
Tsogo, Gabon
Tsonga, Mozambique
Tsou, Taiwan (81)
Tswa, Mozambique
Tswa, Zimbabwe
Tswana, Namibia
Tswana, Zimbabwe
Tucano, Brazil
Tumawo, Indonesia
Tunebo, Cobaria, Colombia
Tung-Chia, China (81)
Tunya, Central African Republic
Tupuri, Cameroon
Turkana, Kenya
**Turkana Fishing Community, Kenya
  (79)
Turu, Tanzania
Turu, Indonesia
Tuyuca, Brazil
Udmurt, Soviet Russia
Uduk, Sudan
Uhunduni, Indonesia
Ukaan, Nigeria
Ukpe-Bayobiri, Nigeria
Ukwuani-Aboh, Nigeria
Urarina, Peru
Urhobo, Nigeria
Uria, Indonesia
Uruangnirin, Indonesia
Urubu, Brazil
Urupa, Brazil
Uspanteco, Guatemala
Utugwang, Nigeria
Uvbie, Nigeria
Uzekwe, Nigeria
Vagala, Ghana

Vaikino, Indonesia
Vale, Central African Republic
Venda, Zimbabwe
***Vere, Nigeria
Vere, Cameroon
Vidunda, Tanzania
Vinza, Tanzania
Vute, Nigeria
Wa, Burma
Wabo, Indonesia
Waimiri, Brazil
Waiwai, Brazil
**Wajita, Tanzania
Wala, Ghana
Walamo, Ethiopia
Wambon, Indonesia
**Wanchoo, India
Wanda, Tanzania
Wandamen, Indonesia
Wandji, Gabon
Wanggom, Indonesia
Wanji, Tanzania
Wano, Indonesia
Wapishana, Brazil
Wapishana, Venezuela
Warao, Venezuela
Ware, Mali
Warembori, Indonesia
Waris, Indonesia
*Warjawa, Nigeria
Warkay-Bipim, Indonesia
Waropen, Indonesia
Wasi, Tanzania
Watchi, Togo
Waura, Brazil
Wayana, Surinam
*Wazinza, Tanzania
Wetawit, Ethiopia
Wewewa, Indonesia
Widekum, Cameroon
**Wimbum, Cameroon
Wobe, Ivory Coast
Wodani, Indonesia
Woi, Indonesia
Wongo, Zaire
Wumbvu, Gabon
Wungu, Tanzania
Xavante, Brazil
Xerente, Brazil
Xokleng, Brazil
Xu, Namibia
Yafi, Indonesia
Yagua, Peru
Yahadian, Indonesia
Yaka, Zaire
Yakoma, Central African Republic
**Yala, Nigeria
Yaly, Indonesia
Yambasa, Cameroon
Yaminahua, Peru
*Yanomamo in Brazil, Brazil (79)
Yanomamo in Venezuela, Venezuela
Yans, Zaire
**Yao, Thailand (79)
*Yao Refugees from Laos, Thailand
Yaoure, Ivory Coast
Yaruro, Venezuela
Yasing, Cameroon
Yaur, Indonesia

Yava, Indonesia
**Yei, Botswana
Yei, Indonesia
Yela, Zaire
Yelmek, Indonesia
Yeretuar, Indonesia
Yidinit, Ethiopia
Yin-Kyar, Burma
Yin-Nett, Burma
Yinga, Cameroon
Yoabu, Benin
Yogad, Philippines
Yonggom, Indonesia
Yotafa, Indonesia
Yuana, Venezuela
Yucateco, Guatemala
Yukpa, Colombia
Yukpa, Venezuela
Yuracare, Bolivia
Yuruti, Colombia
Zanaki, Tanzania
Zande, Zaire
**Zaranda Hill Peoples, Nigeria
Zayse, Ethiopia
Zemi Naga of Assam, India (81)
Zigwa, Tanzania
Zilmamu, Ethiopia
Zimba, Zaire
Zoliang, India
Zowla, Ghana
Zulu, Malawi
Zuni, United States of America

BAHAISM

Bahais in Teheran, Iran (82)

BUDDHISM

*Barbers in Tokyo, Japan (82)
Bhutias, Bhutan
*Chinese in Thailand, Thailand
Danu, Burma
Government officials, Thailand
Hkun, Burma
Japanese in Brazil, Brazil (79)
Kachin in Shan State, Burma
Kae Sung Natives in Seoul,
    Korea, Republic of (82)
Kalmytz, Soviet Russia
Koreans in Manchuria, China (81)
**Lahaulis in Punjab, India
*Lao, Laos (79)
**Lepers of N.E. Thailand,
    Thailand
Newar in Kathmandu, Nepal (82)
Palaung, Burma (79)
Pao, Burma
*Ramkamhaeng Un. Students,
    Thailand
Shan, Burma

*Sherpa, Nepal
Sinhalese, Sri Lanka
*Slum Dwellers of Bangkok,
    Thailand
Soka Gakkai Believers, Japan
Taungyoe, Burma
*Thai University Students,
    Thailand (81)
*Tibetan Refugees, India
*Tibetans, China
Tibetans in Bhutan, Bhutan (81)
Vietnamese, Laos
**Vietnamese in the USA, United
    States of America
**Vietnamese Refugees, Thailand

BUDDHIST-ANIMIST

*Ami, Taiwan (81)
**Banai, Bangladesh
Buriat, Soviet Russia
*Cambodians, Thailand
*Central Thailand Farmers,
    Thailand (81)
*Chakmas of Mizoram, India (81)
*Chang-Pa of Kashmir, India (81)
Chaungtha, Burma
Chin, Asho, Burma
Chin, Falam, Burma
Chin, Haka, Burma
Chin, Khumi, Burma
Chin, Ngawn, Burma
Chin, Tiddim, Burma
Chinbok, Burma
Dai, Burma
Evenks, Soviet Russia
Gheko, Burma
Hallam, Burma
Hrangkhol, Burma
Intha, Burma
Kebumtamp, Bhutan
**Khmer Refugees, Thailand
Kokant, Burma
*Kui, Thailand
Lama, Burma
*Lao Refugees, Thailand
Lawa, Eastern, Thailand (81)
Lawa, Mountain, Thailand
**Lepers of Cen. Thailand,
    Thailand (81)
Loven, Laos (81)
Lu, China
Maghi, Burma
Mon, Burma (81)
Monpa, India
Mun, Burma
Norra, Burma
Pai, China (81)
Phu Thai, Laos
Purum, Burma
Ralte, Burma
Riang-Lang, Burma
Senthang, Burma
Shan, Thailand
Shan Chinese, Burma

Sharchagpakha, Bhutan
Street Vendors in Saigon, Viet
  Nam (82)
Taman, Burma
Taungyo, Burma
Tawr, Burma
Thai Northern, Thailand
Thai of Bangkok, Thailand
Thai, North East, Thailand
Thai, Southern, Thailand
Thai-Ney, Burma
Tuvinian, Soviet Russia
Yangbye, Burma
Yinchia, Burma
Yos, Burma
Zome, Burma

CHRISTO-PAGANISM

Abaknon, Philippines
Aeta, Philippines
Akawaio, Guyana
Alangan, Philippines
**Ampeeli, Papua New Guinea
Amuzgo, Guerrero, Mexico
Amuzgo, Oaxaca, Mexico
**Apayao, Philippines
Arawak, Guyana
Ati, Philippines
Aymara, Carangas, Chile
***Azteca, Mexico (79)
***Bagobo, Philippines
**Balangao, Philippines
Bantuanon, Philippines
Batak, Palawan, Philippines
**Bidayuh of Sarawak, Malaysia
  (81)
***Bipim, Indonesia
**Black Caribs, Belize, Belize
  (79)
**Black Caribs, Guatemala,
  Guatemala
**Black Caribs, Honduras, Honduras
**Bontoc, Southern, Philippines
Buglere, Panama
Buhid, Philippines
Caluyanhon, Philippines
***Cebu, Middle-Class, Philippines
***Ch'ol Sabanilla, Mexico
Chamorro, Turks and Caicos
  Islands
Chamula, Mexico (79)
Chatino, Nopala, Mexico
Chatino, Panixtlahuaca, Mexico
Chatino, Tataltepec, Mexico
Chatino, Yaitepec, Mexico
Chatino, Zacatepec, Mexico
Chatino, Zenzontepec, Mexico
**Chayahuita, Peru
Chinanteco, Tepinapa, Mexico
Chinanteco, Ayotzintepec, Mexico
Chinanteco, Chiltepec, Mexico
Chinanteco, Comaltepec, Mexico
Chinanteco, Lalana, Mexico
Chinanteco, Lealao, Mexico

Chinanteco, Ojitlan, Mexico
Chinanteco, Palantla, Mexico
Chinanteco, Quiotepec, Mexico
Chinanteco, Sochiapan, Mexico
Chinanteco, Tepetotutla, Mexico
Chinanteco, Usila, Mexico
Chocho, Mexico
Chuj, San Mateo Ixtatan, Mexico
Chulupe, Paraguay
Cocopa, Mexico
Cora, Mexico
Cuicateco, Tepeuxila, Mexico
Cuicateco, Teutila, Mexico
Cuyonon, Philippines
Davaweno, Philippines
Djuka, Surinam
*Favelados-Rio de Janeiro, Brazil
  (82)
Gagauzes, Soviet Russia
Galla of Bucho, Ethiopia
*Guanano, Colombia (79)
Guarayu, Bolivia
Guarojio, Mexico
Gypsies, Soviet Russia
Hanonoo, Philippines
Huasteco, Mexico
**Huave, Mexico
Huichol, Mexico
*Ibataan, Philippines
Inga, Colombia
Iraya, Philippines
Itawit, Philippines
Itneg, Adasen, Philippines
Itneg, Binongan, Philippines
Itneg, Masadiit, Philippines
Ixil, Guatemala
Jemez Pueblo, United States of
  America
**Jivaro (Achuara), Venezuela
Ka'mis, Papua New Guinea
Kaagan, Philippines
*Kaffa, Ethiopia (80)
Kaingang, Brazil
**Kalinga,Northern, Philippines
  (81)
**Kekchi, Guatemala
Kikapoo, Mexico
Kinaray-A, Philippines
Komi-Permyat, Soviet Russia
Komi-Zyrian, Soviet Russia
**Kunimaipa, Papua New Guinea
Lacandon, Mexico
Lionese, Indonesia
*Lokoro, Sudan
Lubang Islanders, Philippines
  (81)
**Mam Indian, Guatemala
**Mamanua, Philippines (81)
**Mansaka, Philippines
Mapuche, Chile
Mari, Soviet Russia
Matlatzinca, Atzingo, Mexico
Mayo, Mexico
**Mazahua, Mexico
***Mestizos in La Paz, Bolivia (82)
*Mimika, Indonesia
Miskito, Nicaragua
**Mixes, Mexico
Mixteco, Amoltepec, Mexico

Mixteco, Apoala, Mexico
Mixteco, Central Puebla, Mexico
Mixteco, Eastern, Mexico
Mixteco, Eastern Putla, Mexico
Mixteco, Huajuapan, Mexico
Mixteco, Silacayoapan, Mexico
Mixteco, Southern Puebla, Mexico
Mixteco, Southern Putla, Mexico
Mixteco, Tututepec, Mexico
Mixteco, Yosondua, Mexico
*Mixteco,San Juan Mixtepic, Mexico
**Mopan Maya, Guatemala
**Mopan Maya, Belize
Mutu, Venezuela
*Nahua, North Pueblo, Mexico
Ngada, Indonesia
Northern Cagayan Negrito, Philippines
Otomi, Eastern, Mexico
Otomi, Mezquital, Mexico
Otomi, Northwestern, Mexico
Otomi, Southeastern, Mexico
Otomi, State of Mexico, Mexico
Otomi, Tenango, Mexico
Otomi, Texcatepec, Mexico
***Paez, Colombia
Paipai, Mexico
Pame, Central Chichimeca, Mexico
Pame, Chichimeca-Jonaz, Mexico
Pame, Northern, Mexico
Paranan, Philippines
Patamona, Guyana
Pima Bajo, Mexico
**Plantation Workers, Papua New Guinea
Pocomchi, Eastern, Guatemala
Pocomchi, Western, Guatemala
Popoloca, Ahuatempan, Mexico
Popoloca, Coyotepec, Mexico
Popoloca, Eastern, Mexico
Popoloca, Northern, Mexico
Popoloca, Southern, Mexico
Popoloca, Western, Mexico
Popoluca, Oluta, Mexico
Popoluca, Sayula, Mexico
Popoluca, Sierra, Mexico
Popoluca, Texistepec, Mexico
**Puyuma, Taiwan (81)
**Quechua, Peru
**Quechua, Bolivia
**Quiche, Guatemala (79)
**Quichua, Ecuador
Rabinal-Achi, Guatemala
Saramaccan, Surinam
Seri, Mexico
***Shankilla (Kazza), Ethiopia
**Suena, Papua New Guinea
Sumba, Indonesia
Sumu, Nicaragua
Tagbanwa, Kalamian, Philippines
Tarahumara, Northern, Mexico
Tarahumara, Rocoroibo, Mexico
Tarahumara, Samachique, Mexico
Tarasco, Mexico
Tepehua, Huehuetla, Mexico
Tepehua, Pisa Flores, Mexico
Tepehua, Veracruz, Mexico
Tepehuan, Northern, Mexico

Tepehuan, Southeastern, Mexico
Tepehuan, Southwestern, Mexico
**Teribe, Panama
Tlapaneco, Malinaltepec, Mexico
Tojolabal, Mexico
Totonaco, Northern, Mexico
Totonaco, Oxumatlan, Mexico
Totonaco, Papantla, Mexico
Totonaco, Sierra, Mexico
Totonaco, Yecuatla, Mexico
Trique, San Juan Copala, Mexico
**Tsachila, Ecuador
Tubar, Mexico
Tukude, Indonesia
Tzeltal, Bachajon, Mexico
Tzeltal, Highland, Mexico
Tzotzil, Chenalho, Mexico
Tzotzil, Huistan, Mexico
Tzutujil, Guatemala
Ulithi-Mall, Turks and Caicos Islands
Waiwai, Guyana
Wapishana, Guyana
Woleat, Turks and Caicos Islands
Yaghan, Chile
Yaquis, Mexico
Yucateco, Mexico
*Yucuna, Colombia
Zinacantecos, Mexico (79)
Zoque, Chimalapa, Mexico
Zoque, Copainala, Mexico
Zoque, Francisco Leon, Mexico
Zoque, Tabasco, Mexico

FOLK RELIGION

*Alars, India
**Apartment Residents-Seoul, Korea, Republic of
*Deviant Youth in Taipei, Taiwan (82)
Druzes, Israel (79)
*Gabbra, Ethiopia
Gabbra, Kenya
*Gypsies in Spain, Spain (79)
Indust.Workers Yongdungpo, Korea, Republic of
*Koreans of Japan, Japan
*Prisoners in Antananarivo, Madagascar (82)
Romany, Turkey
Spiritists, Brazil (79)
**Vietnamese Refugees, Australia

HINDU-ANIMIST

Abujmaria in M.P., India
Aimol in Assam, India
Ajmeri in Rajasthan, India
Aranadan in Tamil Nadu, India
Bagelkhandi in M.P., India

Balinese, Indonesia
Bangaru in Punjab, India
Bhakta, India
Bhattri, India
Bhilala, India
Bhoyari in Maharashtra, India
Bhumij in Assam, India
Bhunjia in Madhya Pradesh, India
Bijori in Bihar, India
Binjhwari in Bihar, India
Birhor in Bihar, India
**Bodo Kachari, India
Cham, Viet Nam
Chamari in Madhya Pradesh, India
Chameali in H.P., India
Chenchu in Andhra Pradesh, India
Chodhari in Gujarat, India
Churahi in H.P., India
**Dhodias, India
Dhurwa, India
Dorlin in Andhra Pradesh, India
**Dubla, India
Gadaban in Andhra Pradesh, India
Gaddi in Himachal Pradesh, India
Galong in Assam, India
Gamti in Gujarat, India
Gangte in Assam, India
Gawari in Andhra Pradesh, India
Grasia in Gujarat, India
**Hajong, Bangladesh
Halbi in Madhya Pradesh, India
Harauti in Rajasthan, India
Ho in Bihar, India
Holiya in Madhya Pradesh, India
**Indian Tamils - Colombo, Sri
    Lanka (82)
Jagannathi in A.P., India
Jatapu in Andhra Pradesh, India
Jaunsari in Uttar Pradesh, India
Kadar in Andhra Pradesh, India
Kahluri in Andamans, India
Kaikadi in Maharashtra, India
Kamar in Madhya Pradesh, India
Kanikkaran in Kerala, India
Kanjari in Andhra Pradesh, India
**Karbis, India
Karmali in Dihar, India
Katakari in Gujarat, India
Kawar in Madhya Pradesh, India
Keer in Madhya Pradesh, India
Khandesi, India
Kharia in Bihar, India
Khirwar in Madhya Pradesh, India
Khowar, India
Kisan in Bihar, India
Kishanganjia in Bihar, India
Kishtwari in Jammu, India
**Koch, Bangladesh
Koda in Bihar, India
**Kohli, Wadiara, Pakistan
Kol in Assam, India
*Kolam, India
Kom in Manipur, India
Konda-Dora in A.P., India
Konkani in Gujarat, India
Koraga in Kerala, India
Korwa in Bihar, India
Kota in Tamil Nadu, India
Kotia in Andhra Pradesh, India

Koya in Andhra Pradesh, India
Kudiya, India
*Kuknas, India
Kumauni in Assam, India
Kupia in Andhra Pradesh, India
Kurichiya in Kerala, India (81)
Kuruba in Tamil Nadu, India
Kurux in Bihar, India
Kuvi in Orissa, India
Lodhi in Bihar, India
Lushai in Assam, India
**Magar, Nepal
Mahali in Assam, India
Maithili, Nepal
Majhwar in Madhya Pradesh, India
Malakkaras of Kerela, India (81)
Malankuravan in Kerala, India
Malapandaram in Kerala, India
Malaryan in Kerala, India
Mali in Andhra Pradesh, India
Malki in Bihar, India
Malpaharia in Assam, India
Malvi in Madhya Pradesh, India
Manna-Dora in A.P., India
Mannan in Kerala, India
Mara in Assam, India
Maria in Andhra Pradesh, India
Marwari in Gujarat, India
**Mawchis, India
**Miching, India
Mina in Madhya Pradesh, India
Mirdha in Orissa, India
Mishmi in Assam, India
Multani in Punjab, India
Mundari in Assam, India
Muria in Andhra Pradesh, India
Muthuvan in A.P., India
Muwasi in Madhya Pradesh, India
Naga, Kalyokengnyu, India
Nagar in Madhya Pradesh, India
Nihali in Madhya Pradesh, India
Ojhi in Madhya Pradesh, India
Ollari in Orissa, India
Ong in Andamans, India
Pahari Garhwali in U.P., India
Paite in Assam, India
Panika, India
Pardhan in Andhra Pradesh, India
Parengi in Orissa, India
Patelia in Gujarat, India
Pengo in Orissa, India
Pnar in Assam, India
Rabha in Assam, India
*Rai, Danuwar, Nepal
Rajbansi, Nepal
Sadan in Andamans, India
Sondwari in M.P., India
Takankar, India
Tengger, Indonesia
Thakur, India
Thar in Bihar, India
Toda in Tamil Nadu, India
Tokkaru in Tamil Nadu, India
Tugara, India
Ullatan in Kerala, India
Urali in Kerala, India
Vishavan in Kerala, India
Waddar in Andhra Pradesh, India
Wagdi in Rajasthan, India

Yanadi in Andhra Pradesh, India
Yerava in Karnataka, India
Yerukala in A.P., India
Zangskari in Kashmir, India

HINDU-BUDDHIST

Kanauri in Uttar Pradesh, India
Khamti in Assam, India
Labans, India
Labhani in Andhra Pradesh, India
Ladakhi in Jammu, India
Lalung in Assam, India
**Lepcha, Sikkim
Naga, Mao, India
Naga, Nruanghmei, India
Naga, Sangtam, India
Naga, Tangkhul, India
Naga, Wancho, India
*Newari, Nepal
Nimadi in Madhya Pradesh, India
Pao in Madhya Pradesh, India
Rai, Nepal
Riang in Assam, India
Sikkimese, India
Sulung, India
*Tamang, Nepal
Tamaria in Bihar, India
Thado in Assam, India
Vaiphei in Assam, India
Zome in Manipur, India

HINDUISM

Adiyan in Kerala, India
Agariya in Bihar, India
Anga in Bihar, India
Arya in Andhra Pradesh, India
Babri, India
Bagri, Pakistan
Bajania, Pakistan (79)
Balmiki, Pakistan
Bareli in Madhya Pradesh, India
Bathudi in Bihar, India
**Bhil, Pakistan
*Bhojpuri, Nepal
Bondo in Orissa, India
*Gorkha, India
Gujarati, United Kingdom
Gurung, Nepal
Indians in Dubai, United Arab
   Emirates (82)
Indians in Fiji, Fiji (79)
*Indians In Rhodesia, Zimbabwe
**Indians, East, Trinidad and
   Tobago (79)
Iravas in Kerala, India
***Irulas in Kerala, India
Jharia in Orissa, India
Juang in Orissa, India
Kachchi in Andhra Pradesh, India

Khasi in Assam, India
**Kohli, Kutchi, Pakistan
**Kohli, Tharadari, Pakistan
**Kohlis, Parkari, Pakistan
*Kudisai Vagh Makkal, India
**Kuluis in Himachal Prades, India
   (81)
*Labourers of Jhoparpatti, India
Lohar, Pakistan
Malavedan in Kerala, India
Mangs in Maharashtra, India
***Matharis, India
**Meghwar, Pakistan (79)
*Meitei, India (79)
**Nepalese in India, India
*Nepali, Nepal
Od, Pakistan
*Rava in Assam, India
**Saiva Vellala, India
*Shourastra in Tamil Nadu, India
*Sindhis of India, India
Sochi, Pakistan
Sora in Orissa, India
Tamil (Ceylonese), Sri Lanka
*Tamil in Yellagiri Hills, India
**Tamil Laborers in Bombay, India
   (82)
***Tamil Plantation Workers,
   Malaysia
*Tamils (Indian), Malaysia
**Tamils (Indian), Sri Lanka (79)
Tharu, Nepal
Totis, India
Vagari, Pakistan

ISLAM

Abazin, Soviet Russia
Abialang, Sudan
Abkhaz, Turkey
Abong, Nigeria
Abu Leila, Sudan
Achehnese, Indonesia (80)
Acheron, Sudan
Achipa, Nigeria
Adygei, Soviet Russia
Afitti, Sudan
**African Students in Cairo, Egypt
Afshars, Iran
Agajanis, Iran
Agul, Soviet Russia
Ahir in Maharashtra, India
**Ahl-i-Haqq in Iran, Iran (79)
Ahmadis in Lahore, Pakistan (82)
Aja, Sudan
Alaba, Ethiopia
*Alawites, Syria (79)
*Albanian Muslims, Albania (80)
*Albanians in Yugoslavia,
   Yugoslavia
Algerian (Arabs), Algeria (80)
Algerian Arabs in France, France
*Anatolian Turks-Istanbul, Turkey
   (82)
Ara, Indonesia

Harari, Ethiopia
**Hazara in Kabul, Afghanistan (82)
Heiban, Sudan
Hezareh, Iran
Hui, China (80)
**Hunzakut, Pakistan (79)
Hwana, Nigeria
Hyam, Nigeria
Ikulu, Nigeria
Inallu, Iran
Ingushes, Soviet Russia
*Int'l Stud., Los Banos, Philippines
Jamshidis, Iran
Jara, Nigeria
Jati, Afghanistan
**Javanese of Pejompongan, Indonesia
Jera, Nigeria
Jimbin, Nigeria
**Jimini, Ivory Coast
Kabyle, Algeria (79)
Kadugli, Sudan
Kagoma, Nigeria
Kaibu, Nigeria
Kaka, Nigeria
Kakwa, Sudan
Kamo, Nigeria
Kanga, Sudan
Kanuri, Nigeria (80)
Karakalpak, Soviet Russia (80)
Karekare, Nigeria
Kariya, Nigeria
Karko, Sudan
**Kashmiri Muslims, India (79)
Katab, Nigeria
Katcha, Sudan
Katla, Sudan
Kazakhs, Iran (80)
Keiga, Sudan
Keiga Jirru, Sudan
Khalaj, Iran
Khasonke, Mali
Khojas, Agha Khani, India
Kilba, Nigeria
Kirghiz, Afghanistan
Kirgiz, China
Kirifi, Nigeria
Kita, Mali
Koma, Central, Sudan
Kono, Nigeria
Kotokoli, Benin
Kuda-Chamo, Nigeria
Kunama, Ethiopia
Kurds in Iran, Iran (80)
Kurds in Kuwait, Kuwait
*Kurds of Turkey, Turkey (79)
Kushi, Nigeria
Kuteb, Nigeria
Kuturmi, Nigeria
Kuzamani, Nigeria
Kwa, Nigeria
Kyibaku, Nigeria
Laamang, Nigeria
Labbai, India
Lafofa, Sudan
Lakians, Soviet Russia
Lakka, Nigeria

Lame, Nigeria
Laro, Sudan
Laru, Nigeria
Lebong, Indonesia
Libyans, Libya
Ligbi, Ivory Coast
Ligbi, Ghana
Longuda, Nigeria
Lori, Sudan
Lors, Iran (80)
Lotsu-Piri, Nigeria
Luac, Sudan
Lubu, Indonesia
Luwu, Indonesia
Lwo, Sudan
Maba, Sudan
Maban-Jumjum, Sudan
Madi, Sudan
Madurese, Indonesia (79)
Maguindano, Philippines (80)
*Mahrah, Yemen, Democratic
Makonde, Tanzania
Malays of Singapore, Singapore (79)
Mamasani, Iran
Mandar, Indonesia
Mandara, Nigeria
Mandingo, Liberia (79)
Manggarai Muslims, Indonesia (81)
Mappillas, India
Maranao, Philippines (79)
Marghi Central, Nigeria
Marka, Upper Volta
Masakin, Sudan
Masalit, Sudan
Masenrempulu, Indonesia
Matakam, Nigeria
Matumbi, Tanzania
Maures, Senegal
Mazandaranis, Iran
Mboi, Nigeria
Mbula-Bwazza, Nigeria
Meos of Rajasthan, India (80)
Midob, Sudan
Minangkabau, Indonesia (80)
Miri, Sudan
Mober, Nigeria
Modo, Sudan
Mogholi, Afghanistan
Montol, Nigeria
Moor Malays, Sri Lanka (79)
Moors in Mauritania, Mauritania
Moqaddam, Iran
Moreb, Sudan
Mori, Indonesia (81)
Moru, Sudan
Mumbake, Nigeria
Munji-Yidgha, Afghanistan
Muslim Community of Bawku, Ghana
Muslim Gypsies in Skoplje, Yugoslavia (82)
**Muslim Immigrants in U.K., United Kingdom
Muslim Malays, Malaysia (80)
Muslims (West Nile Dist.), Uganda
Muslims in U.A.E., United Arab Emirates (79)

Muslims of Jordan, Jordan
Nafar, Iran
Naka, Sudan
Nandu-Tari, Nigeria
Nginyukwur, Sudan
Ngirere, Sudan
Ngizim, Nigeria
Ngok, Sudan
Ngunduna, Sudan
Nguqwurang, Sudan
Ngwoi, Nigeria
Ninzam, Nigeria
Njalgulgule, Sudan
North Africans in Belgium,
  Belgium (80)
Numana-Nunku-Gwantu, Nigeria
**Nupe, Nigeria
Nuristani, Afghanistan (80)
Nyamusa, Sudan
Nyarueng, Sudan
Nzanyi, Nigeria
Otoro, Sudan
Ouaddai, Chad
Palembang, Indonesia
Paloc, Sudan
Pankhu, Bangladesh
Pashtuns, Iran (80)
Pero, Nigeria
Persians of Iran, Iran (80)
Pishagchi, Iran
Piti, Nigeria
Piya, Nigeria
Polci, Nigeria
Pongu, Nigeria
Poouch in Kashmir, India
***Prasuni, Afghanistan
Puku-Geeri-Keri-Wipsi, Nigeria
Punjabis, Pakistan (80)
Purig-Pa of Kashmir, India (81)
Qajars, Iran
Qara'i, Iran
Qaragozlu, Iran
Qashqa'i, Iran (80)
Rajasthani Muslims-Jaipur, India
  (82)
Redjang, Indonesia (80)
Rukuba, Nigeria
Rumaya, Nigeria
Ruruma, Nigeria
Rut, Sudan
Rutul, Soviet Russia
**Saguye, Kenya
Sama Pangutaran, Philippines
  (80)
Sanga, Nigeria
Sangil, Philippines
Sarakole, Senegal (80)
Sasanis, Iran
Sau, Afghanistan
Saya, Nigeria
Sayyids, Yemen, Arab Republic
Sere, Sudan
Shahsavans, Iran (80)
Shatt, Sudan
Shawiya, Algeria
**Shihu, United Arab Emirates
Shilluk, Sudan
Shughni, Afghanistan
Shuwa Arabic, Nigeria

Shwai, Sudan
Siri, Nigeria
Solorese Muslims, Indonesia (81)
Somali, Ethiopia
Somali, Somalia (79)
Somali, Ajuran, Kenya (79)
Somali, Degodia, Kenya
Somali, Gurreh, Kenya
Somali, Ogadenya, Kenya
Soninke, Gambia
Soninke, Mali
Soninke, Mauritania
Sopi, Sudan
Sukur, Nigeria
Sumbawa, Indonesia
Sura, Nigeria
Surubu, Nigeria
Swatis, Pakistan (79)
Tabasaran, Soviet Russia
Tajik, Iran (80)
Tajik, Afghanistan
Tajik, Soviet Russia
Takestani, Iran
Tal, Nigeria
Talish, Iran
Talodi, Sudan
Tamil Muslims in Madras, India
  (82)
Tangale, Nigeria
Tangchangya, Bangladesh
Tat, Soviet Russia
Tatars, Soviet Russia (80)
Taucouleur, Senegal (80)
Tausug, Philippines (80)
Teda, Chad (80)
Teda, Libya
Tegali, Sudan
Teimuri, Iran
Teimurtash, Iran
Tem, Togo
Temein, Sudan
Tera, Nigeria
Ternatans, Indonesia
*Tertiary Level Youth, Iran
Thoi, Sudan
Thuri, Sudan
Tippera, Bangladesh
Tira, Sudan
Tirma, Sudan
*Toussian, Upper Volta
Tsakhur, Soviet Russia
Tuareg, Niger (79)
Tula, Nigeria
Tulishi, Sudan
Tumale, Sudan
Tumma, Sudan
Tumtum, Sudan
Turkish Immigrant Workers,
  German Federal Rep. (79)
Turkish Workers, Belgium (80)
Turkomans, Iran (80)
Turks in Basel, Switzerland (82)
Turks, Anatolian, Turkey
Turkwam, Nigeria
Twi, Sudan
Uighur, Afghanistan
Uigur, China (80)
Umm Dorein, Sudan
Umm Gabralla, Sudan

*Vai, Liberia (80)
**Vohras of Yavatmal, India
Waja, Nigeria
Weda, Indonesia
Winji-Winji, Benin
Woro, Sudan
Yao, Mozambique
Yemenis, Yemen, Arab Republic (79)
Yeskwa, Nigeria
Yoruk, Turkey
Yulu, Sudan
Yungur, Nigeria
Zaghawa, Libya
Zaghawa, Sudan
Zari, Nigeria
Zenaga, Mauritania

ISLAM-ANIMIST

Abe, Ivory Coast
Abidji, Ivory Coast
Abou Charib, Chad
Abure, Ivory Coast
Achode, Ghana
Adele, Togo
Adyukru, Ivory Coast
Afar, Ethiopia (79)
Agutaynon, Philippines
Ahlo, Togo
Akan, Brong, Ivory Coast
***Akhdam, Yemen, Arab Republic
Akpafu, Ghana
Aladian, Ivory Coast
Alas, Indonesia
Ana, Togo
Animere, Togo
Anyanga, Togo
Attie, Ivory Coast
Avatime, Ghana
Avikam, Ivory Coast
Awutu, Ghana
Ayana, Kenya
Bagirmi, Chad
Bajau, Land, Malaysia
Bakwe, Ivory Coast
Balantak, Indonesia
Bali, Nigeria
Bambara, Ivory Coast
Banyum, Senegal
Bariba, Nigeria
Basila, Togo
Bata, Nigeria
Bayot, Gambia
Bayot, Guinea-Bissau
Bayot, Senegal
Bidyogo, Guinea-Bissau
Bilala, Chad
Bile, Nigeria
Bimoba, Ghana
Bimoba, Togo
Bira, Indonesia
Birifor, Upper Volta
Bitare, Nigeria
Bolon, Upper Volta

Bomou, Chad
Boran, Ethiopia
**Boran, Kenya
Boran, Kenya
Bousansi, Upper Volta
Bowili, Togo
Bugis, Indonesia (80)
Buli, Indonesia
Buli, Upper Volta
Bullom, Northern, Sierra Leone
Bullom, Southern, Sierra Leone
Butung, Indonesia
Chala, Ghana
Chamba Daka, Nigeria
Chamba Leko, Nigeria
Cirebon, Indonesia
Dagari, Upper Volta
**Dagomba, Ghana
Daju of Dar Dadju, Chad
Daju of Dar Sila, Chad
Dan, Liberia
Dangaleat, Chad
Dass, Nigeria
Dida, Ivory Coast
Diola, Senegal
Dirim, Nigeria
Doghosie, Upper Volta
Dyan, Upper Volta
Dyerma, Niger (80)
Dyola, Gambia
Dyola, Guinea-Bissau
Dyola, Senegal
Ebira, Nigeria
Ebrie, Ivory Coast
Eotile, Ivory Coast
Fula, Upper Volta
Fula, Cunda, Gambia
Fulani, Cameroon (79)
*Fulani, Benin
*Fulbe, Ghana
Gabri, Chad
*Galla (Bale), Ethiopia
Gambai, Chad
Gan, Upper Volta
Gangam, Togo
Gayo, Indonesia (80)
Gidar, Chad
Gola, Liberia
Gola, Sierra Leone
Golo, Chad
Gonja, Ghana
Gosha, Kenya
Gouin-Turka, Upper Volta
Goulai, Chad
Guere, Ivory Coast
Gujars of Kashmir, India (81)
Gujars of Kashmir, India (81)
Gula, Chad
Gurage, Ethiopia (80)
Gurma, Upper Volta
Gwa, Ivory Coast
Hwela-Numu, Ivory Coast
Icen, Nigeria
Igbira, Nigeria (80)
Jama Mapun, Philippines (80)
Jambi, Indonesia
**Javanese (rural), Indonesia (79)
**Javanese of Central Java, Indonesia

Jongor, Chad
Kanembu, Chad
Kanembu, Niger
Karachay, Soviet Russia
Karanga, Chad
Kari, Chad
Kasanga, Guinea-Bissau
Kasele, Togo
Kasem, Upper Volta
**Kaur, Indonesia
Kazakhs, China (81)
Kebu, Togo
Kendari, Indonesia
Kenga, Chad
Kera, Chad
Kerinchi, Indonesia
Kibet, Chad
Kim, Chad
Kirgiz, Soviet Russia (80)
Kissi, Southern, Sierra Leone
Klaoh, Liberia
Kobiana, Guinea
Koke, Chad
Kolbila, Cameroon
Komering, Indonesia
Komono, Upper Volta
Konyagi, Guinea
**Koranko, Sierra Leone
Kotoko, Chad
Kotokoli, Togo
Kouya, Ivory Coast
Kpelle, Guinea
Kposo, Togo
Krachi, Ghana
Krim, Sierra Leone
Krio, Gambia
Krobou, Ivory Coast
Kubu, Indonesia (81)
Kuka, Chad
Kulele, Ivory Coast
Kullo, Ethiopia
Kulung, Nigeria
Kunante, Guinea-Bissau
Kurumba, Upper Volta
Kuwaa, Liberia
Laka, Chad
Lampung, Indonesia (80)
Landoma, Guinea
Landoma, Guinea-Bissau
Lele, Chad
Lele, Upper Volta
Lelemi, Ghana
Liguri, Sudan
Logba, Ghana
Loko, Guinea
Loko, Sierra Leone
Maba, Chad
Majingai-Ngama, Chad
Mamprusi, Ghana
Mandyak, Gambia
Mangbai, Chad
Maninka, Guinea-Bissau
Maninka, Sierra Leone
Mankanya, Guinea-Bissau
Mankanya, Senegal
Maou, Ivory Coast
Maranao, Lanad, Philippines
Mararit, Chad
Marba, Chad

Masalit, Chad
Massalat, Chad
Maure, Mali
Mbai, Chad
Mbum, Chad
Mende, Liberia
Mesengo, Ethiopia
Mesme, Chad
Mesmedje, Chad
Mimi, Chad
Mo, Ivory Coast
Mogum, Chad
*Molbog, Philippines
Mona, Ivory Coast
Moru, Ivory Coast
Mubi, Chad
Muna, Indonesia
Mundang, Chad
Musei, Chad
Musgu, Chad
Musi, Indonesia
Nalu, Guinea
Nancere, Chad
Naoudem, Togo
Nara, Ethiopia
Natemba, Togo
Natioro, Upper Volta
Nchumbulu, Ghana
Nchumunu, Ghana
Ndunpa Duupa, Cameroon
Nielim, Chad
Nkonya, Ghana
Ntrubo, Togo
Nunuma, Upper Volta
Nyangbo, Ghana
Nzema, Ivory Coast
Nzema, Ghana
Ogan, Indonesia
Oubi, Ivory Coast
Palara, Ivory Coast
Papel, Guinea-Bissau
Pashayi, Afghanistan
Prang, Ghana
Puguli, Upper Volta
Pye, Ivory Coast
Rataning, Chad
Rendille, Kenya
Runga, Chad
Safaliba, Ghana
Sakuye, Kenya
Sama Bangingi, Philippines (80)
Sama, Siasi, Philippines
Sama, Sibuku, Philippines
Sama-Badjaw, Philippines (79)
Samo, Northern, Upper Volta
Santrokofi, Ghana
Sarwa, Chad
Sasak, Indonesia (80)
Sekayu, Indonesia
Sekpele, Ghana
**Serawai, Indonesia (81)
Serere-Non, Senegal
Serere-Sine, Senegal
Shilha, Morocco
Shina, Afghanistan
**Shluh Berbers, Morocco
Sidamo, Ethiopia
Sindhi Muslims in Karachi,
   Pakistan (82)

Sisala, Upper Volta
Siwu, Ghana
Somrai, Chad
Songhai, Niger
Songhai, Upper Volta
Subanun,Lapuyan, Philippines
**Sundanese, Indonesia (80)
Sungor, Chad
Susu, Guinea-Bissau
Susu, Sierra Leone
Tafi, Togo
Tagwana, Ivory Coast
*Talo, Indonesia
Tama, Chad
Tamazight, Morocco
Tana, Chad
Teda, Niger
Tepo, Ivory Coast
Thai Islam (Malay), Thailand (80)
*Thai Islam (Thai), Thailand
Tidorese, Indonesia
Tiefo, Upper Volta
Trepo, Ivory Coast
Tunya, Chad
Tupuri, Chad
Tura, Ivory Coast
**Uzbeks, Afghanistan (79)
Vagla, Ghana
Vai, Sierra Leone
Vige, Upper Volta
Voko, Cameroon
Wara, Upper Volta
Win, Upper Volta
Wolio, Indonesia
Wolof, Senegal (80)
Wolof, Gambian, Gambia
Wom, Nigeria
Yakan, Philippines (80)
*Yalunka, Sierra Leone (80)
Yandang, Nigeria
Yanga, Togo
**Yao, Malawi
Zaghawa, Chad
Zaramo, Tanzania

JAIN

Jains, India

JUDAISM

**Falasha, Ethiopia (79)
*Jewish Imgrnts.-American, Israel
*Jewish Imgrnts.-Argentine, Israel
*Jewish Imgrnts.-Australia, Israel
*Jewish Imgrnts.-Brazilian, Israel
*Jewish Imgrnts.-Mexican, Israel
*Jewish Imgrnts.-Uruguayan, Israel
*Jewish Immigrants, Other, Israel
Jews in Venice, Italy (82)
Jews of Iran, Iran
Jews of Montreal, Canada
Jews, Sephardic, Canada
Ladinos, Lebanon
Targum, Israel

NOMINAL CHRISTIAN

Baguio Area Miners, Philippines (81)
**Batangeno, Philippines
***Bolinao, Philippines
*Casiguranin, Philippines
**Chicanos in Denver, United States of America (82)
***Copacabana Apt. Dwellers, Brazil
*Drug Addicts in Sao Paulo, Brazil (82)
**Hotel Workers in Manila, Philippines (81)
**Ishans, Nigeria
*Jeepney Drivers in Manila, Philippines (81)
*Jeepney Drivers in Manila, Philippines (81)
**Kalinga, Tanudan, Philippines
**Middle Class-Mexico City, Mexico (82)
**Military Personnel, Ecuador
*Universitarios - Rosario, Argentina (82)
**Urban Mestizos, Ecuador

PEYOTE RELIGION

Paiute, Northern, United States of America

SECULARISM

Aborigines in Brisbane, Australia (82)
*Americans in Geneva, Switzerland
Amsterdam Boat Dwellers, Netherlands
**Auberge Crowd in Geneva, Switzerland (82)
**Bachelors in Lagos, Nigeria (82)
**Bus Girls in Seoul, Korea, Republic of (82)

*Casual Laborers-Atlanta, United States of America (82)
**Chinese in Boston, United States of America (82)
*Chinese in Korea, Korea, Republic of
*Chinese in West Germany, German Federal Rep.
*Chinese Mainlanders, Taiwan
**Chinese Stud., Australia, Australia
*Coloureds in Eersterust, South Africa (82)
*Danchi Dwellers in Tokyo, Japan (82)
Dead-End Kids - Amsterdam, Netherlands (82)
**Ex-Mental Patients in NYC, United States of America (82)
*Expatriates in Riyadh, Saudi Arabia (82)
Gays in San Francisco, United States of America (82)
Geishas in Osaka, Japan (82)
*Industrial Workers, Taiwan (81)
**Jamaican Elite, Jamaica
**Japanese Students In USA, United States of America
**Korean Prisoners, Korea, Republic of
Nurses in St. Louis, United States of America (82)
*Parsees, India (81)
Pension Students-Madrid, Spain (82)
**Portuguese in France, France
**Pro Hockey Players, United States of America (82)
**Racetrack Residents, United States of America (79)
Seychellois, Seychelles
Students in Cuiaba, Brazil
**Suriguenos, Philippines
Taiwan-Chinese Un. Stud., Taiwan
*University Students, France (79)
*University Students, German Federal Rep. (79)

TRADITIONAL CHINESE

Ach'ang, China
Buriat, China
Burig, China
Ch'iang, China
Chin, China
Chinese Businessmen, Hong Kong (81)
Chinese Factory Workers, Hong Kong
Chinese Fishermen, Malaysia
**Chinese Hakka of Taiwan, Taiwan (79)
**Chinese in Australia, Australia
*Chinese in Austria, Austria

**Chinese in Brazil, Brazil
Chinese in Burma, Burma
**Chinese in Hong Kong, Hong Kong
**Chinese in Indonesia, Indonesia
*Chinese in Japan, Japan
*Chinese in Laos, Laos
*Chinese in Malaysia, Malaysia
*Chinese in New Zealand, New Zealand
**Chinese in Panama, Panama
Chinese in Puerto Rico, Puerto Rico
**Chinese in Sabah, Malaysia
**Chinese in Sarawak, Malaysia
*Chinese in South Africa, South Africa
*Chinese in Taiwan, Taiwan
**Chinese in United Kingdom, United Kingdom
**Chinese in United States, United States of America
**Chinese in Vancouver B.C., Canada
*Chinese of W. Malaysia, Malaysia
*Chinese Refugees in Macau, Macau (81)
**Chinese Refugees, France, France (79)
*Chinese Restaurant Wrkrs., France
**Chinese Students Glasgow, United Kingdom
Chinese Villagers, Hong Kong
Chingp'o, China
Chungchia, China
Chwang, China
Dagur, China
Evenki, China
Fishing Village People, Taiwan
Hani, China
**High School Students, Hong Kong
Jyarung, China
Kalmytz, China
Kam, China
Kelao, China
Khalka, China
Kham, China
Lahul, China
Laka, China
Lati, China
Li, China
Manchu, China (81)
Mongour, China
Nahsi, China
Nanai, China
Nosu, China
Nung, China
Oirat, China
Oronchon, China
Paongan, China
Pu-I, China
Punu, China
Rawang, China
Salar, China
Santa, China
Sibo, China
Sui, China
Wa, China

*Women Laborers, Taiwan
Yellow Uighur, China
Yuku, China

TRADITIONAL JAPANESE

Farmers of Japan, Japan
*Industry Laborers-Japan, Japan
*Inland Sea Island Peoples, Japan
*Japanese in Korea, Korea,
  Republic of
*Ryukyuan, Japan
**Univ. Students of Japan, Japan

ZOROASTRIANISM

*Parsis in Bombay, India (82)

OTHER

**Lotuka, Sudan
*Yanyula, Australia

UNKNOWN

Abkhaz, Soviet Russia
Akhavakh, Soviet Russia
Alutor, Soviet Russia
Andi, Soviet Russia
Archin, Soviet Russia
Bangangte, Cameroon
Basaa, Cameroon
Batsi, Soviet Russia
Botlikh, Soviet Russia
Budug, Soviet Russia
**Bus Drivers, South Korea, Korea,
  Republic of
Chamalin, Soviet Russia
*Chinese in Amsterdam,
  Netherlands
Chinese in Costa Rica, Costa
  Rica
*Chinese in Holland, Netherlands
Chinese Merchants, Ghana
Chukot, Soviet Russia
Didoi, Soviet Russia
Dolgans, Soviet Russia
*Factory Workers, Hong Kong
Gilyak, Soviet Russia
*Havasupai, United States of
  America
Itelmen, Soviet Russia
Izhor, Soviet Russia

Kapuchin, Soviet Russia
Karagas, Soviet Russia
Karaim, Soviet Russia
Karakalpak, Soviet Russia
Karatin, Soviet Russia
Ket, Soviet Russia
Khakas, Soviet Russia
Khana, Nigeria
Khanti, Soviet Russia
Khinalug, Soviet Russia
Khvarshin, Soviet Russia
Kongo, Angola
***Koreans in Germany, German
  Federal Rep.
Koryak, Soviet Russia
Kryz, Soviet Russia
Kvanadin, Soviet Russia
Liv, Soviet Russia
Lugbara, Uganda
Mansi, Soviet Russia
Mingat, Soviet Russia
Naga, Sema, India
Nanai, Soviet Russia
Nentsy, Soviet Russia
Nganasan, Soviet Russia
Nivkhi, Soviet Russia
Oroch, Soviet Russia
Orok, Soviet Russia
Saams, Soviet Russia
Selkup, Soviet Russia
Shor, Soviet Russia
Svan, Soviet Russia
Tindin, Soviet Russia
Udegeis, Soviet Russia
Udin, Soviet Russia
Ulchi, Soviet Russia
Veps, Soviet Russia
Yagnobi, Soviet Russia
Yazgulyam, Soviet Russia
Yukagirs, Soviet Russia
Yurak, Soviet Russia

NOT REPORTED

Balanta, Senegal
Bamum, Cameroon
Lunda, Ndembu, Zambia
Mancang, Senegal
Manding, Senegal
Manjack, Senegal
Mulimba, Cameroon
Ndogo, Sudan
Pular, Senegal
Tandanke, Senegal
Tsaangi, Congo

Index by
Language

INDEX BY LANGUAGE

Groups are listed according to their primary vernacular language. In many cases, groups are bilingual or trilingual, speaking several languages including a more commonly known trade language.

Aja	Aja, Sudan
Ajmeri	Ajmeri in Rajasthan, India
Aka	Aka, India
Akan, Brong	Akan, Brong, Ivory Coast
Akawaio	Akawaio, Guyana
Ake	Ake, Nigeria
**Akha	Akha, Thailand (79)
Akhavakh	Akhavakh, Soviet Russia
Akpa-Yache	Akpa-Yache, Nigeria
Akpafu	Akpafu, Ghana
Akrukay	Akrukay, Papua New Guinea
Alaban	Alaba, Ethiopia
Aladian	Aladian, Ivory Coast
Alago	Alago, Nigeria
Alak	Alak, Laos
Alamblak	Alamblak, Papua New Guinea
Alangan	Alangan, Philippines
Alatil	Alatil, Papua New Guinea
Alauagat	Alauagat, Papua New Guinea
Albanian (Gheg)	*Albanians in Yugoslavia, Yugoslavia
Albanian Tosk	*Albanian Muslims, Albania (80)
Aledjo	*Nyantruku, Benin
Alege	Alege, Nigeria
Allar	*Alars, India
Alor, Kolana	Alor, Kolana, Indonesia (81)
Altaic	Ewenkis, China (81)
Alur	Alur, Zaire
Alutor	Alutor, Soviet Russia
Ama	Ama, Papua New Guinea
Amahuaca	Amahuaca, Peru
Amaimon	Amaimon, Papua New Guinea
Amanab	Amanab, Indonesia
	Amanab, Papua New Guinea
Amar	Amar, Ethiopia
Amarakaeri	Amarakaeri, Peru
Amasi	Amasi, Cameroon
Ambai	Ambai, Indonesia
Ambasi	Ambasi, Papua New Guinea
Amber	Amber, Indonesia
Amberbaken	Amberbaken, Indonesia
Ambo	Ambo, Zambia
Ambonese	Ambonese, Netherlands
	Ambonese, Indonesia
Ami	*Ami, Taiwan (81)
Amo	Amo, Nigeria
Amoy	Fishing Village People, Taiwan
	*Women Laborers, Taiwan
Ampale	**Ampeeli, Papua New Guinea
Amto	Amto, Papua New Guinea
Amuesha	Amuesha, Peru
Amuzgo, Guerrero	Amuzgo, Guerrero, Mexico
Amuzgo, Oaxaca	Amuzgo, Oaxaca, Mexico
Ana	Ana, Togo
Anaang	Anaang, Nigeria
Anal	Anal in Manipur, India
Andarum	Andarum, Papua New Guinea
Andha	Andha in Andhra Pradesh, India
Andi	Andi, Soviet Russia
Andoque	Andoque, Colombia
Anem	Anem, Papua New Guinea
Anga	Anga in Bihar, India
Angaataha	Angaataha, Papua New Guinea
Angal Heneng, South	Angal Heneng, South, Papua New Guinea
Angal Heneng, West	Angal Heneng, West, Papua New Guinea
Angal, East	Angal, East, Papua New Guinea
Angas	Angas, Nigeria
Angaua	Angaua, Papua New Guinea
Anggor	Anggor, Papua New Guinea
Angoram	Angoram, Papua New Guinea

Animere	Animere, Togo
Ankave	Ankave, Papua New Guinea
Ankwai	Ankwe, Nigeria
Anor	Anor, Papua New Guinea
Ansus	Ansus, Indonesia
Anuak	Anuak, Ethiopia
	Anuak, Sudan
Anuki	Anuki, Papua New Guinea
Anyanga	Anyanga, Togo
Apalai	Apalai, Brazil
Apartani	**Apatani in Assam, India
Apinaye	Apinaye, Brazil
Apurina	Apurina, Brazil
Ara	Ara, Indonesia
Arabela	Arabela, Peru
Arabic	***Akhdam, Yemen, Arab Republic
	*Alawites, Syria (79)
	Algerian (Arabs), Algeria (80)
	Algerian Arabs in France, France
	Arab Immigrants in Bangui, Central African Republic (82)
	Arab-Jabbari (Kamesh), Iran
	Arab-Shaibani (Kamesh), Iran
	**Arabs in New Orleans, United States of America (82)
	Arabs of Khuzestan, Iran
	**Auberge Crowd in Geneva, Switzerland (82)
	Chinese in Saudi Arabia, Saudi Arabia
	Circassians in Amman, Jordan (82)
	Druzes, Israel (79)
	**Hadrami, Yemen, Democratic
	Libyans, Libya
	Masalit, Sudan
	Maures, Senegal
	Muslims in U.A.E., United Arab Emirates (79)
	Muslims of Jordan, Jordan
	North Africans in Belgium, Belgium (80)
	Sayyids, Yemen, Arab Republic
Arabic (Eastern)	Yemenis, Yemen, Arab Republic (79)
Arabic (Hassani)	Moors in Mauritania, Mauritania
Arabic dialect	Arabs in Morocco, Morocco
Arafundi	Arafundi, Papua New Guinea
Aranadan	Aranadan in Tamil Nadu, India
Aranatan	*Arnatas, India
Arandai	Arandai, Indonesia
Arapesh, Bumbita	Arapesh, Bumbita, Papua New Guinea
Arapesh, Mountain	Arapesh, Mountain, Papua New Guinea
Arapesh, Muhiang	Arapesh, Muhiang, Papua New Guinea
Arawak	Arawak, Guyana
Arawe	Arawe, Papua New Guinea
Arbore	Arbore, Ethiopia
Archin	Archin, Soviet Russia
Arecuna	Arecuna, Venezuela
Argobba	Argobba, Ethiopia
Arguni	Arguni, Indonesia
Arifama-Miniafia	Arifama-Miniafia, Papua New Guinea
Arigibi	Arigibi, Papua New Guinea
Arinua	Arinua, Papua New Guinea
Arop	Arop, Papua New Guinea
Aruop	Aruop, Papua New Guinea
Arusha	Arusha, Tanzania
Arya	Arya in Andhra Pradesh, India
Asaro	Asaro, Papua New Guinea
Asat	Asat, Papua New Guinea
Asienara	Asienara, Indonesia
Asmat	*Asmat, Indonesia (79)
Assamese	Assamese, Bangladesh
Assumbo	Assumbo, Cameroon

Asu	Asu, Tanzania
Asuri	Asuri in Bihar, India
Asurini	Kuatinema, Brazil
Ata	Ata, Papua New Guinea
Aten	Aten, Nigeria
Ati	Ati, Philippines
Atoc	Atoc, Sudan
Atruahi	Atruahi, Brazil
Atta	*Atta, Philippines
Attie	Attie, Ivory Coast
Atuot	Atuot, Sudan
Atye	*Atye, Ivory Coast
Au	Au, Papua New Guinea
Aunalei	Aunalei, Papua New Guinea
Auyana	Auyana, Papua New Guinea
Avatime	Avatime, Ghana
Avikam	Avikam, Ivory Coast
Avukaya	Avukaya, Sudan
Awa	Awa, Papua New Guinea
Awar	Awar, Papua New Guinea
Awara	Awara, Papua New Guinea
Awin	Awin, Papua New Guinea
Awngi	Awngi, Ethiopia
Awutu	Awutu, Ghana
Awyi	Awyi, Indonesia
Awyu	Awyu, Indonesia
Ayana	Ayana, Kenya
Aymara	**Aymara, Bolivia
Aymara, Carangas	Aymara, Carangas, Chile
Ayoreo	Ayoreo, Paraguay
Ayu	Ayu, Nigeria
Azera	Azera, Papua New Guinea
Azerbaijani	**Azerbaijani, Afghanistan
Azerbaijani (Shahsavani)	Shahsavans, Iran (80)
Azerbaijani Turkish	Azerbaijani Turks, Iran (80)
Baali	Baali, Zaire
Babajou	Babajou, Cameroon
Babri	Babri, India
Baburiwa	Baburiwa, Indonesia
Bachama	Bachama, Nigeria
Bada	Bada, Nigeria
Badagu	Badagu in Nilgiri, India
Bade	Bade, Nigeria
Badyara	Badyara, Guinea-Bissau
Bafut	Bafut, Cameroon
Bagelkhandi	Bagelkhandi in M.P., India
Baghati	Baghati in H.P., India
Bagirmi	Bagirmi, Chad
Bagobo	***Bagobo, Philippines
Bagri	Bagri, Pakistan
Baham	Baham, Indonesia
Bahasa Jawa	**Javanese of Pejompongan, Indonesia
Bahasa Malaysia	Muslim Malays, Malaysia (80)
Bahawalpuri	Bahawalpuri in M.P., India
Bahinemo	Bahinemo, Papua New Guinea
Bai	Bai, Sudan
Baibai	Baibai, Papua New Guinea
Baiga	Baiga in Bihar, India
Baining	Baining, Papua New Guinea
Bajau, Indonesian	Bajau, Indonesian, Indonesia
Bajaus	Bajau, Land, Malaysia
Baka	Baka, Cameroon
	Baka, Zaire
Bakairi	Bakairi, Brazil
Bakhtiaris	Bakhtiaris, Iran (80)
Bakwe	Bakwe, Ivory Coast
Bakwele	Bakwele, Congo
Balangao	**Balangao, Philippines
Balangaw	Balangaw, Philippines

Balanta	Balanta, Senegal
	Balante, Guinea-Bissau
Balantak	Balantak, Indonesia
Bali	Bali, Nigeria
Bali-Vitu	Bali-Vitu, Papua New Guinea
Balinese	Balinese, Indonesia
Balkar	Balkars, Soviet Russia
Balti	Balti in Jammu, India
Baluchi	Baluchi, Iran (80)
Bam	Bam, Papua New Guinea
Bambara	Bambara, Mali
	Bambara, Ivory Coast
Bambuka	Bambuka, Nigeria
Bamougoun-Bamenjou	Bamougoun-Bamenjou, Cameroon
Bamum	Bamum, Cameroon
Banaro	***Banaro, Papua New Guinea
Bandawa-Minda	Bandawa-Minda, Nigeria
Bandi	Bandi, Liberia
	Gbande, Guinea
Bandjoun	Bandjoun, Cameroon
Banen	Banen, Cameroon
Banga	Banga, Nigeria
Bangba	Bangba, Zaire
Banggai	Banggai, Indonesia
Bangri	Bangaru in Punjab, India
Baniwa	Baniwa, Brazil
Banoni	Banoni, Papua New Guinea
Bantuanon	Bantuanon, Philippines
Banyum	Banyum, Senegal
Banyun	Banyun, Guinea-Bissau
Barai	Barai, Papua New Guinea
Barambu	Barambu, Sudan
Barasano	Barasano, Colombia
Barasano, Northern	Barasano, Northern, Colombia
Barau	Barau, Indonesia
Bare'e	Bare'e, Indonesia
Bareli	Bareli in Madhya Pradesh, India
Bari	Bari, Sudan
Bariai	Bariai, Papua New Guinea
Bariba	*Bariba, Benin (80)
	Bariba, Nigeria
Bariji	Bariji, Papua New Guinea
Barim	Barim, Papua New Guinea
Barok	Barok, Papua New Guinea
Baruga	Baruga, Papua New Guinea
Baruya	Baruya, Papua New Guinea
Basaa	Basaa, Cameroon
Basari	Basari, Togo
	Basari, Guinea
	Basari, Senegal
Bashar	Bashar, Nigeria
Bashgali	Bashgali, Afghanistan
Basila	Basila, Togo
Basketo	Basketo, Ethiopia
Bassa	*Bassa, Liberia
	**Bassa, Nigeria
Bata	Bata, Nigeria
Batak, Angkola	*Batak, Angkola, Indonesia (80)
Batak, Karo	Batak, Karo, Indonesia
Batak, Palawan	Batak, Palawan, Philippines
Batak, Simalungun	Batak, Simalungun, Indonesia
Batak, Toba	Batak, Toba, Indonesia
Batanga-Ngolo	Batanga-Ngolo, Cameroon
Bateg	Bateg, Malaysia
Bathudi	Bathudi in Bihar, India
Batsi	Batsi, Soviet Russia
Batu	Batu, Nigeria
Bau	Bau, Papua New Guinea
Baule	***Baoule, Ivory Coast

Baushi	Baushi, Nigeria
Bauwaki	Bauwaki, Papua New Guinea
Bawm	Bawm, Bangladesh
Bayat	Bayats, Iran
Bayot	Bayot, Gambia
	Bayot, Guinea-Bissau
	Bayot, Senegal
Bazigar	Bazigar in Gujarat, India
Bebeli	Bebeli, Papua New Guinea
Bediya	Bediya in Bihar, India
Bedoanas	Bedoanas, Indonesia
Beja	Beja, Ethiopia
	Beja, Sudan
Bekwarra	Bekwarra, Nigeria
Bembe	Bembe, Zaire
Bembi	Bembi, Papua New Guinea
Bena	Bena, Tanzania
Benabena	Benabena, Papua New Guinea
Bencho	Bencho, Ethiopia
Bende	Bende, Tanzania
Bene	Bene, Cameroon
Benga	Benga, Gabon
Bengali	**Banai, Bangladesh
	Bengali, Bangladesh (80)
	Bengalis in London, United Kingdom (82)
	**Hajong, Bangladesh
	**Koch, Bangladesh
Berba	Berba, Benin
Berik	Berik, Indonesia
Berom	Berom, Nigeria
Besisi	Besisi, Malaysia
Bete	Bete, India
	*Bete, Ivory Coast
Bethen	Bethen, Cameroon
Betsinga	Betsinga, Cameroon
Bette-Bende	Bette-Bende, Nigeria
Bhakta	Bhakta, India
Bharia	Bharia in Madhya Pradesh, India
Bhatneri	Bhatneri, India
Bhattri	Bhattri, India
Bhilala	Bhilala, India
Bhojpuri	*Bhojpuri, Nepal
	Tharu, Nepal
Bhoyari	Bhoyari in Maharashtra, India
Bhuiya	Bhuiya in Bihar, India
Bhumij	Bhumij in Assam, India
Bhunjia	Bhunjia in Madhya Pradesh, India
Biafada	Biafada, Guinea-Bissau
Biak	Biak, Indonesia
Biaka	Biaka, Papua New Guinea
Biangai	Biangai, Papua New Guinea
Biatah	**Bidayuh of Sarawak, Malaysia (81)
Bibling	Bibling, Papua New Guinea
Biduanda	Biduanda, Malaysia
Bidyogo	Bidyogo, Guinea-Bissau
	**Bijogo, Guinea-Bissau
Bijori	Bijori in Bihar, India
Biksi	Biksi, Indonesia
Bilaan	**Bilan, Philippines
Bilala	Bilala, Chad
Bile	Bile, Nigeria
Bilen	Bilen, Ethiopia
Biliau	Biliau, Papua New Guinea
Bima	Bimanese, Indonesia
Bimin	Bimin, Papua New Guinea
Bimoba	Bimoba, Ghana
	Bimoba, Togo
	Moba, Ghana
	Moba, Togo

Boya	Boya, Sudan
Bozo	Bozo, Mali
Brahui	Brahui, Pakistan
Braj	Braj in Uttar Pradesh, India
Brao	Brao, Laos (79)
Brat	Brat, Indonesia
Breri	Breri, Papua New Guinea
Bruneis	Bruneis, Malaysia
Bua	Bua, Chad
Bual	Bual, Indonesia
Buamu (Bobo Wule)	Bwa, Upper Volta (80)
Buang, Central	Buang, Central, Papua New Guinea
Buang, Mangga	Buang, Mangga, Papua New Guinea
Bube	Bube, Equatorial Guinea
Budibud	Budibud, Papua New Guinea
Budu	Budu, Zaire
Budug	Budug, Soviet Russia
Buduma	Buduma, Nigeria
Bugis	Bugis, Indonesia (80)
Buglere	Buglere, Panama
Bugombe	Bugombe, Zaire
Buhid	Buhid, Philippines
Buin	Buin, Papua New Guinea
Buja	Buja, Zaire
Buka-khwe	Bushmen in Botswana, Botswana
Bukaua	Bukaua, Papua New Guinea
Buli	Builsa, Ghana
	Buli, Indonesia
	Buli, Upper Volta
Bulia	Bulia, Zaire
Bullom, Northern	Bullom, Northern, Sierra Leone
Bullom, Southern	Bullom, Southern, Sierra Leone
Bulu	Bulu, Papua New Guinea
Buna	Buna, Papua New Guinea
Bunabun	Bunabun, Papua New Guinea
Bunak	Bunak, Indonesia
Bunama	Bunama, Papua New Guinea
Bunan	Bunann in Kashmir, India
Bungku	Bungku, Indonesia
Bunu	Bunu, Nigeria
Bura	Bura, Cameroon
Bura (Babur)	**Babur Thali, Nigeria (80)
Burak	Burak, Nigeria
Buraka-Gbanziri	Buraka-Gbanziri, Congo
Buriat	Buriat, China
	Buriat, Soviet Russia
Burig	Burig, China
	Burig in Kashmir, India
Burji	Burji, Ethiopia
Burmese	Danu, Burma
	Kachin in Shan State, Burma
	Taungyoe, Burma
Buru	Buru, Indonesia
Burum	Burum, Papua New Guinea
Burun	Burun, Sudan
Burungi	Burungi, Tanzania
Burushaski	**Hunzakut, Pakistan (79)
Busa	Busa, Papua New Guinea
Busa (Bokobarn Akiba)	Busa, Nigeria (80)
Busami	Busami, Indonesia
Bushoong	Bushoong, Zaire
Bussa	Bussa, Ethiopia
Buta	Butawa, Nigeria
Butung	Butung, Indonesia
Buwid	Buwid, Philippines (81)
Bviri	Bviri, Sudan
Bwa	Bwa, Zaire
Bwaidoga	Bwaidoga, Papua New Guinea
Bwisi	Bwisi, Zaire

Chik-Barik	Chik-Barik in Bihar, India
ChiKalanga	*Kalanga, Botswana
Chin	Chin, China
Chin, Asho	Chin, Asho, Burma
Chin, Falam	Chin, Falam, Burma
Chin, Haka	Chin, Haka, Burma
Chin, Khumi	Chin, Khumi, Burma
Chin, Ngawn	Chin, Ngawn, Burma
Chin, Tiddim	Chin, Tiddim, Burma
Chinanteco, Ayotzintepec	Chinanteco, Ayotzintepec, Mexico
Chinanteco, Chiltepec	Chinanteco, Chiltepec, Mexico
Chinanteco, Comaltepec	Chinanteco, Comaltepec, Mexico
Chinanteco, Lalana	Chinanteco, Lalana, Mexico
Chinanteco, Lealao	Chinanteco, Lealao, Mexico
Chinanteco, Ojitlan	Chinanteco, Ojitlan, Mexico
Chinanteco, Palantla	Chinanteco, Palantla, Mexico
Chinanteco, Quiotepec	Chinanteco, Quiotepec, Mexico
Chinanteco, Sochiapan	Chinanteco, Sochiapan, Mexico
Chinanteco, Tepetotutla	Chinanteco, Tepetotutla, Mexico
Chinanteco, Tepinapa	Chinanteco, Tepinapa, Mexico
Chinanteco, Usila	Chinanteco, Usila, Mexico
Chinbok	Chinbok, Burma
Chinese dialects	*Chinese in Malaysia, Malaysia
	Chinese Merchants, Ghana
	**Chinese Stud., Australia, Australia
Chinga	Chinga, Cameroon
	Chinga, Cameroon
Chingp'o	Chingp'o, China
Chip	Chip, Nigeria
Chipaya	Chipaya, Bolivia
Chiquitano	Chiquitano, Bolivia
ChiTonga	*Tonga, Zimbabwe
	Tonga, Gwembe Valley, Zambia (79)
Chiyao	**Yao, Malawi
Chodhari	Chodhari in Gujarat, India
Chokobo	Chokobo, Nigeria
Chokwe	Chokwe, Zambia
	Chokwe (Lunda), Angola
Chopi	Chopi, Mozambique
Chorote	Chorote, Argentina
	Chorote, Paraguay
Chorti	Chorti, Guatemala
Chuang	Chuang, China (81)
Chuave	Chuave, Papua New Guinea
Chuj	Chuj, Guatemala
	Chuj of San Mateo Ixtatan, Guatemala
Chuj, San Mateo Ixtatan	Chuj, San Mateo Ixtatan, Mexico
Chukot	Chukot, Soviet Russia
Chulupe	Chulupe, Paraguay
Chungchia	Chungchia, China
Churahi	Churahi in H.P., India
Chwabo	Chuabo, Mozambique
Chwang	Chwang, China
Cinta Larga	Cinta Larga, Brazil
Circassian	Circassian, Turkey
Citak	Citak, Indonesia
Citak (Asmat)	***Citak, Indonesia
Cocama	Cocama, Peru
Cocopa	Cocopa, Mexico
Cofan	Cofan, Colombia
Cogui	Cogui, Colombia
Colorado	**Tsachila, Ecuador
Comorian (Shingazidja)	*Comorians, Comoros (79)
Cora	Cora, Mexico
Coreguaje	**Coreguaje, Colombia
	Coreguaje, Colombia
Cotabato Manobo	**Manobo, Cotabato, Philippines
Creole	Seychellois, Seychelles
Cubeo	Cubeo, Colombia

Dida	Dida, Ivory Coast
	**Dida, Ivory Coast
Didinga	Didinga, Sudan
	Didinga, Sudan
Didoi	Didoi, Soviet Russia
Digo	Digo, Tanzania
	Digo, Kenya
Dimasa	Dimasa in Cachar, India
Dime	Dime, Ethiopia
Dimir	Dimir, Papua New Guinea
Dinka	Dinka, Sudan
Dinka, Agar	Dinka, Agar, Sudan
Diodio	Diodio, Papua New Guinea
Diola	Diola, Senegal
	Diola, Guinea-Bissau (80)
Dirim	Dirim, Nigeria
Dirya	Dirya, Nigeria
Divehi	Divehi, Maldives (80)
Djuka	Djuka, Surinam
Dobu	Dobu, Papua New Guinea
Doe	Doe, Tanzania
Doga	Doga, Papua New Guinea
Doghosie	Doghosie, Upper Volta
Dogon	*Dogon, Mali (79)
Dogoro	Dogoro, Papua New Guinea
Dolgan	Dolgans, Soviet Russia
Dom	Dom, Papua New Guinea
Dompago	Dompago, Benin
Domu	Domu, Papua New Guinea
Domung	Domung, Papua New Guinea
Dongjoi	Dongjoi, Sudan
Dongo	Dongo, Sudan
	Dongo, Zaire
Doohyaayo	**Doohwaayo, Cameroon
Dorli	Dorlin in Andhra Pradesh, India
Doromu	Doromu, Papua New Guinea
Dorze	Dorze, Ethiopia
Doura	Doura, Papua New Guinea
Duala	Balong, Cameroon
Duan	Duna, Papua New Guinea
Duau	Duau, Papua New Guinea
Dubu	Dubu, Indonesia
Duguri	Duguir, Nigeria
Duguza	Duguza, Nigeria
Dukanci	**Duka, Nigeria
Duma	Duma, Gabon
Dumagat	*Dumagat , Casiguran, Philippines (81)
Dungan	Dungan, Soviet Russia
Duru	Duru, Cameroon
Dusun	**Sugut, Malaysia
Dutch	Amsterdam Boat Dwellers, Netherlands
	Dead-End Kids - Amsterdam, Netherlands (82)
Duvele	Duvele, Indonesia
Dyan	Dyan, Upper Volta
Dyerma	Dyerma, Niger (80)
	Dyerma, Nigeria
Dyola	Dyola, Gambia
	Dyola, Guinea-Bissau
	Dyola, Senegal
Ebira	Ebira, Nigeria
Ebrie	Ebrie, Ivory Coast
Edawapi	Edawapi, Papua New Guinea
Edo	Edo, Nigeria
Efik	Efik, Nigeria
Efutop	Efutop, Nigeria
Eggon	Eggon, Nigeria
Eivo	Eivo, Papua New Guinea
Ejagham	Ejagham, Nigeria
Ekagi	Ekagi, Indonesia

	Fula, Sierra Leone
	Fula, Cunda, Gambia
Fula, Macina	Fula, Macina, Mali
Fula, Peuhala	Fula, Peuhala, Mali
Fulani	Adamawa, Cameroon
	Fulah, Upper Volta
	Fulani, Cameroon (79)
	*Fulani, Benin
	*Fulbe, Ghana
Fuliro	Fuliro, Zaire
Fulnio	Fulnio, Brazil
Fungom, Northern	Fungom, Northern, Cameroon
	Fungom, Northern, Cameroon
Fungor	Fungor, Sudan
Furu	Furu, Zaire
Fuyuge	Fuyuge, Papua New Guinea
Fyam	Fyam, Nigeria
Fyer	Fyer, Nigeria
Ga-Dang	Ga-Dang, Philippines
Gabri	Gabri, Chad
Gabrinja	*Gabbra, Ethiopia
Gadaba	Gadaban in Andhra Pradesh, India
Gaddi	Gaddi in Himachal Pradesh, India
Gade	Gade, Nigeria
Gadsup	Gadsup, Papua New Guinea
Gagou	Gagu, Ivory Coast
Gaguaz	Gagauzes, Soviet Russia
Gahuku	Gahuku, Papua New Guinea
Gaikundi	Gaikundi, Papua New Guinea
Gaina	Gaina, Papua New Guinea
Gal	Gal, Papua New Guinea
Galambi	Galambi, Nigeria
Galeshi	Galeshis, Iran
Galla	Gabbra, Kenya
	*Galla (Bale), Ethiopia
	**Saguye, Kenya
Galler	Galler, Laos
Gallinya	Galla, Harar, Ethiopia
Gallinya (Oromo)	Galla of Bucho, Ethiopia
Galong	Galong in Assam, India
Gambai	Gambai, Chad
Gamei	Gamei, Papua New Guinea
Gamti	Gamti in Gujarat, India
Gan	Gan, Upper Volta
Gane	Gane, Indonesia
Gangam	Gangam, Togo
Ganglau	Ganglau, Papua New Guinea
Gangte	Gangte in Assam, India
Garuh	Garuh, Papua New Guinea
Garus	Garus, Papua New Guinea
Garuwahi	Garuwahi, Papua New Guinea
Gasari	Basari, Senegal
Gawar-Bati	Gawar-Bati, Afghanistan
Gawari	Gawari in Andhra Pradesh, India
Gawwada	Gawwada, Ethiopia
Gayo	Alas, Indonesia
	Gayo, Indonesia (80)
Gbari	Gbari, Nigeria (80)
Gbaya	Gbaya, Nigeria
Gbaya-Ndogo	Gbaya-Ndogo, Sudan
Gbazantche	Gbazantche, Benin
Gberi	Gberi, Sudan
Ge	**Adja, Benin
	Watchi, Togo
Gedaged	Gedaged, Papua New Guinea
Gedeo	Gedeo, Ethiopia
Geji	Geji, Nigeria
Genagane	Genagane, Papua New Guinea
Gende	Gende, Papua New Guinea

Guduf	Guduf, Nigeria
Guere	Guere, Ivory Coast
	*Krahn, Ivory Coast
Gugu-Yalanji	Gugu-Yalanji, Australia
Guhu-Samane	Guhu-Samane, Papua New Guinea
Gujarati	Dawoodi Muslims, India
	**Dubla, India
	Gujarati, United Kingdom
	*Indians In Rhodesia, Zimbabwe
	Khojas, Agha Khani, India
	*Parsees, India (81)
	**Vohras of Yavatmal, India
Gujarati Dialect	Bajania, Pakistan (79)
	Lohar, Pakistan
	Vagari, Pakistan
Gujarati, Koli	**Kohli, Kutchi, Pakistan
	**Kohli, Tharadari, Pakistan
	**Kohli, Wadiara, Pakistan
	**Kohlis, Parkari, Pakistan
Gujari	Gujars of Kashmir, India (81)
	Gujars of Kashmir, India (81)
Gujuri	Gujuri, Afghanistan
Gula	Gula, Chad
Gulfe	Gulfe, Cameroon
	Gulfe, Cameroon
Gumasi	Gumasi, Papua New Guinea
Gumine	Gumine, Papua New Guinea
Gumuz	Gumuz, Ethiopia
	Gumuz, Sudan
Gurage Dialects	Gurage, Ethiopia (80)
Gure-Kahugu	Gure-Kahugu, Nigeria
Gurenne	Gurensi, Ghana
Gurma	Gurma, Upper Volta
Gurung	Gurung, Nepal
Guruntum-Mbaaru	Guruntum-Mbaaru, Nigeria
Gusap	Gusap, Papua New Guinea
Guwot	Guwot, Papua New Guinea
Gwa	Gwa, Ivory Coast
Gwandara	Gwandara, Nigeria
Gwari Matai	Gwari Matai, Nigeria
Gwedena	Gwedena, Papua New Guinea
Gwere	Gwere, Uganda
Ha	Ha, Tanzania
Hadiyya	Hadiyya, Ethiopia
Hadza	Dorobo, Tanzania
Hahon	Hahon, Papua New Guinea
Hakka	**Chinese Hakka of Taiwan, Taiwan (79)
	**Chinese in Brazil, Brazil
	Chinese in Puerto Rico, Puerto Rico
	**Chinese in Sabah, Malaysia
	*Chinese in Thailand, Thailand
Halbi	Halbi in Madhya Pradesh, India
Halia	Halia, Papua New Guinea
Hallam	Hallam, Burma
Hamtai	Hamtai, Papua New Guinea
Hangaza	Hangaza, Tanzania
Hani	Hani, China
Hanonoo	Hanonoo, Philippines
Harari	Harari, Ethiopia
Harauti	Harauti in Rajasthan, India
Hatsa	Hatsa, Tanzania
Hausa	Arawa, Nigeria
	Kurfei, Niger
	***Maguzawa, Nigeria (79)
	Mauri, Niger
	Muslim Community of Bawku, Ghana
Hausa, Ghana	Havu, Zaire
Havu	Havunese, Indonesia
Havunese	Haya, Tanzania
Haya	

Hazaragi	**Hazara in Kabul, Afghanistan (82)
Hebrew	*Jewish Imgrnts.-American, Israel
	*Jewish Imgrnts.-Argentine, Israel
	*Jewish Imgrnts.-Australia, Israel
	*Jewish Imgrnts.-Brazilian, Israel
	*Jewish Imgrnts.-Mexican, Israel
	*Jewish Imgrnts.-Uruguayan, Israel
	*Jewish Immigrants, Other, Israel
Hehe	Hehe, Tanzania
Heiban	Heiban, Sudan
Heikum	Bushmen (Heikum), Namibia
Helong	Helong, Indonesia
Herero	Herero, Botswana
Heso	Heso, Zaire
Hewa	**Hewa, Papua New Guinea (79)
Hezara'i	Hezareh, Iran
Higi	***Higi, Nigeria
Hindi	Jains, India
Hindustani	Balmiki, Pakistan
	Indians in Fiji, Fiji (79)
Hixkaryana	Hixkaryana, Brazil
Ho	Ho in Bihar, India
Hohodene	Hohodene, Brazil
Hokkien	Chinese Fishermen, Malaysia
Holiya	Holiya in Madhya Pradesh, India
Holoholo	Holoholo, Tanzania
Holu	Holu, Angola
Hopi	Hopi, United States of America
Hote	Hote, Papua New Guinea
Hrangkhol	Hrangkhol, Burma
Huachipaire	Huachipaire, Peru
Huambisa	Huambisa, Peru
Huasteco	Huasteco, Mexico
Huave	**Huave, Mexico
Hui-hui-yu	Hui, China (80)
Huichol	Huichol, Mexico
Huila	**Huila, Angola
Huitoto, Meneca	Huitoto, Meneca, Colombia
Huitoto, Murui	Huitoto, Murui, Peru
Hukwe	Hukwe, Angola
Hula	Hula, Papua New Guinea
Huli	Huli, Papua New Guinea
Humene	Humene, Papua New Guinea
Hunde	Hunde, Zaire
Hunjara	Hunjara, Papua New Guinea
Hupda Maku	Hupda Maku, Colombia
Hwana	Hwana, Nigeria
Hwela-Numu	Hwela-Numu, Ivory Coast
Hyam	Hyam, Nigeria
Iatmul	Iatmul, Papua New Guinea
Ibaji	Ibaji, Nigeria
Iban	**Iban, Malaysia (81)
Ibanag	Ibanag, Philippines
Ibataan	*Ibataan, Philippines
Ibibio	Ibibio, Nigeria
Ica	Ica, Colombia
Icen	Icen, Nigeria
Icheve	Ihceve, Nigeria
Idi	Idi, Papua New Guinea
Idoma	Idoma, Nigeria
Idoma, North	Idoma, North, Nigeria
Ifugao	*Ifugao, Philippines
	Ifugao in Cababuyan, Philippines
Ifugao, Ambanad	Ifugao, Ambanad, Philippines
Ifugao, Kiangan	Ifugao, Kiangan, Philippines
Ifumu	Ifumu, Congo
Igala	Igala, Nigeria
Igbirra	Igbira, Nigeria (80)
Igede	Igede, Nigeria

Ignaciano	Ignaciano, Bolivia
Igora	Igora, Papua New Guinea
Igorot	Igorot, Philippines
Iha	Iha, Indonesia
Ijo	Ijo, Central-Western, Nigeria
	Ijo, Northeast, Nigeria
	Ijo, Northeast Central, Nigeria
Ikalahan	Ikalahan, Philippines
Ikobi-Mena	Ikobi-Mena, Papua New Guinea
Ikulu	Ikulu, Nigeria
Ikundun	Ikundun, Papua New Guinea
Ikwere	Ikwere, Nigeria
Ila	Ila, Zambia
Ilianen Manobo	*Manobo, Ilianen, Philippines
Ilocano	Baguio Area Miners, Philippines (81)
Ilongot	Ilongot, Philippines
Inanwatan	Inanwatan, Indonesia
Indinogosima	Indinogosima, Papua New Guinea
Indonesian	**Chinese in Indonesia, Indonesia
	Jambi, Indonesia
	Musi, Indonesia
	Ogan, Indonesia
	Sekayu, Indonesia
Inga	Inga, Colombia
Ingush	Ingushes, Soviet Russia
Insinai	Insinai, Philippines
Intha	Intha, Burma
Ipiko	Ipiko, Papua New Guinea
Ipili	Ipili, Papua New Guinea
Irahutu	Irahutu, Indonesia
Iraqw	Iraqw, Tanzania
	Iraqw, Tanzania
Iraya	Iraya, Philippines
Iresim	Iresim, Indonesia
Iria	Iria, Indonesia
Irigwe	Irigwe, Nigeria
Irula	***Irulas in Kerala, India
Irumu	Irumu, Papua New Guinea
Isaalin	**Sisaala, Ghana
Isanzu	Isanzu, Tanzania
Isebe	Isebe, Papua New Guinea
Isekiri	Isekiri, Nigeria
Isneg	**Apayao, Philippines
Isneg, Dibagat-Kabugao	Isneg, Dibagat-Kabugao, Philippines
Isneg, Karagawan	Isneg, Karagawan, Philippines
Isoko	Isoko, Nigeria
Italian	Jews in Venice, Italy (82)
	Pension Students-Madrid, Spain (82)
Itawit	Itawit, Philippines
Itelmen	Itelmen, Soviet Russia
Itik	Itik, Indonesia
Itneg, Adasen	Itneg, Adasen, Philippines
Itneg, Binongan	Itneg, Binongan, Philippines
Itneg, Masadiit	Itneg, Masadiit, Philippines
Itonama	Itonama, Bolivia
Ivbie North-Okpela-Atte	Ivbie North-Okpela-Atte, Nigeria
Iwa	Iwa, Zambia
Iwaidja	*Iwaidja, Austria
Iwal	Iwal, Papua New Guinea
Iwam	Iwam, Papua New Guinea
Iwam, Sepik	Iwam, Sepik, Papua New Guinea
Iwur	Iwur, Indonesia
Iyon	Iyon, Nigeria
	Iyon, Cameroon
	Iyon, Cameroon
Izarek	Izarek, Nigeria
Izhor	Izhor, Soviet Russia
Izi	**Izi, Nigeria
Jaba	Jaba, Nigeria

Kadazans	Kadazans, Malaysia
Kadiweu	Kadiweu, Brazil
Kadugli	Kadugli, Sudan
Kaeti	Kaeti, Indonesia
Kaffenya (Kefa)	*Kaffa, Ethiopia (80)
Kafiristani (Bashgali)	**Kafirs, Pakistan (79)
Kagoma	Kagoma, Nigeria
Kagulu	Kagulu, Tanzania
Kahluri	Kahluri in Andamans, India
Kaian	Kaian, Papua New Guinea
Kaibu	Kaibu, Nigeria
Kaiep	Kaiep, Papua New Guinea
Kaikadi	Kaikadi in Maharashtra, India
Kaili	Kaili, Indonesia
Kaingang	Kaingang, Brazil
Kairi	Kairi, Papua New Guinea
Kairiru	Kairiru, Papua New Guinea
Kaiwai	Kaiwai, Indonesia
Kajang	Kajang, Indonesia
Kaka	Kaka, Nigeria
	Kaka, Central African Republic
	Kaka, Cameroon
	Kaka, Cameroon
Kakoa	Kakoa, Papua New Guinea
Kakuna-Mamusi	Kakuna-Mamusi, Papua New Guinea
Kakwa	Kakwa, Sudan
	Kakwa, Uganda
	Kakwa, Zaire
Kalagan	**Kalagan, Philippines
Kalanga	Kalanga, Zimbabwe
Kalangoya	**Ifugao (Kalangoya), Philippines
Kaliko	Kaliko, Zaire
Kalimga,Sumadel-Tinglayan	*Kalinga, Southern, Philippines
Kalinga	**Kalinga, Tanudan, Philippines
	**Kalinga,Northern, Philippines (81)
Kalinga, Kalagua	Kalinga, Kalagua, Philippines
Kalinga, Limus-Linan	Kalinga, Limus-Linan, Philippines
Kalinga, Quinaang	Kalinga, Quinaang, Philippines
Kalmytz	Kalmytz, China
	Kalmytz, Soviet Russia
Kalokalo	Kalokalo, Papua New Guinea
Kam	Kam, China
Kamano	Kamano, Papua New Guinea
Kamar	Kamar in Madhya Pradesh, India
Kamayura	Kamayura, Brazil
Kambarci	*Kambari, Nigeria (80)
Kambera	Kambera, Indonesia
Kamberataro	Kamberataro, Indonesia
	Kamberataro, Papua New Guinea
Kambot	Kambot, Papua New Guinea
Kami	Kami, Tanzania
Kamkam	Kamkam, Cameroon
	Kamkam, Cameroon
Kamnum	Kamnum, Papua New Guinea
Kamo	Kamo, Nigeria
Kamoro	Kamoro, Indonesia
Kampung Baru	Kampung Baru, Indonesia
Kamtuk-Gresi	Kamtuk-Gresi, Indonesia
Kamuku	*Kamuku, Nigeria (80)
Kana	Kana, Nigeria
Kanauri	Kanauri in Uttar Pradesh, India
Kandas	Kandas, Papua New Guinea
Kanembu	Kanembu, Chad
	Kanembu, Niger
Kanga	Kanga, Sudan
Kanikkaran	Kanikkaran in Kerala, India
Kaningra	Kaningra, Papua New Guinea
Kanite	Kanite, Papua New Guinea
Kanjari	Kanjari in Andhra Pradesh, India

Kankanay	**Kankanay, Central, Philippines
Kanu	Kanu, Zaire
Kanum	Kanum, Indonesia
	Kanum, Papua New Guinea
Kanuri Dialects	Kanuri, Nigeria (80)
Kaonde	Kaonde, Zaire
	Kaonde, Zambia
Kapin	Kapin, Papua New Guinea
Kapore	Kapore, Papua New Guinea
Kapori	Kapori, Indonesia
Kapriman	Kapriman, Papua New Guinea
Kapuchin	Kapuchin, Soviet Russia
Kara	Kara, Tanzania
	Kara, Papua New Guinea
Karaboro	*Karaboro, Upper Volta
Karachay-Balkan	Karachay, Soviet Russia
Karagas	Karagas, Soviet Russia
Karaim	Karaim, Soviet Russia
Karakalpak	Karakalpak, Soviet Russia (80)
	Karakalpak, Soviet Russia
Karam	Karam, Papua New Guinea
Karanga	Karanga, Chad
Karangi	Karangi, Papua New Guinea
Karas	Karas, Indonesia
Karatin	Karatin, Soviet Russia
Kare	Kare, Papua New Guinea
Karekare	Karekare, Nigeria
Kari	Kari, Chad
	Kari, Central African Republic
	Kari, Zaire
Karipuna Creole	Karipuna Creole, Brazil
Karipuna Do Guapore	Karipuna Do Guapore, Brazil
Kariya	Kariya, Nigeria
Karkar	Karkar, Papua New Guinea
Karko	Karko, Sudan
Karmali	Karmali in Dihar, India
Karo	Kao, Ethiopia
Karon Dori	Karon Dori, Indonesia
Karon Pantai	Karon Pantai, Indonesia
Karre	Karre, Central African Republic
Karua	Karua, Papua New Guinea
Kasanga	Kasanga, Guinea-Bissau
Kasele	Kasele, Togo
Kasem	Kasem, Upper Volta
	**Kasena, Ghana
Kashmiri	**Kashmiri Muslims, India (79)
Kasseng	Kasseng, Laos
Kasua	Kasua, Papua New Guinea
Kasuweri	Kasuweri, Indonesia
Katab	Katab, Nigeria
Katakari	Katakari in Gujarat, India
Katcha	Katcha, Sudan
Kate	Kate, Papua New Guinea
Kati, Northern	Kati, Northern, Indonesia
Kati, Southern	Kati, Southern, Indonesia
Katiati	Katiati, Papua New Guinea
Katla	Katla, Sudan
Katukina, Panoan	Katukina, Panoan, Brazil
Kaugat	Kaugat, Indonesia
Kaugel	Kaugel, Papua New Guinea
Kaur	**Kaur, Indonesia
Kaure	Kaure, Indonesia
Kavwol	Kavwol, Indonesia
	Kavwol, Papua New Guinea
Kaw	Kaw, Burma
Kawar	Kawar in Madhya Pradesh, India
Kawe	Kawe, Indonesia
Kayabi	Kayabi, Brazil
Kayagar	Kayagar, Indonesia

Kayan	Kayan, Malaysia
Kayapo	Kayapo, Brazil
Kaygir	Kaygir, Indonesia
Kayupulau	Kayupulau, Indonesia
Kazakh	Kazakhs, China (81)
Kazakhi	Kazakhs, Iran (80)
Kebu	Kebu, Togo
Kebumtamp	Kebumtamp, Bhutan
Kedayanas	Kedayanas, Malaysia
Keer	Keer in Madhya Pradesh, India
Kei	Kei, Indonesia
Keiga	Keiga, Sudan
Keiga Jirru	Keiga Jirru, Sudan
Kekchi	**Kekchi, Guatemala
Kela	Kela, Zaire
	Kela, Papua New Guinea
Kelabit	Kelabit, Malaysia (81)
Kelao	Kelao, China
Kele	Kele, Gabon
Keley-i	Ifugao, Antipolo, Philippines
Kemak	Kemak, Indonesia
Kembata	Kembata, Ethiopia
Kemok	Kemok, Malaysia
Kenati	Kenati, Papua New Guinea
Kendari	Kendari, Indonesia
Kenga	Kenga, Chad
Kenyah	Kenyah, Indonesia
Keopara	Keopara, Papua New Guinea
Kera	Kera, Chad
	Kera, Cameroon
	Kera, Cameroon
Kerewo	Kerewo, Papua New Guinea
Keriaka	Keriaka, Papua New Guinea
Kerinchi	Kerinchi, Indonesia
Ket	Ket, Soviet Russia
Kewa	*Kepas, Papua New Guinea
Kewa, East	Kewa, East, Papua New Guinea
Kewa, South	Kewa, South, Papua New Guinea
Kewa, West	Kewa, West, Papua New Guinea
Khakas	Khakas, Soviet Russia
Khalaj	Khalaj, Iran
Khalka	Khalka, China
Kham	Kham, China
Khamti	Khamti in Assam, India
Khamu	*Khamu, Thailand
Khana	Khana, Nigeria
Khandesi	Khandesi, India
Khanti	Khanti, Soviet Russia
Kharia	Kharia in Bihar, India
Khasi	Khasi in Assam, India
Khasonke	Khasonke, Mali
Khinalug	Khinalug, Soviet Russia
Khirwar	Khirwar in Madhya Pradesh, India
Khowar	Khowar, India
Khuwar	Chitralis, Pakistan (79)
Khvarshin	Khvarshin, Soviet Russia
Kiari	Kiari, Papua New Guinea
Kibet	Kibet, Chad
Kibiri	Kibiri, Papua New Guinea
Kichepo	Kichepo, Sudan
Kijita	**Wajita, Tanzania
Kikapoo	Kikapoo, Mexico
Kikerewe	Kerewe, Tanzania
Kilba	Kilba, Nigeria
Kilmera	Kilmera, Papua New Guinea
Kim	Kim, Chad
	Kim, Central African Republic
Kimaghama	Kimaghama, Indonesia
Kimbu	Kimbu, Tanzania

Kimyal	*Kimyal, Indonesia
Kinalakna	Kinalakna, Papua New Guinea
Kinaray-A	Kinaray-A, Philippines
Kinga	Kinga, Tanzania
Kinyarwanda	***Banyarwanda, Rwanda
Kirghiz	Kirghiz, Afghanistan
Kirgiz	Kirgiz, Soviet Russia (80)
	Kirgiz, China
Kiriwina	Kiriwina, Papua New Guinea
Kis	Kis, Papua New Guinea
Kisan	Kisan in Bihar, India
Kisankasa	Kisankasa, Tanzania
Kishanganjia	Kishanganjia in Bihar, India
Kishtwari	Kishtwari in Jammu, India
Kisi	Kisi, Tanzania
Kissi	Kissi, Guinea
	*Kissi, Liberia
Kissi, Southern	*Kissi, Sierra Leone
	Kissi, Southern, Sierra Leone
Kiwai, Northeast	Kiwai, Northeast, Papua New Guinea
Kiwai, Southern	Kiwai, Southern, Papua New Guinea
Kiwai, Wabuda	Kiwai, Wabuda, Papua New Guinea
Kizinza	*Wazinza, Tanzania
Klaoh	Klaoh, Liberia
Koalib (Nuba)	Koalib, Sudan (79)
Kobiana	Kobiana, Guinea
Kobon	Kobon, Papua New Guinea
Koda	Koda in Bihar, India
Kodi	Kodi, Indonesia
Koenoem	Koenoem, Nigeria
Kofyar	Kofyar, Nigeria
Kohoroxitari	Kohoroxitari, Brazil
Kohumono	Kohumono, Nigeria
Koiari, Grass	Koiari, Grass, Papua New Guinea
Koiari, Mountain	Koiari, Mountain, Papua New Guinea
Koita	Koita, Papua New Guinea
Kokant	Kokant, Burma
Koke	Koke, Chad
Kol	Kol, Papua New Guinea
	Kol in Assam, India
Kolaka	**Loho Loho, Indonesia
Kolami	**Kolam, India
Kolbila	Kolbila, Cameroon
Kole	Kole, Cameroon
	Kole, Cameroon
Koliku	Koliku, Papua New Guinea
Kolom	Kolom, Papua New Guinea
Kom	Kom in Manipur, India
Kom Komba	*Konkomba, Togo
Koma	Koma, Ghana
	Koma, Nigeria
	Koma, Cameroon
	Koma, Cameroon
Koma, Central	Koma, Central, Sudan
Komba	Komba, Papua New Guinea
Kombio	Kombio, Papua New Guinea
Komering	Komering, Indonesia
	Lampung, Indonesia (80)
Komi-Permyat	Komi-Permyat, Soviet Russia
Komi-Zyrian	Komi-Zyrian, Soviet Russia
Komo	*Komo, Ethiopia
Komono	Komono, Upper Volta
Komutu	Komutu, Papua New Guinea
Konabem	Konabem, Cameroon
	Konabem, Cameroon
Konda-Dora	Konda-Dora in A.P., India
Koneraw	Koneraw, Indonesia
Kongo	Kongo, Angola
Konkani	Konkani in Gujarat, India

Konkomba	Konkomba, Ghana
Kono	**Kono, Sierra Leone
	Kono, Nigeria
Konomala	Konomala, Papua New Guinea
Konongo	Konongo, Tanzania
Konso	Konso, Ethiopia
Konyagi	Konyagi, Guinea
Koraga	Koraga in Kerala, India
Korak	Korak, Papua New Guinea
Korape	Korape, Papua New Guinea
Korapun	Korapun, Indonesia
Korean	**Apartment Residents-Seoul, Korea, Republic of
	**Bus Drivers, South Korea, Korea, Republic of
	**Bus Girls in Seoul, Korea, Republic of (82)
	Indust.Workers Yongdungpo, Korea, Republic of
	Kae Sung Natives in Seoul, Korea, Republic of (82)
	**Korean Prisoners, Korea, Republic of
	***Koreans in Germany, German Federal Rep.
	Koreans in Manchuria, China (81)
	*Koreans of Japan, Japan
Korku	*Korku in Madhya Pradesh, India
Koro	Koro, Nigeria
Koroma	Koroma, Sudan
Korop	Korop, Nigeria
	Korop, Cameroon
	Korop, Cameroon
Korwa	Korwa in Bihar, India
Koryak	Koryak, Soviet Russia
Kosorong	Kosorong, Papua New Guinea
Kota	Kota, Gabon
	Kota in Tamil Nadu, India
	Kotta, India
Kotia	Kotia in Andhra Pradesh, India
Kotogut	Kotogut, Indonesia
Kotoko	Kotoko, Chad
	Kotoko, Cameroon
	Kotoko, Cameroon
Kotokoli	Kotokoli, Benin
	Kotokoli, Togo
	Tem, Togo
Kotopo	Kotopo, Cameroon
Kouya	Kouya, Ivory Coast
Kovai	Kovai, Papua New Guinea
Kove	Kove, Papua New Guinea
Kowaao	**Kowaao, Liberia
Koya	Koya in Andhra Pradesh, India
Koyra	Koyra, Ethiopia
Kpa	Kpa, Cameroon
	Kpa, Cameroon
Kpelle	Kpelle, Liberia
	Kpelle, Guinea
Kposo	Kposo, Togo
Krachi	Krachi, Ghana
Krahn	***Krahn, Liberia
Kreen-Akakore	Kreen-Akakore, Brazil
Krifi	Kirifi, Nigeria
Krio	Krio, Gambia
Krisa	Krisa, Papua New Guinea
Krobou	Krobou, Ivory Coast
Krongo	Krongo, Sudan
Krumen	Krumen, Ivory Coast
Kryz	Kryz, Soviet Russia
Kube	Kube, Papua New Guinea
Kubu	Kubu, Indonesia (81)
Kuda-Chamo	Kuda-Chamo, Nigeria

Kwanyama	Kwanyama, Angola
	Kwanyama, Namibia
Kwaya	Kwaya, Tanzania
Kwe-Etshari	*Bushmen (Hiechware), Zimbabwe
Kwe-etshori	Kwe-etshori, Botswana
	Kwe-Etshori, Zimbabwe
Kwerba	Kwerba, Indonesia
Kwere	Kwere, Tanzania
Kwese	Kwese, Zaire
Kwesten	Kwesten, Indonesia
Kwoma	Kwoma, Papua New Guinea
Kwomtari	Kwomtari, Papua New Guinea
Kyibaku	Kyibaku, Nigeria
Laamang	Laamang, Nigeria
Labaani	Labans, India
Labhani	Labhani in Andhra Pradesh, India
Labu	Labu, Papua New Guinea
Lacandon	Lacandon, Mexico
Ladakhi	Ladakhi in Jammu, India
Ladinos	Ladinos, Lebanon
Laewomba	Laewomba, Papua New Guinea
Lafofa	Lafofa, Sudan
Lahouli	**Lahaulis in Punjab, India
Lahu	*Lahu, Thailand (81)
	Lahu, Burma
Lahul	Lahul, China
Laka	Laka, Cameroon
	Laka, China
	Laka, Central African Republic
Lakal	Laka, Chad
Lakian	Lakians, Soviet Russia
Lakka	Lakka, Nigeria
Lala	Lala, Zambia
Lalia	Lalia, Zaire
Lalung	Lalung in Assam, India
Lama	Lama, Burma
Lamba	Lamba, Togo
	Lamba, Benin
	Lamba, Zaire
	Lamba, Zambia
Lambadi	**Lambadi in Andhra Pradesh, India (81)
Lambi	Lambi, Cameroon
Lambya	Lambya, Malawi
	Lambya, Tanzania
Lame	Lame, Nigeria
Lamogai	Lamogai, Papua New Guinea
Landoma	Landoma, Guinea
	Landoma, Guinea-Bissau
Langi	Langi, Tanzania
Lango	*Lango, Ethiopia
	Lango, Uganda
Lanoh	Lanoh, Malaysia
Lao	*Lao, Laos (79)
	*Lao Refugees, Thailand
Lara	Lara, Indonesia
Laro	Laro, Sudan
Laru	Laru, Nigeria
Latdwalam	Latdwalam, Indonesia
Lati	Lati, China
Latuka	**Lotuka, Sudan
Laudje	Laudje, Indonesia
Lavatbura-Lamusong	Lavatbura-Lamusong, Papua New Guinea
Lavongai	Lavongai, Papua New Guinea
Lawa	Lawa, Mountain, Thailand
Lebgo	Lebgo, Nigeria
Leco	Leco, Bolivia
Lega	Lega, Zaire
Lele	Lele, Chad
	Lele, Upper Volta

Luimbi	Luimbi, Angola
Lukep	Lukep, Papua New Guinea
Lumbu	Lumbu, Gabon
Luna	Luna, Zaire
Lunda	Lunda, Angola
Lunda, Ndembu	Lunda, Ndembu, Zambia
Lundu	Lundu, Cameroon
Lungu	Lungu, Nigeria
Luo	Luo, Tanzania
Luri	Lors, Iran (80)
	Mamasani, Iran
Lushai	Lushai in Assam, India
Luteso	**Teso, Kenya
Luwu	Luwu, Indonesia
Luyana	Luyana, Angola
	Luyana, Zambia
Lwalu	Lwalu, Zaire
Lwena	Lwena, Angola
Lwo	Lwo, Sudan
Ma	Ma, Zaire
Maanyan	Maanyan, Indonesia
Maba	Maba, Chad
	Maba, Sudan
	Ouaddai, Chad
Maban-Jumjum	Maban-Jumjum, Sudan
	Meban, Sudan
Maca	Maca, Paraguay
Machiguenga	Machiguenga, Peru
Macu	Macu, Colombia
Macuna	Macuna, Colombia
Macuxi	**Macuxi, Brazil
Madak	Madak, Papua New Guinea
Madda	Madda, Nigeria
Madi	Madi, Sudan
	Madi, Uganda
Madik	Madik, Indonesia
Madurese	Madurese, Indonesia (79)
Mafaara	**Nafaara, Ghana (79)
Magar	**Magar, Nepal
Maghi	Maghi, Burma
Magori	Magori, Papua New Guinea
Maguindano	Maguindano, Philippines (80)
Mahali	Mahali in Assam, India
Mahri	Mahri, Oman
Mai	Mai, Papua New Guinea
Mailu	Mailu, Papua New Guinea
Maiongong	Maiongong, Brazil
Mairasi	Mairasi, Indonesia
Maisan	Maisan, Papua New Guinea
Maithili	Maithili, Nepal
Maiwa	Maiwa, Papua New Guinea
Majangiir	*Masengo, Ethiopia
Majhwar	Majhwar in Madhya Pradesh, India
Maji	Maji, Ethiopia
Majingai-Ngama	Majingai-Ngama, Chad
	Majingai-ngama, Central African Republic
Maka	Maka, Cameroon
Makarim	Makarim, Papua New Guinea
Makasai	Makasai, Indonesia
Makere	Makere, Uganda
Makian, West	Makian, West, Indonesia
Maklew	Maklew, Indonesia
Makua	Makua, Mozambique
Mala, Pattani	Thai Islam (Malay), Thailand (80)
Malagasy	*Prisoners in Antananarivo, Madagascar (82)
Malalamai	Malalamai, Papua New Guinea
Malamutha	Malakkaras of Kerela, India (81)
Malankuravan	Malankuravan in Kerala, India
Malapandaram	Malapandaram in Kerala, India

	Mankanya, Senegal
Manna-Dora	Manna-Dora in A.P., India
Mannan	Mannan in Kerala, India
Mano	Mano, Liberia
Manobo	*Ata of Davao, Philippines
Manobo, Agusan	Manobo, Agusan, Philippines
Manobo, Ata	Manobo, Ata, Philippines
Manobo, Binokid	Manobo, Binokid, Philippines
	**Manobo, Western Bukidnon, Philippines
Manobo, Binukid	**Bukidnon, Philippines
Manobo, Dibabawon	Manobo, Dibabawon, Philippines
Manobo, Obo	Manobo, Obo, Philippines
Manobo, Pulangi	Manobos, Pulangi, Philippines
Manobo, Sarangani	Manobo, Sarangani, Philippines
Manobo, Tagabawa	Manobo, Tagabawa, Philippines
Manobo, Tigwa	**Manobo, Salug, Philippines
	**Manobo, Tigwa, Philippines
Mansaka	**Mansaka, Philippines
Mansi	Mansi, Soviet Russia
Mantera	Mantera, Malaysia
Mantion	Mantion, Indonesia
Manu Park Panoan	Manu Park Panoan, Peru
Manyika	Manyika, Zimbabwe
Mao, Northern	Mao, Northern, Ethiopia
Maou	Maou, Ivory Coast
Mapoyo	Mapoyo, Venezuela
Mapuche	Mapuche, Chile
Maquiritari	Maquiritari, Venezuela
Mara	Mara in Assam, India
Maranao	Maranao, Philippines (79)
Maranao, Lanad	Maranao, Lanad, Philippines
Mararit	Mararit, Chad
Marathi	*Labourers of Jhoparpatti, India
	Mangs in Maharashtra, India
Marau	Marau, Indonesia
Marba	Marba, Chad
Marghi Central	Marghi Central, Nigeria
Mari	Mari, Soviet Russia
Maria	Maria in Andhra Pradesh, India
Marind	Marind, Indonesia
Marind, Bian	Marind, Bian, Indonesia
Marka	Marka, Upper Volta
Marubo	Marubo, Brazil
Marwari	**Bhil, Pakistan
	Marwari in Gujarat, India
	**Meghwar, Pakistan (79)
Masa	Budugum, Cameroon
	Gisei, Cameroon
	Masa, Chad
Masaba	Masaba, Uganda
Masai	**Maasai, Kenya (79)
Masai, Samburu	Samburu, Kenya
Masakin	Masakin, Sudan
Masalit	Masalit, Chad
Masenrempulu	Masenrempulu, Indonesia
Mashi	Mashi, Zambia
Massalat	Massalat, Chad
Mataco	Mataco, Argentina
Matakam	Matakam, Cameroon
	Matakam, Nigeria
Matawari	Matawari, Surinam
Matbat	Matbat, Indonesia
Matengo	Matengo, Tanzania
Matipuhy-Nahukua	Matipuhy-Nahukua, Brazil
Matlatzinca, Atzingo	Matlatzinca, Atzingo, Mexico
Matumbi	Matumbi, Tanzania
Maure	Maure, Mali
Maviha	Maviha, Mozambique
Mawchi	**Mawchis, India

Mixteco, Eastern Putla	Mixteco, Eastern Putla, Mexico
Mixteco, Huajuapan	Mixteco, Huajuapan, Mexico
Mixteco, Silacayoapan	Mixteco, Silacayoapan, Mexico
Mixteco, Southern Puebla	Mixteco, Southern Puebla, Mexico
Mixteco, Southern Putla	Mixteco, Southern Putla, Mexico
Mixteco, Tututepec	Mixteco, Tututepec, Mexico
Mixteco, Yosondua	Mixteco, Yosondua, Mexico
Miya	Miya, Nigeria
Mo	Mo, Ivory Coast
Mo (Degha)	Mo, Ghana
Mober	Mober, Nigeria
Mocha	***Mocha, Ethiopia
Modo	Modo, Sudan
Mofu	Mofu, Cameroon
Mogholi	Mogholi, Afghanistan
Mogum	Mogum, Chad
Moi	Moi, Indonesia
Moken	Moken, Burma (79)
Mokole	*Mokole, Benin
Molbog	*Molbog, Philippines
Mole	Mossi, Upper Volta (80)
Molof	Molof, Indonesia
Mombum	Mombum, Indonesia
Momoguns	Momoguns, Malaysia
Mon	Mon, Burma (81)
Mona	Mona, Ivory Coast
Mongondow	Mongondow, Indonesia (81)
Mongour	Mongour, China
Moni	Moni, Indonesia
Monjombo	Monjombo, Central African Republic
Mono	Mono, Zaire
Monpa	Monpa, India
Montol	Montol, Nigeria
Mopan Maya	**Mopan Maya, Guatemala
	**Mopan Maya, Belize
Moqaddam	Moqaddam, Iran
Mor	Mor, Indonesia
Moreb	Moreb, Sudan
Moreno	**Black Caribs, Belize, Belize (79)
	**Black Caribs, Guatemala, Guatemala
	**Black Caribs, Honduras, Honduras
Mori	Mori, Indonesia (81)
Moru	Moru, Ivory Coast
	Moru, Sudan
Morunahua	Morunahua, Peru
Morwap	Morwap, Indonesia
Mosi	Mosi, Tanzania
Motilon	Motilon, Colombia
	Motilon, Venezuela
Movima	Movima, Bolivia
Mpoto	Mpoto, Malawi
	Mpoto, Tanzania
Mualthuam	Mualthuam, India
Mubi	Mubi, Chad
Muinane	Muinane, Colombia
Mulimba	Mulimba, Cameroon
Multani	Multani in Punjab, India
Mumbake	Mumbake, Nigeria
Mumuye	Mumuye, Nigeria
Mun	Mun, Burma
Muna	Muna, Indonesia
Munda	**Mundas in Bihar, India
Mundang	Mundang, Chad
Mundari	Mundari in Assam, India
Mundu	Mundu, Zaire
Munduruku	Munduruku, Brazil
Mungaka	Mungaka, Cameroon
Munggui	Munggui, Indonesia
Munji-Yidgha	Munji-Yidgha, Afghanistan

Ndom	Ndom, Indonesia
Ndomde	Ndomde, Tanzania
Ndoolo	Ndoolo, Zaire
Ndop-Bamessing	Ndop-Bamessing, Cameroon
Ndoro	**Ndoro, Nigeria
	Ndoro, Cameroon
Nduga	Nduga, Indonesia
Ndunga	Ndunga, Zaire
Ndunpa Duupa	Ndunpa Duupa, Cameroon
Nentsy	Nentsy, Soviet Russia
Nepali	**Nepalese in India, India
	*Nepali, Nepal
Nevo	Neyo, Ivory Coast
Newari	Newar in Kathmandu, Nepal (82)
	*Newari, Nepal
Ngada	Ngada, Indonesia
Ngalik, North	Ngalik, North, Indonesia
Ngalik, Southern	Ngalik, Southern, Indonesia
Ngalum	Ngalum, Indonesia
Ngamo	**Ngamo, Nigeria
Nganasan	Nganasan, Soviet Russia
Ngando	Ngando, Central African Republic
	Ngando, Zaire
Ngasa	Ngasa, Tanzania
Ngayaba	Ngayaba, Cameroon
Ngbaka	Ngbaka, Zaire
Ngbaka Ma'bo	Ngbaka Ma'bo, Central African Republic
	Ngbaka Ma'bo, Zaire
Ngbandi	Ngbandi, Zaire
Ngbee	Ngbee, Zaire
Ngemba	Ngemba, Cameroon
Ngen	*Ngen, Ivory Coast
Ngeq	Ngeq, Laos
Ngi	Ngi, Cameroon
Ngindo	Ngindo, Tanzania
Nginyukwur	Nginyukwur, Sudan
Ngirere	Ngirere, Sudan
Ngiri	Ngiri, Zaire
Ngizim	Ngizim, Nigeria
Ngok	Ngok, Sudan
Ngombe	**Ngombe, Zaire
Ngoni	Ngoni, Tanzania
	Ngoni, Zambia
Ngulu	Ngulu, Malawi
	Ngulu, Tanzania
Ngumba	Ngumba, Cameroon
Ngumbi	Ngumbi, Equatorial Guinea
Ngunduna	Ngunduna, Sudan
Nguqwurang	Nguqwurang, Sudan
Ngurimi	Ngurimi, Tanzania
Nguu	Nguu, Tanzania
Ngwo	Ngwo, Cameroon
Ngwoi	Ngwoi, Nigeria
Nharon	Nharon, Botswana
Nhengatu	Nhengatu, Brazil
Nias	Nias, Indonesia
Nielim	Nielim, Chad
Nihali	Nihali in Madhya Pradesh, India
Nilamba	Nilamba, Tanzania
Nimadi	Nimadi in Madhya Pradesh, India
Nimboran	Nimboran, Indonesia
Ninam	Ninam, Brazil
Ningerum	*Ningerum, Papua New Guinea
Ninggrum	Ninggrum, Indonesia
Ninzam	Ninzam, Nigeria
Nisa	Nisa, Indonesia
Nivkhi	Nivkhi, Soviet Russia
Njadu	Njadu, Indonesia
Njalgulgule	Njalgulgule, Sudan

Nkem-Nkum	Nkem-Nkum, Nigeria
Nkom	Nkom, Cameroon
Nkonya	Nkonya, Ghana
Nkutu	Nkutu, Zaire
Nocte	***Nocte, India
Nohu	Nohu, Cameroon
Norra	Norra, Burma
North Thai Dialect	Thai Northern, Thailand
Northeast Thai	**Lepers of N.E. Thailand, Thailand
Northern Cagayan Negrito	Northern Cagayan Negrito, Philippines
Northern Kamer	*Cambodians, Thailand
Northern Kankanay	Kankanay, Northern, Philippines
Nosu	Nosu, China
Nouni	*Nouni, Upper Volta
Nsenga	Nsenga, Zimbabwe
	Nsenga, Zambia
Nso	Nso, Cameroon
Nsongo	Nsongo, Angola
Ntomba	Ntomba, Zaire
Ntrubo	Ntrubo, Ghana
	Ntrubo, Togo
	Ntrubs, Ghana
Nuer	*Nuer, Ethiopia
	*Nuer, Sudan (79)
Numana-Nunku-Gwantu	Numana-Nunku-Gwantu, Nigeria
Nung	Nung, China
Nungu	Nungu, Nigeria
Nunuma	Nunuma, Upper Volta
Nupe	**Nupe, Nigeria
Nyabwa	**Nyabwa, Ivory Coast
Nyaheun	Nyaheun, Laos
Nyakyusa	Nyakyusa, Malawi
	Nyakyusa, Tanzania
Nyambo	Nyambo, Tanzania
Nyamusa	Nyamusa, Sudan
Nyamwezi	Nyamwezi, Tanzania (80)
Nyaneka	Nyaneka, Angola
Nyang	Nyang, Cameroon
Nyanga-Li	Nyanga-Li, Zaire
Nyangbo	Nyangbo, Ghana
Nyanja	Nyanja, Zimbabwe
Nyankole	Nyankole, Uganda
Nyarueng	Nyarueng, Sudan
Nyaturu	Turu, Tanzania
Nyemba	Nyemba, Angola
Nyiha	Nyiha, Tanzania
	Nyiha, Zambia
Nyoro	Nyoro, Uganda
Nyuli	Nyuli, Uganda
Nyungwe	Nyungwe, Mozambique
Nzakara	Nzakara, Central African Republic
Nzanyi	Nzanyi, Nigeria
Nzebi	Nzebi, Congo
Nzema	Nzema, Ivory Coast
	Nzema, Ghana
O'ung	O'ung, Angola
Obanliku	Obanliku, Nigeria
Obolo	Obolo, Nigeria
Ocaina	Ocaina, Peru
Odki	Od, Pakistan
Odual	Odual, Nigeria
Odut	Odut, Nigeria
Ogbia	Ogbia, Nigeria
Oi	Oi, Laos
Oirat	Oirat, China
Ojhi	Ojhi in Madhya Pradesh, India
Okobo	Okobo, Nigeria
Okpamheri	Okpamheri, Nigeria
Ollari	Ollari in Orissa, India

Olulumo-Ikom	Olulumo-Ikom, Nigeria
Ong	Ong in Andamans, India
Onin	Onin, Indonesia
Orang Kanak	Orang Kanak, Malaysia
Orang Laut	Orang Laut, Malaysia
Orang Ulu	Orang Ulu, Malaysia
Orejon	Orejon, Peru
Oring	Oring, Nigeria
Ormu	Ormu, Indonesia
Oroch	Oroch, Soviet Russia
Orok	Orok, Soviet Russia
Oron	Oron, Nigeria
Oronchon	Oronchon, China
Oso	Oso, Cameroon
Ot Danum	Ot Danum, Indonesia
Otank	Otank, Nigeria
Otomi	Otomi, State of Mexico, Mexico
Otomi, Eastern	Otomi, Eastern, Mexico
Otomi, Mezquital	Otomi, Mezquital, Mexico
Otomi, Northwestern	Otomi, Northwestern, Mexico
Otomi, Southeastern	Otomi, Southeastern, Mexico
Otomi, Tenango	Otomi, Tenango, Mexico
Otomi, Texcatepec	Otomi, Texcatepec, Mexico
Otoro	Otoro, Sudan
Oubi	Oubi, Ivory Coast
Oyampipuku	Oyampipuku, Brazil
Oyda	Oyda, Ethiopia
Padaung	Kayan, Burma
Paez	***Paez, Colombia
Pahari Garhwali	Pahari Garhwali in U.P., India
Pai	Pai, Nigeria
Paite	Paite in Assam, India
Paiute, Northern	Paiute, Northern, United States of America
Pakaasnovos	Pakaasnovos, Brazil
Pakabeti	***Pakabeti of Equator, Zaire
Pala'wan	*Pala'wan, Philippines (81)
Palara	Palara, Ivory Coast
Palaung	Palaung, Burma (79)
Palawano	Palawano, Philippines
Palawano, Central	Palawano, Central, Philippines
Palembang	Palembang, Indonesia
Palikur	Palikur, Brazil
Paloc	Paloc, Sudan
Pambia	Pambia, Central African Republic
Pame, Central Chichimeca	Pame, Central Chichimeca, Mexico
Pame, Northern	Pame, Northern, Mexico
Pamiri	Tajik, Afghanistan
Pana	Pana, Central African Republic
Panare	Panare, Venezuela
Pande	Pande, Congo
Pangwa	Pangwa, Tanzania
Panika	Panika, India
Paniyan	**Paniyan of Kerela, India (81)
Panjabi	Ahmadis in Lahore, Pakistan (82)
Pankhu	Pankhu, Bangladesh
Pantu	Pantu, Indonesia
Pao	Pao, Burma
	Pao in Madhya Pradesh, India
Paongan	Paongan, China
Pape	Pape, Cameroon
Papel	Papel, Guinea-Bissau
Papuma	Papuma, Indonesia
Parakanan	Parakanan, Brazil
Paranan	Paranan, Philippines
Pardhan	Pardhan in Andhra Pradesh, India
Pare	Pare, Tanzania
Parengi	Parengi in Orissa, India
Paresi	Paresi, Brazil
Parintintin	Parintintin, Brazil

Purum	Purum, Burma
Puyuma	**Puyuma, Taiwan (81)
Pwo Karen	Karen, Pwo, Thailand
Pye	Pye, Ivory Coast
Pyu	Pyu, Indonesia
Qajar	Qajars, Iran
Qara'i	Qara'i, Iran
Qaragozlu	Qaragozlu, Iran
Qashqa'i	Qashqa'i, Iran (80)
Quaiquer	Quaiquer, Colombia
Quechua	**Quechua, Peru
	**Quechua, Bolivia
Quechua, Huancayo	**Quechua, Huanco, Peru
Quiche	**Quiche, Guatemala (79)
Quichua	**Quichua, Ecuador
Rabha	Rabha in Assam, India
Rabinal Achi	Rabinal-Achi, Guatemala
Rai	Rai, Nepal
Rajasthani	Meos of Rajasthan, India (80)
Rajbansi	Rajbansi, Nepal
Ralte	Ralte, Burma
Ratahan	Ratahan, Indonesia
Rataning	Rataning, Chad
Rava	*Rava in Assam, India
Rawang	Rawang, China
Redjang-Lebong	Lebong, Indonesia
Rejang	Redjang, Indonesia (80)
Rendille	Rendille, Kenya
Reshe	Reshe, Nigeria
Reyesano	Reyesano, Bolivia
Riang	Riang in Assam, India
Riang-Lang	Riang-Lang, Burma
Riantana	Riantana, Indonesia
Rikbaktsa	Rikbaktsa, Brazil
Rom	*Gypsies in Spain, Spain (79)
Romany	Romany, Turkey
Romany (Serbian Kaldnash)	Gypsies in Yugoslavia, Yugoslavia
Romany Dialect	Gypsies in Jerusalem, Israel (82)
Romany Dialects	Muslim Gypsies in Skoplje, Yugoslavia (82)
Ronga	Ronga, Mozambique
	Ronga, South Africa
Ruihi	Ruihi, Tanzania
Rumaya	Rumaya, Nigeria
Runga	Runga, Chad
	Runga, Central African Republic
Rungi	Rungi, Tanzania
Rungwa	Rungwa, Tanzania
Ruruma	Ruruma, Nigeria
Rusha	Rusha, Tanzania
Rut	Rut, Sudan
Rutul	Rutul, Soviet Russia
Rwamba	Rwamba, Uganda
	Rwamba, Zaire
Ryukyuan	*Ryukyuan, Japan
Saamia	Saamia, Uganda
Saams	Saams, Soviet Russia
Saberi	Saberi, Indonesia
Sadan	Sadan in Andamans, India
Sadang	Sadang, Indonesia
Safaliba	Safaliba, Ghana
Safwa	Safwa, Tanzania
Sagala	Sagala, Tanzania
Saija	Saija, Colombia
Saisiat	Saisiat, Taiwan (81)
Sakata	Sakata, Zaire
Sakuye	Sakuye, Kenya
Sala	Sala, Zambia
Salampasu	Salampasu, Zaire
Salar	Salar, China

Saliba	Saliba, Colombia
Sama Pangutaran	Sama Pangutaran, Philippines (80)
Sama, Mapun	Sama, Mapun, Philippines
Sama, Siasi	Sama, Siasi, Philippines
Sama, Sibuku	Sama, Sibuku, Philippines
Samal dialects	Sama-Badjaw, Philippines (79)
Samarkena	Samarkena, Indonesia
Samburu	El Molo, Kenya
Samo	*Samo-Kubo, Papua New Guinea
Samo, Northern	Samo, Northern, Mali
	Samo, Northern, Upper Volta
Samogho	Samogho, Mali
San	San, Namibia
Sanapana	Sanapana, Paraguay
Sandawe	Sandawe, Tanzania
Sanga	Sanga, Nigeria
	Sanga, Zaire
Sangil	Sangil, Philippines
Sangir	Sangir, Indonesia
Sangke	Sangke, Indonesia
Sangu	Sangu, Gabon
	Sangu, Tanzania
Santa	Santa, China
Santhali	**Santhali, Nepal
Sanuma	*Sanuma, Brazil
	Sanuma, Venezuela
Sanza	Sanza, Zaire
Saramaccan	Saramaccan, Surinam
Sarwa	Sarwa, Chad
Sasak	Sasak, Indonesia (80)
Sasani	Sasanis, Iran
Sasaru-Enwan Igwe	Sasaru-Enwan Igwe, Nigeria
Satere	Satere, Brazil
Sau	Sau, Afghanistan
Sause	Sause, Indonesia
Save (Yoruba)	**Save, Benin
Sawi	**Sawi, Indonesia
Saya	Saya, Nigeria
Secoya	Secoya, Ecuador
Sekar	Sekar, Indonesia
Seko	Seko, Indonesia
Sekpele	Sekpele, Ghana
Selakau	**Selakau of Sarawak, Malaysia
Sele	Santrokofi, Ghana
Selkup	Selkup, Soviet Russia
Semelai	Semelai, Malaysia
Sempan	Sempan, Indonesia
Sena	Sena, Malawi
	Sena, Mozambique
Senari	Senufo, Ivory Coast (80)
Senggi	Senggi, Indonesia
Sentani	Sentani, Indonesia
Senthang	Senthang, Burma
Serawai (Pasemah)	**Serawai, Indonesia (81)
Serbo-Croation	*Bosnian, Yugoslavia (80)
Sere	Sere, Sudan
Serere	Serere, Senegal (79)
Serere-Non	Serere-Non, Senegal
Serere-Sine	Serere-Sine, Senegal
Seri	Seri, Mexico
Serui-Laut	Serui-Laut, Indonesia
Sgaw Karen	Karen, Thailand (79)
Sha	Sha, Nigeria
Shamatali	Yanomamo in Venezuela, Venezuela
Shambala	Shambala, Tanzania
Shan	Hkun, Burma
	Shan, Thailand
	Shan, Burma
	Shan Chinese, Burma

	Thai-Ney, Burma
Shan Dialects	Yin-Kyar, Burma
	Yin-Nett, Burma
Shanga	Shanga, Nigeria
Shankilla (Kazza)	***Shankilla (Kazza), Ethiopia
Sharanahua	Sharanahua, Peru
Sharchagpakha	Bhutias, Bhutan
	Sharchagpakha, Bhutan
Shatt	Shatt, Sudan
Shawiya	Shawiya, Algeria
Sheko	Sheko, Ethiopia
Sherpa	*Sherpa, Nepal
Shihu	**Shihu, United Arab Emirates
Shilha	Shilha, Morocco
Shilluk	Shilluk, Sudan
Shina	Shina, Afghanistan
Shinasha	Shinasha, Ethiopia
Shinkoya	*Nkoya, Zambia
Shipibo	Shipibo, Peru
Shirishana	**Shirishana, Brazil
Shor	Shor, Soviet Russia
Shourastra	*Shourastra in Tamil Nadu, India
Shrina	*Dog-Pa of Ladakh, India (81)
Shua	Shua, Botswana
Shughni	Shughni, Afghanistan
Shuwa Arabic	Shuwa Arabic, Nigeria
Shwai	Shwai, Sudan
Siagha-Yenimu	Siagha-Yenimu, Indonesia
Sibo	Sibo, China
Sidamo	Sidamo, Ethiopia
Sikhule	Sikhule, Indonesia
Sikka	Sikanese, Indonesia
Sikkimese	Sikkimese, India
Simaa	Simaa, Zambia
Sinama Bangini	Sama Bangingi, Philippines (80)
Sindebele	**Ndebele, Zimbabwe (79)
Sindhi	Sindhi Muslims in Karachi, Pakistan (82)
	*Sindhis of India, India
	Sochi, Pakistan
Sinhala	Sinhalese, Sri Lanka
Siona	Siona, Colombia
Sira	Sira, Gabon
Siri	Siri, Nigeria
Siriano	Siriano, Colombia
Siriono	Siriono, Bolivia
Sisala	Sisala, Upper Volta
siSwati	**Swazi, South Africa
Siwu	Siwu, Ghana
So	So, Laos
	*So, Thailand (81)
	So, Cameroon
Sobei	Sobei, Indonesia
Soga	Soga, Uganda
Soli	Soli, Zambia
Solor	Solorese Muslims, Indonesia (81)
Somagai	*Somahai, Indonesia
Somahai	Somahai, Indonesia
Somali	Somali, Ethiopia
	Somali, Somalia (79)
	Somali, Degodia, Kenya
	Somali, Gurreh, Kenya
	Somali, Ogadenya, Kenya
	Somali, Ajuran, Kenya (79)
Somali (Ajuran)	
Somba (Detammari)	**Somba, Benin
Somrai	Somrai, Chad
	Somrai, Central African Republic
Sondwari	Sondwari in M.P., India
Songe	Songe, Zaire
Songhai	Songhai, Mali

Susu	Susu, Guinea-Bissau
	Susu, Sierra Leone
Svan	Svan, Soviet Russia
Swaga	Swaga, Zaire
Swahili	Ikizu, Tanzania
Swaka	Swaka, Zambia
Swati	Swatis, Pakistan (79)
T'in	T'in, Thailand (81)
Ta-Oi	Ta-Oi, Laos
Tabasaran	Tabasaran, Soviet Russia
Tabi	Ingassana, Sudan
	Tabi, Sudan
Tacana	Tacana, Bolivia
Tadjio	Tadjio, Indonesia
Tadyawan	Tadyawan, Philippines
Tae'	Toraja, Southern, Indonesia (81)
Tafi	Tafi, Togo
Tagal	Tagal, Malaysia (81)
Tagalog	**Batangeno, Philippines
Tagbanwa	**Tagbanwa, Aborlan, Philippines
Tagbanwa, Kalamian	Tagbanwa, Kalamian, Philippines
Tagin	***Tagin, India
Tagwana	Tagwana, Ivory Coast
Taikat	Taikat, Indonesia
Taiwanese	*Deviant Youth in Taipei, Taiwan (82)
Taiwanese (Hoklo)	*Industrial Workers, Taiwan (81)
Taiwanese (Minnan, Amoy)	*Chinese in Taiwan, Taiwan
Takankar	Takankar, India
Takemba	Takemba, Benin
Takestani	Takestani, Iran
Tal	Tal, Nigeria
Talish	Talish, Iran
Talo	*Talo, Indonesia
Talodi	Talodi, Sudan
Tama	Tama, Chad
Tamachek	Tuareg, Niger (79)
Tamagario	Tamagario, Indonesia
Taman	Taman, Burma
Tamang	*Tamang, Nepal
Tamaria	Tamaria in Bihar, India
Tamazight	Tamazight, Morocco
Tambas	Tambas, Nigeria
Tambo	Tambo, Zambia
Tamil	**Indian Tamils - Colombo, Sri Lanka (82)
	*Kudisai Vagh Makkal, India
	Labbai, India
	Moor Malays, Sri Lanka (79)
	**Saiva Vellala, India
	Tamil (Ceylonese), Sri Lanka
	*Tamil in Yellagiri Hills, India
	**Tamil Laborers in Bombay, India (82)
	Tamil Muslims in Madras, India (82)
	***Tamil Plantation Workers, Malaysia
	*Tamils (Indian), Malaysia
	**Tamils (Indian), Sri Lanka (79)
Tampulensi	Tampulma, Ghana
Tana	Tana, Chad
	Tana, Central African Republic
Tanahmerah	Tanahmerah, Indonesia
Tancouleur	Taucouleur, Senegal (80)
Tandanke	Tandanke, Senegal
Tandia	Tandia, Indonesia
Tangale	Tangale, Nigeria
Tangchangya	Tangchangya, Bangladesh
Tangsa	**Tangsa, India
Tanimuca-Retuama	Tanimuca-Retuama, Colombia
Taori-Kei	Taori-Kei, Indonesia
Tara	Tara, Indonesia
Tarahumara, Northern	Tarahumara, Northern, Mexico

Tarahumara, Rocoroibo   Tarahumara, Rocoroibo, Mexico
Tarahumara, Samachique   Tarahumara, Samachique, Mexico
Taram   Taram, Cameroon
Tarasco   Tarasco, Mexico
Targum   Targum, Israel
Tarof   Tarof, Indonesia
Tarok   Tarok, Nigeria
Tarpia   Tarpia, Indonesia
Tashilhait   **Shluh Berbers, Morocco
Tat   Tat, Soviet Russia
                               Tindin, Soviet Russia
                               Bashkir, Soviet Russia (80)
Tatar   Tatars, Soviet Russia (80)
Tatar dialects   Barabaig, Tanzania (79)
Tatoga   Tatoga, Tanzania
Tatuyo   **Tatuyo, Colombia
Taungyo   Taungyo, Burma
Taurap   Taurap, Indonesia
Tausug   Tausug, Philippines (80)
Tawr   Tawr, Burma
Tayaku   Tayaku, Benin
Tboli   **T'boli, Philippines (81)
Tchang   Tchang, Cameroon
Teda   Teda, Chad (80)
                               Teda, Libya
                               Teda, Niger
Teen   *Tense, Ivory Coast
Tegali   Tegali, Sudan
Tehit   Tahit, Indonesia
Teimuri   Teimuri, Iran
Teimurtash   Teimurtash, Iran
Teke, Eastern   Teke, Eastern, Zaire
Teke, Northern   Teke, Northern, Congo
Teke, Southwestern   Teke, Southwestern, Congo
Telugu   ***Matharis, India
Tembe   Tembe, Brazil
Tembo   Tembo, Zaire
Temein   Temein, Sudan
Temira   Temira, Malaysia
Temne   **Temne, Sierra Leone (80)
Tenggerese   Tengger, Indonesia
Tepehua, Huehuetla   Tepehua, Huehuetla, Mexico
Tepehua, Pisa Flores   Tepehua, Pisa Flores, Mexico
Tepehua, Veracruz   Tepehua, Veracruz, Mexico
Tepehuan, Northern   Tepehuan, Northern, Mexico
Tepehuan, Southeastern   Tepehuan, Southeastern, Mexico
Tepehuan, Southwestern   Tepehuan, Southwestern, Mexico
Tepeth   Tepeth, Uganda
Tepo   Tepo, Ivory Coast
Tera   Tera, Nigeria
Terena   Terena, Brazil
Teribe   **Teribe, Panama
Ternate   Ternatans, Indonesia
Teso   Teso, Uganda
Tewa (Jemez)   Jemez Pueblo, United States of America
Thado   Thado in Assam, India
Thai   *Central Thailand Farmers, Thailand (81)
                               Government officials, Thailand
                               **Lepers of Cen. Thailand, Thailand (81)
                               *Ramkamhaeng Un. Students, Thailand
                               *Slum Dwellers of Bangkok, Thailand
                               *Thai University Students, Thailand (81)
                               Thai of Bangkok, Thailand
Thai, Central   *Thai Islam (Thai), Thailand
Thai, Southern   Thakur, India
Thakur   Thar in Bihar, India
Thar   Thoi, Sudan
Thoi   Thuri, Sudan
Thuri   *Tibetan Refugees, India
Tibetan

	*Tibetans, China
	Tibetans in Bhutan, Bhutan (81)
Tibetan Dialect	*Chang-Pa of Kashmir, India (81)
Tibeto-Burman	Jinuos, China (81)
	Lisu, China (81)
Tibeto-Burman Dialect	Lawa, Eastern, Thailand (81)
Ticuna	Ticuna, Brazil
Tidore	Tidorese, Indonesia
Tiefo	Tiefo, Upper Volta
Tien-Chiu	**Chinese Refugees, France, France (79)
Tiene	Tiene, Zaire
Tigon	Tigon, Cameroon
Tikar	Tikar, Cameroon
Tila Chol	Ch'ol Tila, Mexico
Timorese	Timorese, Indonesia
Tippera	Tippera, Bangladesh
Tira	Tira, Sudan
Tirma	Tirma, Sudan
Tiro	Tiro, Indonesia
Tiruray	Tiruray, Philippines
Tlapaneco, Malinaltepec	Tlapaneco, Malinaltepec, Mexico
Toala	Toala, Indonesia
Toba	Toba, Argentina
Toda	Toda in Tamil Nadu, India
Tofi	*Tofi, Benin
Togbo	Togbo, Zaire
Tojolabal	Tojolabal, Mexico
Tokkaru	Tokkaru in Tamil Nadu, India
Tol	Tol, Honduras
Tombulu	Tombulu, Indonesia
Tomini	Tomini, Indonesia
Tondanou	Tondanou, Indonesia
Tonga	Tonga, Botswana
	Tonga, Malawi
	Tonga, Mozambique
Tongwe	Tongwe, Tanzania
Tonsea	Tonsea, Indonesia
Tontemboa	Tontemboa, Indonesia
Toposa	*Topotha, Sudan
Toposa, Donyiro	Nyzatom, Sudan
Totonaco, Northern	Totonaco, Northern, Mexico
Totonaco, Oxumatlan	Totonaco, Oxumatlan, Mexico
Totonaco, Papantla	Totonaco, Papantla, Mexico
Totonaco, Sierra	Totonaco, Sierra, Mexico
Toussian	*Toussian, Upper Volta
Towei	Towei, Indonesia
Trepo	Trepo, Ivory Coast
Tribal dialects	***Halam in Tripura, India
Tribal Languages	**Bachelors in Lagos, Nigeria (82)
Trio	Trio, Surinam
Trique, San Juan Copala	Trique, San Juan Copala, Mexico
Tsaangi	Tsaangi, Congo
Tsakhur	Tsakhur, Soviet Russia
Tsamai	Tsamai, Ethiopia
Tshiluba	**Bakuba, Zaire
Tsimane	Tsimane, Bolivia
Tsogo	Tsogo, Gabon
Tsonga	Tsonga, Mozambique
Tsou	Tsou, Taiwan (81)
Tswa	Tswa, Mozambique
	Tswa, Zimbabwe
Tswana	Tswana, Namibia
	Tswana, Zimbabwe
Tubar	Tubar, Mexico
Tucano	Pacu, Brazil
	Piratapuyo, Brazil
	Quarequena, Brazil
	Seuci, Brazil

Vaikino	Vai, Sierra Leone
Vaiphei	Vaikino, Indonesia
Vale	Vaiphei in Assam, India
Various dialects	Vale, Central African Republic
	**African Students in Cairo, Egypt
	**Mangyan, Philippines
Venda	Venda, Zimbabwe
Veps	Veps, Soviet Russia
Vere	***Vere, Nigeria
	Vere, Cameroon
Vidunda	Vidunda, Tanzania
Vietnamese	*Int'l Stud., Los Banos, Philippines
	Street Vendors in Saigon, Viet Nam (82)
	Vietnamese, Laos
	**Vietnamese in the USA, United States of America
	**Vietnamese Refugees, Thailand
	**Vietnamese Refugees, Australia
Vige	Vige, Upper Volta
Vinza	Vinza, Tanzania
Vishavan	Vishavan in Kerala, India
Vute	Vute, Nigeria
Wa	Wa, China
	Wa, Burma
Wabo	Wabo, Indonesia
Waddar	Waddar in Andhra Pradesh, India
Waffa Dialect	Ka'mis, Papua New Guinea
Wagdi	Wagdi in Rajasthan, India
Waimiri	Waimiri, Brazil
Waiwai	Waiwai, Brazil
	Waiwai, Guyana
Waja	Waja, Nigeria
Walamo	Walamo, Ethiopia
Wali	Wala, Ghana
Wambon	Wambon, Indonesia
Wanchoo	**Wanchoo, India
Wanda	Wanda, Tanzania
Wandamen	Wandamen, Indonesia
Wandji	Wandji, Gabon
Wanggom	Wanggom, Indonesia
Wanji	Wanji, Tanzania
Wano	Wano, Indonesia
Wapishana	Wapishana, Brazil
	Wapishana, Guyana
	Wapishana, Venezuela
Wara	Wara, Upper Volta
Warao	Warao, Venezuela
Ware	Ware, Mali
Warembori	Warembori, Indonesia
Waris	Waris, Indonesia
Warji	*Warjawa, Nigeria
Warkay-Bipim	Warkay-Bipim, Indonesia
Waropen	Waropen, Indonesia
Wasi	Wasi, Tanzania
Waura	Waura, Brazil
Wayana	Wayana, Surinam
Weda	Weda, Indonesia
Wetawit	Wetawit, Ethiopia
Wewewa	Wewewa, Indonesia
Widekum	Widekum, Cameroon
Win	Win, Upper Volta
Winji-Winji	Winji-Winji, Benin
Wobe	Wobe, Ivory Coast
Wodani	Wodani, Indonesia
Woi	Woi, Indonesia
Woko	Voko, Cameroon
Woleat	Woleat, Turks and Caicos Islands
Wolio	Wolio, Indonesia
Wolof	Wolof, Senegal (80)

Wolof, Gambian	Wolof, Gambian, Gambia
Wom	Wom, Nigeria
Won Chow	*Chinese Restaurant Wrkrs., France
Wongo	Wongo, Zaire
Woro	Woro, Sudan
Wumbvu	Wumbvu, Gabon
Wungu	Wungu, Tanzania
Xavante	Xavante, Brazil
Xerente	Xerente, Brazil
Xokleng	Xokleng, Brazil
Xu	*Bushmen (Kung), Namibia (79)
	Xu, Namibia
Yafi	Yafi, Indonesia
Yaghan	Yaghan, Chile
Yagnobi	Yagnobi, Soviet Russia
Yagua	Yagua, Peru
Yahadian	Yahadian, Indonesia
Yaka	Yaka, Zaire
Yakan	Yakan, Philippines (80)
Yakoma	Yakoma, Central African Republic
Yala	**Yala, Nigeria
Yalunka	*Yalunka, Sierra Leone (80)
Yaly	Yaly, Indonesia
Yambasa	Yambasa, Cameroon
Yaminahua	Yaminahua, Peru
Yanadi	Yanadi in Andhra Pradesh, India
Yandang	Yandang, Nigeria
Yanga	Yanga, Togo
Yangbye	Yangbye, Burma
Yanomam (Waica)	*Yanomamo in Brazil, Brazil (79)
Yans	Yans, Zaire
Yanyula (Yanjula)	*Yanyula, Australia
Yao	Yao, Mozambique
	*Yao Refugees from Laos, Thailand
Yao (Mien Wa)	**Yao, Thailand (79)
Yaoure	Yaoure, Ivory Coast
Yaqui	Yaquis, Mexico
Yaruro	Yaruro, Venezuela
Yasing	Yasing, Cameroon
Yaur	Yaur, Indonesia
Yava	Yava, Indonesia
Yazgulyam	Yazgulyam, Soviet Russia
Yei	**Yei, Botswana
	Yei, Indonesia
Yela	Yela, Zaire
Yellow Uighur	Yellow Uighur, China
Yelmek	Yelmek, Indonesia
Yerava	Yerava in Karnataka, India
Yeretuar	Yeretuar, Indonesia
Yerukala	Yerukala in A.P., India
Yeskwa	Yeskwa, Nigeria
Yi	Lolo, China (81)
	Pai, China (81)
Yidinit	Yidinit, Ethiopia
Yinchia	Yinchia, Burma
Yinga	Yinga, Cameroon
Yoabu	Yoabu, Benin
Yogad	Yogad, Philippines
Yonggom	Yonggom, Indonesia
Yos	Yos, Burma
Yotafa	Yotafa, Indonesia
Yuana	Yuana, Venezuela
Yucateco	Yucateco, Guatemala
	Yucateco, Mexico
Yucuna	*Yucuna, Colombia
Yukagir	Yukagirs, Soviet Russia
Yukpa	Yukpa, Colombia
	Yukpa, Venezuela
Yuku	Yuku, China

Yulu	Yulu, Sudan
Yungur	Yungur, Nigeria
Yuracare	Yuracare, Bolivia
Yurak	Yurak, Soviet Russia
Yuruti	Yuruti, Colombia
Zaghawa	Zaghawa, Chad
	Zaghawa, Libya
	Zaghawa, Sudan
Zanaki	Zanaki, Tanzania
Zande	Zande, Zaire
Zangskari	Zangskari in Kashmir, India
Zaramo	Zaramo, Tanzania
Zari	Zari, Nigeria
Zayse	Zayse, Ethiopia
Zenaga	Zenaga, Mauritania
Zighvana(Dghwede)	*Dghwede, Nigeria
Zigwa	Zigwa, Tanzania
Zilmamu	Zilmamu, Ethiopia
Zimba	Zimba, Zaire
Zome	Zome, Burma
	Zome in Manipur, India
Zoque, Chimalapa	Zoque, Chimalapa, Mexico
Zoque, Copainala	Zoque, Copainala, Mexico
Zoque, Francisco Leon	Zoque, Francisco Leon, Mexico
Zoque, Tabasco	Zoque, Tabasco, Mexico
Zulu	Zulu, Malawi
Zuni	Zuni, United States of America

Index by
Country

INDEX BY COUNTRY

Groups are listed by the countries for which information has been reported by questionnaires. In most cases, this means they are listed in the country where they are primarily located. Many peoples are found in several countries. This listing is limited to the country for which the MARC files have information. Groups are listed alphabetically under each country listed. Please note that not all countries will be found in this index. Peoples have not been reported from every country. Cambodia is listed under its new name, Kampuchea. The Republic of China is listed as Taiwan. Dahomey is listed under its current name, Benin. The population estimate given is an indication of the size of that people in that one country. In some cases, it is only a part of a large people to be found in several other countries as well.

Belgium	North Africans in Belgium (80)	90,000
	Turkish Workers (80)	60,000
Belize	**Black Caribs, Belize (79)	10,000
	**Mopan Maya	4,000
Benin	**Adja	250,000
	*Bariba (80)	400,000
	Berba	44,000
	**Boko	40,000
	Dendi	40,000
	Dompago	19,000
	*Fulani	70,000
	Gbazantche	9,000
	Gu	173,000
	Kabre	35,000
	Kotokoli	75,000
	Lamba	29,000
	*Mokole	7,000
	*Nyantruku	4,000
	**Pila	50,000
	**Save	15,000
	**Somba	60,000
	Soruba	5,000
	Takemba	10,000
	Tayaku	10,000
	*Tofi	33,000
	Winji-Winji	5,000
	Yoabu	8,000
Bhutan	Bhutias	780,000
	Kebumtamp	400,000
	Sharchagpakha	400,000
	Tibetans in Bhutan (81)	5,000
Bolivia	**Aymara	850,000
	Chacobo	250
	Chipaya	850
	Chiquitano	20,000
	***Guarani (79)	15,000
	Guarayu	5,000
	Ignaciano	5,000
	Itonama	110
	Leco	200
	***Mestizos in La Paz (82)	400,000
	Movima	1,000
	**Quechua	1,000,000
	Reyesano	1,000
	Siriono	500
	Tacana	3,500
	Tsimane	5,500
	Yuracare	2,500
Botswana	"Au"ei	5,000
	Buka-khwe	9,000
	Bushmen in Botswana	30,000
	Herero	10,000
	*Kalanga	150,000
	Kwe-etshori	3,000
	Nharon	3,000
	Shua	400
	Tonga	6,000
	**Yei	10,000
Brazil	Apalai	100
	Apinaye	210
	Apurina	1,000
	Arapaco	310
	Atruahi	500
	Bakairi	300
	Baniwa	2,440
	*Bororo	500
	Caiwa	7,000
	Canela	1,400
	**Chinese in Brazil	45,000

Balong	4,500
Bamougoun-Bamenjou	31,000
Bamum	75,000
Bandjoun	60,000
Banen	28,000
Bangangte	475,000
Basaa	170,000
Batanga-Ngolo	9,000
Bene	60,000
Bethen	10,000
Betsinga	10,000
Bitare	50,000
Bobe	600
Bokyi	87,000
Bomboko	2,500
Bonkeng-Pendia	1,500
Budugum	10,000
Bura	100,000
Chinga	12,600
Daba	31,000
Dghwede	13,000
**Doohwaayo	15,000
Duru	20,000
Eton	112,000
Fali	50,000
Fulani (79)	250,000
Fungom, Northern	15,000
Gidar	50,000
Gisei	10,000
Gisiga	30,000
Gouwar	5,000
Gude	100,000
Gulfe	36,000
Iyon	4,000
Kaalong	50,000
Kaka	2,000
Kamkam	800
Kera	15,000
Kolbila	1,000
Kole	300
Koma	15,000
Konabem	3,000
Korop	10,000
Kotoko	31,000
Kotopo	10,000
Kpa	17,000
Kutin	400
Kwakum	3,000
Laka	10,000
Lambi	1,000
Lue	4,000
Lundu	24,000
Maka	51,000
Mambila	40,000
Mangisa	14,000
Matakam	140,000
Mbembe	25,000
Mbimu	nr
Mbo	22,500

	Xokleng	250
	*Yanomamo in Brazil (79)	3,000
Burma	Chaungtha	34,600
	Chin, Asho	11,000
	Chin, Falam	92,000
	Chin, Haka	85,000
	Chin, Khumi	30,000
	Chin, Ngawn	5,000
	Chin, Tiddim	38,000
	Chinbok	21,000
	Chinese in Burma	600,000
	Dai	10,000
	Danu	70,000
	Gheko	4,000
	Hallam	11,000
	Hkun	20,000
	Hrangkhol	8,500
	Intha	80,000
	Kachin in Shan State	80,000
	Kaw	30,000
	Kayan	18,000
	Kokant	50,000
	Lahu	40,000
	Lama	3,000
	Maghi	309,000
	Moken (79)	5,000
	Mon (81)	350,000
	Mun	10,000
	Myaung-Ze	7,000
	Norra	10,000
	Palaung (79)	150,000
	Pao	100,000
	Purum	300
	Ralte	17,000
	Riang-Lang	20,000
	Senthang	10,000
	Shan	800,000
	Shan Chinese	20,000
	Taman	10,000
	Taungyo	159,200
	Taungyoe	18,000
	Tawr	700
	Thai-Ney	5,000
	Wa	50,000
	Yangbye	326,650
	Yin-Kyar	2,000
	Yin-Nett	2,000
	Yinchia	4,000
	Yos	4,500
	Zome	30,000
Burundi	Pygmy (Binga)	30,000
Cameroon	Adamawa	380,000
	Age	5,000
	Aghem	7,000
	Amasi	10,000
	Assumbo	10,000
	Babajou	500
	Bafut	25,000
	Baka	15,000

	Menemo-Mogamo	35,000
	Menka	10,000
	Mofu	33,000
	Mulimba	3,000
	Mungaka	14,000
	Namshi	30,000
	Ndjem	25,000
	Ndop-Bamessing	17,000
	Ndoro	10,000
	Ndunpa Duupa	1,000
	Ngayaba	1,000
	Ngemba	33,500
	Ngi	10,000
	Ngumba	10,000
	Ngwo	10,000
	Nkom	30,000
	Nohu	6,500
	Nso	100,000
	Nyang	10,000
	Oso	25,000
	Pape	1,000
	Podokwo	25,000
	So	6,000
	Su	500
	Suga	10,000
	Taram	3,000
	Tchang	100,000
	Tigon	25,000
	Tikar	12,500
	Tupuri	70,000
	Vere	20,000
	Voko	1,000
	Widekum	10,000
	**Wimbum	50,000
	Yambasa	26,000
	Yasing	25,000
	Yinga	300
Canada	**Chinese in Vancouver B.C.	80,000
	Jews of Montreal	120,000
	Jews, Sephardic	26,000
Central African Republic	Arab Immigrants in Bangui (82)	5,000
	Day	1,600
	Kaba	11,000
	Kaba Dunjo	17,000
	Kaka	37,000
	Kari	4,000
	Karre	40,000
	Kim	5,000
	Laka	40,000
	Majingai-ngama	47,000
	Mbai	73,000
	Mbati	15,000
	Monjombo	11,000
	Ndam	670
	Ndogo	3,500
	Ngando	2,000
	Ngbaka Ma'bo	17,000
	Nzakara	3,000
	Pambia	2,000
	Pana	20,000
	Pygmy (Binga)	2,000
	Runga	13,000
	Somrai	50,000
	Tana	35,000
	Tunya	800
	Vale	1,400
	Yakoma	5,300
Chad	Abou Charib	25,000
	Bagirmi	40,000

	Bilala	42,000
	Bomou	15,000
	Bua	20,000
	Daju of Dar Dadju	27,000
	Daju of Dar Sila	33,000
	Dangaleat	20,000
	Daza	159,000
	Gabri	20,000
	Gambai	200,000
	Gidar	50,000
	Golo	3,400
	Goulai	30,000
	Gula	2,500
	Jongor	16,000
	Kanembu	2,250
	Karanga	57,000
	Kari	40,000
	Kenga	25,000
	Kera	5,000
	Kibet	22,000
	Kim	5,000
	Koke	1,000
	Kotoko	31,000
	Kuka	38,000
	Laka	40,000
	Lele	30,000
	Maba	56,000
	Majingai-Ngama	47,000
	Mangbai	2,000
	Mararit	42,000
	Marba	30,000
	Masa	80,000
	Masalit	73,500
	Massalat	23,000
	Mbai	73,000
	Mbum	20,000
	Mesme	28,000
	Mesmedje	11,000
	Mimi	15,000
	Mogum	6,000
	Mubi	36,000
	Mundang	100,000
	Musei	60,000
	Musgu	75,000
	Nancere	35,000
	Nielim	2,000
	Ouaddai	320,000
	Rataning	10,000
	Runga	13,000
	Sarwa	400
	Somrai	50,000
	Sungor	39,000
	Tama	60,000
	Tana	35,000
	Teda (80)	10,000
	Tunya	800
	Tupuri	60,000
	Zaghawa	61,000
Chile	Aymara, Carangas	20,000
	Mapuche	300,000
	Yaghan	50
China	Ach'ang	10,000
	Buriat	26,500
	Burig	148,000
	Ch'iang	77,000
	Chin	95,500
	Chingp'o	101,850
	Chuang (81)	12,000,000
	Chungchia	1,500,000

	Chwang	7,785,410
	Dagur	22,600
	Evenki	7,200
	Ewenkis (81)	10,000
	Hani	138,000
	Hui (80)	5,200,000
	Jinuos (81)	10,000
	Jyarung	70,000
	Kalmytz	70,000
	Kam	825,320
	Kazakhs (81)	700,000
	Kelao	23,000
	Khalka	68,000
	Kham	11,400
	Kirgiz	90,000
	Koreans in Manchuria (81)	3,000,000
	Lahul	1,600
	Laka	6,000
	Lati	450
	Li	1,000,000
	Lisu (81)	470,000
	Lolo (81)	4,800,000
	Lu	400,000
	Manchu (81)	200,000
	Miao (81)	2,800,000
	Mien (81)	740,000
	Mongour	50,000
	Nahsi	155,750
	Nanai	1,000
	Nosu	556,000
	Nung	100,000
	Oirat	60,000
	Oronchon	2,400
	Pai (81)	1,000,000
	Paongan	8,000
	Pu-I	1,311,020
	Punu	220,000
	Rawang	60,000
	Salar	31,000
	Santa	155,500
	Sibo	21,000
	Sui	160,310
	*Tibetans	3,000,000
	Tung-Chia (81)	1,100,000
	Uigur (80)	4,800,000
	Wa	286,160
	Yellow Uighur	4,000
	Yuku	4,000
Colombia	Achagua	100
	Andoque	100
	Barasano	400
	Barasano, Northern	450
	Barasano, Southern	400
	Bora	400
	Cacua	150
	Camsa	2,000
	Carapana	200
	Chami	3,000
	Cofan	250
	Cogui	4,000
	**Coreguaje	500
	Coreguaje	500
	Cubeo	2,000
	Cuiba	2,000
	*Cuna (79)	600
	Cuna	600
	Curipaco	2,500
	Embera, Northern	2,000
	Guajibo	15,000

	Dorze	3,000
	**Falasha (79)	30,000
	*Gabbra	nr
	*Galla (Bale)	750,000
	Galla of Bucho	1,500
	Galla, Harar	1,305,400
	Gawwada	4,000
	Gedeo	250,000
	**Ghimeera	50,000
	Gidicho	500
	Gobato	1,000
	Gobeze	22,000
	Gumuz	53,000
	Gurage (80)	750,000
	Hadiyya	700,000
	Harari	13,000
	Janjero	1,000
	Kachama	500
	*Kaffa (80)	320,000
	Kao	600
	Kembata	250,000
	*Komo	20,000
	Konso	30,000
	Koyra	5,000
	Kullo	82,000
	Kunama	70,000
	*Lango	8,000
	Maji	15,000
	Male	12,000
	Mao, Northern	13,000
	*Masengo	7,000
	Me'en	38,000
	Mesengo	28,000
	***Mocha	170,000
	Mursi	6,000
	Nao	5,000
	Nara	25,000
	*Nuer	70,000
	Oyda	3,000
	Reshiat	10,000
	***Shankilla (Kazza)	20,000
	Sheko	23,000
	Shinasha	4,000
	Sidamo	857,000
	Somali	1,000,000
	**Suri	30,000
	Tsamai	7,000
	Walamo	908,000
	Wetawit	28,000
	Yidinit	600
	Zayse	21,000
	Zilmamu	3,000
Fiji	Indians in Fiji (79)	265,000
France	Algerian Arabs in France	804,000
	**Chinese Refugees, France (79)	100,000
	*Chinese Restaurant Wrkrs.	50,000
	**Portuguese in France	150,000
Gabon	*University Students (79)	800,000
	Benga	nr
	Duma	10,000
	Kele	15,000
	Kota	nr
	Lumbu	12,000
	Mbaama	12,000
	Mbede	45,000
	Minduumo	4,000
	Sangu	18,000
	Sira	17,000
	Tsogo	15,000

	Cakchiquel, Central	300,000
	Chorti	25,000
	Chuj	15,000
	Chuj of San Mateo Ixtatan	17,000
	Ixil	45,000
	Jacalteco	12,000
	**K'anjobal of San Miguel	18,000
	**Kekchi	270,000
	**Mam Indian	470,000
	**Mopan Maya	2,000
	Pocomchi, Eastern	20,000
	Pocomchi, Western	25,000
	**Quiche (79)	500,000
	Rabinal-Achi	21,000
	Tzutujil	5,000
	Uspanteco	15,000
	Yucateco	3,000
Guinea	Basari	3,500
	Fula	1,500,000
	Gbande	66,000
	Kissi	266,000
	Kobiana	300
	Konyagi	85,000
	Kpelle	250,000
	Landoma	4,000
	Loko	16,000
	Loma	180,000
	Nalu	10,000
Guinea-Bissau	Badyara	10,000
	Balante	100,000
	Banyun	15,000
	Bayot	3,000
	Biafada	15,000
	Bidyogo	10,000
	**Bijogo	25,000
	Diola (80)	15,000
	Dyola	nr
	Kasanga	420
	Kunante	6,000
	Landoma	5,000
	Maninka	65,000
	**Manjaco	80,000
	Mankanya	35,000
	Papel	36,300
	Susu	2,000
Guyana	Akawaio	3,000
	Arawak	5,000
	Patamona	1,000
	Waiwai	1,000
	Wapishana	4,000
Honduras	**Black Caribs, Honduras	20,000
	Paya	300
	Tol	200
Hong Kong	Chinese Businessmen (81)	10,000
	Chinese Factory Workers	500,000
	**Chinese in Hong Kong	4,135,000
	Chinese Villagers	500,000
	*Factory Workers	40,000
	**High School Students	453,000
India	Abujmaria in M.P.	11,000
	***Adi	80,300
	Adiyan in Kerala	2,500
	Agariya in Bihar	11,790
	Ahir in Maharashtra	132,520
	Aimol in Assam	110
	Ajmeri in Rajasthan	580
	Aka	2,257
	*Alars	400
	Anal in Manipur	6,590

Grasia in Gujarat	27,160
Gujars of Kashmir (81)	150,000
***Halam in Tripura	20,000
Halbi in Madhya Pradesh	349,260
Harauti in Rajasthan	334,380
Ho in Bihar	749,800
Holiya in Madhya Pradesh	3,090
Iravas in Kerala	3,700,000
***Irulas in Kerala	10,000
Jagannathi in A.P.	1,310
Jains	2,000,000
Jatapu in Andhra Pradesh	36,450
Jaunsari in Uttar Pradesh	56,560
Jharia in Orissa	2,060
Juang in Orissa	12,170
Kachchi in Andhra Pradesh	470,990
Kadar in Andhra Pradesh	800
Kahluri in Andamans	66,190
Kaikadi in Maharashtra	11,850
Kamar in Madhya Pradesh	10,110
Kanauri in Uttar Pradesh	28,500
Kanikkaran in Kerala	10,000
Kanjari in Andhra Pradesh	55,390
**Karbis	300,000
Karmali in Dihar	69,620
**Kashmiri Muslims (79)	3,060,000
Katakari in Gujarat	4,950
Kawar in Madhya Pradesh	33,770
Keer in Madhya Pradesh	2,890
Khamti in Assam	300
Khandesi	14,700
Kharia in Bihar	88,900
Khasi in Assam	384,010
Khirwar in Madhya Pradesh	34,250
Khojas, Agha Khani	175,000
Khowar	6,960
Kisan in Bihar	73,850
Kishanganjia in Bihar	56,920
Kishtwari in Jammu	12,170
Koda in Bihar	14,140
Kol in Assam	82,900
**Kolam	60,000
Kom in Manipur	6,970
***Kond	900,000
Konda-Dora in A.P.	15,650
Konkani in Gujarat	1,522,680
Koraga in Kerala	1,500
*Korku in Madhya Pradesh	250,000
Korwa in Bihar	14,250
Kota in Tamil Nadu	860
Kotia in Andhra Pradesh	15,000
Kotta	1,200
Koya in Andhra Pradesh	211,880
*Kudisai Vagh Makkal	1,000,000
Kudiya	100
*Kuknas	125,000
**Kuluis in Himachal Prades (81)	200,000
Kumauni in Assam	1,234,940
Kupia in Andhra Pradesh	4,000
Kurichiya in Kerala (81)	12,130
Kuruba in Tamil Nadu	7,900
Kurux in Bihar	1,240,400
Kuvi in Orissa	190,000
Labans	nr
Labbai	nr
Labhani in Andhra Pradesh	1,203,340
*Labourers of Jhoparpatti	1,500
Ladakhi in Jammu	56,740

Poouch in Kashmir	
Purig-Pa of Kashmir (81)	500,000
Rabha in Assam	nr
Rajasthani Muslims-Jaipur (82)	10,000
*Rava in Assam	3,500
Riang in Assam	45,000
Sadan in Andamans	74,930
**Saiva Vellala	807,180
Satnamis in M.P.	1,500,000
*Shourastra in Tamil Nadu	30,000
Sikkimese	200,000
*Sindhis of India	36,580
Sondwari in M.P.	3,000,000
Sora in Orissa	31,490
Sulung	221,710
***Tagin	nr
Takankar	25,000
Tamaria in Bihar	10,960
*Tamil in Yellagiri Hills	5,050
**Tamil Laborers in Bombay (82)	3,500
Tamil Muslims in Madras (82)	3,000
**Tangsa	50,000
Thado in Assam	10,700
Thakur	42,340
Thar in Bihar	99,000
*Tibetan Refugees	8,790
Toda in Tamil Nadu	nr
Tokkaru in Tamil Nadu	770
Totis	1,298,860
Tugara	nr
Ullatan in Kerala	43,680
Urali in Kerala	1,500
Vaiphei in Assam	1,080
Vishavan in Kerala	12,210
**Vohras of Yavatmal	150
Waddar in Andhra Pradesh	10,000
Wagdi in Rajasthan	35,900
**Wanchoo	756,790
Yanadi in Andhra Pradesh	nr
Yerava in Karnataka	205,380
Yerukala in A.P.	10,870
Zangskari in Kashmir	67,550
Zemi Naga of Assam (81)	5,000
Zoliang	16,000
Zome in Manipur	50,000

Indonesia	Abau	30,000
	Achehnese (80)	3,390
	Aghu	2,200,000
	Aibondeni	3,000
	Aikwakai	150
	Airo-Sumaghaghe	400
	Airoran	2,000
	Alas	350
	Alor, Kolana (81)	30,000
	Amanab	90,000
	Ambai	2,800
	Amber	6,000
	Amberbaken	300
	Ambonese	5,000
	Ansus	80,000
	Ara	3,000
	Arandai	75,000
	Arguni	2,000
	Asienara	200
	*Asmat (79)	700
	Awyi	30,000
	Awyu	400
	Baburiwa	18,000
	Baham	160
		500

Kamberataro	970
Kamoro	8,000
Kampung Baru	400
Kamtuk-Gresi	5,000
Kanum	320
Kapori	60
Karas	200
Karon Dori	5,000
Karon Pantai	2,500
Kasuweri	1,200
Kati, Northern	8,000
Kati, Southern	4,000
Kaugat	1,000
**Kaur	50,000
Kaure	800
Kavwol	500
Kawe	300
Kayagar	9,000
Kaygir	4,000
Kayupulau	570
Kei	30,000
Kemak	50,000
Kendari	500,000
Kenyah	37,500
Kerinchi	170,000
Kimaghama	3,000
*Kimyal	7,000
Kodi	25,000
Komering	400,000
Koneraw	300
Korapun	4,000
Kotogut	1,000
Kubu (80)	6,000
Kubu (81)	25,000
Kurudu	1,100
Kwansu	350
Kwerba	2,000
Kwesten	2,480
Lampung (80)	1,500,000
Lara	12,000
Latdwalam	860
Laudje	125,000
Lebong	nr
Letti	6,000
Lionese	100,000
**Loho Loho	10,000
Loinang (81)	100,000
Lore	140,000
Lubu	1,000,000
Luwu	500,000
Maanyan	15,000
Madik	1,000
Madurese (79)	7,000,000
Mairasi	1,000
Makasai	70,000
Makian, West	12,000
Maklew	120
Mambai	80,000
Mandar	302,000
Mander	100
Manem	400
Manggarai Muslims (81)	25,000
**Manikion	8,000
Mantion	12,000
Marau	1,200
Marind	7,000
Marind, Bian	900
Masenrempulu	250,000
Matbat	550

Sowanda	1,100
Sumba	400,000
Sumbawa	114,000
**Sundanese (80)	20,000,000
Tadjio	100,000
Tahit	6,000
Taikat	600
*Talo	90,000
Tamagario	3,500
Tanahmerah	3,200
Tandia	350
Taori-Kei	140
Tara	125,000
Tarof	600
Tarpia	560
Taurap	160
Tengger	400,000
Ternatans	42,000
Tidorese	26,000
Timorese	300,000
Tiro	75,000
Toala	100
Tombulu	40,000
Tomini	50,000
Tondanou	35,000
Tonsea	90,000
Tontemboa	140,000
Toraja, Southern (81)	250,000
Towei	120
Tukude	45,000
Tumawo	350
Turu	800
Uhunduni	14,000
Uria	1,200
Uruangnirin	250
Vaikino	14,000
Wabo	900
Wambon	2,000
Wandamen	4,000
Wanggom	1,000
Wano	1,700
Warembori	350
Waris	1,480
Warkay-Bipim	250
Waropen	6,000
Weda	900
Wewewa	55,000
Wodani	3,000
Woi	1,300
Wolio	25,000
Yafi	180
Yahadian	700
Yaly	12,000
Yaur	350
Yava	4,500
Yei	1,000
Yelmek	400
Yeretuar	250
Yonggom	2,000
Yotafa	2,460

Iran

Afshars	290,000
Agajanis	1,000
**Ahl-i-Haqq in Iran (79)	500,000
Arab-Jabbari (Kamesh)	13,000
Arab-Shaibani (Kamesh)	16,000
Arabs of Khuzestan	520,000
Azerbaijani Turks (80)	6,000,000
Bahais in Teheran (82)	45,000
Baharlu (Kamesh)	7,500

	Bakhtiaris (80)	590,000
	Baluchi (80)	1,100,000
	Bayats	nr
	Bovir-Ahmadi	110,000
	Galeshis	2,000
	Gilakis	1,950,000
	Goudari	2,000
	Hezareh	nr
	Inallu	5,000
	Jamshidis	1,000
	Jews of Iran	93,000
	Kazakhs (80)	3,000
	Khalaj	20,000
	Kurds in Iran (80)	2,000,000
	Lors (80)	600,000
	Mamasani	110,000
	Mazandaranis	1,620,000
	Moqaddam	1,000
	Nafar	3,500
	Pashtuns (80)	3,000
	Persians of Iran (80)	2,000,000
	Pishagchi	1,000
	Qajars	3,000
	Qara'i	2,000
	Qaragozlu	2,000
	Qashqa'i (80)	350,000
	Sasanis	1,000
	Shahsavans (80)	180,000
	Tajik (80)	15,000
	Takestani	220,000
	Talish	20,000
	Teimuri	10,000
	Teimurtash	7,000
	*Tertiary Level Youth	nr
	Turkomans (80)	550,000
Israel	Druzes (79)	33,000
	Gypsies in Jerusalem (82)	300
	*Jewish Imgrnts.-American	25,797
	*Jewish Imgrnts.-Argentine	17,686
	*Jewish Imgrnts.-Australia	1,257
	*Jewish Imgrnts.-Brazilian	4,005
	*Jewish Imgrnts.-Mexican	1,065
	*Jewish Imgrnts.-Uruguayan	2,720
	*Jewish Immigrants, Other	5,520
	Targum	5,000
Italy	Jews in Venice (82)	650
Ivory Coast	Abe	28,500
	Abidji	23,000
	Abure	25,000
	Adyukru	50,450
	Akan, Brong	50,000
	Aladian	14,770
	Attie	160,000
	*Atye	210,000
	Avikam	7,940
	Bakwe	5,060
	Bambara	1,000,000
	***Baoule	1,200,000
	*Bete	300,000
	***Dan	270,000
	**Dida	120,000
	Ebrie	50,000
	Eotile	4,000
	Gagu	25,000
	***Godie	20,000
	**Gouro	200,000
	Guere	117,870
	Gwa	8,300

	Hwela-Numu	50,000
	**Jimini	42,000
	Kouya	5,690
	*Krahn	250,000
	Krobou	3,400
	Krumen	17,000
	Kulango	60,000
	Kulele	15,000
	Ligbi	20,000
	Lobi	40,000
	Maou	80,000
	Mo	800
	Mona	5,570
	Moru	10,000
	Neyo	5,000
	*Ngen	20,000
	Ngere	150,000
	**Nyabwa	30,000
	Nzema	24,080
	Oubi	1,340
	Palara	10,000
	Pye	6,120
	Senufo (80)	300,000
	Tagwana	43,000
	*Teenbu	5,000
	*Tense	5,000
	Tepo	20,000
	Trepo	3,400
	Tura	19,230
	Wobe	40,000
	Yaoure	14,000
Jamaica	**Jamaican Elite	800,000
Japan	*Barbers in Tokyo (82)	220,000
	*Chinese in Japan	50,000
	*Danchi Dwellers in Tokyo (82)	2,500,000
	Farmers of Japan	24,988,740
	Geishas in Osaka (82)	nr
	*Industry Laborers-Japan	21,000,000
	*Inland Sea Island Peoples	1,000,000
	*Koreans of Japan	600,000
	*Ryukyuan	1,000,000
	Soka Gakkai Believers	6,500,000
	**Univ. Students of Japan	2,000,000
Jordan	Circassians in Amman (82)	17,000
	Muslims of Jordan	1,000,000
Kampuchea, Democratic	*Cham (Western) (80)	90,000
Kenya	Ayana	5,000
	**Boran	37,000
	Boran	40,000
	Digo	168,000
	Dorobo	22,000
	El Molo	1,000
	Gabbra	12,000
	Giryama	335,900
	Gosha	3,000
	**Maasai (79)	100,000
	Rendille	20,000
	Sabbra	18,000
	**Saguye	30,000
	Sakuye	8,000
	Samburu	60,500
	Somali, Ajuran (79)	25,374
	Somali, Degodia	68,667
	Somali, Gurreh	54,165
	Somali, Ogadenya	99,129
	Suk	133,200
	**Teso	110,000
	Turkana	224,000
	**Turkana Fishing Community (79)	20,000

	*Chinese of W. Malaysia	3,500,000
	Dusun (81)	160,000
	**Iban (81)	30,000
	Juhai	400
	Kadazans	110,000
	Kayan	12,000
	Kedayanas	25,000
	Kelabit (81)	17,000
	Kemok	400
	Lanoh	400
	Mantera	4,000
	**Melanau of Sarawak (80)	61,000
	Menri	400
	Momoguns	110,000
	Murut	37,500
	Muslim Malays (80)	5,500,000
	Orang Kanak	4,000
	Orang Laut	4,000
	Orang Ulu	4,000
	Penan, Western (81)	2,600
	**Selakau of Sarawak	5,300
	Semelai	3,000
	**Senoi (81)	337,400
	**Sugut	10,000
	Tagal (81)	19,000
	***Tamil Plantation Workers	137,150
	*Tamils (Indian)	600,000
Maldives	Temira	7,000
Mali	Divehi (80)	120,000
	Bambara	1,000,000
	Bobo Fing	3,000
	Bobo Wule	366,000
	Bozo	nr
	*Dogon (79)	312,000
	Fula, Macina	50,000
	Fula, Peuhala	450,000
	Kagoro	30,000
	Khasonke	71,000
	Kita	150,000
	Maure	58,000
	Minianka	300,000
	Samo, Northern	50,000
	Samogho	10,000
	Songhai	125,100
	Soninke	283,000
	Suppire	300,000
Mauritania	Ware	2,000
	Moors in Mauritania	1,000,000
	Soninke	22,000
Mexico	Zenaga	16,000
	Amuzgo, Guerrero	20,000
	Amuzgo, Oaxaca	5,000
	***Azteca (79)	250,000
	***Ch'ol Sabanilla	20,000
	Ch'ol Tila	38,000
	Chamula (79)	50,000
	Chatino, Nopala	7,500
	Chatino, Panixtlahuaca	4,500
	Chatino, Tataltepec	2,000
	Chatino, Yaitepec	2,000
	Chatino, Zacatepec	500
	Chatino, Zenzontepec	4,000
	Chinanteco, Tepinapa	3,000
	Chinanteco, Ayotzintepec	2,000
	Chinanteco, Chiltepec	3,000
	Chinanteco, Comaltepec	1,500
	Chinanteco, Lalana	10,000
	Chinanteco, Lealao	5,000
	Chinanteco, Ojitlan	10,000

	Tojolabal	14,000
	Totonaco, Northern	15,000
	Totonaco, Oxumatlan	1,300
	Totonaco, Papantla	50,000
	Totonaco, Sierra	100,000
	Totonaco, Yecuatla	500
	Trique, San Juan Copala	8,000
	Tubar	100
	Tzeltal, Bachajon	20,000
	Tzeltal, Highland	25,000
	Tzotzil, Chenalho	16,000
	Tzotzil, Huistan	11,000
	Yaquis	14,000
	Yucateco	500,000
	Zinacantecos (79)	10,000
	Zoque, Chimalapa	6,000
	Zoque, Copainala	10,000
	Zoque, Francisco Leon	12,000
	Zoque, Tabasco	400
Morocco	Arabs in Morocco	5,250,000
	Shilha	3,000,000
	**Shluh Berbers	2,000,000
	Tamazight	1,800,000
Mozambique	Chopi	400,000
	Chuabo	250,000
	Kunda	60,000
	Lomwe	1,000,000
	Makua	1,200,000
	Maviha	70,000
	Nyungwe	700,000
	Podzo	45,000
	Ronga	400,000
	Sena	85,000
	Tonga	10,000
	Tsonga	1,500,000
	Tswa	200,000
	Yao	220,000
Namibia	Bushmen (Heikum)	16,000
	*Bushmen (Kung) (79)	10,000
	Herero	40,000
	Kwambi	30,000
	Kwanyama	150,000
	Nama	10,000
	San	6,000
	Tswana	11,300
	Xu	8,000
Nepal	*Bhojpuri	806,480
	Gurung	172,000
	**Magar	300,000
	Maithili	1,000,000
	*Nepali	6,060,758
	Newar in Kathmandu (82)	100,000
	*Newari	500,000
	Rai	232,000
	*Rai, Danuwar	12,000
	Rajbansi	15,000
	**Santhali	nr
	*Sherpa	20,000
	*Tamang	nr
	Tharu	495,000
Netherlands	Ambonese	30,000
	Amsterdam Boat Dwellers	7,500
	*Chinese in Amsterdam	15,000
	*Chinese in Holland	35,000
	Dead-End Kids - Amsterdam (82)	30,000
New Zealand	*Chinese in New Zealand	12,500
Nicaragua	Miskito	20,000
	Sumu	2,000
Niger	Dyerma (80)	1,000,000

Dirya	3,750
Duguir	12,000
Duguza	2,000
**Duka	10,000
Dyerma	50,000
Ebira	325,000
Edo	430,000
Efik	26,300
Efutop	10,000
Eggon	80,000
Ejagham	100,000
Ekajuk	15,000
Eket	22,000
Ekpeye	30,000
Eleme	16,000
Emai-Iuleha-Ora	48,000
Engenni	10,000
Epie	12,000
Esan	200,000
Etulo	2,900
Evant	5,000
**Fakai	15,000
**Fali	25,000
Fyam	14,000
Fyer	3,000
Gade	25,000
Galambi	1,000
Gbari (80)	500,000
Gbaya	350,000
Geji	2,650
Gera	13,300
Geruma	4,700
Ghotuo	9,000
**Glavda	19,000
Goemai	80,000
Gokana	54,000
Gude	40,000
Gudu	1,200
Guduf	21,300
Gure-Kahugu	5,000
Guruntum-Mbaaru	10,000
Gwandara	25,000
Gwari Matai	200,000
***Higi	150,000
Hwana	20,000
Hyam	60,000
Ibaji	20,000
Ibibio	2,000,000
Icen	7,000
Idoma	300,000
Idoma, North	56,000
Igala	350,000
Igbira (80)	400,000
Igede	70,000
Ihceve	5,000
Ijo, Central-Western	338,700
Ijo, Northeast	395,300
Ijo, Northeast Central	8,400
Ikulu	6,000
Ikwere	200,000
Irigwe	15,000
Isekiri	33,000
**Ishans	25,000
Isoko	20,000
Ivbie North-Okpela-Atte	20,000
Iyon	2,000
Izarek	30,000
**Izi	200,000
Jaba	60,000

Janjo	6,100
Jara	40,000
**Jarawa	150,000
Jera	23,000
Jerawa	70,000
*Jibu	20,000
Jimbin	1,500
Jukun	20,000
Kadara	40,000
Kagoma	6,250
Kaibu	650
Kaka	2,000
Kamantan	5,000
*Kambari (80)	100,000
Kamo	3,000
*Kamuku (80)	20,000
Kana	90,000
Kanuri (80)	3,000,000
Karekare	39,000
Kariya	2,200
Katab	32,370
Khana	90,000
Kilba	80,000
Kirifi	14,000
Koenoem	3,000
Kofyar	40,000
Kohumono	11,870
Koma	15,000
Kono	1,550
Koro	35,000
Korop	10,000
Kuda-Chamo	4,000
Kugbo	2,000
Kukele	31,700
Kulere	8,000
Kulung	15,000
Kushi	4,000
Kuteb	26,000
Kuturmi	2,950
Kuzamani	1,000
Kwa	1,000
Kyibaku	20,000
Laamang	40,000
Lakka	500
Lame	2,000
Laru	1,000
Lebgo	30,000
Lo	2,000
Longuda	32,000
Lotsu-Piri	2,000
Lungu	10,000
Madda	30,000
***Maguzawa (79)	100,000
Mama	20,000
Mandara	19,300
Marghi Central	135,000
Matakam	2,000
Mbe	14,300
Mbembe (Tigong)	2,900
Mboi	3,200
Mbula-Bwazza	7,900
Migili	10,000
Miya	5,200
Mober	44,800
Montol	20,000
Mumbake	10,000
Mumuye	200,000
Nandu-Tari	4,000
Naraguta	3,000

391

Nde-Nsele-Nta	10,000
Ndoe	3,000
**Ndoro	10,000
**Ngamo	18,000
Ngizim	39,200
Ngwoi	1,000
Ninzam	35,000
Nkem-Nkum	16,700
Numana-Nunku-Gwantu	15,000
Nungu	25,000
**Nupe	600,000
Nzanyi	14,000
Obanliku	19,800
Obolo	70,000
Odual	9,000
Odut	700
Ogbia	22,000
Okobo	11,200
Okpamheri	30,000
Olulumo-Ikom	9,250
Oring	25,000
Oron	48,300
Otank	3,000
Pai	2,000
Pero	20,000
Piti	1,600
Piya	2,500
Polci	6,150
Pongu	3,680
Puku-Geeri-Keri-Wipsi	15,000
Reshe	30,000
Rukuba	50,000
Rumaya	1,800
Ruruma	2,200
Sanga	5,000
Sasaru-Enwan Igwe	3,780
Saya	50,000
Sha	500
Shanga	5,000
Shuwa Arabic	100,000
Siri	2,000
Sukur	10,000
Sura	40,000
Surubu	1,950
Tal	10,000
Tambas	3,000
Tangale	100,000
Tarok	60,000
Tera	46,000
Tula	19,000
Turkwam	6,000
Ukaan	18,000
Ukpe-Bayobiri	12,000
Ukwuani-Aboh	150,000
Urhobo	340,000
Utugwang	12,000
Uvbie	6,000
Uzekwe	5,000
***Vere	20,000
Vute	1,000
Waja	30,000
*Warjawa	70,000
Wom	10,000
**Yala	60,000
Yandang	10,000
Yeskwa	13,000
Yungur	44,300
**Zaranda Hill Peoples	10,000
Zari	3,950

Oman	Mahri	50,000
Pakistan	Ahmadis in Lahore (82)	60,000
	Bagri	20,000
	Bajania (79)	20,000
	Balmiki	20,000
	**Bhil	800,000
	Brahui	745,000
	Chitralis (79)	120,000
	**Gagre	40,000
	**Hunzakut (79)	10,000
	**Kafirs (79)	3,000
	**Kohli, Kutchi	50,000
	**Kohli, Tharadari	40,000
	**Kohli, Wadiara	40,000
	**Kohlis, Parkari	100,000
	Lohar	nr
	**Meghwar (79)	100,000
	Od	40,000
	Punjabis (80)	49,000,000
	Sindhi Muslims in Karachi (82)	350,000
	Sochi	nr
	Swatis (79)	600,000
	Vagari	30,000
Panama	Buglere	2,000
	**Chinese in Panama	25,000
	**Teribe	1,000
Papua New Guinea	Abau	3,400
	Abie	580
	Abulas	33,000
	Adjora	2,100
	Aeka	3,000
	Agarabi	12,000
	Agob	1,100
	Aiku	800
	Aiome	850
	Aion	800
	Akrukay	150
	Alamblak	1,500
	Alatil	400
	Alauagat	300
	Ama	380
	Amaimon	370
	Amanab	2,800
	Ambasi	500
	**Ampeeli	1,000
	Amto	200
	Andarum	725
	Anem	1,000
	Angaataha	750
	Angal Heneng, South	15,000
	Angal Heneng, West	25,000
	Angal, East	10,000
	Angaua	1,800
	Anggor	1,250
	Angoram	4,000
	Ankave	1,500
	Anor	580
	Anuki	540
	Arafundi	1,080
	Arapesh, Bumbita	2,000
	Arapesh, Mountain	5,000
	Arapesh, Muhiang	8,070
	Arawe	2,200
	Arifama-Miniafia	2,150
	Arigibi	300
	Arinua	1,700
	Arop	1,500
	Aruop	470
	Asaro	12,000

Asat	660
Ata	1,000
Au	3,900
Aunalei	1,800
Auyana	6,500
Awa	1,500
Awar	570
Awara	900
Awin	6,500
Azera	360
Bahinemo	325
Baibai	315
Baining	4,500
Bali-Vitu	6,660
Bam	600
***Banaro	2,500
Banoni	1,000
Barai	1,500
Bariai	1,500
Bariji	260
Barim	600
Barok	1,425
Baruga	1,050
Baruya	4,400
Bau	1,790
Bauwaki	380
Bebeli	600
Bembi	360
Benabena	14,000
Biaka	400
Biangai	1,100
Bibling	1,500
Biliau	620
Bimin	400
Binahari	770
Binandere	3,000
Bine	2,000
Binumarien	190
Bisis	355
Bitara	100
Biyom	400
Boanaki	1,700
Bohutu	1,065
Boikin	31,000
Bola	4,600
Bom	1,130
Bongu	415
Bonkiman	250
Bosavi	350
Bosilewa	350
Bosngun	715
Breri	720
Buang, Central	6,100
Buang, Mangga	2,500
Budibud	170
Buin	9,000
Bukaua	5,000
Bulu	200
Buna	935
Bunabun	500
Bunama	5,000
Burum	3,200
Busa	230
Bwaidoga	5,380
Chambri	935
Chenapian	150
Chuave	20,000
Dadibi	5,500
Daga	5,500

Dahating	920
Dami	1,100
Daonda	100
Dawawa	1,700
Dedua	4,400
Degenan	500
Dia	1,850
Dimir	1,270
Diodio	1,200
Dobu	8,000
Doga	200
Dogoro	120
Dom	8,860
Domu	480
Domung	850
Doromu	840
Doura	300
Duau	7,100
Duna	11,000
Edawapi	3,800
Eivo	1,120
Elkei	1,400
Emerum	460
Emira	3,650
Endangen	450
Enga	110,000
Ewage-Notu	10,000
Fagululu	415
Faiwol	2,500
Fas	1,600
Fasu	850
Finungwan	400
Foi	2,585
Foran	800
Fore	16,000
Fuyuge	13,000
Gadsup	7,000
Gahuku	8,390
Gaikundi	700
Gaina	1,130
Gal	210
Gamei	930
Ganglau	200
Garuh	1,730
Garus	2,100
Garuwahi	225
Gedaged	2,765
Genagane	1,165
Gende	8,000
Gidra	1,600
Gimi	18,000
Ginuman	775
Gira	400
Girawa	3,820
Giri	1,540
Gitua	450
Gizra	600
Gobasi	1,000
Gogodala	10,000
Guhu-Samane	4,000
Gumasi	250
Gumine	24,715
Gusap	400
Guwot	1,000
Gwedena	2,400
Hahon	1,300
Halia	13,200
Hamtai	32,200
**Hewa (79)	1,500

Hote	
Hula	2,500
Huli	3,000
Humene	54,000
Hunjara	440
Iatmul	4,300
Idi	8,000
Igora	900
Ikobi-Mena	880
Ikundun	650
Indinogosima	880
Ipiko	3,450
Ipili	200
Irumu	6,000
Isebe	1,800
Iwal	770
Iwam	1,500
Iwam, Sepik	2,000
Jabem	3,500
Jimajima	2,900
Ka'mis	540
Kabadi	50
Kaian	1,500
Kaiep	230
Kairi	300
Kairiru	650
Kakoa	2,800
Kakuna-Mamusi	6,870
Kalokalo	2,900
Kamano	720
Kamberataro	47,000
Kambot	690
Kamnum	4,380
Kandas	400
Kaningra	480
Kanite	330
Kanum	16,000
Kapin	320
Kapore	1,700
Kapriman	600
Kara	1,165
Karam	2,255
Karangi	11,000
Kare	200
Karkar	340
Karua	1,200
Kasua	850
Kate	1,200
Katiati	5,600
Kaugel	2,300
Kavwol	35,000
Kela	500
Kenati	1,500
Keopara	600
*Kepas	16,420
Kerewo	5,000
Keriaka	2,200
Kewa, East	990
Kewa, South	20,000
Kewa, West	5,000
Kiari	20,000
Kibiri	1,180
Kilmera	1,100
Kinalakna	1,880
Kiriwina	220
Kis	14,000
Kiwai, Northeast	215
Kiwai, Southern	3,700
Kiwai, Wabuda	9,700
	1,700

Kobon	6,800
Koiari, Grass	1,800
Koiari, Mountain	1,700
Koita	2,300
Kol	1,900
Koliku	300
Kolom	120
Komba	10,500
Kombio	2,150
Komutu	500
Konomala	600
Korak	170
Korape	4,200
Kosorong	1,350
Kovai	2,800
Kove	3,000
Krisa	485
Kube	4,000
Kukuwy	1,230
Kumai	3,940
Kuman	66,000
Kumdauron	400
Kumukio	300
Kuni	2,400
**Kunimaipa	9,000
Kunua	1,340
Kuot	900
Kurada	935
Kwale	720
Kwanga	5,110
Kwoma	2,235
Kwomtari	780
Labu	800
Laewomba	1,840
Lamogai	1,000
Lavatbura-Lamusong	1,300
Lavongai	9,365
Leron	500
Lihir	4,790
Lohiki	850
Lou-Baluan-Pam	1,280
Lugitama	520
Lukep	600
Madak	2,690
Magori	200
Mai	210
Mailu	4,700
Maisan	1,800
Maiwa	1,300
Makarim	1,500
Malalamai	340
Malas	190
Malasanga	400
Malek	1,200
Maleu	4,000
Malon	3,330
Mamaa	200
*Ningerum	3,000
**Plantation Workers	5,000
*Samo-Kubo	1,500
**Suena	2,000

Paraguay

Ayoreo	700
Chamacoco, Bahia Negra	1,000
Chorote	nr
Chulupe	8,000
Guaiaqui	350
Guana	3,000
Lengua, Northern	95,000
Maca	600

Peru	Sanapana	4,000
	Achual	5,000
	Aguaruna	22,000
	Amahuaca	1,500
	Amarakaeri	500
	Amuesha	5,000
	Arabela	200
	Campa	5,000
	Candoshi	3,000
	Capanahua	500
	Cashibo	1,500
	Chamicuro	150
	**Chayahuita	6,000
	Cocama	18,000
	Cujareno	100
	Huachipaire	215
	Huambisa	5,000
	Huitoto, Murui	800
	Iquito	150
	Jaqaru	2,000
	Jebero	3,000
	Machiguenga	10,000
	Manu Park Panoan	200
	Mayoruna	1,000
	Morunahua	150
	Ocaina	250
	Orejon	300
	Piro	2,500
	**Quechua	3,000,000
	**Quechua, Huanco	275,000
	Sharanahua	1,500
	Shipibo	15,000
	Urarina	3,500
	Yagua	4,000
	Yaminahua	1,200
Philippines	Abaknon	10,000
	Aeta	500
	Agutaynon	7,000
	Alangan	6,000
	**Apayao	12,000
	*Ata of Davao	10,000
	Ati	1,500
	*Atta	1,000
	***Bagobo	35,000
	Baguio Area Miners (81)	40,000
	**Balangao	4,500
	Balangaw	5,000
	Bantuanon	50,000
	Batak, Palawan	390
	**Batangeno	nr
	**Bilan	75,000
	***Bolinao	26,000
	**Bontoc, Central (81)	20,000
	**Bontoc, Southern	12,000
	Buhid	6,000
	**Bukidnon	100,000
	Buwid (81)	6,000
	Caluyanhon	30,000
	*Casiguranin	10,000
	***Cebu, Middle-Class	500,000
	Cuyonon	49,000
	Davaweno	13,000
	*Dumagat , Casiguran (81)	1,000
	Ga-Dang	5,500
	Hanonoo	6,000
	**Hotel Workers in Manila (81)	11,000
	Ibanag	319
	*Ibataan	500
	Ifuago, Antipolo	5,000

	**Subanen, Sindangan (80)	80,000
	Subanun,Lapuyan	25,000
	**Suriguenos	23,000
	**T'boli (81)	150,000
	Tadyawan	1,000
	**Tagbanwa, Aborlan	10,000
	Tagbanwa, Kalamian	4,500
	Tao't Bato	150
	Tausug (80)	500,000
	Tiruray	30,000
	Yakan (80)	97,000
	Yogad	7,000
Puerto Rico	Chinese in Puerto Rico	200
Rwanda	***Banyarwanda	4,000,000
Saudi Arabia	Chinese in Saudi Arabia	20,000
	*Expatriates in Riyadh (82)	nr
Senegal	Balanta	49,200
	Banyum	9,000
	Basari	8,000
	Basari	8,000
	Bayot	4,000
	Diola	266,000
	Dyola	nr
	Mancang	35,200
	Manding	208,400
	Manjack	44,200
	Mankanya	16,000
	Maures	57,000
	Pular	281,900
	Sarakole (80)	67,600
	Serere (79)	700,000
	Serere-Non	70,000
	Serere-Sine	315,000
	Tandanke	1,000
	Taucouleur (80)	464,700
	Wolof (80)	1,500,000
Seychelles	Seychellois	51,000
Sierra Leone	Bullom, Northern	167,000
	Bullom, Southern	40,000
	Fula	250,000
	Gola	1,400
	*Kissi	48,000
	Kissi, Southern	58,000
	**Kono	133,000
	**Koranko	103,000
	Krim	3,400
	Limba	233,000
	Loko	80,000
	Loko	60,700
	Maninka	64,200
	Mende	600,000
	Susu	86,500
	**Temne (80)	1,000,000
	Vai	2,800
	*Yalunka (80)	25,000
Sikkim	**Lepcha	18,000
Singapore	Malays of Singapore (79)	300,000
Somalia	Somali (79)	2,500,000
South Africa	Cape Malays in Cape Town (82)	150,000
	*Chinese in South Africa	9,000
	*Coloureds in Eersterust (82)	20,000
	Nama	15,000
	Ronga	600,000
	**Swazi	500,000
Soviet Russia	Abazin	25,000
	Abkhaz	83,000
	Adygei	100,000
	Agul	8,800

Akhavakh	5,000
Alutor	2,000
Andi	9,000
Archin	900
Balkars	60,000
Bashkir (80)	1,200,000
Batsi	3,000
Botlikh	3,500
Budug	2,000
Buriat	315,000
Chamalin	5,500
Cherkess	40,000
Chukot	14,000
Dargin	231,000
Didoi	7,000
Dolgans	4,900
Dungan	39,000
Evenks	25,000
Gagauzes	157,000
Gilyak	4,400
Gypsies	175,000
Ingushes	158,000
Itelmen	1,300
Izhor	1,100
Kalmytz	137,000
Kapuchin	2,500
Karachay	173,000
Karagas	600
Karaim	1,000
Karakalpak (80)	277,000
Karakalpak	236,000
Karatin	6,000
Ket	1,200
Khakas	67,000
Khanti	21,000
Khinalug	1,500
Khvarshin	1,800
Kirgiz (80)	1,700,000
Komi-Permyat	153,000
Komi-Zyrian	322,000
Koryak	7,500
Kryz	6,000
Kvanadin	5,500
Lakians	86,000
Liv	1,500
Mansi	7,700
Mari	599,000
Mingat	4,000
Nanai	12,400
Nentsy	29,000
Nganasan	1,000
Nivkhi	4,400
Oroch	1,100
Orok	400
Rutul	12,000
Saams	1,900
Selkup	4,300
Shor	16,000
Svan	35,000
Tabasaran	55,000
Tajik	2,500,000
Tat	17,000
Tatars (80)	6,000,000
Tindin	5,000
Tsakhur	11,000
Tuvinian	139,000
Udegeis	1,500
Udin	3,700
Udmurt	704,000

	Ulchi	2,400
	Veps	16,000
	Yagnobi	2,000
	Yazgulyam	2,000
	Yukagirs	nr
	Yurak	29,000
Spain	*Gypsies in Spain (79)	200,000
	Pension Students-Madrid (82)	1,500
Sri Lanka	**Indian Tamils - Colombo (82)	nr
	Moor Malays (79)	895,322
	SinhaTese	9,146,679
	Tamil (Ceylonese)	1,415,567
	**Tamils (Indian) (79)	1,195,368
Sudan	Abialang	7,200
	Abu Leila	4,100
	Acheron	1,300
	Afitti	3,000
	Aja	1,000
	Anuak	30,000
	Atoc	5,200
	Atuot	8,000
	Avukaya	5,200
	Bai	2,500
	Barambu	46,000
	Bari	340,000
	Beja	91,000
	Binga	1,000
	Biti	280
	Bongo	2,400
	Bor Gok	5,800
	Boya	15,000
	Burun	5,000
	Bviri	16,000
	Dair	225
	Daju of Dar Fur	12,000
	Daju of West Kordofan	6,000
	Didinga	30,000
	Didinga	3,000
	Dinka	1,940,000
	Dinka, Agar	16,000
	Dongjoi	9,000
	Dongo	100
	Fungor	4,500
	Gbaya-Ndogo	1,800
	Gberi	600
	Ghol	2,000
	Ghulfan	3,300
	Gumuz	40,000
	Heiban	25,000
	Ingassana	35,000
	*Jiye	7,000
	Kadugli	19,000
	Kakwa	84,000
	Kanga	6,400
	Karko	2,200
	Katcha	6,000
	Katla	8,700
	Keiga	6,000
	Keiga Jirru	1,400
	Kichepo	16,000
	Koalib (79)	320,000
	Koma, Central	3,000
	Koroma	30,000
	Krongo	121,000
	Lafofa	2,000
	Laro	3,000
	Liguri	2,000
	*Lokoro	22,000
	Lori	1,000

*Deviant Youth in Taipei (82)	80,000
Fishing Village People	150,000
*Industrial Workers (81)	500,000
**Puyuma (81)	7,300
Saisiat (81)	2,900
Taiwan-Chinese Un. Stud.	308,800
Tsou (81)	4,100
*Women Laborers	1,200,000

Tanzania

Arusha	110,000
Asu	110,000
Barabaig (79)	49,000
Bena	150,000
Bende	9,000
Bondei	30,000
Burungi	20,000
Chagga	800,000
Dhaiso	12,000
Digo	30,000
Doe	8,000
Dorobo	3,000
Fipa	78,000
Gogo	280,000
Goroa	180,000
Ha	286,000
Hangaza	54,000
Hatsa	2,000
Haya	276,000
Hehe	192,000
Holoholo	5,000
Ikizu	9,000
Iraqw	218,000
Iraqw	103,000
Isanzu	12,000
Jiji	3,000
Jinja	66,000
Jita	71,000
Kagulu	59,000
Kami	180,000
Kara	32,000
Kerewe	35,000
Kimbu	15,000
Kinga	57,000
Kisankasa	3,600
Kisi	3,600
Konongo	20,000
Kuria	75,000
Kutu	17,000
Kwaya	35,000
Kwere	63,000
Lambya	7,000
Langi	95,000
Luo	1,522,000
Makonde	550,000
Malila	175,000
Mambwe-Lungu	16,000
Manda	10,000
Matengo	58,000
Matumbi	72,000
Mbugwe	8,000
Mbunga	10,000
Mosi	240,000
Mpoto	36,000
Mwanga	27,000
Mwera	110,000
Nata	9,500
Ndali	57,000
Ndamba	19,000
Ndengereko	53,000
Ndomde	12,000

	Thai of Bangkok	4,500,000
	*Thai University Students (81)	nr
	Thai, North East	15,500,000
	Thai, Southern	4,000,000
	**Vietnamese Refugees	140,000
	**Yao (79)	19,867
Togo	*Yao Refugees from Laos	7,000
	Adele	3,000
	Ahlo	2,900
	Ana	36,000
	Animere	250
	Anyanga	3,000
	Basari	100,000
	Basila	4,750
	Bimoba	70,000
	Bowili	3,300
	Chakossi in Togo	20,000
	Gangam	16,000
	Kabre	273,000
	Kasele	20,000
	Kebu	20,000
	*Konkomba	25,000
	Kotokoli	150,000
	Kposo	45,000
	Lamba	29,000
	Moba	70,000
	Naoudem	90,000
	Natemba	17,000
	Ntrubo	3,000
	Tafi	1,000
	Tem	100,000
	Watchi	1,000,000
	Yanga	nr
Trinidad and Tobago	**Indians, East (79)	400,000
Turkey	Abkhaz	12,400
	*Anatolian Turks-Istanbul (82)	2,000,000
	Circassian	113,370
	*Kurds of Turkey (79)	1,900,000
	Romany	20,000
	Turks, Anatolian	31,000,000
	Yoruk	600,000
Turks and Caicos Islands	Chamorro	15,000
	Ulithi-Mall	2,000
	Woleat	1,000
Uganda	Acholi	nr
	Adhola	200,000
	Chiga	272,000
	Gwere	162,000
	Jiye	34,000
	Kakwa	573,000
	Kumam	100,000
	Kupsabiny	60,000
	Lango	560,000
	Lugbara	260,000
	Madi	114,000
	Makere	17,500
	Masaba	110,000
	Meje	13,200
	Muslims (West Nile Dist.)	45,000
	Nyankole	810,000
	Nyoro	620,000
	Nyuli	140,000
	Pokot	170,000
	Rwamba	60,000
	Saamia	124,000
	Soga	780,000
	Tepeth	4,000
	Teso	830,000
United Arab Emirates	Indians in Dubai (82)	24,000

	Yanomamo in Venezuela	nr
	Yaruro	5,000
	Yuana	300
	Yukpa	3,000
Viet Nam	Cham	45,000
	**Chrau	15,000
	Street Vendors in Saigon (82)	nr
Yemen, Arab Republic	***Akhdam	nr
	Sayyids	nr
	Yemenis (79)	5,600,000
Yemen, Democratic	**Hadrami	151,000
	*Mahrah	50,000
Yugoslavia	*Albanians in Yugoslavia	1,500,000
	*Bosnian (80)	1,740,000
	Gypsies in Yugoslavia	800,000
	Muslim Gypsies in Skoplje (82)	23,000
Zaire	Alur	19,000
	Baali	38,000
	Baka	2,600
	**Bakuba	75,000
	Bangba	29,000
	Bembe	50,000
	Binji	64,000
	Bira	35,000
	Bolondo	1,000
	Boma	15,000
	Budu	83,000
	Bugombe	12,000
	Buja	200,000
	Bulia	45,000
	Bushoong	100,000
	Bwa	35,000
	Bwisi	6,000
	Dengese	4,000
	Dongo	5,000
	Enya	7,000
	Fuliro	56,000
	Furu	5,000
	Havu	262,000
	Heso	6,000
	Hunde	33,500
	Kakwa	20,000
	Kaliko	18,000
	Kanu	3,500
	Kaonde	20,000
	Kari	1,000
	Kela	100,000
	Kumu	60,000
	Kusu	26,000
	Kwese	60,000
	Lalia	30,000
	Lamba	80,000
	Lega	150,000
	Lele	26,000
	Lendu	250,000
	Lese	20,000
	Liko	26,000
	Logo	54,000
	Lombi	8,100
	Lombo	10,000
	Lugbara	350,000
	Luna	50,000
	Lwalu	21,000
	Ma	4,700
	Mamvu-Efe	40,000
	Mangbutu	8,000
	Mba	20,000
	Mbala	200,000
	Mbangwe	2,000

	Mbanja	81,000
	Mbo	2,000
	Mbole	100,000
	Mono	30,000
	Mundu	5,000
	Nandi	310,000
	Ndaaka	4,700
	Ndo	13,000
	Ndoolo	5,000
	Ndunga	2,500
	Ngando	121,000
	Ngbaka	700,000
	Ngbaka Ma'bo	17,000
	Ngbandi	137,000
	Ngbee	30,000
	Ngiri	6,000
	**Ngombe	5,000
	Nkutu	40,000
	Ntomba	50,000
	Nyanga-Li	25,000
	***Pakabeti of Equator	3,000
	Pende	200,000
	Peri	40,000
	Poke	46,000
	*Pygmy (Mbuti) (79)	40,000
	Rwamba	48,000
	Sakata	75,000
	Salampasu	60,000
	Sanga	35,000
	Sanza	15,000
	Songe	500,000
	Songomeno	40,000
	Songoora	1,300
	Suku	74,000
	Swaga	121,000
	Teke, Eastern	71,000
	Tembo	30,000
	Tiene	24,500
	Togbo	5,500
	Wongo	8,000
	Yaka	200,000
	Yans	165,000
	Yela	33,000
	Zande	467,000
	Zimba	50,000
Zambia	Ambo	1,000
	Bisa	83,000
	Cewa	200,000
	Chokwe	25,000
	Ila	39,000
	Iwa	15,000
	Kaonde	116,000
	Kunda	21,000
	Kunda	8,000
	Lala	125,000
	Lamba	89,000
	Lenje	79,000
	Lima	12,000
	Lozi	215,000
	Luano	4,000
	Luchazi	34,000
	Lunda, Ndembu	102,000
	Luyana	50,000
	Mambwe-Lungu	121,000
	Mashi	21,000
	Ngoni	257,000
	*Nkoya	nr
	Nsenga	191,000
	Nyiha	59,000

	Sala	11,000
	Simaa	40,000
	Soli	32,000
	Swaka	33,000
	Tambo	7,000
	Tonga, Gwembe Valley (79)	86,000
Zimbabwe	*Bushmen (Hiechware)	1,600
	*Indians In Rhodesia	9,600
	Kalanga	87,000
	Kunda	40,000
	Kwe-Etshori	1,800
	Lozi	8,100
	Manyika	350,000
	**Nambya	40,000
	Ndau	178,000
	**Ndebele (79)	1,000,000
	Nsenga	16,100
	Nyanja	252,000
	*Tonga	90,000
	Tswa	300,000
	Tswana	30,000
	Venda	38,000

Appendices

HING THE UNREACHED

program being carried out jointly by the Strategy Working Group of the
Committee for World Evangelization and MARC, the Missions Advanced
and Communication Center, which is a ministry of World Vision International.

919 West Huntington Drive, Monrovia, California, USA

There are over 3 billion people in the world who do not know Jesus Christ as Lord and Savior. Large numbers of these people are not being reached by the gospel because they are hidden among larger populations or because the gospel message has not been expressed in ways that they can understand and respond to.

They are unreached people.

It has been estimated that there are at least 15,000 major unreached people groups, the vast majority of which have not been identified as to where they are and how they can be reached. This is a task for Christ's Church throughout the world. This is *your* task.

In order to understand and locate these unreached people the Strategy Working Group of the Lausanne Committee for World Evangelization has been working with the Missions Advanced Research and Communication Center (MARC). The early results of this research were presented at the Lausanne Congress on World Evangelization in 1974. Since then this worldwide effort has continued.

The on-going results are published annually in a directory entitled *Unreached Peoples*. As new information comes in from around the world, basic data about each group is listed and some 80 to 100 groups are described in detail. Information on each group is available for your use from MARC.

By publishing whatever information is available, the *Unreached Peoples* directory acts as a bridge between those who are discovering new unreached people, and those whom God has chosen to seek them out with the good news. Your contribution is important!

This questionnaire has been designed to make that task as simple as possible. We ask that you supply whatever information you can, trusting that the Lord of the Harvest has others who will supply what is missing.

Thank you for being a part of this grand vision that every person in the world may have an opportunity to know Jesus Christ.

52479A

FINDING THE UNREACHED: YOU CAN HELP!

You can help locate unreached people groups

You are part of a worldwide network of concerned Christians. There are millions upon millions of people in the world who have had little or no contact with the gospel of Jesus Christ. Because of this, we are asking you to help the Church locate and identify these peoples so it can reach them.

Within each country there are distinct and unique groups of people who may be unreached. This questionnaire is designed to help you describe such groups so that Christians everywhere may pray and consider how these groups might be reached with the gospel. This information will be continuously compiled and made available to the Church and her mission agencies. It appears each year in an annual directory, *Unreached Peoples*, produced by David C. Cook.

There are many different groups of people in the world. How varied they are! Consequently, this questionnaire may not always ask the best questions for understanding a particular people. The questions have been asked in a way that will give comparative information to as large a number of Christians as possible. Where you feel another form of question would better suit your situation, please feel free to comment.

What is a "people group"?

A people group is a part of a society that has some basic characteristics in common that cause it to feel a sense of oneness, and set it apart from other groups. It may be unified by language, religion, economic status, occupation, ethnic origin, geographic location, or social position. For example, a distinct group based on ethnic, language and geographic characteristics might be the Quechua of Bolivia; a sociological group might be the urban university and college students of Colombia, or the urban industrial workers of France. It is important to see that groups may share a common way of life and sense of oneness because of social, occupational or economic characteristics, as well as because of language or ethnic origin. Therefore, whenever possible, *describe the smallest number of persons who make up a distinct group,* that is, don't say that all persons in a region or province are a group, rather describe the specific subgroups within that region or province.

Who are the "unreached and unevangelized people"?

Christians have different definitions of the terms "unreached" or "unevangelized." For the purposes of this worldwide effort, we describe an unreached or unevangelized people as a people who has not received or responded to the gospel. This unresponsiveness may be due to lack of opportunity, to lack of understanding, or because the people has not received enough information about the gospel message in its own language through the eyes of its own culture so that it can truly respond to Christ.

We consider a people "unreached" when less than 20 percent of the members of the group are *practicing* Christians, that is, are active members of the Christian community. By "Christian" we mean adherents (church members, families and followers) of the historic Christian communions; Protestant, Anglican, Roman Catholic, Orthodox and such independent groups as may claim the Bible as the basis of faith and Jesus Christ as Lord and Savior. A group less than 20 percent Christian may yet need Christians from outside the group to help with the evangelism task.

How you can provide information

The attached questionnaire has two parts. If you only have information for the first part, send that in now.

Please fill in one questionnaire for *each* people group with which you are familiar. Do not put several groups on one questionnaire. (If you need more questionnaires, ask for extra copies or photocopy this one, or typewrite the questions you are answering on a separate sheet of paper.) We realize that one person may not have all the answers to these questions. Just answer what you can. PLEASE DO NOT WAIT UNTIL YOU HAVE ALL THE INFORMATION REQUESTED ON THIS QUESTIONNAIRE. SEND WHAT YOU HAVE. Other people may provide information that you do not have. Thank you for your help!

When you have completed this questionnaire, please return it to:

Unreached Peoples Program Director
c/o MARC, 919 W. Huntington Drive, Monrovia, CA 91016 U.S.A.

SURVEY QUESTIONNAIRE FOR UNEVANGELIZED AND UNREACHED PEOPLES

Do you see a group of people who are unreached or unevangelized? Identify them! As the Lord spoke to Ezekiel of ▮ld, so He speaks to us today. "Son of man, What do you see"?

Answers to the questions on these two pages will provide the minimum information needed to list this people group in ▮he *Unreached Peoples* annual.

After you have read the directions, type or print your answers so they can be easily read. It is unlikely that you will have ▮ll the information requested. Do the best you can. What information you are lacking others may supply. If your infor-▮nation is a best guess or estimate, merely place an "E" after it. Send in what you have as soon as possible. Please ignore ▮he small numbers next to the answers. They help others prepare your answers for the *Unreached Peoples* annual.

reason I bow
▮es before the
▮, from whom
▮ily in heaven
▮d on earth is
named . . ."
3:14-15 (RSV)

1. Name of the group or people:_____

2. Alternate name(s) or spelling: _____

3. Country where located: _____

4. Approximate size of the group in this country: _____

5. Vernacular or common language: _____

6. Lingua franca or trade language: _____

7. Name of religious groups found among this people:

	% who are adherents of this religion	% who practice this religion
CHRISTIAN GROUPS:		
Protestant	____ %	____ %
Roman Catholic	____ %	____ %
Eastern Orthodox	____ %	____ %
Other Christian: _____ *(name)*	____ %	____ %
NON-CHRISTIAN GROUPS OR SECULARISM:		
_____	____ %	____ %
_____	____ %	____ %
_____	____ %	____ %
_____	____ %	____ %
_____	____ %	____ %
TOTAL FOR ALL GROUPS:	100 %	

▮ren, My heart's
▮e and prayer to
▮ them is that
may be saved."
Romans 10:1
(RSV)

8. In your opinion, what is the attitude of this people toward Christianity?

(01)☐ Strongly favorable   (02)☐ Somewhat favorable   (03)☐ Indifferent   (04)☐ Somewhat opposed   (05)☐ Strongly opposed

TURN THIS SHEET OVER FOR PAGE 2

52479B

9. Questionnaire completed by:

Name: _____ Date: _____

Organization: _____

Address: _____

_____

10. Who else might be able to provide information about this people?

Name   Organization (if any)   Address

_____

_____

_____

11. If you are aware of any publications describing this people, please give title and author.

_____

12. What other information do you have that could help others to understand this people better? What do you would help in evangelizing them?   *(Use additional sheet if necessary.)*

"And how are they to believe in him of whom they have never heard? And how are they to hear without a preacher?"
Romans 10:14 (RSV)

13. Are you also sending in pages 3 and 4? ☐ Yes   ☐ No

Please send whatever information you have immediately. Do not wait until you have every answer.

Mail to:

Unreached Peoples Program Director
c/o MARC, 919 W. Huntington Drive, Monrovia, CA 91016 USA

Name of people group described_____ Your name _____ Date ____

If you have any more information about this people group, please complete the following two pages as best you can. If not, please send in pages one and two now. If you can obtain more information later, send it in as soon as possible.

PEOPLE DISTINCTIVES—What makes them different? Why are they a people group?

14. A number of different things contribute to create a distinctive people or group, one that in some way shares a common way of life, sees itself as a particular group having an affinity toward one another, and differs to some extent from other groups or peoples. What would you say makes the people you are describing distinctive? Check the appropriate box of as many of the following descriptions as *are important* in making this people distinctive. Use the following scale: "High" importance, "Medium" importance, "Low" importance. For example, if you thought that the fact that they had a common political loyalty was of medium importance in unifying and making a group distinctive, you would place an "X" in the middle box under "Medium".

Importance
High Medium Low

(01)☐ ☐ ☐ Same language
(02)☐ ☐ ☐ Common political loyalty
(03)☐ ☐ ☐ Similar occupation
(04)☐ ☐ ☐ Racial or ethnic similarity
(05)☐ ☐ ☐ Shared religious customs
(06)☐ ☐ ☐ Common kinship ties
(07)☐ ☐ ☐ Strong sense of unity
(08)☐ ☐ ☐ Similar education level
(09)☐ ☐ ☐ Other(s) _____
(please write in)

Importance
High Medium Low

(10)☐ ☐ ☐ Common residential area
(11)☐ ☐ ☐ Similar social class or caste
(12)☐ ☐ ☐ Similar economic status
(13)☐ ☐ ☐ Shared hobby or special interest
(14)☐ ☐ ☐ Discrimination from other groups
(15)☐ ☐ ☐ Unique health situation
(16)☐ ☐ ☐ Distinctive legal status
(17)☐ ☐ ☐ Similar age
(18)☐ ☐ ☐ Common significant problems

15. How rapidly would you say the lifestyle of this people is changing? (check one)

(01)☐ Very Slow Change   (02)☐ Slow Change   (03)☐ Moderate Change   (04)☐ Rapid Change   (05)☐ Very Rapid Change

*to him was given
on and glory and
kingdom, that all
oles, nations, and
ages should serve
Daniel 7:14 (RSV)*

PEOPLE LANGUAGES—What do they speak?

Please list the various languages used by the members of this people:

LANGUAGE TYPE	Primary name(s) of their language(s)	Approximate % who *speak* this language	Approximate % of people over 15 years of age who *read* this language
16. Vernacular or common language:	_____	_____ %	_____ %
17. Lingua franca or trade language:	_____	_____ %	_____ %
18. Language used for instruction in schools:	_____	_____ %	_____ %
19. Language suitable for presentation of the gospel:	_____	_____ %	_____ %

20. If there is Christian witness at present, what language(s) is being used? _____

21. Place an "x" in the boxes that indicate the status of Scripture translation *in the language you consider mos* *suitable for communicating the gospel* (question 19):

	CURRENT STATUS			AVAILABLE		
	Not available	In process	Completed	In oral form	In print	On cassette or records
(POR)New Testament portions	☐	☐	☐	☐	☐	☐
(NT)Complete New Testament	☐	☐	☐	☐	☐	☐
(OT)Complete Old Testament	☐	☐	☐	☐	☐	☐

22. Of the <u>Christians</u> present among this people, what percent *over 15 years of age can and do read any languag*

_____ %

52479

CHRISTIAN WITNESS TO THIS PEOPLE—Who is trying to reach them?

23. If there are Christian churches or missions (national or foreign) now active *within the area or region whe*
    people is concentrated, please give the following information:
    (If there are none, check here: ☐)

CHURCH OR MISSION Name of church, denomination	YEAR Year work began in this area	MEMBERS Approximate number of full members from this people	ADHERENTS Approximate number of adherents (community including children)	WORKERS Approximate numbers of trained pastors and evangelists from this people
_____	_____	_____	_____	_____
_____	_____	_____	_____	_____
_____	_____	_____	_____	_____

24. What is the growth rate of the total Christian community among this people group?

    (01)☐ Rapid growth   (02)☐ Slow growth   (03)☐ Stable   (04)☐ Slow decline   (05)☐ Rapid decline

25. In your opinion, what is the attitude of this people to religious change of any kind?

    (01)☐ Very open   (02)☐ Somewhat open   (03)☐ Indifferent   (04)☐ Somewhat closed   (05)☐ Very closed

26. In your opinion, what is the attitude of this people toward Christianity?

    (01)☐ Strongly favorable   (02)☐ Somewhat favorable   (03)☐ Indifferent   (04)☐ Somewhat opposed   (05)☐ Strongly opposed

27. Most people move through a series of more or less well-defined stages in their attitude toward Christianity. Parts
    people group will be further along than other parts. Here are ten categories that attempt to show this progres
    However, locating people in some of these categories can be difficult, so to make things simpler some categ
    are combined in the questions that follow.

    In your estimation, what percentage of this people can be described as those who: (These percentages
    exclusive. Do not include people more than once. Your total should add up to 100%.)

Have no awareness of Christianity . . . . ____

Have awareness of the existence of Christianity . . . . ____

Have some knowledge of the gospel . . . . ____

Understand the message of the gospel . . . . ____

See the personal implications of the gospel . . . . ____

Recognize a personal need that the gospel can meet . . . . ⎫
                                                                                                                ⎬ ____
Are being challenged to receive Christ . . . . ⎭

Have decided for Christ, but are not incorporated into a fellowship
  (may be evaluating their decision) . . . . ____

Are incorporated into a fellowship of Christians . . . . ____

Are active propagators of the gospel . . . . ____

                                                                                          TOTAL   10

28. On the whole, how accurate is the information you have given us?

    (V)☐ Very accurate   (F)☐ Fairly accurate   (E)☐ Good estimate   (G)☐ Mainly guesses

29. Are you willing to have your name publically associated with this information?

    ☐ No   ☐ Yes   ☐ Yes, with qualifications: _____

APPENDIX B:

Recommended Bibliography: Selected and Annotated by Ray Bakke

Introductory note

Because most urban evangelization is an adaptation of principles and strategies hardly unique to cities, the following list of works deals specifically with issues and data that enable evangelists and pastors to understand the urban context.

Banfield, Edward C., *The Unheavenly City Revisited*, Little Brown, 1974.

Rather controversial but cogent discussion of significant urban issues impacting on the church and its mission in the city.

Berry, Brian J. L. ed., *Urbanization and Counter-Urbanization*, Sage Publications, 1976.

A series of essays describing then differentiating urbanization in the developed and less developed world.

Butterworth, Douglas, and Chance, John K., *Latin American Urbanization*, Cambridge University Press, 1981.

A comprehensive work, strong on urban migration phenomena and its significance. This is one of a new series of works called "Urbanization in Developing Countries" edited by Kenneth Little, an acknowledged expert in West African urban studies.

Eames, Edwin, and Goode, Judith Granich, *Anthropology of the City: An Introduction to Urban Anthropology*, Prentice Hall, 1977.

A superb discussion of urban typologies and roles written in ways that will help formerly rural persons understand the differences environments make in behavior.

Greeley, Andrew, *Why Can't They Be Like Us?: America's White Ethnic Groups*, Dutton, 1975.

Our perceptions of ethnics govern the way we deal with them. Greeley, both priest and sociologist, includes a helpful description of six steps from accommodation to assimilation with the attendant consequences.

Jones, Ronald, *Essays on World Urbanization*, George Philip and Son, Ltd. (n.d.).

Papers on the processes and patterns of urbanization worldwide with excellent documentation and resources for further study of specific regions.

Miller, Randall M., and Marzik, Thomas D., *Immigrants and Religion in Urban America*, Temple University Press, 1977.

How religion functions for a variety of ethnic groups in American cities, with implications for those seeking to understand urban gospel communication patterns and possibilities among immigrants and migrants.

Novak, Michael, *The Rise of the Unmeltable Ethnics*, Macmillan, 1972.

A treatment of urban white ethnics which includes a "WASP" critique which, upon reflection, helps explain why so many evangelization strategies of evangelicals fail in cities.

Phi Delta Kappa, *Why Do Some Urban Schools Succeed?*, 1980.

Eight marvelous case studies of elementary schools from medium to large cities which by analogy offer significant implications for urban church renewal, especially in areas of institutional structures, policies, leadership perceptions, and styles.

Tapinos, Georges, and Piotrow, Phyllis T., eds., *Six Billion People: Demographic Dilemmas and World Politics,* McGraw-Hill, 1978.

One of thirty projected volumes by the 1980s Project/Council on Foreign Relations, with population tables for specific cities and regions.

Thernstrom, Stephan, ed., *Harvard Encyclopedia of American Ethnic Groups,* Harvard University Press, 1980.

A remarkable source of up-to-date research on U.S. ethnicity, with applications for anyone doing urban ministry, though the book is not exclusively urban.

Warren, Rachelle B., and Warren, Donald I. *The Neighborhood Organizers Handbook,* University of Notre Dame Press, 1977.

A practical guide to the understanding of five types of urban neighborhoods, complete with diagnostic steps and communication strategies.

Weber, Max, *Politics as Vocation,* Fortress, 1965.

A discussion of two kinds of ethics and attitudes common among leaders, i.e., the disengaged and the responsible. The disengaged try to maintain purity at all costs; the responsible get involved and are subject to taint. A thoughtful essay on a classic issue.

Worley, Robert, *A Gathering of Strangers: Understanding the Life of Your Church,* Westminster, 1976.

A discussion about forms of power, styles, environments, and their relationship to the theory and practice of ministry. The charts and graphs are especially helpful for those engaged in church renewal.

Younger, George, *The Church and the Urban Power Structure,* Westminster, 1963.

A theologically sensitive discussion of how American cities function and churches respond.

Ziegenhalls, Walter E., *Urban Churches in Transition: Reflections on Selected Problems and Approaches to Churches and Communities in Racial Transition Based on the Chicago Experience,* Pilgrim Press, 1978.

In addition to the case studies, the dialog and bibliographic resources listed in the notes are very valuable.

APPENDIX C

Expanded Descriptions in
Unreached Peoples '79, '80, and *'81*

INDEX OF PEOPLE GROUPS WITH EXPANDED DESCRIPTIONS IN *UNREACHED PEOPLES '79*

INDEX OF PEOPLE GROUPS WITH DESCRIPTIONS
IN *UNREACHED PEOPLES '80*

INDEX OF PEOPLE GROUPS WITH DESCRIPTIONS IN *UNREACHED PEOPLES '81*

APPENDIX D

Urban Unreached Peoples: Issues and Questions

1. Can we define cities in helpful ways or describe them in typologies for the benefit of large-city evangelization strategists, laity, and local pastors alike, that account for the similarities and differences on each continent?

2. Can we identify and facilitate evangelization in international urban migrant streams? What resources are available to assist us?

3. Can we identify and network urban training centers and inventory some urban evangelization resources that could be shared widely?

4. Most ministry assumes leisure time versus work-based or vocational strategies. Large cities work twenty-four hours with massive population groups passing each other like ships in the night. Can we develop strategies appropriate to the urban calendar and clock?

5. Can we identify urban "gatekeepers" or opinion leaders who may become special targets of witness strategies?

Gatekeeping roles are common in urban neighborhoods and familiar to anthropologists who study cultures.

6. What are some appropriate roles for denominations and mission agencies in large-city evangelization?

7. How shall we relate to the renewal movements (Catholic, Orthodox, Coptic, et al.)?

8. Contemporary urbanology defines at least four kinds of urban planning models for addressing the problems or prospects of cities. Each has its own rationale, value system, and scenario. Do these have implications for multiple strategies for large-city evangelization and mission strategies of churches or parachurch agencies? Can we test and prioritize them?

9. Can we find ways to identify recycle mission resources into urban settings (both persons and funds)? What are the consequences and difficulties of such policies?

10. Can we identify a unique set of skills for urban pastoral ministry?

11. Can we reflect on biblical and historical experiences of urban and cross-cultural evangelism and mission in ways that give guidance to our present scene?

12. Can we teach neighborhood analysis? Community organizers in the U.S.A. are taught to identify some five distinct types of neighborhoods with different types of social organization, communication patterns, functions, and leadership styles. Moreover, patterns of community change or decline can be charted in identifiable steps as well as in industrial cities. Does this transfer to Third World cities? Is it helpful in exegeting the context of our work?

13. Can we teach people-group analysis? Cultural anthropology offers insights to the identification of groups. Strategists have shared much of this material (see *That Everyone May Hear, Unreached Peoples* volumes, MARC). How shall we apply this knowledge in the large cities?

14. Can we design resource centers for groups that desperately want to know what's happening in their city and what they might do to be more effective in large-city evangelization?

15. Can we describe personal and family resources and models for urban living where stress factors test the ability to cope?

16. Can we discover ways historic mission organizations function in cities? Many mission agencies have "user relationships" or locate in bridge cities as jumping-off points to mission in the hinterlands. This is fine, but can those mission agencies come together to design strategies for urban evangelization in cooperative ways?

17. Many cities contain huge and rapidly growing numbers of unemployed persons with rising expectations (a "social time bomb"). Marxism sets up house in these environments. What are we doing?

18. Missions have confronted violent cultures in the past, but in largely rural settings and then with patience and at great cost. What lessons can we learn or transfer from that history to confront urban guerilla movements?

19. How can we facilitate Christians and congregations in Muslim or Marxist environments?

20. Can we learn to think theologically about the evangelization of large cities? Do we have biblical and historical resources for our contemporary challenge? What is your theological rationale for urban witness?

21. Can you locate and begin to pray daily for the world's largest cities and the mission of the church within them? Can you gain a working knowledge of the urban world?

22. Can you construct a list of unanswered questions or unaddressed concerns you may have pertaining to large-city evangelization theory or practice?

23. Thoughtful, compassionate analysis will be called for on these and other issues which have enormous significance for our urban brothers and sisters worldwide. Can you begin to share some of your own responses to these and other related concerns?

APPENDIX E

FOLLOW-UP INFORMATION

It appears that there is the following error/omission on page _____

of *Unreached Peoples '82:* _____

_____

_____

_____

_____

_____

I would like to receive more information on the _____

_____(name of people group).

Additional Comments: _____

_____

_____

Name_____

Date _____

Address _____

Please detach, insert in an envelope, and mail to:

Missions Advanced Research and
Communication Center
919 West Huntington Drive
Monrovia, CA 91016
U.S.A.

The Unreached Peoples Series

"Much more than just tables of statistics and regional [classi]sifications. Some of the best minds in missions have b[een] tapped." **Alliance Witness**

"A treasury of world information." **Presbyterian Jou[rnal]**

UNREACHED PEOPLES '79, the first volume in this an[nual] series, was honored by *Occasional Bulletin of Missio[ns] Research* as one of the fifteen outstanding books in the [field] of missiology for the year 1978.

Unreached Peoples '80, focus on the Muslim world
Unreached Peoples '81, focus on peoples of Asia
Unreached Peoples '82, focus on urban peoples
FUTURE VOLUMES
Unreached Peoples '83, focus on refugees
Unreached Peoples '84, focus on peoples of Africa

The Editors

EDWARD R. DAYTON is the founder of the Missions [Ad]vanced Research and Communication Center (MARC) [a] ministry of World Vision International. He is also vi[ce] president for missions and evangelism with World Vision a[nd] has written extensively on management and mission strate[gy].

SAMUEL WILSON is the current director of MARC. He [has] served on the mission field in Peru for over a decade, [and] following his doctoral work in sociology at Cornell Univers[ity] he served for eight years as a professor at Nyack College a[nd] the Alliance School of Theology and Missions.

Special Consultant

RAYMOND J. BAKKE is a professor of ministry at North[ern] Baptist Theological Seminary in Lombard, Illinois, and is [the] founder of the Seminary Consortium for Urban Pastoral E[du]cation (SCUPE). He has taught Bible at Trinity College; chu[rch] history and urban ministry at McCormick Theological Se[mi]nary, and has over twenty years of urban ministry experien[ce] including a ten-year inner-city pastorate. In 16[80 Bak]served as the international coordinator [for the] consultation on large cities at the consult[ation on world] Evangelization in Pattaya, Thailand.

The **UNREACHED PEOPLES** series is a join[t effort of the] Strategy Working Group of the Lausanne Com[mittee for World] Evangelization and the MARC ministry of Wor[ld Vision Inter]national.

5475 A3127
[I]SBN 0-89191-838-8

Unreached Peoples '82